NO STICKS or STONES NO BROKEN BONES

Healing cPTSD when the trauma wasn't physical

It was naCCT:
- *non-physically assaultive*
- *attachment-based*
- *Chronic*
- *Covert*
- *Trauma*

Dr. Ricia Fleming

Ph.D. English Literature
Licensed Mental Health Counselor

No Sticks or Stones, No Broken Bones:
Healing cPTSD when the trauma wasn't physical,
It was naCCT: Non-physically-assaultive, attachment-based Chronic Covert Trauma

Published by ThriveAlive International

Visit the website at ChronicCovertTrauma.com

Note to Readers:
The stories and characters in this book are not real-life case monographs. With the exception of myself and specific people referenced and cited in the text, they are fictional artifacts created for the purpose of illustrating psychoeducational material. Any resemblance in circumstances, characteristics, names, conditions, appearance and so forth to real people is entirely coincidental.
The content in this book is for educational and informational purposes only, and not for the purpose of providing individualized mental health advice nor intended as a substitute for consulting with your physician, psychotherapist or other qualified healthcare professional. Your purchase, downloading and/or reading of these materials do not create a therapist-client relationship between the book, the author, and you. Neither the publisher nor the author shall be liable or responsible for any loss or damage allegedly arising from any information or suggestion in this book.
If you have questions concerning your emotional, physical, or mental health, or about the application of the information described in this book, consult a qualified healthcare professional.

ISBN: 978-0-578-29026-3

NAMING THE TRAUMA WITH NO NAME

I coined the formal descriptive term *non-physically-assaultive, attachment-based Chronic Covert Trauma, (naCCT* for short). The precision of the name clearly distinguishes these traumas from others.

"n" = **"non-physically-assaultive,"** because it is *not* the result of beating, hitting, punching, sexual attack, or any other form of physical assault.

"a" = **"attachment-based,"** because it happens in the essential relationship between children and their mothers, fathers, or other essential Lifeline People, without whose care the child would die.

"C" = **"Chronic,"** because it doesn't stop. It is ongoing, repetitive, and cumulative rather than a single event or set of events.

"C" = **"Covert,"** because it is so hidden, subtle, secret, and difficult to identify.

"T" = **"Trauma,"** because it is an experience that:
(1) overwhelms one's mental, physical, and emotional resources at the time it occurs, and

(2) may result in characteristic mental, social, physical, and spiritual wounds of PTSD that may continue to cause pain and disability long afterward.

Ten Things You Can Do
to
Raise Public Awareness
about
The NaCCT Category of Trauma

You can contribute to creating a broader and deeper social context that will support your own healing and pave the way for others to heal. Here are ten ways you can do that:

1. Casually mention, "I'm reading an interesting book that says we need to take intangible traumas seriously,"
2. Use the words "intangible trauma" and the acronym "naCCT,"
3. Make a "Patron's Book Request" for *No Sticks or Stones* at your local library,
4. Reach out to your friends, family, and colleagues, both on-line and face-to-face,
5. Tell your therapist, physician, or other health professional about cPTSD from naCCT,
6. Offer some clarifying psychoeducation — maybe about People-Triggers, or naCCT Body-State Triggers — to someone who might benefit from it,
7. Start a group to do the reader activities in this book together,
8. Help someone to self-identify as an naCCT survivor with cPTSD and thereby get on the road to recovery,
9. Share your thoughts about your experience reading this book by posting a review on Amazon, Goodreads, or your favorite book forum,
10. Come on over to the community at the website: **ChronicCovertTrauma.com.**

I dedicate this work to brave little Patty F
who never, never, never, never, never gave up.

Table of Contents

PROLOGUE

TAKING NACCT SERIOUSLY

"My parents did not beat me or abuse me. They fed me, bought me clothes, sent me to good schools and wished the best for me. As a result I was unable to point to any tangible cause"

FAQ:

Q: WHAT'S THE HARDEST THING ABOUT HEALING FROM INTANGIBLE TRAUMAS FROM CHILDHOOD?

A: TAKING THEM SERIOUSLY.

If you have trouble validating your emotional pain from intangible childhood traumas and taking it seriously today, you're not alone. I did too. For a long time I deprived myself of the deep healing I needed. Why? Because I believed I hadn't suffered enough.

It has taken me over twenty years to get the courage to offer you this book about these seemingly inconsequential childhood experiences; over twenty years to go public with my conviction that these small events from long ago cause serious problems today.

And even now, it's sometimes hard for me to validate the traumatic nature of such intangibles as emotional neglect, psychological abandonment, lack of comforting touch and soothing physical presence, or even well-intentioned but unempathic and overwhelming parental involvement.

It's hard to believe that these are real traumas, that I'm not just a "cry-baby making mountains out of molehills."

After all, there are no bruises when a baby is left crying in the dark, no broken bones when a sensitive infant recoils from a parent's impatient touch or unconscious hostility, no trips to the emergency room when a child's heart is broken by a yet another forgotten promise. No viral videos rally public outrage when a child's development is damaged by pressure to serve as a buddy to a lonely parent, entertain a depressed parent, or become a showpiece that will elevate a parent's social status or compensate for a parents' failed ambitions.

So, what gave me the courage to go public with this book? *You!* An image of you relieved, empowered, strong. You benefiting from reading what I've learned both as a therapist and as someone whose life has been affected by these intangible traumas from my own childhood.

Maybe you too feel you haven't suffered enough. And if you feel that way, I wrote this book for you.

৽৶

HEALING BEGINS WITH TAKING IT SERIOUSLY

"Is this story too shocking for a book about trauma that doesn't involve any physical assault?" I asked a colleague.

"Let's hear it," she said.

Here's the story I told her: What do you think?

TIME TRAVEL: BACK TO EARLY SUMMER, 1996:

"It's horrifying," says my friend Carol, bounding into the coffee shop and squeezing into the booth next to me.

"And it's linked to the very thing you're afraid to take seriously." She shakes the current issue of the *New Yorker* in front of my face. "Read it."

I take the magazine. Carol reads along over my shoulder. What I read about Harvard pre-med student Sinedu Tadesse indeed addresses the very thing I've been struggling to take seriously. And what I read is indeed horrifying.

Sinedu had tried unsuccessfully to get help with what she described as her "hellish" life. Desperate, she had written a letter begging for help and snail-mailed copies to strangers picked at random from the addresses listed in a phone book.

Alone with her journal, Sinedu had struggled to understand what was wrong, to find relief before it was too late.

She had grown up in a family of mother, father, and four siblings, but the ordinary comforts of home seemed alien and incomprehensible to her. Instead of warmth, security, and love, in her family she had experienced "a lot of pain and trauma."

But the cause of Sinedu's pain and trauma baffled her: "My parents did not beat me or abuse me," she wrote. "They fed me, bought me clothes, sent me to good schools and wished the best for me. As a result I was unable to point to any tangible cause."

Carol reaches across the page and taps on the words "unable to point to any tangible cause." Looking directly into my eyes, she says, "I've heard you say those exact words."

Yes, I have said those exact words. For a survivor of intangible traumas, these puzzled words are typical.

But what Sinedu did next is not at all typical:

In her Harvard University dormitory early one Sunday morning, Sinedu Tadesse, still desperate, picked up a knife, went to the bed where her roommate was sleeping, and stabbed her sleeping roommate forty-five times. Then she went into the bathroom and hanged herself.

TIME TRAVEL: RETURN TO THE PRESENT

Today, twenty-three years later, I finish reading this story to my colleague and wait for her response.

Silence.

Betsy is a seasoned psychotherapist and a good friend. Like me, she has worked with the results of many kinds of traumas in her thirty years of helping people. Her opinion matters to me.

"So, what do you think?" I ask. "Should I tell the story?"

More silence.

Finally: "It's an awful story," she says. "And it makes the point you needed to hear back then, a point your readers might need to hear today: These intangible traumas are *not trivial*.

"They're *real* problems with *real* consequences that can be devastating. Sinedu's story –unusual and shocking as it is — shows these intangible traumas are really serious. And they *should* be taken seriously.

"Tell the story."

TAKING INTANGIBLE TRAUMA SERIOUSLY TODAY

Although intangible traumas often result in pain and confusion, rarely do the pain and confusion erupt with such horror. Most people who have lived through these intangible traumas do not murder other people or kill themselves.

But many suffer from despair so profound they feel they "might as well be dead." Many battle constantly with anxiety, depression, or even rage. Feelings of dread, panic, and exhaustion may seem to come out of the blue sky and make everyday living feel like tap-dancing in a mine field.

However, most survivors are troupers. Rather than giving in to self-pity or resorting to parent-bashing, they tend to soldier on, perhaps with the help of psychiatric medication or alcohol, perhaps by simply grinning and bearing it, and adopting the mindset that "life is difficult." Many even succeed more and enjoy it less with each passing year, living productive lives of quiet desperation.

Part I:

Introduction and Orientation

CHAPTER 1

WHAT IS NACCT?

Widespread, deadly, seldom traced to their hidden roots, the aftereffects of intangible trauma in crucial childhood relationships are implicated in diverse adult problems: Physical, emotional, social, even spiritual well-being can be undermined by the long-term aftereffects of unidentified, untreated, and unhealed intangible trauma.

The name given to these unhealed aftereffects of trauma is Post-Traumatic Stress Disorder, PTSD for short.

PTSD from intangible, interpersonal trauma blunts a survivor's ability to live and love fully and completely. It cripples the ability to love oneself, to bond with others, to belong to society, and to reach that sense of love and connection that gives meaning to life and forms the core of authentic spirituality. To make matters worse, post-traumatic terror hinders the ability to receive the love that would heal these wounds.

Sometimes people wake up at midlife, feeling empty and only half alive. Walled up behind coping strategies and defenses, one's true "soul," that which gives ordinary life depth and value, is often held hostage to hidden PTSD. If depth is blocked with post-traumatic pain, one is forced to live on the surface.

PTSD from intangible trauma also takes a toll on the body, contributing to any or all of the following widespread problems:

- Substance abuse and its devastating psychological, physical, and social complications,

- Numerous medical conditions, including obesity and chronic physical pain, and

- Mood disorders such as anxiety and depression.

JENNA LEE IS A TYPICAL SURVIVOR

Jenna Lee arrived at her first therapy session unhappy and confused.

"There is no good reason why I get so upset," said thirty-two-year-old Jenna Lee at our first psychotherapy session. "I've thought about my family a lot, and I've read a lot of self-help and recovery books. Nothing in my childhood explains why I'm having such a hard time today."

As she slumped in the chair opposite mine, the words seemed to tumble out of her mouth: "I don't know what's wrong with me. Sometimes I go to Al-Anon because I feel the same fear, doubt, and insecurity that people with alcoholic parents do, but there was no alcohol in my family. Also no drugs, no physical abuse, no incest."

She paused for a moment, shrugged her shoulders, and with a wry smile summed it up for me. "The only really dysfunctional thing about my family is *me*."

When I asked what brought her to therapy, she fluffed her hair nervously and replied, "I'm stuck; I try to stay balanced and take life in stride, but I keep getting upset. Then I calm down and feel ashamed of how upset I got. It's finally getting to me."

After a moment's pause, she pointed to red and purple paint splotches on her low-heeled shoes and said, "Then there's work — kid's poster paint on my practical shoes. I'm working as a teacher's aide in a special education class, even though I'm certified to teach. I probably could get a better job if I made more of an effort."

Sinking further into her chair, she stuffed her hands into the pockets of her oversized sweater, brought out a bit of folded gold paper that she began to unfold. "My life's just not working the way it should. I'm in a relationship on and off. Right now it's off, but it's always rocky. I'm sensitive to criticism, and sometimes I can get to acting pretty needy."

As she placed the shiny gold paper on her gray wool covered knee and smoothed it slowly with her thumb, she continued: "Since Mike and I broke up, which we do regularly, I just go to work, come home, watch TV, and try to cheer myself up with chocolate. I guess you could say I'm kind of depressed. I used to ride my bike after work, but now it's rusting in chains on the bike rack."

Again she busied herself with the gold paper, folding it in half and running her finger down the fold, folding it again into a tinier square. Looking intently at the square, she said, "Mike used to tease me about those happy TV families — the ones from the 50's, like *Ozzie and Harriet*. He thought they were just media myths until he met my parents. Mike's parents are divorced. Like the parents of half my friends. My parents never even fought.

"My parents worked things out, compromised. Even my name is a compromise: Dad wanted Jennifer and Mom wanted Lisa and here I am: Jennifer Lisa, both names equally shortened to Jenna Lee."

Jenna Lee paused, lost in thought, gazing despondently out the window.

Then she stuffed the folded paper back into her pocket, pushed her whole body up so she sat tall in her chair and spoke, "I did have it really easy. Nothing upset Mom: She was the original "keep calm and carry on" woman.

"Dad had a good job in high-tech and we had a nice house in the suburbs. I took dance classes and skating lessons. They took an interest in my projects and chauffeured me around to activities.

"Maybe I was spoiled."

"TRAUMA SURVIVOR WITH PTSD? ME? NO WAY!"

Jenna Lee's belief that her distress is somehow not justified is common. I've talked with hundreds of people in my thirty-plus years as a psychotherapist, both in private practice and in hospital groups. In these many years, I've heard many variations on Jenna Lee's stern, self-condemning refrain. The wording may vary —

"Compared to most people, I have nothing to complain about,"

"I can't blame anyone but myself for my bad attitude,"

"I had it so easy as a kid, I've got no excuse for having such a hard time."

However, the core meaning remains the same: "Nothing was really wrong with my childhood; so there must be *something really wrong with me*."

Shame, frustration, guilt, and self-disgust often accompany this attitude.

Many survivors don't even think of exploring a connection between today's suffering and possible intangible traumas they may have endured in childhood. And if they do think of it, they rule it out.

"Trauma," these survivors say, "That's what happens to shell-shocked combat veterans and rape victims, not to me."

Survivors of intangible interpersonal trauma are prone to feel their distress is illegitimate because there is no tangible evidence or cause for their pain. Traumas such as emotional disconnection from parents, constant but subtle coercion, smothering overstimulation, emotional abandonment or indifference leave no obvious physical traces.

Furthermore, there's limited social context for taking intangible trauma seriously:

- No social worker comes to investigate when a child is confused by parents' contradictory messages or squelched by a parent's inability to tolerate sorrow or fear.

- No tabloid headlines scream "Preteen micromanaged by helicopter mom using criticism labeled help."

- No child protective services intervene and remove a child from parents who don't hug their children or say "I love you."

With no physical evidence and no social context supporting and validating intangible trauma, many survivors understandably conclude that they are just defective. Many blame their innate character or genetically malfunctioning body chemistry for their continuing unhappiness.

Meanwhile, the hidden legacy of unacknowledged and unhealed intangible trauma continues to create serious problems in their lives.

TRAUMA SURVIVOR WITH PTSD? ME? MAYBE

Intangibles can produce the characteristic overwhelming terror of trauma and the long-term psychological problems characteristic of complex PTSD.

However, unlike blatant physical traumas involving direct physical assault, intangible traumas involve *indirect* threats to a child's safety.

A baby's attachment to a caregiver is a matter of life and death. A baby's attachment bond is a lifeline. After the physical lifeline of the umbilical cord is cut, a new *interpersonal lifeline* is formed between the newborn and mother, father, or other caregiver. These essential people function as lifelines. They are Lifeline Caregivers.

All healthy babies are born knowing this in their bones. It's as if we're born with a prewired survival strategy: "Cling for your life to your Lifeline Caregiver."

The intangible traumas of childhood often originate in commonplace, sometimes even imperceptible, breaks in the responsive care a young dependent child needs in order to stay alive. Failures of empathy, threats to abandon, or inattention to the real needs of the totally dependent child cause that child to wordlessly fear that no one will come. And if no one comes, death will eventually follow.

Threats to these life sustaining bonds can occur both in quiet, orderly, nonviolent homes and in chaotic homes full of drugs, violence, and sexual abuse.

The threat of danger can arise from many causes, intentional and accidental. The danger can be caused both by the presence of something bad and by the absence of something good, both by traumatic action and by traumatic failure to act.

These threats range across a spectrum from very mild and well-intentioned to severe hidden hostilities that could properly be labeled covert traumatic abuse. On that extreme end would be acts like intentionally inviting a mean child for a playdate and embodied hostilities like rough impatient handling, failure to get timely relief for sicknesses, or sadistic pleasure in a child's pain, such as harshly brushing the tangles out of a child's long hair every morning, but not allowing the child to have a short haircut.

This threat can arise when a child is exposed to coldness, rigidity, inauthenticity, favoritism, or unempathic overprotection.

This threat can also arise from early experiences of potentially deadly disconnection, signaled by a parent's slight pulling back, a glare, or by a cringing, collapsing parent who just "went away" psychologically when the child become upset.

So, for the child, there is a constant dread of losing that life sustaining connection.

This constant dread of deadly disconnection explains how children can grow into adults who experience mortal terror if they start to cry, don't perform perfectly, lose control, or fail to get a response.

AND TODAY'S ADULT PROBLEMS COULD BE PTSD

When these intangible interpersonal traumas are not recognized as traumas, adults who suffered from these traumas as children don't recognize the magnitude of their wounds.

These adults have been the ignored trauma victims: seriously traumatized, yet discounted because their trauma didn't involve a *direct physical* assault.

The problems of these forgotten trauma victims get misdiagnosed. And, therefore, tragically but not surprisingly, because they are misdiagnosed, their wounds remain unhealed.

NAMING THE TRAUMA WITHOUT A NAME

One of the reasons for this unfortunate misdiagnosis has been the lack of a name for this category of trauma.

Without a name, it's hard to talk about something, or even think about it. Or even feel like it's real.

Having a name can make what we're talking about seem real.

Having a name can help us to share vital information, compare notes, and learn from each other's experience.

Having a name can help us to discover that we aren't "the only one," that other people have similar problems.

We have long needed a name that distinguishes intangible traumas such as psychological isolation and emotional abuse from blatant physical traumas such as combat, rape and natural disasters.

Many names exist for childhood traumas involving parents and other Lifeline Caregivers. As you continue to investigate this kind of trauma, you may hear "infantile trauma," "relational trauma," "developmental trauma," "emotional trauma," "interpersonal trauma," "psychological trauma," and "psychosocial trauma," to mention a few of the names currently in use.

However, you'll notice that none of these names specify that physical assault is not their cause. Any of those names could refer to blatant physically assaultive traumas.

The distinction is crucial between traumas that involve physical assault and those that don't. The intangible traumas we're talking about here present a unique set of injuries and demand a unique kind of healing.

They need their own name. So, to help us talk to each other about this problem, I gave them one.

NACCT: "NON-PHYSICALLY-ASSAULTIVE, ATTACHMENT-BASED CHRONIC COVERT TRAUMA"

I coined the formal descriptive term "non-physically-assaultive, attachment-based Chronic Covert Trauma," naCCT for short.

Some people will complain about this name: They will say it's too long and complicated. It *is* a big complicated name because it is a big complicated problem. It is a serious formal name for something that deserves to be taken seriously.

Most importantly, the precision of the name "non-physically-assaultive, attachment-based Chronic Covert Trauma" clearly distinguishes this category of trauma.

Each specific characteristic in the name matters. Each one deserves a place in your awareness as we go forward. Let's itemize those characteristics of an naCCT.

Each letter stands for one characteristic:

- **"n"** = **"non-physically-assaultive,"** because it is *not* the result of beating, hitting, punching, sexual attack, or any other form of physical assault.

- **"a"** = **"attachment-based,"** because it happens in the essential relationship between children and their mothers, fathers, or other essential Lifeline People without whose care the child would die.

  The word "attachment" in psychology has come to refer to the deep bond between a baby and the baby's caregiver. These traumas are based on that very early Lifeline Relationship.

- **"C"** = **"Chronic,"** because it doesn't stop. It is ongoing, repetitive, and cumulative rather than a single event or set of events.

  A child who suffers from naCCT has been slowly overwhelmed and incapacitated by the cumulative impact of subtle emotional traumas with mothers, fathers, or other Lifeline Caregivers.

Instead of having the trauma end and healing begin, the traumatic experience goes on and gets worse.

Only temporarily relieved by the usual strategies — pep talks, sports events, sex, romance, shopping, food, alcohol, internet, exercise, or massage — the misery returns. And when it returns, it undermines attempts to find successful relationships, radiant health, satisfying work, and authentic meaning and happiness in life. And the recurring problems deepen the wounds. Which lead to more problems well into adulthood.

It's a vicious cycle: unidentified, unaddressed, and unhealed, these naCCT wounds continue to fuel problems and continue to undermine the positive effects of medication, self-help, and behavioral self-management.

- **"C" = "Covert,"** because it is so hidden, subtle, secret, difficult to identify. This kind of trauma has been compared to cancer, radon, and toxic waste: hidden, undetected, insidiously growing and doing its damaging work.

  The naCCT wound itself is covert.

  The cause can be so subtle that someone standing next to you might not even realize that you were being traumatized.

  The connection between what happened then and what's troubling today is so obscure and insidious that it's functionally covert.

  The most insidious wound from non-physically-assaultive, attachment-based, Chronic Covert Trauma is the traumatized person's lack of awareness that the trauma wound even exists.

  Some understandable human forces are at work keeping these traumas covert. In some ways, we *want* to keep them hidden. Children understandably try to forget the painful experience of the trauma. Try to keep the trauma a secret even from themselves.

  As adults, we also hide these traumas from ourselves by dismissing them or trivializing them with the belittling cliché "I'm making a mountain out of a molehill."

  (And parents hide upsetting truths to protect their children. They withhold disturbing information from their children and kindly bite their tongues when their kids displease them. And parents have secrets even from themselves — maybe unconscious disgust, or embarrassing neediness. Of course, children can see into the nooks and crannies of their parents' hearts, and what they see there can terrify them.)

- **"T"** = **"Trauma,"** because it is an experience that:
     (1) overwhelms the terrified victim's mental, physical, and emotional resources at the time it occurs, and
     (2) may result in characteristic mental, social, physical, and spiritual wounds of PTSD that may continue to cause pain and disability long afterward.

I don't use the formal name "non-physically-assaultive, attachment-based, Chronic Covert Trauma" every time I refer to this category of trauma. Sometimes I shorten it to the acronym "naCCT."

And sometimes I refer to "intangible, interpersonal traumas." And sometimes I just use the more casual phrase "these intangible traumas" or "these attachment traumas." Or even "No Sticks or Stones type traumas." Even when I use the more casual names for them, the traumas in this book are non-physically-assaultive, attachment-based, Chronic Covert Traumas.

A survivor of naCCT uses a simpler working definition: "Stuff other people didn't think was so terrible had a terrible effect on *me*. That's naCCT."

Any name, even a long complicated formal name, enables us to talk. With a name, we can find our voices and put an end to the silence.

SOME TRAUMA IS NOT ABUSE

Some people ask: "Why do you say 'trauma' instead of 'abuse?'"

I know that sometimes people equate trauma with abuse. They might, for instance, speak of "emotional abuse" when they refer to intangible, attachment-based Chronic Covert Traumas. Equating trauma with abuse can be confusing and result in people concluding that as children their family lives had been completely free of trauma.

For example, Jenna Lee would say, "Trauma? No way! My parents weren't abusive. I was the center of their lives! They really tried and they are basically good people. I couldn't have been traumatized."

Here's why I say "trauma" instead of "abuse":

Trauma and abuse are not identical. It's important to distinguish between them and honor the different connotations attached to each one.

The word "abuse" tends to be judgmental, and in many cases — perhaps like Jenna Lee's — "abuse" or "emotional abuse" just doesn't ring true to the situation.

The word "abuse" tends to invite blame, moral condemnation, and outrage about a wrong done. And it tends to focus on the person causing the wound.

The word "trauma," on the other hand, tends to focus on the wounded person and invite healing and compassion. For healing purposes, I'll go with the focus on extending healing and compassion to the wounded person.

THE TRAGEDY OF UNINTENTIONAL TRAUMA

And here's another reason I use the word "trauma" rather than "abuse:" People think of interpersonal trauma as something atrocious caused by awful people. Abusers aren't generally thought of as "nice" and abuse isn't considered well-intentioned. But, in fact, people who introduce trauma into a child's life are often nice and well-intentioned.

We tend to deny that good intentions could ever result in trauma. However, the world is complex. It's not so simply divided into the evil people who abuse and traumatize their children versus the good people who never abuse or traumatize their children.

The sad truth is that, as children, many people were subjected to serious psychological trauma by the ordinary human failings of well-intentioned people. Born as we are into an imperfect world, it's nearly impossible for parents to completely avoid hurting their children. It seems to be the fate of all children to be hurt sometimes by their parents. None of us completely escape this sad experience.

Serious psychological trauma can even be caused by good intentions gone awry, as when a fragile parent takes on more than she can handle, collapses from emotional fatigue, and leaves her child feeling abandoned.

Parents or other well-meaning Lifeline People might not have had a clue that their behavior was distressing. In fact, they may have been trying really hard to be good parents. Naive parents, fragile parents, or sick parents, all "without a mean bone in their bodies," can cause severe unintentional naCCT in their children.

Parents are often unaware of the trauma they are inflicting. For example, well-meaning parents who use rigid coping strategies to survive emotionally may inadvertently cause psychological trauma to their children. While they intend to help their children by passing on their fear-based strategies like "always be cheerful" or "never trust anyone outside the family," they may inadvertently constrict, frighten, and covertly traumatize the child they love.

> *"NaCCT IS THE HELL TO WHICH*
> *THE ROAD IS PAVED WITH GOOD INTENTIONS."*

TRAUMATIC IMPACT WITHOUT BLAME

There may be a temperamental mismatch between parent and child, one being very sturdy, sanguine, and extroverted, while the other is very sensitive, introverted, and temperamentally delicate. This situation can lead to frustration and a natural tendency to clash between the needs of the child and the parent's desire to provide loving care. In these cases, a parent's struggle to respond empathically is often truly heroic. But sadly, the child's emotional isolation resulting from the caregiver's unattunement may nevertheless be traumatic.

A very bright child might suffer from the chronic trauma of unattunement simply because her well-intentioned caregiver doesn't understand her well enough to guide and limit her effectively.

Megan was a very bright child who was chronically traumatized by the responses of her beloved grandmother who gradually developed early undiagnosed Alzheimer's. Granny couldn't remember what Megan had told her, forgot what she had promised Megan, and frightened Megan with her confusing responses. Megan felt alone, bewildered, terrified, and helpless. She needed to hear someone say, "How awful that must have been for you, that she couldn't understand you, and you felt so alone with her." Thus, Megan was traumatized but not abused.

Consider the following situations: Does the connotation of "abuse" fit?

- Jim was mild-mannered and an excellent provider. Jim's wife thought Jim had Asperger's or high functioning autism. Jim thought other people put too much emphasis on emotions and engaged in pointless and annoying small talk. Jim's son agreed with him. Jim's daughter had a history of painful relationships with people who focused on work and belittled her emotions.

- Becky's mother believed babies need to cry to strengthen their lungs. Mom told Becky's sister to let the baby cry. "Failure to let the baby cry," she said, "deprives a baby of the opportunity to develop strength needed in later life." Her pediatrician agreed, and so did her friends.

- Marilyn loved her children. But she did not feel comfortable with touch. "I'm just not one of those touchy-feely people," she says. "I don't like the handshaking and hugging that goes on in the middle of our church service. I didn't use the massage gift certificate I won at the raffle." Marilyn's teenage daughter Josie sometimes longed for touch, and sometimes used sex to get some physical affection.

Would you say Jim or Becky's mom or Marilyn were "abusive?" These are instances where the connotation of "abuse" just doesn't seem to fit.

A child may suffer from chronic covert trauma due to undiagnosed vision or hearing problems that lead to behaviors labeled "timid" or even "stupid." Undiagnosed dyslexia, attention deficit and hyperactivity disorder, or sensory processing disorder often result in kids being labeled "defiant" or "oppositional."

Take Frank, for example. He had an undiagnosed vision problem which caused headaches whenever he tried to read for too long. He was doubly traumatized: first, by the headaches and second, by his parents' and teachers' assumption that he just wasn't trying hard enough — because, in fact, he tried really hard, and the harder he tried, the worse his headaches got. But was he abused? Once his problem was diagnosed, his parents wasted no time in getting the surgery and vision training needed to correct it.

So, there you have my long explanation of why I use the word "trauma" rather than "abuse." I want to validate your experience, not serve as attorney for the prosecution of those who traumatized you. I want to help you, not hurt them.

Takeaway to remember: Trauma can have other causes besides abuse. You can be traumatized without being abused. If you look only for abuse, you'll miss problematic traumas or disqualify them because nice, well-intentioned people caused them.

THE PROCESS OF "RUPTURE AND REPAIR"

Immediate Spontaneous Repair:

Sometimes these misfortunes that cause psychological traumas are healed as soon as they occur, as when a little child gets lost in the mall. The child's obvious terror is so understandable, and the parents are so relieved, that, once the child is found, a joyful, emotional reunion takes place. The terrified child is soothed by warm hugs and a special treat to eat. The terror is released in a good cry. The child gets to process the psychological trauma, and healing happens quickly and naturally.

Sometimes parents are able to acknowledge and help their children process and heal from more subtle psychological traumas. Parents help when they acknowledge they've been harsh, or careless, or hurtful after an impatient outburst. They repair the rupture with an apology, some comforting, and maybe even some amends. Far from causing PTSD, this process of "rupture and repair" may actually strengthen the Lifeline bond.

"Better Late than Never" Repair:

Sometimes a ruptured relationship is repaired soon after the rupture is recognized.

This happened when Frank's vision problem was finally diagnosed: His parents and his teachers said things to him like: "How awful for you that we accused you of not trying hard enough, when you were so good and trying so hard. Of course you got hurt and mad at us. We were unfair and just plain wrong, and we are so very sorry."

And sometimes a ruptured relationship is repaired after many years have gone by.

This happened when Marilyn was able to talk with her daughter Josie, after many years passed, about her discomfort with touch. Josie still felt touch-hungry, but she didn't feel crazy, and what she called her "sex addiction" made sense. And she felt closer to Marilyn after their talk.

A woman I spoke to praised her mother's loving willingness to be accountable: "She was able to say to me many years later, 'I'm really sorry I wasn't there for you while I was struggling to stay afloat after Grandma died; I know that made it extra hard for you'."

Yet another woman remembers her mother saying to her, "I was so afraid of not being accepted in the community when we first moved here that I overcontrolled you and squashed your spontaneity. When I got scared and turned away from you, I really scared you, and I'm truly sorry."

No Repair

It's more common, however, for the rupture never to be addressed and repaired. Instead, it's ignored. Minimized. Dismissed as inconsequential. The child is told to "suck it up." "You don't really feel that way." "You aren't going to let a little thing like that upset you." "Offer it up." "Get over it." "Let it go."

The episode of naCCT is unacknowledged, ungrieved, and unhealed, and the results sink into the child's being as PTSD.

WHAT THIS MEANS FOR A SURVIVOR

In the tapestry of childhood, trauma threads and golden threads are often woven tightly together.

Parents and other caregivers often were loving, protective, supportive, and growth promoting. It is good to feel gratitude where gratitude is due. It's appropriate, and it feels good.

In my own case, I am really grateful for all the diapers my mom changed and the meals she cooked. I'm also truly grateful for lovely home and the college education my parents provided for me.

In complicated situations, too, gratitude and pride have a place. Here are two such situations:

- The grown child has reason to be grateful, and the mother has reason to be proud of her restraint in walking out of the room when she was tempted to throw something, even though her leaving meant her child felt abandoned.

- The grown daughter, looking back with adult information and wisdom, may have reason to be grateful and her divorced dad has reason to be proud of his restraint in never touching her sexually when she reached puberty and there were only the two of them in his apartment, even though his strategy involved keeping a painful distance between them.

Regardless of a caregivers' intent, you got the treatment you got, and it may have been horribly traumatizing. You don't need to prove they were rotten and abusive (although they may well have been rotten and abusive) in order to have your legitimate feelings of rage and hate. You get to have your feelings about what happened that shouldn't have, or about what didn't happen but should have, whether the agents of these events were well-intentioned, indifferent, or downright hateful.

This mixed caregiving, with no clearcut good guys and bad guys, adds to the naCCT survivor's challenges: For most of us, acknowledging and healing from naCCT will involve living in a complex world of good, bad, and neutral all mixed in together, in the very same people. It requires mature wisdom to live with those contradictions and oppositions.

JENNA LEE DESCRIBES HER FAMILY BACKGROUND

Let's see how this applied to Jenna Lee.

She'd said she had no good reason to be upset, but was that true? I wondered: Could Jenna Lee have a good reason to be upset? Could Jenna Lee have a history of intangible trauma that could have led to complex PTSD?

Maybe it had been difficult for Jenna Lee when she'd been upset in her family growing up. What had happened when things didn't go well in her family? What did her mom and dad do with the wellnigh inevitable ruptures in family relationships, the disagreements and conflicts, the difficult emotions, the problem behaviors and hurt feelings? Had Jenna Lee's upset been harshly dealt with? Or not dealt with at all?

Putting out a little exploratory feeler, I asked, "So your boyfriend thought your family was a mythic happy family, like Ozzie-and-Harriet's TV family. What do *you* think? How was it for you growing up?"

Her eyes darted first out the window, then jumped from object to object in the room, looking for a safe place to rest.

Finally she spoke: "Well, we always had fun. And I had plenty of friends. People even called me 'Sunshine' because I was always smiling. Not like now. . . .What happened between then and now?. . . ."

Shifting slightly in her seat, she corrected herself: "Well, lots of people *still* think I'm cheerful, even when I'm miserable inside.

"Anyway, growing up in my family. Everybody pitched in and kept things running along smoothly. We looked at the bright side of things, and we didn't dwell on our troubles. . . .

"Actually, we didn't have any real troubles. Dad was a natural salesman, so friendly and enthusiastic and persuasive; he did really well at sales and marketing.

"With Mom's gift for staying calm and carrying on, and Dad's upbeat attitude — always right there with a homey joke or inspirational saying — my parents didn't get upset much. . . . I'm the only one. . . . and they certainly didn't stay upset. . . . . No, I didn't *stay* upset either: I always managed to somehow get over it."

As she spoke, she seemed to rearrange her own features into a forced, frozen smile.

Picturing a parent coaxing a teary child to "turn that frown upside down," I wondered if Jenna Lee had learned to manufacture this smile in her "happy" family. "So you had a pretty happy childhood?" I asked.

"Really, nothing was wrong — I'm just feeling sorry for myself," she responded, with a harsh tone creeping into her voice. "I know I have this tendency to feel sorry for myself. Mom used to notice that sometimes. I get so annoyed with myself when I get like this, just making life unpleasant for myself and everyone around me."

NACCT BACKGROUND: NO BLATANT PHYSICALLY ASSAULTIVE TRAUMA

I let myself conjecture about the story Jenna Lee might tell as our work together unfolded.

Jenna Lee said nobody in her family had ever physically assaulted her, or even threatened to assault her. In time, maybe she would remember instances of blatant trauma that she had forgotten or repressed, and maybe she would not.

However, it was quite possible, perhaps even likely, that she had felt chronically threatened with another terror: disconnection and the loss of her life-sustaining bond with her family. I could imagine how that threat might have come about.

Although there are many possible causes for her troubles, here I share with you my thoughts focused on naCCT as a possible cause.

As we've seen, a home in which the only trauma a child suffers is covert may appear happy, peaceful, even enviable. The parents may be successful and kind, active in the community and involved in their children's lives; the house itself may be attractive, even expensive, and well-kept; the life within the house calm, well-mannered and free from alcohol, incest, or physical abuse.

The parents may value parenting and make a conscious effort to give their children the best.

NaCCT in these homes may be so imperceptible that even the traumatized child may think, and believe, "I am so lucky, and I am so miserable; what's wrong with me?" However, after meeting with hundreds of therapy clients who have come from these "happy" homes, it is clear through their compelling stories that while "nothing was the matter" in these homes, something was very wrong.

That mysterious "something very wrong" was often naCCT.

Children in these homes may have learned that if they want to be loved and responded to, they must organize themselves around their Lifeline Caregiver's moods, fears, needs, interests, and belief systems. These children become musical, thin, smart, funny, serious, beautiful, athletic, responsible, productive, defiant, sassy, adventurous, entertaining, clumsy — and also severely traumatized — in response to almost microscopic caregiver disappointments, disapprovals, and rejections.

Survivors who did not experience blatant physically assaultive trauma in their families growing up may view their family as basically fine. Maybe a little weird. Sometimes annoying. But not traumatic.

This is especially true if the emotional, psychological, and social traumas were subtle naCCTs. Flagrant narcissism, verbal abuse, shunning and scapegoating may have been identified. But without flagrant intangible abuse or gross neglect, these survivors are quite likely to think their families were OK.

With no concept of naCCT and nothing tangible to point to, these survivors have trouble getting to the starting line of healing. They can't identify subtle intangible trauma. They tend to shoulder the responsibility for any relationship troubles that do exist. They have limited skill in holding the other person accountable, let alone blaming where blaming might be due.

These survivors end up stuck with the belief: "My Lifeline Caregiver — [mommy or daddy or whoever else] — is good, and if they don't love me it's because I'm bad."

If we listen closely, we may even hear echoes of exasperated, impatient parents' voices in these survivors' exasperation with themselves.

MY CONJECTURES ABOUT JENNA LEE'S FAMILY BACKGROUND

Jenna Lee's words and tone suggested that no loving compassion flowed toward her distress. As we've seen, a survivor's combination of self-blame and impatience with their own distress is, sad to say, typical of people living with PTSD in the aftermath of intangible trauma.

"I make myself sick," is not an unusual comment to hear from a survivor. Serving as everyone else's defense attorneys, they may prosecute themselves unmercifully. This habit of letting everything and everyone except themselves off the hook has deep roots in their naCCT histories.

Even in our first meeting, Jenna Lee's words and gestures suggested that her home was ruled by the silent principle, "No unhappiness allowed," as if her family had a welcome mat featuring a crying face in a circle with a red line slashing diagonally through it. Jenna Lee might have learned, probably from her parents, who probably learned it from their parents, that expressions of sadness and fear were taboo.

Maybe Jenna Lee's parents struggled ("for the sake of the kids") not to raise their voices in front of them and to hide some disappointment in each other and their marriage. Maybe her parents felt good that they were able to protect her from their grief and they struggled "not to let her see them get upset." They practiced what they preached, and even if it was difficult, if they "didn't have something nice to say, they didn't say anything at all."

Jenna Lee might have learned about this taboo as a tiny baby, left to "cry it out" in her crib by parents who believed this would help her develop independence.

She might have learned about the family taboo directly from tenseness in her mother's body as she picked up baby Jenna Lee and tried to hush her when she cried.

With an infant's life-preserving sensitivity to nuances in her caregiver, baby Jenna Lee might have sensed her mother's fear and become frightened herself. Using her innate human capacity to learn how to survive, baby Jenna Lee might have learned without words "if you cry, you get that danger feeling, so don't cry."

As Jenna Lee grew older, her mom might have calmly urged her to dry her eyes and given her sensible practical suggestions that showed she "really had nothing to cry about."

Her upbeat dad might have greeted her tears with an uplifting saying and a little jollying, giving her the message, "Smile and the whole family smiles with you; cry and you cry alone." If she hadn't wanted to lose her place in the family, she would have had to quickly find a way to put on a happy face.

To make matters worse, if Jenna Lee's "happy" family had had no room for unhappiness, then nobody would have helped little Jenna Lee learn how to handle unhappiness. She would have been left alone to fend for herself with her unacknowledged fear and upset.

Being alone and unhelped with fear and upset is traumatic in itself, especially for a little child

What if being upset had been more than little Jenna Lee could handle by herself? In a family that had no room for upset, she would have been in a terrible predicament. She would have been at risk of being cut off from the people she needed in order to stay alive.

And this risk would have added another layer of upset for little Jenna Lee to deal with. Upset on top of upset.

Extreme upset on top of upset is known as "emotional dysregulation" in the mental health and psychotherapy communities. You may have heard the phrase. It's used a lot these days. It appears, for instance, in the name of a new childhood diagnostic category for extreme irritability, anger, and frequent, intense temper outbursts: Disruptive Mood Dysregulation Disorder (DMDD). And some people now use the term "Emotional Dysregulation Disorder" as an unofficial diagnosis.

"Emotional dysregulation" means that someone has trouble controlling thoughts, feelings, and actions in response to what happens to them. It's a fancy way of talking about getting upset and having trouble calming down.

This "getting upset" or "emotional dysregulation" is central to naCCT.

Like Jenna Lee, people who struggle with the aftereffects of naCCT often present themselves in therapy with "emotional dysregulation:" intense emotions such as anger, tears, fear, and helplessness; racing thoughts; all worked up; super- sensitive to subtle disturbances, thoughtlessness, and slights. All the stuff we mean when we say "really upset."

And like Jenna Lee, people who struggle with the aftereffects of naCCT of become afraid of this painful state. She faced the internal threat of her emotional dysregulation and the external threat of not belonging to her family. If she failed to "turn the corners of her mouth up," she would have risked a painful encounter with that mental image of disconnection from her composed, pleasant parents.

To prevent this terrifying disconnection, she would have had to show them she wasn't upset. She might have tried to hide the upset that she couldn't handle and to cover it over with a smiley face.

These images of possible disconnection could have become a chronic threat for Jenna Lee. Experiences like these in Jenna Lee's early life would explain why her smile looked frozen: she could be petrified of what would happen if she failed to smile.

NACCT BACKGROUND: DOUBLE SURVIVORS OF BOTH BLATANT PHYSICALLY ASSAULTIVE TRAUMA AND NACCT

And what about people who've survived both overt physically assaultive trauma and naCCT? People who either remember or suspect that they have endured overt traumas such as physical or sexual abuse?

A man I'll call Tom survived both types of trauma. He tells his story:

"My mother swung between violent anger and helpless despair. When she got furious, she would hurl whatever she was holding at me — books, ashtrays, even the can of corn she was opening for dinner.

"I knew this was traumatic, but what was even worse was when she'd be lying on our old green sofa in front of the TV with the sound turned way down. Even in summer, she'd have this old quilt pulled up around her.

"Then I would forget how scared I'd been of her rage.

"She would look at me out of her watery gray eyes, desperate. She would sob: 'I don't want to go on living. Please, do something; please, help me.' I was so afraid she'd die, and I didn't know what to do to help her.

"I'd feel myself sinking down into blankness, darkness, dizziness. Doomed. Those times were even worse than the trauma."

The way Tom tells his story is very revealing. Seeing his mother in that state of despair, having the terrifying responsibility of providing psychological life support for her thrust upon him, and fearing that if he failed he would lose her may be "worse than the trauma," but Tom doesn't call those times "trauma" at all.

As Tom tells it, living through his mother's angry assaults is "the trauma," and those times when she turned to him in despair? Well, he just knew those times "were even worse than the trauma."

Those "worse times" were, in fact, times Tom experienced naCCT.

Like Tom, people who've experienced blatant physically assaultive trauma in their families of origin have probably come to view their family as problematic, to say the least. They *know* something traumatic happened to them and they *know* that it is normal to be affected by it. They may already identify themselves as trauma survivors. Maybe they've used words like "traumatic" or "abusive." Other people may have gasped when they told their stories; those other people might have even used the word "trauma." These trauma survivors may even be working hard already to grieve and to heal the resulting complex PTSD.

But, also like Tom, they may only have addressed healing the blatant, physically-assaultive trauma.

The profound intangible interpersonal naCCT that accompanies blatant overt trauma may never have been addressed.

You would think it would go without saying that if, for example, a parent's overtly traumatic physical abuse sends a child to the emergency room with a broken rib, that parent has also caused naCCT by violating the child's emotional well-being and rupturing the safe bond between parent and child. Isn't it obvious that a parent whose physical assault traumatizes their child also *psychologically* traumatizes the child?

But NaCCT is often overlooked, even by the victims themselves. How can this be?

Does the obvious terror of blatant trauma sometimes blind people to the hidden terror of intangible trauma?

Have NaCCTs been rendered invisible by the glare of physical assault or in the dark chaos of incest?

Like Tom, survivors of physically assaultive traumas need to acknowledge naCCT is real trauma, not merely some incidental annoyance that they "probably shouldn't be too upset about."

This book will help you who, like Tom, have survived both overt and covert trauma. You may be surprised to find how much pain your subtle intangible traumas have caused you.

You will learn that it is legitimate to grieve naCCTs as well as blatant physical traumas. Working this book with a focus on intangible traumas will help you to validate that pain and heal the PTSD those traumas may have caused.

FORTUNATELY, THERE'S HOPE FOR HEALING THE AFTEREFFECTS OF NACCT

If you're struggling with the aftermath of these intangible traumas from your childhood lifeline relationships, you deserve help.

For many survivors of naCCT, the help that's been offered has felt like a hit-or-miss jumble of partial solutions thrown at an unclear mix of troubles. These attempts at help may have missed the mark because they failed to identify and address the naCCT problem at the root. If so, it's no wonder the help hasn't been too helpful.

The aftereffects of naCCT can be properly treated if they are properly diagnosed. I have listened to many stories of intangible interpersonal traumas and helped people chip away at the huge task of resolving them. After thirty-plus years of providing psychosocial counseling to more than two thousand people, and many more years investigating my own mysterious stuckness, I can say with confidence that people can heal.

A solution can be implemented if the problem is correctly identified. And the problem can be identified if you know what to look for and what to do.

JOIN ME. I'LL SHARE WHAT WORKED FOR ME AND MY CLIENTS

You'll learn to come alongside yourself.

You'll learn that you make sense.

You'll stop feeling ashamed of being stuck.

You'll learn your grief and pain are legitimate.

You'll learn to apply the tools and techniques traumatologists have used to help survivors of overt physical trauma.

You'll uncover the treasure that got buried along with the trauma inside of you.

"WE NEED A BOOK OF OUR OWN"

From autobiographical memoirs to psychological self-help, books on blatant trauma abound. These books often provide valuable information about the impact of trauma on body, mind, and spirit and suggest ways of healing.

However, these books fail to acknowledge naCCT. They offer no direct help either to survivors like Tom, who acknowledged his physically-assaultive trauma but was blind to his naCCT, or to those like Jenna Lee, who viewed her family history as basically fine.

When survivors who have no blatant trauma in their past read these books, they sometimes try to squeeze their own histories into the overt trauma model. In the process, they find they distort the truth of their own experience.

They are often distressed by having to analogize from so-called "real traumas" to their own. As one naCCT survivor put it, "I felt like I was trespassing when I read Ellen Bass' and Laura Davis' great book *The Courage to Heal* (1988, New York: Harper and Row). Even though I could relate to so much of what those incest survivors talked about, I felt like I was sneaking healing meant for others.

These naCCT survivors say, "We need a book of our own."

Here's that book. If you are a survivor of naCCT, you now have a book of your own.

HOW THIS BOOK WILL SERVE YOU

The information in this book is intended to help all survivors of naCCT take it seriously. Take back your self respect. You are not a feeble organism with bad genes. You were dealt a serious blow. The key to recovery is accurate acknowledgement of the serious impact the trauma had on you.

This book focuses on the specific and unique problems that arise from naCCT. It is designed to empower you with both awareness and action, so you know what to look for and what to do. It will offer you validation, guidance, and encouragement that will help you to dignify your distress and extend well-deserved compassion to yourself.

This book will also help you reclaim the parts of yourself that you have lost along the way —scared child parts that went into exile, parts that went underground for safety.

Don't wait until you remember some "objectively" awful memory of tangible abuse, start honoring your pain today; if it hurts, the pain is real and deserves care.

If you are struggling with PTSD from intangible trauma, this book will help you take the necessary steps to heal your wounds and begin to lead a full, meaningful, connected life.

It's hard work. Stop feeling ashamed of failing at something easy, and start feeling proud of hanging in there and not giving up on something really difficult.

This book will help you roll up your sleeves and continue to fight for your right to be fully alive, passionate, and free. Take pride in how well you have managed so far. And eventually you will be legitimately proud of succeeding at something very hard

THIS BOOK FOCUSES ON WHAT YOU CAN DO FOR YOURSELF

You can use this book with therapy. But relationships — even therapy relationships — are fraught with triggers, and sometimes therapy for naCCT gets very tangled and difficult. This book can help you take care of yourself when or if that happens. It helps you understand triggers and manage them — even when they happen in therapy.

IDEALLY:

Once you reach a place of understanding your experience and trusting your perception of what happened, you can feel empowered to act in your own best interests. You will become fully present in your own life, making profoundly wise choices based on your deepest truth. You may find that your deepest self is still excited, still curious, still filled with wonder, love, and delight.

REALISTICALLY:

Complex PTSD is complex, as the name indicates. The process of your recovery will also be complex, most likely made up of many small healing moments. It most likely won't be easy, it won't be fast, but it can be done.

To lift your spirits, dear reader, here's a typical example of one of those small healing moments:

JENNA LEE BRINGS COMPASSION HOME TO HERSELF

There would come a time when I could talk with Jenna Lee about what happened when she got upset and dysregulated. We've seen and heard how she blamed herself, sank into shame, became impatient, went numb, or pasted on a happy mask and exerted rigid self-control.

A moment of relief from her upset and self-blame would be a blessing for Jenna Lee.

As a teacher, she was wise and skillful in dealing with discouraged or frustrated kids. She could handle upset. As often happens, Jenna Lee had grown up to give others what she herself had needed as a child and still needed as an adult: gentle empathy and responsive assistance when she was upset.

Maybe she could bring this skillful caring home to herself.

Tentatively, I began, "Children often feel upset like you do right now, and they aren't shy about letting their feelings show. I wonder. . . do you have to deal with kids who are having a hard time, all distraught and dysregulated?"

Jenna Lee brightened. "Oh, just about every day some kid gets really upset," she said. "My heart goes out to them. . . I squat right down to their eye-level. I talk in a soft voice and try to connect with them and understand what they're all upset about."

She stopped abruptly. "Oh, wait a minute!. . . . I don't tell them they're wrong or bad for feeling upset."

"So you comfort a child who feels upset like you do now," I said, "and you try to understand what they're all upset about?"

Tears filled her hazel eyes and hung there, glistening. Jenna Lee's frozen smile yielded to a slight quiver in her lower lip, almost as if another person lived behind her sunshine mask, peeking out and eavesdropping on our conversation with interest and even hope.

She said quietly, "When those kids are upset, I'm really gentle with them." Again she reached up and fluffed her hair.

WHAT JENNA LEE'S HEALING MOMENT SHOWS US

As she got in touch with her emotional pain, a tender new shoot of awareness stirred in her: maybe she, Jenna Lee, *also* deserved love, comfort, and understanding rather than shame, blame, and harshness when she felt upset.

Although I knew that at some point in the future she might balk and backtrack, for now Jenna Lee came alongside herself and gave herself an island of soothing from which she could plan and act to improve the quality of her life.

THE NEED TO COME COMPASSIONATELY AND EFFECTIVELY ALONGSIDE YOURSELF

This work of becoming effectively responsive to oneself is core work in the healing of naCCT. Its absence is one of the major wounds of naCCT. Healing this wound is difficult, and it is helpful to start addressing it right from the beginning.

When Jenna Lee described her response to upset kids, she summed up a crucial response to distress and the challenges of recovering from Chronic Covert Trauma. Remember her saying:

- My heart goes out to them.

- I squat right down to their eye-level.

- I talk in a soft voice.

- I try to connect with them and understand what they're all upset about.

When she gave herself the same empathic tenderness she gave to her troubled special education students, Jenna Lee's healing began. We would all do well to remember Jenna Lee's words when we're upset. Coming kindly and effectively alongside ourselves, trying to connect and understand.

NOW YOUR TURN

Now you've been introduced to naCCT. Congratulate yourself on reading this far. You've been able to hold in your awareness the connection between adult problems and childhood trauma, the intangible roots of present problems. That's a significant accomplishment. Claim it.

Reflect on what this reading experience has felt like for you. Check in with yourself. Would you benefit from squatting down to your own eye level and giving yourself some understanding attention?

Does what you read shed some light on some of your experiences?

Could you be among the people whose adult lives are diminished by the aftereffects of unidentified childhood naCCT, especially those people who have tried to change and feel stuck?

Is there someone you want to tell about what you've read, felt, and thought about here?

If you struggle with anxiety, hopelessness, depression, addictions, physical problems, unhappy relationships, unsatisfying work, and if you have strengths such as being a good neighbor, good citizen and good friend; being empathetic, helpful, reliable, cooperative, and finding yourself able to keep on functioning while feeling distressed; and if you find yourself resonating with trauma "for no reason", perhaps you too have some naCCT in your past that is still a force in your present life today.

If you're grappling with these problems, you can turn to this book for assistance.

When you feel ready to move on, the next chapter will help you identify "Is this You?"

CHAPTER 2

IS THIS YOU?

Could you be someone whose current happiness is undermined by PTSD from non-physically-assaultive, attachment-based Chronic Covert Trauma from childhood?

Perhaps you have some naCCT in your past that is still a force in your present life today. Could some of your problems be trauma wounds? Read on.

You may have already said, "Yes, this is me." If so, read this section for the purpose of coming alongside yourself and taking stock of your challenges and resources.

YOUR COURAGEOUS COMMITMENT TO HELPING YOURSELF

POSITIVE SELF-HELP ATTRIBUTES:

Because you've picked up this book and read this far, my hunch is you're someone who's willing to take some pains to honor this precious gift of life you've been given. You'll roll up your sleeves and do some heavy work because you seek out truth. You commit to soul-searching. You're willing to dig deep and work hard.

You're psychology-minded, open to new points of view. In some ways you are flexible and strong. You're able to stand back and reflect on people and circumstances. You take responsibility for your mental health. You're psychologically responsible, pro-active, investigative.

Are you a pretty reflective, self-help reader? A seeker of transformational growth? With the capacity for self-reflection, and the ability to speak about your thoughts and feelings.

You may already be someone who explores deep transformational work in the present by examining the impact of childhood experiences on adult life.

In the area of self-help, far from being a "couch potato," you're probably more of a self-help go-getter. You've probably done some committed personal growth work already, whether it's been twelve-step or other recovery groups, extensive reading, classes, on-line websites and forums, or psychotherapy.

Maybe you're also a healer yourself: maybe a professional therapist, a very sympathetic hairdresser or bartender, or simply the person other people come to with their troubles.

You may or may not be an action hero, but you are definitely a soul hero. You've shown courage to come this far, and you're gathering courage to push even further in this heroic quest of self-awareness and awakening.

WHAT BROUGHT YOU TO THIS BOOK?

Are you drawn to this book because you already suspect that you might have PTSD from early naCCT? Do you suspect from how they relate to you and other people today that mother, father, or other Lifeline Caregivers were problems for you as a child? Maybe one was immature or controlling or downright abusive, or diagnosed with narcissistic personality disorder, borderline personality disorder, Asperger's or autism, or Sensory Processing Disorder.

Maybe you are drawn to this book by some mixture of the usual stuff that psychotherapists call "presenting problems" — those problems that are right there in your face every day, demanding attention and undercutting the quality of your life.

Specific "presenting problems" vary from one naCCT survivor to another. A few typical ones are listed below. Mentally check the ones that apply to you:

- Mood disorder: depression, anxiety

- Chronic pain or other physical problems with a stress component

- Unsatisfying relationships; co-dependence
- Substance or behavioral addictions
- Issues with work, career, money
- Troublesome thoughts and feelings about yourself

With many threads snarled into a painful tangle of bewildered hopelessness and self-blame, these problems may be on-going, almost a part of your nature. Or they may be intermittent, popping up at inopportune times and tormenting you.

You may think, "I've tried everything," but have you tried addressing PTSD from those early non-physically-assaultive, attachment-based, Chronic Covert Traumas?

CHARACTERISTIC NACCT TIP-OFFS

Along with the challenge of these presenting problems, you may also be aware of some deep issues that may be tip-offs signaling: "Look for naCCT". Recognizing these deep issues, coming alongside them, and working with them can lead to more than problem management. Doing so can lead to deep life transformation.

Here are 5 tip-offs that naCCT is a factor you could address to improve your life.

TIP-OFF #1: MYSTERIOUS STUCKNESS

What was supposed to work, didn't. Or at least didn't work the way you hoped it would. Do you still feel stuck after some stress management or mindfulness training, attending a self-help group, or exploring an on-line transformational package? A pain management program? Body-based approaches like yoga or a change in diet or exercise?

Willpower alone hasn't worked over the long haul?

Psychiatric medications may only have been of moderate help or none at all, and you're left wondering, "Did they give me the placebos?"

Something is keeping you stuck.

Even after psychotherapy, you might still feel stuck. Maybe the therapy went bad. Maybe it just petered out.

Some recent research results are enlightening here. Guess who is helped least by traditional psychotherapy? People whose primary form of childhood trauma was "emotional abuse and/or emotional neglect."[1]

So, getting stuck in therapy may be an additional tip-off that naCCT is at work in your presenting problems.

TIP-OFF #2: NEGATIVE ATTITUDES TOWARD THIS MYSTERIOUS STUCKNESS

Being stuck with unsolved problems is bad enough.

Some naCCT survivors have another challenging layer of troubles to deal with: harsh negative judgmental attitudes toward their problems, towards themselves for having them, and for being stuck and failing to solve them.

Typical troubling feelings and thoughts about being stuck with unsolved problems include these:

- **Confusion and bewilderment:** "I've put a lot of effort into self-help and therapy, and yet I still have these troubles. How can that be? I must be mental. I don't make sense."

- **Self-disgust and contempt:** "I make myself sick."

- **Shame:** "I must be defective. There is no good reason for me to still have this problem.'"

- **Guilt:** "I must not be trying hard enough."

- **Aggravated, contemptuous impatience:** "Hurry up! Are you STILL having a hard time? Get over it!"

- **Sad futility:** "There's nothing to do but cry. Why bother?"

- **Resignation; discouraged but philosophical:** "I'm hopeless. Nothing will help. That's just the way I am, and that's just the way it is."

- **Apathy:** "I don't care. It doesn't matter."

Negative layers of problematic feelings, thoughts, and attitudes keep building up.

For example, you may feel ashamed of feeling afraid. Or you might go into a fog when you feel angry. Or berate yourself for getting upset. Or find yourself worrying about worrying. Or being afraid of being afraid.

These negative attitudes towards yourself for having those problems persist. Affirmations haven't shifted them. Logic has proven powerless in the face of these negative attitudes. It's another place you find yourself stuck.

These persistent negative attitudes are further tipoffs that naCCT is at work.

TIP-OFF #3: PROBLEMS HANDLING UPSETS

We need soothing and effective help when we're upset. Many of us naCCT survivors have a hard time providing that for ourselves.

What happens when you get upset? What happens inside of you? Do you come alongside yourself and give yourself comfort in a wholesome, healing way?

Maybe there are times when you can't help yourself at all. Maybe you even get so upset that you find yourself in that "emotionally dysregulated" state discussed in the previous chapter.

To review, "emotional dysregulation" is that state of being caught in such a vicious cycle that instead of calming down, you get more and more upset. You even get upset about being upset. You go numb, get hyper-worked up, or go rigid. You can't calm down or regulate your thinking, your feelings, your impulses and desires. You definitely can't plan your most effective next steps. Even your body resonates this upset.

Some naCCT survivors ward off emotional dysregulation in ways that have some powerfully negative aspects themselves: turning to food undermines your health and attractiveness; shutting down and going numb also shuts down your joy and vitality; "keeping busy" annoys your family, produces very little, and leaves you exhausted.

To make matters worse, many naCCT survivors tend to have trouble being helped by other people with their upset.

Try asking yourself, "What happens with other people when I'm upset? Do I turn to anyone for help? If so, who? What is their response? How do I feel when they respond that way?"

And then try asking the most crucial questions: "What happened when I was upset when I was little? Did I turn to anyone for help? What happened? How did they react to me? Were they caring? Comforting? Helpful? Impatient? So flummoxed they didn't know what to do? Did they offer suggestions?"

Many survivors remember some responses that were helpful: Being taken care of when they were sick. Being helped out with money.

Some survivors remember different people responding in different ways — for example, the stereotypical tender mother and the tough "suck it up" dad. Some remember tension as the different caregivers disagreed with each other about how to respond to being upset.

Some remember anger or coldness or panic.

Many remember feeling alone, doing their best to calm themselves down on their own and get done what needed to be done.

When you're disturbed — from uneasy to outraged — by thinking about what happened when you were upset growing up, look for some naCCT.

TIP-OFF #4: RESONANCE WITH PTSD

For people with blatant, physically-assaultive trauma in their histories, resonance with PTSD is to be expected. However, these survivors can be puzzled because the areas of life where the resonance is felt often differ from the areas of life where the blatant trauma occurred.

For people with no blatant trauma in their childhood history, this resonance with PTSD feels downright inexplicable. Even though they may not have lived through combat or rape or beatings, they may feel a kinship with a film portrayal of a combat veteran trying to adjust to civilian life, or a man trying to reclaim his spirituality after an assault by a pedophile priest, or an incest survivor struggling to be in an intimate relationship.

This resonance with PTSD in the absence of blatant physically-assaultive trauma suggests that addressing naCCT would have a big payoff in your current life.

Here are some of the specific ways you might resonate with PTSD:

YOU MAY EXPERIENCE A NAMELESS DREAD, AN ATMOSPHERE OF IMPENDING HORROR AND DOOM

As though an ominous horror movie soundtrack is playing in the background as you go forward in your life, you might resonate with the dread and terror felt by people with PTSD.

Your dread may not be front and center. It may be flitting across your

IS THIS YOU? 41

field of awareness. It may be a vague ominous undertone to daily life, especially when you aren't rushed and busy. It may be lurking, about to spring out and pounce. It may be there when you lie in bed at night or when you wake up. It may be a flutter in your stomach, or your hair standing on end. It may be the feeling like a sudden death threat, right in the midst of daily life.

It's not necessarily a fear of anything. It's just fear.

You may feel that you're always on at least yellow alert, with irritability, isolation, and nervousness accompanying a feeling that a crisis could erupt at any moment so you always need to be prepared and vigilant.

YOU MAY EXPERIENCE REACTIONS THAT ARE AMPED WAY UP OR TONED WAY DOWN

Maybe you tell yourself — or people tell you — that you overreact. You're extremely sensitive. A "Drama Queen."

Although you probably don't do anything dramatic and hyper like diving under a table when you hear a helicopter, you may experience the hair-trigger, "wired" jumpiness and sudden explosions of activity that often seem to go with PTSD.

Or maybe you tell yourself — or people tell you — that you *underreact*. That you're extremely *insensitive*. A "Cold Fish." Maybe you manage intimations of danger by avoiding situations or trying to shut down your reactions and anesthetize yourself.

You might resonate with the way PTSD drives people to swing back and forth between being hyper and being numb.

YOU MAY EXPERIENCE INTRUSIVE PTSD SYMPTOMS

The most famous PTSD symptoms are the intrusive ones: bad moods, bad dreams, flashbacks, and out-of-character behavior that makes you ask afterwards "What got into me?"

Do you have bad dreams? Do the bad feelings from the dreams linger and ruin your day? Does the fear of bad dreams deprive you of sleep?

Flashbacks can be mood flashbacks, emotional flashbacks, or entire State-of-Being Flashbacks where it's as though you're reliving a traumatic experience or back in a traumatic relationship.

Does a difficult mood, attitude, or impulse come over you "out of the blue?" When you reflect on something you've done or said, do you find yourself apologizing, "I'm so sorry, my buttons just got pushed." Do you wonder, "I don't know why I picked up the phone when I swore I'd never call him again" or "I don't know why I find myself saying 'yes, OK' when I'm really feeling 'no way!'"

Do invasive memories, impulses, moods, mental pictures, thoughts, fears and other feelings just take over?

One survivor quipped: "I need a pair of chocolate shoes because I so often put my foot in my mouth with some dumb insensitive remark."

Another survivor laments: ""Sometimes I feel like I'm not the boss of my own life. It's all bad dreams and awful moods. Sometimes I even act against what I know are my own best interests."

Another intrusive PTSD symptom is a drop in energy level. Dread may be hidden behind an urge to sleep, to escape into oblivion rather than face some vague challenge that could be overwhelming, unbearable. You might feel very fatigued. You might experience a desire for a general anesthesia, as you vaguely anticipate something awful, painful, even unendurable, looming up ahead and mentally request, "Just numb me out."

YOU MAY EXPERIENCE CONSTRICTIVE SYMPTOMS

Constrictive symptoms of PTSD are often subtle. They include avoidance, shutting out, pushing away, staying away, isolation, hiding out, hunkering down, and not doing things or going places. Constrictive symptoms may even extend to social phobia or agoraphobia (the fear of going out into the outside world.)

Have people said you're uptight? Rigid? A "stick in the mud?"

Do you feel bound? Trapped? Claustrophobic? Constrictive symptoms can lead people to:

- **Refuse opportunities:** "I automatically say 'No!'"

- **Inhibit action:** "The consequences of the smallest action I might take could be disastrous."

- **Not quite connect with people:** "Something blocks real intimacy."

- **Procrastinate:** "I put things off, lose things, generally screw up."

- **Avoid making the most of your own potential:** "I'm a 'gifted underachiever' and underearner."

- **Block thoughts and feelings:** "I tune stuff out."

- **Block desires:** "I don't know what I want. Wanting feels really dangerous. To be safe, I put my appetite to sleep, numbed it out with Novocain."

- **Block authentic engagement in life itself:** "I have a buried self somewhere, a buried life."

Are you stuck in a comfort zone that sometimes feels like a confinement zone? Or worse, sometimes feels like a captivity zone?

THE ANALOGY TO THE PET PROTECTION SYSTEM, THE "INVISIBLE FENCE"

One of my friend's dogs ran out into the road and almost got hit by a car. So my friend installed one of those hidden underground pet protection systems.

"I love it," he says. "There's no ugly fence to ruin the landscaping, and the dogs can run free in the yard. No more risking their lives running out into the road. I had to install an underground electrical field around the yard and put special collars on the dogs. . . . comfortable collars that give a mild shock when one of them tries to run out of the yard and into the road. . ."

The Invisible fence is the perfect metaphor for the constrictive symptoms of PTSD.

Without knowing it, have *you* set up a personal "electronic pet protection system" with a shock collar and a hidden electronic fence for yourself? Do *you* get a mild shock in the form of negative thoughts or feelings if you start to go outside the fenced-in "comfort zone?"

Has this ever happened to you? You embark on a project with the best intentions, a lot of enthusiasm and commitment. Maybe for self-improvement, better relationships, community engagement, or spiritual development. It really feels like you're following your bliss. Then you come up against a snag. You get scared, or lose interest, get bogged down, maybe even get sick.

Or maybe the irresistible impulse to party or watch another sitcom undermines the next action step toward your dream. A series of fearful thoughts breaks into your agenda for expansion, so you stay small and drop your ambition. The nightmare about what might happen if you pursue your vision squashes the vision altogether.

People are generally not even aware of this "pet protection" system at work. Once it's installed, we don't think about the hidden fence, don't actually *feel* the shock collar. We may have learned to stay so far away from the outer edge of the fenced-in area that we never get "shocks." We have trained ourselves well to stay safe inside our fenced-in yards.

Overall, the atmosphere of dread, the over- or under-reactions, the bad dreams and flashbacks, the constrictive symptoms, the hidden fence and shock collar, all these resonances with PTSD can be tip-offs to investigate naCCT.

TIP-OFF #5: NOT TAKING INTANGIBLE ATTACHMENT INJURIES SERIOUSLY AND DISQUALIFYING THEM AS TRAUMA

The "Molehill" Problem: Dismissing attachment injuries as trivial. You remember being distressed as a child, but disqualify the distressing experience as trauma.

This tip-off is quite prevalent for naCCT survivors who grew up in families where there wasn't blatant physically-assaultive trauma.

Do you compare yourself to people who've endured what you call "real trauma" and then feel guilty, ashamed, or confused?

NaCCT survivors who *did* experience blatant physically assaultive trauma may disqualify their intangible attachment traumas by comparing them to their own blatant, physically-assaultive "real" traumas. They may take their blatant trauma wounds seriously, but dismiss and invalidate their naCCTs.

"BUT HOW COULD I HAVE PTSD?"

Maybe you relate somewhat to the tip-offs listed above.

But you wonder: "How could I have PTSD"

You tell yourself: "I've had a pretty decent childhood. I had it pretty good, pretty caring caregivers. Pinning my problems on my upbringing would be unrealistic and unfair. None of my grievances are legitimate."

Like Jenna Lee in the first chapter, you find yourself puzzled. Like Sinedu at Harvard, you "can't point to any tangible cause." You weren't subjected to incest, or alcoholism, or violence in your family. In fact, you weren't ever hit. You can't think of a time when you were threatened with death or any form of physical attack.

You wonder, "If my childhood was so easy, why am I finding life today so *hard?*"

Do you sometimes think: "Maybe something happened to cause these problems I have today," but you can't pinpoint memories of anything that seems dire enough to cause the persistence and strength of your challenges today.

Do you sometimes feel confused and puzzled, wondering: "There were some quirks in the family I grew up in, but no big traumas, certainly no physical attacks with material damage to my tissues. Nothing was really traumatically wrong in my family when I was a child, so what can be wrong with me today?"

SO, "IS THIS YOU?"

If you are an naCCT survivor with PTSD, very likely underneath whatever present-day problems and aspirations motivate you to read this book, you are faced with this cluster of stuckness, self-blame, spiraling upset and dysregulation around relationships, and inexplicable resonance with PTSD. Any of these can tip you off to the possible presence of intangible trauma and PTSD. . . . and suggest you'll benefit from investigating further.

Now I'm going to tell you how books, or what my librarian friends refer to as my "friends in books," helped me understand my problem. And then it will be *your* turn to think about whether this applies to you.

HERE'S HOW IT WAS FOR ME, RICIA

PERHAPS LIKE YOU, I HAD MANY OF THESE INDICATORS

If this book had existed when I was struggling to improve my life many years ago, my answer to all the questions earlier in this chapter would have been "Yes, this is pretty much me."

Yes, possibly like you, I was a pretty reflective, psychology-minded self-help reader and personal growth seeker.

Yes, I had some positive self-help attributes: persistent, determined not to give up on my own well-being, resourceful.

I had some big areas of effective, even happy, living and loving...both now AND in my childhood.

Perhaps like some of you, I had had a pretty good, calm, nonviolent childhood.

I thought my family of origin was basically fine, maybe with a few quirks due to my parents' idiosyncrasies and a few glitches due to the infant care practices in vogue when I was born. But basically fine.

I was in the prevailing ethnic group in the USA when I grew up: White. Protestant. Middle class. Both parents healthy and still living together. No booze. No beatings. No sexual violations. Things ran smoothly in our house.

My parents gave me rides to friends' houses, the library, and Sunday school. They showed interest in my school work and helped when I got stuck. They sent me to Girl Scout camp and swimming lessons. Helped me memorize my lines for the class play. Had snacks ready when my friends came over after school.

Other kids liked to come to my house. They said my parents were nice. In fact, my parents *were* nice.

Maybe a little too much "go along to get along" existed where assertiveness would have worked better. Maybe my parents were a little uptight and prudish, but who wasn't in those days?

But even with all those positives, something was wrong. With no book like this to explain to me what it was, I felt confused and wondered, "If nothing was traumatically wrong in my family when I was a child, what can be wrong with me today?"

My answers to the five deep, foundational tip-offs to naCCT would have been "yes:"

MY TIP-OFF #1: MYSTERIOUS STUCKNESS? DEFINITE "YES!"

Troubling symptoms and challenges mysteriously persisted in spite of a lot of therapy and self-help work. As a therapist, I attended many professional workshops and trainings. Someone could have accused me of being a personal growth junkie, I went to so many growth groups, seminars, yoga classes, and journaling workshops. Almost as if I was in "self-help overload."

I knew there were therapies for trauma, a whole toolbox of them. I was a psychotherapist, licensed as both a mental health counselor and social worker. I worked with people dealing with chronic physical pain, and resolving early trauma often played a role in healing their pain.

However, *I didn't feel legitimate using those tools myself.*

MY TIP-OFF #2: NEGATIVE ATTITUDES TOWARDS THIS MYSTERIOUS STUCKNESS? YUP!

Definitely "Yes." Impatient. Aggravated. "What's wrong with you? Just try harder!" Sometimes self-indulgent. Sometimes "Don't bother; you're hopeless; give up!"

Sometimes making a big push for positive change, and sometimes just feeling resigned, mildly despairing yet philosophical: "That's just the way I am, and that's just the way it is." (And then go find something good to eat.)

I could not figure out why I had such a persistently hard time making the needed changes, and often felt ashamed having such a *hard* time with such an *easy* life.

MY TIP-OFF #3: PROBLEMS HANDLING UPSETS

What happened when I was upset as a child? I was carefully helped with practical problems like schoolwork and sickness. I received mega-help if I was upset about something I had to do that my mother liked to help me do, such as a scrapbook or a science project, or coming up with creative solutions to small practical problems. My parents liked, no, they *loved* helping me with those upsets.

But when I was upset over emotional or social problems, I was pretty much on my own.

MY TIP-OFF #4: PUZZLING, INEXPLICABLE RESONANCE WITH PTSD? "YES" TO THIS TOO!

- **The nameless dread and doom** could come over me for no apparent reason.

- **The mixture of overreactions and underreactions,** the sudden upsets over trivial rudeness; the moments when I'd reflect on my actions and ask myself, "What got into me?"

- **The intrusive symptoms:** The bad dreams; the sudden low energy state; or the appearance of a mighty inner critic.

- **The constrictive symptoms:** The Shock Collar keeping me hunkered down inside that invisible fence. The failure to follow through on opportunities.

MY TIP-OFF #5: NOT TAKING INTANGIBLE ATTACHMENT INJURIES SERIOUSLY AND DISQUALIFYING THEM AS TRAUMA

"BUT HOW COULD I HAVE PTSD?"

I minimized my troubles and disqualified them as trauma.

I've been a licensed psychotherapist for a long time. I've known my way around diagnoses for a long time. For years, I poured over the qualifying symptoms of PTSD in the American Psychiatric Association's *Diagnostic and Statistical Manual of Mental Disorders*, generally referred to as "*the DSM.*"

I did not seem to qualify as a valid PTSD sufferer because I could not point to any qualifying threat to my life or physical integrity. Furthermore, the nature of the qualifying PTSD symptoms seemed to be jumpy, nervous, and hyper, not depressed like my troubles tended to be.

Along with the shame and guilt I felt for being so stuck when I'd had it so relatively easy, I felt *more* shame and guilt if I even *thought* of claiming PTSD when my symptoms didn't seem to fit the description, and I had experienced no "real" trauma.

Back then, I wasted a lot of time and energy because I didn't know that trauma could happen without a horrific physical assault.

Of course I wondered if there *was* some ("real," qualifying physically assaultive) trauma I had repressed.

I repeatedly fell back into the quagmire of mysterious stuckness mixed with a bad attitude towards it that kept me even more stuck.

BACK THEN, I LONGED FOR A VALIDATING CHAMPION

I had no book like this to explain what was going on with me. But I *did* have a powerful longing for some explanation that would help me get unstuck.

I longed for a strong validating champion to come along, take me by the shoulders, look me in the eyes, and assert with absolute conviction,

"You aren't just spoiled, lazy, thin-skinned, without willpower or stick-to-it-ive-ness, depressed for no good reason. In reality, there *is* a good reason you're having such a hard time: Something *did* happen. Something *did* traumatize you."

❧

I RECEIVED A VICARIOUS, INDIRECT DIAGNOSIS OF TRAUMA

Help came from my "friends in books."

Maybe you are a person who gets help from books. You're here now, reading this book and I hope it's helping you. I definitely am a person who gets help from books. Especially in the days before the internet.

My initial help arrived via a psychiatric case study in a book. There I got my validating champion.

In their book *"Ego Psychology: Theory and Practice,"* Doctors Gertrude and Rubin Blanck, a married couple and professional psychotherapy team in New York City, present the case of a man in his early 20's whom they call Mr. Baker.[2]

I IDENTIFIED WITH MR. BAKER

Mr. Baker's case was ordinary, somewhat prosaic, and sensitively told. Maybe because his case was so ordinary, I was really identifying with it.

Mr. Baker, the oldest of four children, had grown up in a middle class American family. No physical abuse existed in his family, no alcoholism, not even divorce. His parents, like mine, were still alive, still married to each other. Like mine, his parents took good material care of him, even providing him with a college education.

I ALSO IDENTIFIED WITH MR. BAKER'S THERAPY

Mr. Baker's therapy was pretty ordinary too. Interesting to psychology-minded folk, but not the material for an action film. Not even much of a melodrama.

Mr. Baker sought therapy when he found himself socially isolated and anxious after graduating from college.

I could relate. Who didn't feel somewhat lost after transitioning from school to the wide, unstructured world outside?

Mr. Baker's therapy was not dramatic. No suicide threats, no overdoses, no cutting himself, no drug addiction, no arrests. The big dramatic "action" involved Mr. Baker getting anxious and angry when his therapist revealed her vacation plans.

Mr. Baker's therapist soothed him. She encouraged him to talk about how frightened and angry he felt about her going away and abandoning him.

As they explored his upset together, he told her about the terror he'd felt as a three-year-old when his parents went out for the evening. His therapist showed compassion for the little boy who spent the whole evening crouched in a corner, sweating in fear that before his parents came home, wolves would get him and eat him.

In contrast to his parents, Mr. Baker's therapist helped him handle his abandonment fears. She understood how horrible she seemed to him for leaving, how angry this made him, and how his anger at her frightened him.

He slowly learned that she could stand hearing about these feelings. And he slowly learned that he could stand feeling them.

He gradually became comfortable and secure enough in their relationship that when she finally left on vacation, he calmly wished her a good time.

I enjoyed reading Mr. Baker's story. I imagined receiving caring empathy from this capable therapist, who understood the hurt and anger that comes up when a therapist "has the nerve to go on vacation."

I enjoyed feeling his relief. I could feel how safe he felt, having his therapist hang in there till he got secure enough to say "have a good time" when she left.

Engrossed, identifying with his story, I was cruising along, when suddenly I read something that stunned me. I read that Mr. Baker's adult problems had roots in his childhood, when he had "suffered the chronic trauma of unattunement." (p. 102)

What!?! "The chronic trauma of unattunement?" I was startled, almost shocked.

Not the "pesky annoyance of unattunement." Not even "the significant discomfort of unattunement." These experts had clearly said that Mr. Baker had suffered a *trauma* of unattunement.

I was shocked and confused: "This ordinary everyday life I've been identifying with is *traumatic*? Did I miss something in my reading? A drunken episode? A violent outburst?"

I went back through his case history, looking for something really bad, really "traumatic."

I found only plain vanilla upsets. Ordinary commonplace troubles. Like my own.

- *Like him*, I'd been scared when my parents went out for the evening.
- *Like him*, I'd been terrified when I got separated from my mother in a store.
- *Like him*, I'd felt some abandonment and rejection when my little sibling came along.

(Mr. Baker and I even had in common the experience of being called by aunts' and uncles' names. His father and my mother often used their siblings' names when addressing us. But mixing up family names wasn't that unusual, was it? Kind of quirky. Funny. Cute, actually. Wasn't it?)

Mr. Baker's parents and family life seem like mine too.

Like my parents, his parents had been physically present. Like mine, his mother stayed home with her children and kept house. His father was involved, interested in Mr. Baker's activities.

The literal physical presence of his parents, according to Mr. Baker's therapist, obscured the depth and seriousness of his deprivation. "Blatant abandonment," the therapist states, "is an acute trauma difficult to deny."

By contrast, Mr. Baker's emotional abandonment is easy to deny. It's a subtle deprivation. His parents just didn't "get" him. But these therapists challenge that denial with the clinical label "chronic trauma of unattunement."

Applying the word "trauma" to something as subtle as unattunement didn't make sense to me at first. The word "trauma," for me, signified something blatantly atrocious and horribly devastating. Certainly it was startling to think that unattunement could be a trauma, a wound, a shock that overwhelms and has serious debilitating consequences, including PTSD.

Mr. Baker's parents didn't seem like monsters. His therapist described them as "moderately unattuned rather than severely damaging."[3] He'd struggled with his mother over early toilet training. Quarreled with an overbearing father. His parents seemed averagely irritating and off.

Overall, in fact, though their styles were different, Mr. Baker's "moderately unattuned" parents didn't seem much different than mine. And Mr. Baker's upset didn't seem that different than mine.

If "chronic trauma of attunement" applied to his life, it could apply to mine.

WHAT IF THESE VERY IMPORTANT PSYCHOTHERAPISTS SAID TO ME, "YOU SUFFERED THE CHRONIC TRAUMA OF UNATTUNEMENT"?

The impact of imagining my distinguished colleagues apply that phrase to a seemingly ordinary, violence- and incest-free childhood like mine cracked something open in me. Some wall of denial broke open.

The experience was as vivid and profound as if they'd come to my house, observed how nice everyone was, and then said directly to me, "Ricia, you haven't suffered blatant acute trauma. Your parents were only moderately unattuned. But you have suffered the trauma of unattunement."

Whew! That's powerful.

HOW READING MR. BAKER'S CHRONIC TRAUMA OF UNATTUNEMENT CASE AFFECTED ME

For quite a while after I read Mr. Baker's story, that phrase "trauma of unattunement" echoed through my mind.

Having that phrase in my mind felt good. Comforting. It reminded me that although Mr. Baker experienced no blatantly traumatic physical attack, the intrusive control and lack of understanding that overwhelmed him as a child and undermined his functioning as an adult was serious. . . .serious enough for his therapists to label it chronic trauma.

My resonance with PTSD no longer seemed so inappropriate or mysterious. Maybe the troubles I was having were legitimate and I made sense.

When my symptoms acted up, I felt the old familiar mental taunts to "get over it." I tried saying to myself: "Maybe you are suffering from the aftereffects of chronic trauma of unattunement. Maybe it's natural and understandable for you to be having a tough time today."

I FINALLY CONCLUDE "HEY! ALL THIS PTSD STUFF APPLIES TO ME," AND MY HEALING BEGINS

In spite of this vicarious diagnosis of "chronic trauma of unattunement," I continued to be very ambivalent about identifying myself as a trauma survivor.

But when I did, my problems seemed legitimate and I made sense. "What's wrong with me?" became "What happened to me?" I could say to myself, "Something happened; you are dealing with the aftermath of something that happened to you."

Just what I'd longed to hear my validating champion say to me.

And when I did consider myself a trauma survivor, my troublesome attitudes towards my problems began to shift toward compassion and even self-respect for having come as far as I had with all the strengths and resources I'd developed.

I stopped calling myself lazy, defective, and self-pitying. I had dignity. And I had hope.

I realized I could be struggling with PTSD. And once you determine that someone has PTSD, you look for a past trauma that hasn't been resolved. And then you help them resolve it.

From my clinical work, I knew that people were healing from even traumatic physical atrocities. And if I were indeed a trauma survivor, then I had hope — realistic hope — that I could heal too.

NOW YOUR TURN

So, what about you? Did you feel kinship with the qualities and challenges described in this chapter? Does the working hypothesis/ tentative diagnosis of PTSD from early intangible traumas in lifeline relationships with mother, father, or other primary caregiver fit you?

Have you identified yourself as a person who might have PTSD as a result of these early intangible attachment traumas I've given the long technical name of NACCT: non-physically assaultive, attachment-based Chronic Covert Trauma? Could trauma be a factor in your life today?

FIRST, REVIEW THE CHAPTER

Look back over your responses. Notice what made you go, "Hey! That's like me!" Did you have:

- Some of the positive attitudes toward self-help?

- Some of the stuckness in spite of efforts to change?

- Troublesome attitudes towards your problems?

- Problems responding to upsets. What happens when you get upset these days? What happened when you were little? Did you turn to someone for help? Who? Did someone take care of you? What did they do? Did it help?

- Mysterious resonance with PTSD? The nameless dread? The amped up or toned down reactions? The intrusive PTSD symptoms such as bad dreams, troublesome thoughts or moods that suddenly come out of the blue? The constrictive PTSD symptoms that keep your life smaller than you'd like?

- The puzzlement about whether your childhood experiences really qualify you as a trauma survivor?

How does it sit with you to have PTSD from childhood naCCT as a possible working hypothesis explaining your troubles?

I invite you to pause for a moment and reflect on any questions or doubts you have about the legitimacy of naCCT. Note the moments as you were reading along when you thought, "Come on, you've got to be kidding. Trauma? Feh!" You don't need to just brush those thoughts aside. Remember that thoughts like this are to be expected. It's reasonable to have doubts about a working hypothesis.

As you consider going forward with this working hypothesis, ask yourself this practical question: "Might exploring PTSD from childhood naCCT help me to feel better and have a happy life?" Try it out and see!

DONE!

You have come to the end of a huge amount of self-reflection. It probably took some time and energy. And maybe it also took some distress tolerance.

So, before finishing this chapter and going on to explore healing PTSD from naCCT, take a moment for self-congratulation. Pat yourself on the back for your willingness to devote this time and energy to your well-being. It's an investment in a very precious outcome: You!

You have taken a survey of yourself and really come alongside yourself in a serious and caring way...even if some not-so-loving feelings and thoughts came up during the process.

It might be time to put this self-discovery work aside and take a break.

Or you might be on a roll, wanting to stand back and contemplate what you've learned about yourself. If you do, here are some legitimate attitudes you can take and ways you can regard what you've learned:

- Respectfully, compassionately

- With optimism, power, and possibility

- With pride and a "good for me for doing this" attitude

- With legitimate savoring of your positives

- With a "Welcome to the Human Race" perspective toward the negatives

- (And remember: A little gentle humor never hurts!)

FIVE TRAUMA WOUNDS THAT CAN HEAL

Try making these statements about these five hard-to-identify trauma wounds that can heal:

1. Not knowing I've been wounded is a trauma wound that can heal.

2. The invisibility of the trauma wound is itself a trauma wound that can heal.

3. Being confined beneath a kind of a psychological glass ceiling with the belief "that's just the way I am and nothing can be done about it" is a trauma wound that can heal.

4. Not knowing there is help available for me is a trauma wound that can heal.

5. Being cut off from actions that could heal my wound is a trauma wound that can heal.

There's truth in every one of those statements. Can you feel that that truth applied to you?

BUT WAIT! BONUS QUESTIONS: DARE TO DREAM!

Clearly, you haven't given up on yourself or your life. The fact that you're still exploring with this book proves that. My conviction that recovery is possible is so strong that before you go on to the next chapter, I invite you to take a few minutes to dare to dream.

Desires:

(Blurt out the answer, fill in the blank, and stash the paper in a safe place where you can come back to it later.)

I love picturing myself being, doing, or having [_____].

What I would like is [_____].

What I want is [_____].

I wonder what it would be like if I could [_____].

I would like to count myself among those who are [_____].

If you could magically change one thing, what would that thing be? [_____].

If you could magically change one OTHER thing, what would that be? [_____].

If you knew you would be supported in finding and following your bliss, what would you do? [_____].

What's your idea of deep happiness in your lifetime? [_____].

What are you joyfully anticipating? [_____].

Double Bonus Question: Fun and delight:

A time when I belly laughed so hard that I snorted, cried, or felt the muscles in my stomach and my face hurt was when [_____].

COMING UP NEXT:

"Your Recovery Begins: Stay Safe and Stable"

NOTES

[1] "When childhood emotional abuse and/or emotional neglect constitutes the primary form or "organizing thread" of an adult survivors' trauma history, ... the response to traditional psychotherapy [is] most recalcitrant." Elizabeth K. Hopper, Frances K. Grossman, et al, *Treating Adult Survivors of Childhood Emotion (New York: Guilford Press, 2019)* p. 16.

[2] Case material from Blanck and Blanck, *Ego Psychology (*New York, Columbia Univ. Press: 1974), p 101-118).

[3] Blanck and Blanck, (109)

Part II:

Your Recovery Begins

CHAPTER 3

STAY SAFE AND STABLE WHILE HEALING

It's time to roll up our sleeves and get to work on what to know and what to do to get un-stuck and heal the wounds of intangible trauma.

By now you've probably realized that the hero of this story is YOU.

Although you didn't cause the aftereffects of trauma, it's up to you to heal them. That hardly seems fair, but that's the way it is. You get to be aggravated about that. Of course.

And amid the aggravation, you can be taking steps to get un-stuck, to heal.

If you like tracking your progress, grab a pen and paper and look over the following list of transformational outcomes. To indicate how much these descriptions apply to your life right now, assign a number from "0," indicating "nothing, no way have I got this" and "100," indicating "I've got this one nailed."

- Have a good relationship with myself
- Know myself
- Take good care of myself
- Am the boss of my own life
- Have good relationships with other people

- Assess people and situations realistically, so my expectations regarding them are realistic
- Use wise and effective routines, habits, and policies to live my life with grace and ease
- Manage risk and security effectively
- Take myself seriously enough, but not too seriously
- Normalize my struggles with the aftereffects of trauma
- Am the author of an increasingly good "next chapter" in the story of my life

As you continue taking healing steps , you can check back with this list of desirable ways of living whenever you want to see that you are making progress.

OK, Let's go!

FIRST, THE GOOD NEWS: YOU'VE ALREADY TAKEN THE FIRST STEP OF HEALING: YOU SURVIVED!

In my first trauma healing class, our first handout began: "Recovery Step One: Survive."

I said to myself, "Isn't this obvious? Of course you have to survive to recover!"

However, seeing it written down *as a recovery step* surprised me. And then it made good sense.

It's useful to recognize that you've survived and that survival really is the first, and essential, step of recovery. Not beginning your recovery at rock bottom feels good. It also provides a head start and gives your recovery some momentum. Your current success builds on your previous successes.

Thinking of surviving as the first step in healing also helps you appreciate your will to survive, your instinct for self-preservation, your life force.

So, take note that you are safe here in the present, alive, reading this book, which means that you have already completed the essential first step of recovery. None of the traumas that you endured have killed you. You lived through the traumatic moments, not unscathed, but you got through alive.

SELF-TALK SCRIPT: "I COPED SUCCESSFULLY!"

"Good For Me, I did it! I coped successfully. I survived everything that happened to me. My instinct for self-preservation works. I appreciate the vitality and brilliance of my total organism, of my mind and my body. Every cell and tissue and organ did what it needed to do to get me through."

Try saying this Self-Talk Script out loud. How does it feel to do that? Put the Self-Talk Script into your phone. Write it on a piece of paper and carry it around with you.

NAME AND CLAIM YOUR STRENGTHS AFTER SURVIVING INTANGIBLE TRAUMA

So, we survived. Non-physically-assaultive, attachment-based Chronic Covert Trauma (naCCT) did not kill us. But what *state* did it leave us in?

People like to say, "What doesn't kill us makes us strong." But, unfortunately, that upbeat saying isn't absolutely true. You and I know from experience that far from making us strong, what doesn't kill us sometimes undermines our strength, even results in PTSD.

We all know people like a man I'll call Joe, who grew up in a family where his spontaneous expressions were routinely mocked with biting contempt labelled "teasing." And if "being teased" made Joe cry, then he heard "We're only kidding" and "What's the matter with you, Joey? Little baby can't take a joke?"

Joe understandably became wary of sharing anything that mattered to him with his family. And as time went by, he became wary of sharing anything that mattered to him with anyone at all.

But Joe *did* become an expert at snappy, razor-sharp comebacks.

The verbal abuse in Joe's family didn't kill him. And, as the upbeat saying asserts: it did "make him strong" in surviving verbal bullying. However, the verbal abuse also weakened his ability to express his ideas, interests, and feelings.

Therefore, to be true to reality, the saying needs to be revised to, "What doesn't kill us *sometimes* makes us strong in *some* ways."

Let's claim those ways.

You have probably already developed an impressive repertoire of coping skills. For example, ask yourself:

- Can I fend for myself if need be?

- Have I developed a keen awareness of when people are not telling the truth?

- Can I put aside my distress and take care of others?

Some of these survivor strengths may occur in uneven patterns, very strong at times, at other times nowhere to be found. For example, collapsing mentally may alternate with overfunctioning. Brilliance may alternate with mental numbness and sluggishness.

Responding to painful pressure to please your family, you may have learned to sing or to shine in athletics or to groom yourself to look extremely attractive. These skills now belong to you. Wherever and whenever and however these survival strengths show up, name them and claim them as positives of your own.

You may, like many survivors, take your own strengths for granted. Beware of the attitude: "If I have them, doesn't everyone? And how great can these strengths be anyway, if I have them?" Sort of like saying: "Any club that wants me for a member is not a club I'd want to join."

Fight that self-denigrating attitude. You *must* inventory and claim your own positives.

For starters, here are some strengths I've observed in survivors of intangible trauma. This list is very long because we naCCT survivors tend to skimp on acknowledging our good points.

Ready? Here are some positive qualities. Your challenge is to spend twenty minutes acknowledging yours. Go!

Are you:

- Often very resourceful, clever, ingenious

- Self-reliant, finding ways of getting what's needed or of doing without

- Responsible

- Helpful

- Skilled at redirecting your attention away from inner states that would interfere with your responsibilities

- Honest about your feelings

- Open and willing to self-reflect and explore
- Skilled at repression or suppression, at either automatically or intentionally removing your attention away from stressors
- Productive, self-disciplined, thorough
- Very resilient, good at "bouncing back"
- Strong, even stoical
- Unflappable; you "keep calm and carry on"
- Careful, capable, organized
- Skilled at dealing with a particular type of difficult person
- Good at "rising above" unpleasantness
- Very observant, tuned in to social and interpersonal nuances
- Empathic, attuned
- Thoughtful, considerate
- Gracious, hospitable
- Emotionally alive and responsive
- Responsible, dependable, diligent
- Co-operative
- Concerned about justice, equality, social good
- Forgiving
- Generous
- Authentic, real, genuine
- Self-aware
- Deep, tender, sensitive, profound
- Accepting, tolerant
- Skilled at redirecting attention, at intentional distraction
- Industrious
- Flexible

- Funny, humorous, witty
- In touch with feelings, beliefs
- Kind, caring, compassionate
- Fair
- Very sensitive to the needs of others
- Good at soldiering on through difficulties
- A good neighbor and good citizen — i.e.: you pay your taxes, don't litter, don't disrupt the neighborhood, keep the hallway clean, recycle your trash

Do you:

- Have compassion for those who suffer
- Put distress aside and function if necessary (and it often feels necessary)
- Have that quality of "heart" or courage; don't give up; don't believe in "I can't;" believe "where there's a will there's a way"
- Practice good self-care: healthy diet and exercise, good financial management
- Handle situations, so people look to you for leadership and guidance

When circumstances seem to warrant these behaviors, can you also strategically:

- Act cheerful, even if you feel lousy on the inside
- Maintain composure even while feeling distressed
- Control yourself and refrain from emotional outbursts
- Avoid self pity
- Avoid burdening others with your difficulties
- Give people the benefit of the doubt

- Muster a "Positive mental attitude"
- Keep your deep self private
- Acknowledge shortcomings

Rejoice that you now have all the strengths that you checked off at your service. Take security from knowing they're always there for you to use. Keep updating this list, and refer to it often!

FROM SHAME TO PRIDE: REDEEMING A RESOURCEFULNESS YOU USED TO FEEL ASHAMED OF

You may even change your attitude toward yourself for finding substances and behaviors that were dangerously (addictively) effective at making intolerable situations tolerable.

Even while renouncing the substance or the behavior that turned against you in the long run, you *can* embrace your intent to care for yourself when there was nothing else between you and the abyss. You can claim your resourcefulness in finding something that "got you through the night."

For me, it was cigarettes. Oh, how I loved those cigarettes! And marijuana. And coffee. Loaded with cream. And did I mention sugar?

OVERVIEW OF THE HEALING PROCESS

So, with the secure awareness that you did what it took to survive and developed some significant strengths which you legitimately claim as yours, it's time for an overview of trauma healing.

CLASSIC 3-STAGE TREATMENT MODEL

The classic model for healing trauma's aftereffects in psychotherapy has three components, often presented as a sequence of stages.

Since the 1890's, psychotherapists have used some version of this treatment model.

This model was developed primarily for survivors of such blatant overt traumas as physical assaults, car crashes, war, or natural disasters. The model has also been used to treat complex PTSD in survivors of ongoing physical assaults, domestic violence, and incest.

I'll summarize the components here for you:

1. The first component of therapy for healing trauma is "Stay Safe and Stable". This component is dedicated to your safety. You build strengths; develop and use resources; and stay balanced, well regulated, and smoothly functioning. In therapy, you create a safe relationship with your therapist. The work of providing safety and stabilization continues throughout the next stages.

2. In the second component, "Remember and Grieve ," you work on uncovering and narrating the story of what happened to you and what it meant to you. You remember the conclusions you drew about life and re-examine those conclusions to determine if they are still true and useful for you today. You may revise your view of yourself and of the world. This stage often includes grieving over deprivations and losses, feeling almost overwhelming anger and sorrow, and re-experiencing fear, disgust, shame, and despair.

3. In the third component, "Reconnect and Re-engage," both you and your engagement in life are transformed. You re-engage with the world in new and better ways based on the healing work you've done. This stage has a lot in common with what the popular inspirational philosopher Joseph Campbell called "Following Your Bliss." When this transformed engagement in life blossoms from the radical healing work of remembering and grieving what happened, it is firmly anchored in the deep reality of who you are, and it tends to be abiding and strong.

In real life, of course, the stages criss-cross and overlap, depending on what's happening in our lives.

Some therapists stick firmly to a sequence of "Stay Safe and Stable," then "Remember and Grieve," then "Reconnect and Re-engage" in their treatment: "No remembering or grieving what happened until safety and stability are established," they say. Why? To prevent people from "flipping out."

However, I've heard many trauma survivors say this strict adherence to the sequence of stages didn't keep them stable; it triggered and destabilized them instead. Maybe even flipped them out. Here's an illustration of how that could come about.

One survivor — I'll call her "April" — felt destabilized by this rule. As a child, April had been told by her parents not to talk about upsetting things.

April said, "When my therapist told me that I couldn't talk about my trauma until we completed safety and stability work, I felt mad. Squashed and silenced. All my energy started racing around inside me, and I felt the impulse to shout. At the same time, I felt the *opposite* impulse to clam up, like it was life or death, and if I didn't clam up, something terrible would happen."

April's speech reflected her frantic, dysregulated inner state: her words rushed out like escaping prisoners hurrying to deliver a message before they were re-captured and sent back to prison. She rushed on, "The effect of being told I couldn't talk about what happened to me was the same as how I felt when I was little and went to someone for help and instead of really helping me, they tried to distract me or jolly me out of it and I felt like I was invisible and they couldn't hear me and if I couldn't snap out of it and kept on crying and going on about what happened to me and talking about how bad I felt, then they would just walk away."

As a little girl, April had silenced herself to preserve her lifeline relationship with her parents. Now, as an adult, did she again have to silence herself to preserve her an important relationship, this time with her therapist?

Ironically, April's therapist had hoped to maintain stability by prohibiting remembrance and grieving of April's traumatic experiences, but her prohibition brought about the very destabilization it had set out to prevent.

ADAPTING THIS THREE-STAGE MODEL TO HEALING THE AFTEREFFECTS OF NACCT

As your recovery progresses, you'll probably find yourself, like April and her therapist, puzzling over the question: "Should I talk about my trauma story now even though it will probably upset me? Or should I set my story aside and work more on my safety and stability skills?"

In 1992, when psychiatrist Judith Herman re-introduced the classic three stages to the therapy community in her book *Trauma and Recovery*, she said the stages "are a convenient fiction, not to be taken literally. They are an attempt to impose simplicity and order upon a process that is inherently turbulent and complex."

What is the best way to deal with this "inherently turbulent and complex process"? Stick to the sequential order of the components as stages? Or not?

My personal and professional experience indicates that, as April's story illustrates, strictly adhering to an inflexible sequence can present serious concerns for some naCCT survivors.

Life just isn't that orderly. It breaks into the sequence of stages. For example, ordinary life events often trigger naCCT flashbacks, and we're thrown back into our trauma experiences. We saw this happen with April. Her urgent drive to tell what happened to her — (an activity of the "Remember and Grieve " stage) — arose when she was still in the "Stay Safe and Stable" stage.

The realities of life lead to out-of-sequence jumps like the following:

***Out-of-sequence Jumps* from "Stay Safe and Stable" to "Remember and Grieve":** Intangible trauma's triggers are commonplace and found practically everywhere. One of these commonplace triggers might catapult you into vividly remembering and re-experiencing what happened long ago.

***Out-of-sequence Jumps* from "Stay Safe and Stable" to "Reconnect and Re-engage":** Sometimes you'll be inspired to jump to a positive reconnection with the world and re-engagement in life. You'll feel a passionate inspiration to start following your bliss. Sometimes you'll succeed in following through on your inspiration, and sometimes you'll be frustrated when unhealed cPTSD blocks your success.

THE COMPONENT MODEL OF HEALING

If we're going to live and recover in the real world, it's wise to align our plan for healing with how life really happens. So instead of three rigidly sequential stages, I use "Stay Safe and Stable]," "Remember and Grieve," and "Reconnect and Re-engage" as flexible components, to be called upon as needed to meet the demands of real life.

To illustrate how these three healing components weave together in real life recovery, here's the account of a man I'll call Eric.

Eric is very organized. He likes the way the component model helps him organize his understanding of what happens in his recovery. I'll let him tell about how he understood one of the typically small but significant experiences that made up his recovery.

ERIC'S STORY

"I am a recovering 'achievement robot,' so my healing goals include living as a human *being*, instead of a human *doing*. One specific goal is 'learning to hang out.'

"As a teenager, I wasn't popular. I sure didn't just 'hang out' with kids. I was already locked into the achievement way of life.

"What set me off last week was two text messages with two conflicting opportunities for the same Saturday. One was a chance to hang out with some guys. The other was a chance to compete for another accomplishment. I had to choose one and say 'no' to the other.

"My knee-jerk first reaction, of course, was to opt for the accomplishment opportunity.

"But then I remembered my healing goals. I texted back to both invitations, 'Thanks. Let me get back to you.'

"**Stay Safe and Stable Component**: I used all my stabilizing skills to come alongside myself, calm down, and reflect. I let myself really sit with the truth of my situation, that I really *did* have two different opportunities open to me and I *could not* have them both.

"As I came alongside myself, I noticed an urgent churned-up feeling around my stomach and solar plexus. Sort of like nausea. I felt so much pressure, like a weight bearing down on my whole upper body. I *had to* make the right choice.

"I could feel the contradictory pulls: Achieve! No! Hang out with kids! No! Choose! Urgent! Choose! *Now!*

"**Remember and Grieve Component**: As I sat with those physical sensations and urgent thoughts, I remembered something: When I was maybe ten years old, I had this same urgent, pressured feeling. Back then, just like this week with the two invitations, I got a social invitation — a *rare* social invitation — that conflicted with my accomplishment activities.

"My parents very subtly pushed me to say 'no' to that rare opportunity to just hang out, to just be a kid with other kids. They didn't have to *say* anything, because I'd become attuned to their slightest gesture of disapproval, their contempt for frivolous activity. And I'd become addicted to their praise.

"The memory of that long-ago conflict was so vivid, like I'd gone through a science fiction time-warp back to my childhood.

"As I remembered this lost opportunity to be a regular kid with other kids, it surprised me how sad I felt, like an actual weight was pressing down on my sternum. And I felt angry — throbbing temples, pounding heart — about all I'd missed.

"**Stay Safe and Stable Component**: All the time I was remembering that incident, I had to fight to stay safe and stable. I was so worked up it was hard to bring myself back to my present-day conflict and decide which invitation to accept.

I had to go back to my grounding, stabilizing processes again and again.

"I drew my attention back to the present. Slowly, carefully, I let myself feel the pull of the two invitations for the upcoming weekend. How did I *really* feel about each one?

"**Reconnect and Re-engage Component**: In the end, as an adult, I did something new and different from my usual mode of operations: I passed up the achievement opportunity. I said 'yes' to just hanging out with a bunch of guys.

"I aligned with my main recovery goal when I decided to let the achievement invitation go: I became less of a human *doing*; I became more of a human *being*. I actually had *fun* hanging out with those guys."

Eric's story shows how someone can work with the different components: recognizing a trigger or a flashback state; remembering a pattern or incident of long ago trauma; feeling very sad or scared or angry, but not "flipping out;" and responding in a new way to the challenging situation.

The way Eric kept returning to the "Stay Safe and Stable" component also shows how central that component is to the recovery process.

START WITH STAY SAFE AND STABLE

Throughout the process of healing from the wounds of trauma, safety and stability remain top priority. This book focuses on the "Stay Safe and Stable" component.

Exploring trauma is likely to stir up feelings of fear, so let's set a baseline of safety for you right now, with three crucial dimensions: Being, knowing, and feeling.

- **Be safe physically, psychologically, and interpersonally:** "I am objectively safe, right here, right now."

- **Know that you are safe:** "I mentally acknowledge that I am safe. I have secure thoughts about my present situation."

- **Feel safe in your emotions and in your body:** "My emotions and my body feel the safety I'm in. The state of my emotions and my body reflects my safe circumstances."

"WILL I SURVIVE THE HEALING PROCESS?"

Apply the policy "Stay Safe and Stable" to your healing process. You need to know that process itself is safe for you.

This practical application of that policy was inspired by Ellen Bass' and Laura Davis' ground-breaking book *The Courage to Heal.* I was so impressed by their caring wisdom in providing this safety work for incest survivors that I've adapted it here for working with naCCT survivors.

Think about going forward, about reading this book and embarking on the journey of healing and transformation that it represents. Take a minute to notice what endings to the following sentences pop into your mind:

I'm hopeful about going forward because [_____].

I'm confident about going forward because [_____].

I'm eager to go forward because [_____].

What if you also feel some uneasiness about going forward? You may find another sentence creeps into your thinking, something like "Actually, I'm feeling very uneasy about going forward."

If you feel uneasy, first let yourself complete this sentence:

I'm afraid I won't be able to handle reading this book because [_____].

What is the nature of the uneasiness? Is it a feeling? What's it about? Something tangible?

Then brainstorm ways you can address that uneasiness and make the healing process safe enough for yourself.

Here's an outline of the steps in this process:

Complete the sentence prompt:
I'm afraid I won't be able to handle reading this because [_____].

Brainstorm:
Here are ways I can make the process safe enough for myself: [_____].

HERE'S AN EXAMPLE:

And here's an example of how one person used this process to make going on the recovery journey safe for herself:

Complete the sentence prompt:
I'm afraid I won't be able to handle reading this [because I might get triggered by something.]

Brainstorm:
Here are ways I can make the process safe enough for myself:
1. *I won't read it*
2. *I'll get resources for handling triggers so I won't be afraid of them.*
3. *I'll skim ahead to check for potential triggers, to see if going forward looks pretty safe.*
4. *I'll stop reading if I'm starting to get uneasy, like I might be heading into a dangerous area for triggering.*
5. *I know this one's flippant, but I really did think that I get triggered all the time anyway, so what's one more time?*

HERE'S ANOTHER EXAMPLE:

Complete the sentence prompt:

"I'm afraid I won't be able to handle reading this [because I want to start writing in a journal to give myself a place to explore my feelings and express myself, but I'm so nervous about keeping that journal private, safe from prying eyes. Someone read my diary when I was twelve and it was awful.]"

Brainstorm:

Here are ways I can make the process safe enough for myself:

1. *Journal on my computer and protect the document with a password.*
2. *Disguise the journal and hide it under my mattress or in the trunk of my car.*
3. *Shred the pages after I write them.*
4. *I heard of someone who actually drilled a hole through his journal and padlocked it shut. I could do that.*

AND YET ANOTHER EXAMPLE:

Complete the sentence prompt:

"I'm afraid I won't be able to handle reading this [because I'll approach it with my usual perfectionistic standards and force myself to do guided meditations even though they always upset me, especially with my eyes closed.]"

Brainstorm:

Here are ways I can make the process safe enough for myself:

Make a smart, safe, and stable commitment to myself to stop doing anything that doesn't feel safe, no matter how "good for me" that action might seem to be. I can give myself permission to avoid doing any guided meditations, and absolutely avoid doing guided meditations with my eyes closed.

These illustrations show that you can give yourself permission to leave a distressing situation, to set limits, to say "no" to any book chapter or activity here or elsewhere that feels unsafe, that threatens to destabilize, undermine, or weaken you. Never mind other people's opinions. You get to stop and step back and get your bearings. You get to have boundaries. You get to preserve your safety and stability.

NOW YOUR TURN:

Do the "safe enough" process for yourself.

Complete the sentence prompt:
I'm afraid I won't be able to handle reading this because [_____].

Brainstorm:
Here are ways I can make the process safe for myself: [_____].

After you've brainstormed some ways you can keep yourself safe enough as you go forward, choose a way to use this book that seems like it will work for you and commit to doing it.

What ground rules and permissions will you commit to for yourself? The final authority here is *you*. These are *your own* ground rules, policies, and permissions. You don't need to justify or explain them to anyone.

Here are examples of some survivors' commitments to their own safety and stability:

- *I will skip over any disturbing stuff. I'll only do the suggested exercises if they feel right for me.*

- *I'll stop whenever I need to. If I start to numb out or get agitated, or if I "get hungry" or feel an urge to use substances, I'll stop reading right away.*

- *I give myself permission to disagree with anything I read.*

- *I will let myself feel OK if I "accidentally on purpose" lose this book and then decide later to buy a replacement copy.*

Some of these will be absolute "*No. Matter. What!*" boundaries. And some will be more flexible, like guidelines.

OFFICIAL SAFETY AND STABILITY COMMITMENT TO SELF

Some people find it helpful to make a formal, written commitment to themselves. It could be something like this:

"I, [your name], give myself the following permissions and ground rules so I will stay safe and stable as I go forward with this healing work:"

Then list your ground rules and permissions. To make it "official," add your signature and the date.

None of these policies and guidelines are cast in cement. You can revise and update any or all of them as you go along.

SAFE SPACE IMAGERY PROCESS.

After years of belonging to the New England Society for the Treatment of Trauma and Dissociation while working with my clients' and my own traumas, I decided to help out at the organization's annual "Introduction to Treating Trauma and Dissociation," presented by social worker and expert trauma clinician Joanne Twombly.

Guess what she stressed to therapists new to treating PTSD? *Maintain safety!*

She acknowledged that both therapists and clients may regard safety work as "useless" or even "silly" and may want to skip over it and get right to "the real work" of exploring the trauma. She encourages therapists to resist this.

I was impressed with how firmly she emphasized the importance of maintaining safety, and so I pass that firm conviction on to you.

Once again, we're reminded that in trauma recovery, staying safe is bottom-line "real work."

And what was the key tool Twombly recommended for maintaining safety? The Safe Space Imagery process. This is the process of using both imagination and rational thinking to create in our minds the image of a space that we can imagine going to for refuge whenever we need to feel safe.

Twombly was very careful to say "space," because some trauma survivors have unsafe associations to the phrase "safe place," whereas "safe space" tends to feel, well, safer. You can, of course, use either of these phrases or come up with one that works better for you.

This mental image portrays a safe space for your physical body, of course. It also offers safety for your heart. Your mind. Your senses. Your spirit.

NOW YOUR TURN:

To create your own mental Safe Space Image, you might begin by thinking "safe space" and noticing what pops into your mind. Some people get a mental picture. For others, the image is a feeling or a sensation. Some people mentally hear a song or a piece of music.

If you get a memory of a real place, double check to make sure it is *absolutely* safe. If it isn't, either revise it so it is, or go on to create a brand new, entirely imaginary, absolutely safe space instead.

You can always "renovate" your Safe Space Image. You can add imaginary physical protections for your comfort and safety. You can establish boundaries — moats, walls of sound, mighty protective barriers of all sorts — with magical powers to keep out all harm, even to keep out annoyances. No bad smells, no obnoxious noises.

These renovations can involve science-fiction inspired technological innovations such as time-warps that create a protective barrier from any possible harm.

Some people imagine layers of safety, with the outermost layers being tough and fortress-like, and the innermost layers being soft, quiet, and restful.

It's important to thoroughly investigate what's safe for *you*. For example, some people don't want to be outdoors. Others only feel safe outdoors.

Some people want images of safe people or beings such as animal protectors or guardian spirits in their safe space with them. Others want to be completely alone. And some people like to picture having people or other beings "on call," only responding when they are needed.

Some Safe Space Images include the soothing sounds of birdsong, a babbling brook, a purring cat, or gentle rain on the roof. If you find the flickering flame and light of candles peaceful, mentally provide an abundant supply of candles, matches, and holders. If you meditate, you might mentally provide a meditation cushion.

Some people imaginatively fill their safe space with tools and equipment or with entertainment and refreshments. Some people like a minimalist space. Others prefer a Safe Space Image that is overstuffed and cozy.

Here are the safe space images that three different survivors created for themselves:

- A dark, warm, quiet nest, surrounded by soft, downy feathers.

- A "Do Not Disturb" fortress with three layers of magical protective barriers including one that puts a slight time warp between the safe space and the rest of the world.

- A cozy cottage in the woods which is itself enclosed in a protective bubble. Small furry animals come when they are called.

Make your safe space mobile, so you can access it everywhere and mentally feel safe inside wherever you go.

You might have an "Activate and Enter" gesture that works like a password or passkey. Let this be a literal physical gesture you can do without calling attention to yourself, so you can activate and enter your Safe Space Image even when you're being watched by other people in a formal setting. You might, for example, place your thumb and ring finger together, clear your throat, or touch the tip of your tongue to the roof of your mouth. This way you can provide yourself with a safe retreat within, and no one will be the wiser.

You can carry a literal key as a reminder that you always have a safe space image in the privacy of your mind — and the key to access it anytime you choose to — without fear of being ostracized, criticized, or ridiculed.

If you like using guided visualizations, you'll find many on the internet or on audio CDs. But you don't *need* to use a guided meditation. You can use your own intentional creativity to design your safe space. For example, I find images in magazines. Sometimes I paste a safe space image into my journal and put a xerox photo of myself inside it. Just let myself soak in that image.

[I've done some of this safe space imagery work in my own visual journal. Some is posted on the ChronicCovertTrauma.com website to give you more ideas.]

As your healing progresses, you can continue to make renovations to your safe space imagery whenever you get inspired.

And remember, providing safe space for yourself counts as "real" trauma healing work.

OVERVIEW OF KINDS OF SAFETY AS YOU GO FORWARD

As your healing progresses, we'll be mindful to establish and maintain safety and stability in the following areas as healing progresses. *Be* safe, *know* you're safe, and *feel* safe in all these areas:

Physical Safety: Of course, physical safety is important. You want to continue to survive.

Since you are reading this book, you are probably quite literally safe right here, right now. You are free from external threats to life and limb. There probably is no Tyrannosaurus Rex snorting and bellowing hungrily outside your window as you read. Take a minute to notice the truth of that present physical safety. Feel the security that knowledge provides for you. This feeling and knowledge of security is your home base as you explore naCCT. Take a minute to really feel this secure home base. Notice what this safety feels like in your body. You are safe now.

In addition to literal physical safety, we're mindful of these other dimensions of safety:

Intrapsychic Safety: (*intra* = within; *psychic* = psyche or soul) Safe within your psyche; having a safe relationship to yourself, with your own thoughts, feelings, impulses, and sensations. A safe inner world.

Intrapsychic Safety includes having knowledge, information, and empowering psychoeducation that helps to understand, to feel normal, to feel powerful, to have hope. To be safe from ignorance or confusion.

Interpersonal Safety: Safe with other people, including recognizing and coping with your reactions to interpersonal triggers and flashbacks to distressing relationships with other people. Interpersonal safety includes having a safe social context, a "no stigma or invalidation zone" where the traumatic impact and consequences of naCCT are taken seriously, where you're safe from being silenced, where you have language, and a voice, and names for things so they can be thought about, talked about, and planned for. No gas-lighting. No mind-games.

Physiological safety: Safe with the normal functions of your living body; safely handling the bodily aftereffects of intangible traumas, including moods generated by your nervous system, flare-ups of pre-existing conditions, and/or the appearance of new physiological symptoms. Find the safe and stable balance between catastrophizing about them and brushing them off.

PTSD Recovery Safety: Safe going forward with recovery and using this book; Safe coping with PTSD symptoms, including flashbacks, constrictions, social, psychological, and physical aftereffects.

This book is dedicated to helping you develop personal expertise in providing safety and stability for your beloved self in the three areas where naCCT most undermines safety: Intrapsychic Safety, Interpersonal Safety, and Physiological Safety.

CHAPTER 4

PSYCHOEDUCATION ABOUT TRAUMA, NACCT, AND PTSD

Psychoeducation promotes safety and stability. It's easy to dismiss psychoeducation as just a bunch of pamphlets, lectures, and handouts full of small print and big words, something useful only from the neck up, not relevant to real life. But this isn't true.

Psychoeducation does indeed provide factual information about challenging health conditions, including mental health conditions, but *effective* psychoeducation is relevant to real life and improves the quality of that real life by supporting people who are trying to understand and cope with those conditions.

Psychoeducation reconfigures your world and therefore opens up new vistas and pathways for you.

Not understanding what's going on within and around you can feel very scary and unsafe. Many people find that understanding what they're up against and what they can do about it is stabilizing, comforting, and empowering.

Even little kids with PTSD benefit from psychoeducation about trauma. In the Trauma-Focused Cognitive Behavioral Therapy (TF-CBT) training, we learned how to gently provide information to traumatized kids as young as four years old — information to help them understand "how kids feel about the upsetting, confusing thing that happened to them."

You can think of this psychoeducation as "empowering intelligence," as "strategic intel" that deepens your understanding about trauma, naCCT, and PTSD and supports your healing mission.

Because possessing information and the language for talking about it confers a kind of power, psychoeducation offers another significant benefit to naCCT survivors. It empowers them with knowledge and language. For this reason, it breaks down a potentially toxic helping hierarchy, the kind where the authority who knows everything talks down to the uninformed person being helped.

Psychoeducation allows the power that comes with information and language to be shared. With psychoeducation, the helper and the person being helped become more like collaborative partners.

That's how I envision us working together, as collaborative partners in your healing, so let's do some psychoeducation here.

LET'S START WITH THE BASIC QUESTION: "WHAT IS TRAUMA, ANYWAY?"

The word "trauma" is the Greek word for "wound." In medical hospitals, trauma units treat physical wounds. That's pretty clear cut.

In psychology and psychotherapy today, the term "trauma" is not that clear cut.

Many naCCT survivors have a cluster of questions and concerns:

"Just what is trauma, anyway?"

"Does my experience "count" as trauma? Does it qualify as a "real" trauma?"

"Am I *really* a trauma survivor?"

Perhaps more than survivors of other types of trauma, naCCT survivors experience confusion about these questions and have often received contradictory answers to them.

If you, dear reader, sometimes find yourself questioning whether you are a "real" trauma survivor who is legitimately entitled to use all the techniques, processes, and research about trauma and healing PTSD, this chapter will help you understand, at least in part, why you have that feeling of illegitimacy. And it will also provide information to help dispel that feeling of exclusion so you can confidently claim your right to benefit from using methods of trauma healing.

To answer these questions, we'll look at how the psychotherapy community struggles to decide whether or not a person has experienced trauma. Consulting a list of qualifying "trauma events" categories is one way of making that decision.

Here are three examples of such lists:

1. "THE DSM":

Psychotherapists consult the American Psychiatric Association's official *Diagnostic and Statistical Manual of Mental Disorders*, commonly referred to as "*the DSM.*"

In this widely-used professional manual, one of the main criteria for determining if someone had experienced trauma has been the kind of event they experienced. Here are the exact words from the version of "*the DSM-IV-TR*" published in 2000:

> "*The person experienced, witnessed, or was confronted with an event or events that involved actual or threatened death or serious injury, or a threat to the physical integrity of self or others.*"[4]

Applying the criteria enumerated in that unwieldy, abstract statement to real people's real life experiences wasn't easy. Confusion reigned within the psychotherapy community. People wondered, for example, just what specifically constituted a threat of a serious injury? Did the person making the threat have to have a weapon? A gun? And just what real life experience constitutes "a threat to physical integrity?"

Considerable wrangling took place over what events met this requirement, wrangling that sometimes boiled down to:

> "*That wasn't trauma!*"
> "*Yes, it was.*"
> "*No, it wasn't.*"

Thirteen years later, the revised diagnostic manual, *DSM-5*, published in 2013, appeared. But the *DSM-5* didn't stop the wrangling, although it *did* add more event categories, namely: "threatened sexual violence," "learning that a relative or close friend was exposed to a trauma," and "indirect exposure to aversive details of the trauma."[5]

However, the new manual had the same problems the old one had: to be considered "trauma," an experience had to fit into one of the *DSM*'s enumerated categories.

2. "THE ACES":

Another widely-used, official "trauma event list" is the one from the Adverse Childhood Experiences Study, often just referred to as the ACES.[6]

First published in 1998, this study revealed a high correlation between aversive childhood experiences and the occurrence of medical problems later in life.

The ACES questionnaire, which can be accessed on-line, was developed from the ten childhood aversive experiences mentioned most often by a group of about 300 members of the Kaiser Permanente HMO (Health Maintenance Organization.) After its creation, the ACES questionnaire was administered to 17,000 members of the HMO.

The ten aversive experiences on the list break down into the following clusters of childhood events and circumstances:

- Three categories of "abuse" directed toward the child: physical, verbal, and sexual;

- Two categories of "neglect" endured by the child: physical and emotional; and

- Five categories of problems in the child's family: Substance abuse, domestic violence toward the mother, a family member in jail, a family member diagnosed with a mental illness, and the disappearance of a parent because of divorce, death, or abandonment.

The ACES is scored by assigning one point for each category to which an adult taking the test replies "yes," so a person can get a score ranging from zero to ten.

Look over the list. If you experienced naCCT but had no blatant physical assault in your childhood, you may have felt uneasy reading that list. Many naCCT survivors would not even give themselves a score of one.

In my experience, many survivors of naCCT hesitate to give the label "abuse" or "neglect" to their subtle traumatic experiences and would therefore be likely to answer "no" to the first five questions.

And many have not experienced the blatant, undeniably traumatic family situations listed in the five categories of family problems and would therefore answer "no" in response to those questions.

So a survivor of naCCT could easily end up with zero out of ten possible answers and conclude that they hadn't experienced *any* adverse childhood experiences at all.

3. OUR OWN PRIVATE "TRAUMA EVENTS" LISTS:

Official authoritative "trauma event lists" like the ACES and the *Diagnostic and Statistical Manual (DSM)* aren't the only such lists. Many, if not most of us mentally create and use our own private, personal "Trauma Events" lists within which we include some experiences as "real" trauma and exclude others.

What we include and exclude on our personal lists of "real" traumas is of course influenced by the official lists. The culture we live in, what people gasp at, and what the media portrays as shocking also exert their influence on our private "Trauma Events" lists.

Inside our own heads, as in the outer psychotherapy community, wrangling may still go on:

"That's not trauma."

"Yes it is."

"No it isn't."

SO, DOES CONSULTING A "TRAUMA EVENT LIST" WORK FOR US NACCT SURVIVORS?

How has determining trauma by consulting a "Trauma Events" list worked for us naCCT survivors? Not very well. Here's why:

Determining whether a person has survived trauma by consulting a "Trauma Events" list has a serious drawback: It can be unreliable. It can fail to accurately identify who has experienced trauma. It can result in false negatives (when a person who *has* experienced trauma tests negative) and false positives (when a person who *has not* experienced trauma tests positive).

TRAUMA IS RELATIVE

Using a list of "Trauma Events" categories is unreliable because trauma is relative: the same event could be overwhelming and traumatic for one person yet not traumatic at all for someone else.

The relative nature of trauma is illustrated by one athlete's observations: "My lifeguard buddies and I have been known to 'celebrate' someone's birthday by throwing the birthday boy off the dock. We all have such powerful swimming skills, what you therapists call "resources," that there's no way it's a trauma for us. It's just a surprise. For us lifeguards, it's a playful surprise that leads to paybacks and horse-play and, ultimately, a fun party.

"But getting picked up and thrown off a dock would traumatize a young kid, or anyone who couldn't swim. Or, for that matter, anyone who wasn't part of our group of horse-playing lifeguards."

This is a case where the same event impacts different people in different ways. What terrifies one person amuses another.

The event that would terrify the non-swimming landlubber amused the lifeguards because they had resources that the non-swimming landlubber would lack.

Furthermore, the lifeguards' coping-resources weren't limited to knowing how to swim. Their resources included both knowing the ways of the lifeguard horse-play culture and being comfortable interacting with other horse-playing lifeguards.

(Having plenty of resources to meet a challenge — and *knowing* you have these resources — is a wonderful antidote to post-traumatic terror, helplessness, and overwhelm. For this reason, psychotherapists can be justly accused of obsessing over resource-building with clients who have survived trauma.

As you go forward in your own healing, you can follow the therapists' urgings: frequently refer yourself back to the resources you inventoried in the previous two chapters and remember you have these resources available whenever you need them.)

TOO MUCH CHALLENGE, NOT ENOUGH RESOURCES EQUALS TRAUMA

An even balance of challenge to resources often results in easy competence: "I can handle this. I'll take care of it." That even balance of challenge to resources might also be experienced as pleasure: "This is fun!" as with the lifeguards horsing around after work.

A high level of challenge relative to resources is exciting. (Think: extreme sports!) Calling forth the resources to meet the challenge is energizing and growth producing.

Not enough challenge relative to resources is boring. (Remember how the time dragged on your first job?)

And too much challenge relative to resources can be traumatic. When the challenge threatens to overpower your coping resources, trauma happens.

It could be summed up this way: "Challenge bigger than resources equals trauma."

This was the situation for Joe, the verbal-bullying survivor you met in the previous chapter. As a child, he lacked the practical resources to move away from his family. He lacked the inner resources to ignore them. And he lacked social resources: he had no people outside his family to support and protect him.

"PAIN IN THE BUTT" OR THREAT TO SURVIVAL?

Another factor makes using a "Trauma Events" list ineffective for naCCT survivors: Children have way fewer resources than adults do. Because trauma is relative to the person's resources, events that are trivial for adults can easily traumatize children. Here's a common example:

"Even with cell phones, it's a pain in the butt," says an naCCT survivor, reflecting on the relative nature of trauma. "Whenever we go to a festival or a crowded shopping mall, my distractible partner wanders off and gets lost.

"As an adult, I'm mildly aggravated. But compare that to the time I got separated from my family when I was about three years old:

"We were in a store crowded with holiday shoppers. My brother remembers that I was holding his hand one minute. . . .and the next minute I was gone!

"I had evidently darted off just when everyone else in my family was getting onto the escalator. As it carried them up and away from me, they saw me checking out a blue-haired lady and a dog with dyed-blue fur and a flashing collar.

"My family had to ride the escalator to the top, then run to the down escalator. According to them, by the time they got back to me, I was kind of screaming and choking with terror. They remember it taking a lot of hugs and two hot chocolates to calm me down.

"All I remember is seeing legs all around me. I was frantic — lost and alone in a forest of legs.

"That traumatic panic and terror seems natural in a little kid at the mall, doesn't it? Grownups instinctively speak to them in sweet voices, rush to help them find their mommies and daddies, offer them ice cream to calm them down."

Because children's main resources are their parents or other caregivers, kids who get separated from their caregivers haven't enough resources to meet most of the challenges they face. Any separation from their parents is therefore potentially traumatic. Whereas an adult with a cell-phone finds being separated from a partner in a crowd merely "a pain in the butt."

Here's another situation showing that trauma is relative to resources. Compare an adult and a little child trying to get a response from someone and getting ignored instead.

An adult might think, "That was rude. Maybe they're having a bad day." An adult has the option of going away, seeking out another more responsive person, or even coming back to the non-responsive person later and opening up a conversation: "What's up with you today, giving me the cold shoulder?"

On the other hand, a little child getting the cold-shoulder and being ignored by a Lifeline Person like Mommy or Daddy might very realistically react with primal terror: "I'm alone; they'll never come" and, on a very deep survival level, where attachment to a caregiver means life or death, "I could die."

For a poignant demonstration of this, check out Dr. Ed Tronick's "Still face Experiment." It's posted on my website: *ChronicCovertTrauma.com/still-face-experiment*. You'll see a basically secure little child become distressed after only a few seconds of her mother's non-responsiveness. (And you'll see how quickly it's repaired when the mother *does* respond and soothe her little girl.)

Furthermore, just as responses of more-resourced adults differ from those of less-resourced children, so events and circumstances that are relatively trivial for more-resourced older children can be traumatic for less-resourced tiny babies.

So, consulting a "Trauma Events" list isn't a reliable way to determine if someone has experienced trauma, because the same event can be traumatic for one person but not for another.

NACCT SURVIVORS HURT BY RELYING ON TRAUMA EVENTS CATEGORIES TO DETERMINE TRAUMA.

To make matters worse, when we rely on the inclusion of what happened to us on a "trauma event list," some trauma survivors — naCCT survivors in particular — end up not getting help at all.

Here's how that can happen:

Let's say an event overwhelmed my resources, and I experienced a trauma state. If the event I experienced was included on the list I was using, whether an authoritative list like the *Diagnostic and Statistical Manual*'s or a list I've constructed mentally for myself, then I would be considered traumatized.

But what if the event that caused me to experience a trauma state was not on that list? Then the person consulting the list would conclude, "Too bad. That's not on the list of qualifying traumatic event categories. No matter how devastating the impact was on you, what you experienced wasn't trauma."

This would be like an Emergency Room physician saying to a person with a broken leg, "We have a list of events that can cause broken legs. On our list are wars, bar fights, domestic violence, and natural disasters. The event that led to your broken leg was falling down the stairs. That's not on our list of events that cause broken legs, so you don't have a broken leg."

Fortunately, this isn't what happens in emergency rooms. Even using it as an analogy sounds ridiculous.

IF NOT "TRAUMA EVENTS" LISTS, THEN WHAT TO DO INSTEAD?

In real life, what does happen in emergency rooms is sensible and realistic: The leg is examined. If the examination reveals a broken leg, you get diagnosed and treated for a broken leg.

We *need* that same sensible and realistic approach to trauma. Don't examine the list of events; examine the state of the person having the experience.

The results of that examination need to be the basis for the diagnosis. If it reveals a person in an overwhelmed, confused, terrified, helpless state, then consider diagnosing and treating that person for trauma.

Let's take this realistic approach — using the trauma state to determine if a person has experienced a trauma — and apply it to the events in our earlier examples:

- If the person who got thrown off the dock experienced a traumatic state, then for that person, getting thrown off the dock was an actual trauma. So getting thrown off a dock is a traumatic event for the non-swimming landlubber, but not for the horse-playing lifeguards.

- If the person who got separated from companions in the crowded mall experienced a traumatic state, then for that person, getting separated from companions in the crowded mall was an actual trauma. So getting separated from companions in a crowd is a traumatic event for the child, but not for the cell-phone carrying adult.

- If the person who got cold-shouldered and ignored experienced a traumatic state, then for that person, getting cold-shouldered and ignored was an actual trauma. So getting cold-shouldered and ignored is a traumatic event for the child, but not for the adult with many physical, mental, and social resources.

So, here's my answer to the question: "Did I Experience Trauma, or didn't I?" If you've had the experience of being in a traumatic state, of feeling overwhelmed, helpless, and terrified, then you've experienced an actual trauma, and you are entitled to the treatment that will enable you to heal.

❧

TRAUMA CATEGORIES

While consulting a "trauma event list" may not work well for determining trauma, paying attention to trauma events is sometimes very useful.

In fact, paying attention to what happened is so useful that the trauma-healing model's entire second component, the "Remember and Grieve " component, helps survivors attain the deep healing that can come from working with the trauma narrative of "what happened."

Some people are helped by sorting things into categories. They find it brings a calming sense of order.

NaCCT survivors benefit from grouping trauma events into categories and giving those categories names. Survivors can use these names to reach out and communicate with other people who've lived through similar events. They can talk one-on-one and form affinity groups. Connecting with other survivors overcomes isolation and facilitates comparing notes about what they share in common.

Events that cause trauma states can be categorized in a variety of ways. The most common distinction is made between acute and chronic trauma events:

Acute traumas are single incident trauma events, sort of analogous to a broken bone. For example, a car crash, fire, or mugging.

Chronic traumas are prolonged, ongoing or intermittent, sort of analogous to a repetitive strain injury. For example, living in a war zone, a dangerous neighborhood, an abusive relationship, or an emotionally cold home. NaCCTs belong in this category.

Traumas may also be categorized as Overt or Covert:

Overt traumas are blatant traumas, obviously traumatic, difficult to deny.

Covert traumas are hidden traumas, often subtle, difficult to perceive and acknowledge, easy to deny. NaCCTs belong in this category.

NaCCT is a sub-category of chronic, covert trauma (CCT). It's worth repeating here what the individual letters stand for:

"n" = *non-physically-assaultive, because it is not the result of hitting, shaking, sexually attacking, or any other form of tangible assault;*

"a" = *attachment-based, because it happens in the essential relationship between children and their mothers, fathers, or other essential people without whose care the child would die;*

"C" = *Chronic, because it is ongoing, repetitive, and cumulative rather than a single event or set of events;*

"C" = ***Covert****, because it is so difficult to perceive and acknowledge; and*

"T" = ***Trauma****, because (1) it overwhelms the victim's mental, physical and emotional resources at the time it occurs and (2) it may result in characteristic mental, social and spiritual wounds that may continue to cause pain and disability long afterwards.*

Two broad categories of naCCTs are those of omission and those of commission.

NACCTS OF OMISSION:

NaCCTs of Omission happen when the good stuff that was needed didn't happen and a trauma state came about as a result. These NaCCTs of Omission include neglect, deprivation, minimization, cluelessness, indifference, ignoring, dismissing, abandoning and other forms of absence, particularly when experienced by an utterly dependent human baby.

NaCCTs of Omission happen "when nothing is traumatic." Here's a partial list of absences that can be traumatic. A child who doesn't get enough of any of the following can experience naCCT of Omission:

- Attunement
- Responsiveness
- Love
- Touch
- Cuddling
- Soothing
- Delight
- Guidance
- Structure
- Affection
- Play

- Contact

- Validation

- Interest

- Respect

- Empathy

It's easy to ignore the traumas of omission — the neglect, the unattunement, the indifference. But these omissions are profoundly traumatic in their own right. Traumatic absence provides nothing at all to point to. There is *"nothing to be upset about."* The only indicator of traumatic omission may be the trauma state of overwhelming need, distress, or longing endured by the person for whom "nothing is the matter."

Traumas of omission almost invariably accompany traumas of commission. For a glaring instance, traumatic *omission* of care and protection accompanies traumatic *commission* of physical assault. Failure to cherish and protect a child's mental health accompanies reality-twisting or gaslighting.

Intentional withholding, including the classic "Silent Treatment," combines both the interactive intention of naCCTs of commission and the deprivation that causes NaCCTs of omission

NACCTS OF COMMISSION

NaCCTs of Commission happen when the bad stuff that shouldn't have happened, did happen. These naCCTs of Commission include favoritism, over-stimulation, teasing, scapegoating, interrupting, insulting, jostling, exploiting, teasing, "only kidding," comparing, belittling, or one-upping.

NaCCTs of Commission can be further categorized according to specific patterns of interpersonal circumstances and parental behaviors that have been observed to cause these traumas. Here are naCCT names and categories I use:

NaCCTs of Unwholesome Closeness: babying, "helicopter parenting," relating as if the child is the parent's "Golden Child" or "Trophy Child, a stand-in spouse, a best friend, or even the parent's own parent;

NaCCTs of Pathogenic (causing dysfunction) Pleasantness: superficiality; "poisonous positivity;" "fair weather" friend/parent; "nicey-nice;" a "no fear, anger or sadness allowed" mentality; too perfect; too good; too rigidly composed; too relentlessly orderly or cheerful; immature; naïve;

NaCCTs of Reality Twisting: Cognitive NaCCTs, "gaslighting," confusion, double-talking, mind-bending, just not making sense, deceiving by putting on an act or withholding information;

NaCCTs of Hidden hostilities: covert cruelty, unconscious meanness, secret gloating, subtle scapegoating, subtle jabs, insults disguised as concern or innocent ineptitude, harm done "accidentally on purpose." The perpetrator may be the "wolf in sheep's clothing;" the two-faced hypocrite who puts on a good act; the "devil at home, angel abroad."

NACCTS OF UNHELPFUL HELP

When someone seeks help, naCCTs of Unhelpful Help can add another layer of trauma on top of the original trauma.

These naCCTs of Unhelpful Help occur when the person turned to for help with the original trauma doesn't help, perhaps because they refuse or even side with the traumatizer, or, more commonly and tragically, because they mean well and make an effort, but the help they offer fails to help. They may offer invalidation or overly easy solutions, glib inspirational sayings, or moralistic judgments and simplistic advice.

When the help they offer doesn't work, unhelpful helpers may turn away, grow cold, or become frustrated and angry. They may even blame the victim for not benefitting from their help. The person seeking help may feel guilt and shame for not being helped.

YOUR NACCT CATEGORIES

If you felt some resonance with the descriptions in the list of naCCT categories above, experiment with completing this naCCT Resonance Statement:

"As I read over this list of non-physically-assaultive, attachment-based Chronic Covert Traumas, I could relate to the naCCTs of [_____]."

[Note: Sometimes even this much attention to what happened can be disturbing. This disturbance is normal and quite common, which is why some therapists adhere firmly to using the healing components sequentially, avoiding "Remember and Grieve" until the person they're helping has attained great skill with the "Stay Safe and Stable" component.

Fortunately, you've just been reading about maintaining safety in the previous chapter and have that material handy for review now.]

POST-TRAUMATIC STRESS DISORDER (PTSD)

What happens after trauma?

Both the outer events and the inner experiences of the original trauma state can leave their mark on the survivor.

Long after the danger has passed, the trauma may haunt the survivor's heart, mind, and body.

This vast array of significant aftereffects includes alterations in basic mood, pain perception, cognitive style, sleep patterns, energy levels, attitudes and expectations, body chemistry, biological functions, and even the ability to relate and bond with others. These aftereffects may relate to specific relationships, such as "Mother Wounds" and "Father Wounds."

[Hint: Could it be that any or all of the symptoms you inventoried when checking off "Is this You?" statements are aftereffects of trauma?]

If the trauma isn't resolved or healed, these changes linger as a wound that has come to have the name Post-Traumatic Stress Disorder, or PTSD for short. Post-Traumatic stress disorder (PTSD) is not an event; it's a diagnostic term given to the wounded condition.

Many people have the sense of having reacted to something bad that happened to them. PTSD says something bad *did* happen, and you had a normal reaction to it.

Children are particularly vulnerable to PTSD. The younger the child, the fewer resources they have, and the more traumatic the impact of an experience on them is likely to be. One study of children who had been exposed to extremely stressful circumstances revealed the relative numbers: A child under ten years old was three times more likely than a child over twelve to suffer from PTSD.[7]

⊘

HISTORY OF THE PTSD DIAGNOSIS

PTSD has been around for as long as people have experienced trauma and survived. Only the diagnosis is new.

The diagnostic term "Post-Traumatic Stress Disorder" came into use in the 1970's, when it referred to U.S. military veterans of the Vietnam War. Before that, the condition had been given names like "war neurosis," "physioneurosis," or "shell shock."

In 1980, PTSD was officially recognized by the American Psychiatric Association in the third edition of the psychotherapist's professional *Diagnostic and Statistical Manual of Mental Disorders (DSM III)*.

In the 2013 edition of *the DSM*, a new diagnostic category named "Trauma and Stressor-related Disorders" appeared. This new category included PTSD.

PTSD is the only psychiatric diagnosis in *the DSM* in which the disturbing symptoms are linked to an external cause. All the other diagnostic categories are defined and determined by symptoms alone. Only PTSD specifies that the symptoms came as a natural result of something happening to the person suffering from PTSD.

The PTSD diagnosis indicates that any normal person could develop symptoms as a result of experiencing trauma.

To be very precise, the trauma is the cause, the original overwhelming experience of terrifying helplessness in the face of a threat; the PTSD is the resulting condition with its troubling symptoms. In real life, we aren't always that precise, so we say we are healing trauma, but it's good to know that we aren't healing the trauma itself, we are healing the *PTSD symptoms* resulting from that trauma.

YOUR POSSIBLE PTSD SIGNS AND SYMPTOMS

Not everyone who experiences trauma goes on to suffer from PTSD. Sometimes the trauma is repaired when it happens. Sometimes the trauma is even repaired by the very person who caused it.

Problems that aren't repaired and don't resolve as expected could very possibly be entangled in deeply buried, trauma-sourced, psychological scar tissue.

Here are the signs and symptoms of PTSD. Think back to your presenting problems and your responses to the Tip-offs in Chapter Two,

"Is This You?". Do those responses match up with any of these PTSD signs and symptoms?

- Nameless dread and doom; feelings of being in danger and under attack

- Mixture of overreactions and underreactions to present-day people and circumstances

- Intrusive symptoms that break into your present life: memory fragments, dreams, and flashbacks where you relive the past trauma as if it's happening to you right now

- Constrictive symptoms that shrink your present life: stuckness, avoidance

- Physiological symptoms: body troubles, physical disturbances like trembling, chills, headaches, nausea, heart palpitations, panic attacks

- Mood disorders: anxiety, depression

DE-STIGMATIZING "MYSTERIOUS STUCKNESS"

Let's reconsider the naCCT Tip-off #1 of "Mysterious Stuckness," in Chapter Two, "Is This You?" If you relate to "Mysterious Stuckness," if you procrastinate, fail to follow through on your New Year's resolutions, or find yourself in the same relationship bind over and over again, then using the lens of PTSD might help you feel better about your behavior.

It may be that you're protecting yourself by advising yourself, "Don't change anything! You found a way to live through the trauma. That way worked. Leave it just the way it is!"

It's as if your present safety requires absolute adherence to your original time-tested way that kept you alive. As if you can't afford to be flexible. The stakes are too high.

"Being stuck may be bad, but being unstuck could be much worse!"

If placating, going numb, or even snarling and growling at people kept you safe in an important relationship, and if some enthusiastic helper with a bright idea then came along and suggested, "Let's try doing it this other way instead," you probably wouldn't say, "Sure, let's give it a whirl."

You'd be more likely to reply to suggestions for change: "No way! I found a way that got me through. Don't mess with it! Go away!"

Holding in mind the usefulness of adhering to a method that got you through a tough naCCT situation, you could reframe stuckness. Instead of "stuck," you could regard it as "firm," as "rock-solid adherence to life-preserving policies and procedures."

Instead of saying, "I'm stuck," and adding the nasty corollaries "I have no will power; I take terrible care of myself; I am hopeless," you might be saying to yourself, "I take care of myself by holding firm to my life-preserving procedures. My adherence to these procedures doesn't waver. Nothing can force me to abandon the tried and true ways that have kept me safe."

Framing your stuckness this way puts you in the driver's seat, and from there you are in charge.

COMPLEX PTSD

Complex Post-Traumatic Stress Disorder, or complex PTSD, often written "cPTSD," is a subcategory of PTSD that may result from prolonged or repeated trauma. Like PTSD, cPTSD is not a trauma; it's a condition resulting from trauma.

Complex PTSD's lessons have been learned through many traumatic repetitions over a long time. The learning is deep.

Adding the term "complex" to "PTSD" was proposed by psychiatrist Judith Herman in her 1992 book *Trauma and Recovery*. Just as we need the term "naCCT" to distinguish non-physically-assaultive trauma from physically-assaultive trauma, so we need a term that distinguishes PTSD caused by a single trauma from PTSD caused by the accumulation of many ongoing layers and incidents of repeated trauma.

Complex PTSD has not yet been included in the American Psychiatric Association's *DSM*. However, complex PTSD *is* included in the diagnostic manual of the World Health Organization (WHO.) In addition, the UK's National Health Service, the United States Department of Veterans Affairs, and Healthdirect Australia all recognize the diagnosis of complex PTSD.

COMPLEX PTSD RESULTING FROM UNRESOLVED NACCT

The cPTSD subcategory of PTSD includes PTSD resulting from Non-physically-assaultive, attachment-based, Chronic Covert Trauma.

To be clear, the naCCT is the original trauma; the cPTSD is the condition resulting from the trauma. To precisely indicate the connection of symptoms to cause, we can say "cPTSD from naCCT" or "naCCT-sourced cPTSD," or use an arrow going from naCCT to cPTSD, like this:

"naCCT (arrow pointing right) cPTSD"

In practice, we hardly ever make this distinction. Instead, we simply say that we're "healing naCCT." Nevertheless, it is good to keep the distinction in mind. We do not go back in time to heal the trauma; we heal the cPTSD condition in the present.

Unfortunately, discussions of cPTSD typically offer examples involving physical assaults and direct bodily harm, suggesting this is a requirement for being considered "real" cPTSD. The prevalence of this type of example is another reason we need a new term (naCCT) to specify traumas that don't involve direct physical assault.

The kind of cPTSD that may arise from naCCT is a devastating subclass of cPTSD with its own characteristic traits and unique challenges. NaCCT-sourced cPTSD needs a designation of its own.

As mentioned before, complex PTSD from naCCT often goes unidentified and invalidated.

Many naCCT survivors don't know they have a trauma history underlying many of their troubles. So it's very common for survivors of naCCT to think, "I don't have complex PTSD or any kind of PTSD at all because I didn't experience any trauma," and that kind of thinking can tragically result in a person not getting the treatment they need for recovery.

Armed with psychoeducation about naCCT, a survivor can open the way to healing by saying instead, "I could have the kind of complex PTSD that results from non-physically-assaultive, attachment-based, Chronic Covert Trauma," or, more simply put, "I could have cPTSD from naCCT."

❧

NACCT-SOURCED TRIGGERS

One of naCCT-sourced cPTSD's unique challenges is the nature of naCCT-sourced triggers, those reminders of the original traumatic event or situation that activate cPTSD symptoms.

Just as naCCT calls into question the conventional image of trauma — physical, dramatic, overtly menacing (or easily mistaken for something menacing) — so naCCT-sourced triggers call into question the conventional image of PTSD triggers.

Effectively addressing cPTSD triggers from naCCT requires a change in our thinking about triggers.

One common conventional image of PTSD triggers involves those resulting from such traumas as war, car crashes, or natural disasters. Unlike these impersonal triggers, naCCT-sourced triggers, like the naCCTs that cause them, tend to occur in relationships with other people, whether at work, school, family, or community. The specific relationships range from intimate partners to acquaintances and even to people in the media.

Among traumas in relationships with other people, naCCTs are uniquely intangible.

Again, effectively addressing naCCT-sourced triggers calls for a change in our thinking about triggers. The usual conventional image of trauma relating to other people involves blatantly traumatic beatings and incest, but NaCCT triggers, like their naCCT source, require no physical assault whatsoever. They are determined by the traumatic state caused by such non-physically-assaultive interpersonal threats as disconnection from an important person, abandonment, indifference, devaluing, verbal bullying, emotional cruelty, or social shame and exclusion.

NACCT-SOURCED TRIGGERS ARE HARD TO RECOGNIZE

Like their source naCCTs, these triggers tend to be undramatic and subtle, so subtle that they're functionally covert. They're easily missed, overlooked, or rationalized away.

Everyday exchanges with other people are full of pauses, interruptions, miscommunications, lapses in attention and the like. These glitches are so much a part of everyday civilized interactions that while they're annoying, they aren't usually thought of as cPTSD triggers.

However, for naCCT survivors, those ordinary interpersonal glitches could easily be triggers.

Because they're attachment-based — rooted in survivors' unique individual relationships with their unique individual Lifeline Person — each survivor's triggers have essentially been custom-tailored to match their unique individual naCCT. What may trigger one survivor may be neutral for another.

In the case of traumatic unattunement, for example, a survivor's personal triggers may involve perfectly civilized behavior that is jarringly unattuned to their own individual needs and puzzlingly terrifying only to them.

To make matters worse, because naCCT-sourced triggers are so uniquely individualized, the practice of issuing "Trigger Warnings" doesn't usually work for them. They don't shout, "Watch out! Trigger here!" Nor are there universal naCCT trigger words that a caring friend or therapist can be mindful to avoid.

Triggers related to NaCCTs of Omission can be particularly insidious. Like source naCCTs of Omission, these triggers often involve a Lifeline Caregiver's traumatic absence, silence, or failure to do anything at all.

A well-intentioned conversational pause or respectful standing back to give someone their private space can unfortunately trigger a reminder of past traumatic absence, indifference, or similar naCCTs of Omission where "there was nothing to be upset about."

Triggers may also be inner states, such as moments of present-day longing reminiscent of early longing for what was missing from NaCCTs of Omission: for loving responses such as safe touch, thoughtful guidance, or hugs that didn't happen.

Because naCCT-sourced triggers are so ordinary and unremarkable, it's reasonable to expect they won't be recognized as triggers.

Survivors frequently notice they're distressed, perhaps even experiencing an abrupt change into "emotional dysregulation," but they have only a vague sense — or none at all — that "something happened" to trigger that change.

This means that naCCT survivors may easily be triggered without knowing it. They may end up feeling baffled, frantic, frustrated, ashamed, or helpless, yet without a clue as to what's happening to them, why they are so upset, or what to do about it.

In such a predicament, it's not surprising that mystified survivors end up tormenting themselves with futile attempts to discover the source of their troubles in their own bad character, unfortunate genes, or even "repressed or forgotten beatings or incest" that never actually happened.

To help put an end to this suffering, psychoeducation provides you with valuable information about the cPTSD wounds caused by naCCT.

As this psychoeducation chapter draws to a close, reflect on your experience reading about trauma, naCCT, and cPTSD. Do your troubles make more sense to you now? Have you noticed an increase in your compassionate understanding of what the naCCT survivor — maybe you? — has been up against?

UP NEXT: WHERE WE GO FROM HERE

The rest of this book helps you to recognize, acknowledge, care for, and heal these naCCT-sourced cPTSD wounds.

We'll be working within the "Stay Safe and Stable" component, with a special emphasis on building up resources for handling naCCT-sourced triggers in three areas:

1. **Intrapsychic Experience.** First we'll strengthen your inner helping relationship in order to cope with the thoughts and feelings in your inner world.

2. **Interpersonal Experience.** Then we'll tackle naCCT-sourced triggers in the outer social world, in your relationships with other people.

3. **Physiological Experience.** And finally, we'll explore coping with naCCT's impact on your physiology: sensations, physical problems, and body-based mood disorders.

As the name *complex* PTSD indicates, the wound caused by naCCT is a *complex* wound. The process of your recovery will also be complex.

One survivor recovering from naCCT-sourced cPTSD thought for a minute after I asked her what I should be sure to tell you. Then she said, "Be sure to tell them healing is really hard and it's really slow."

So I'm telling you: Healing is really hard, and it's really slow.

Still, you can do it. With this psychoeducation and with persistent work guided by this book, you can — although slowly and with difficulty — ultimately meet the unique challenges of naCCT-sourced cPTSD and succeed in making positive healing changes beyond your wildest dreams.

NOTES

[4] *Diagnostic and Statistical Manual of Mental Disorders (4th ed., Text Revision)*, (Washington, DC: American Psychiatric Association, 2000), quoted in https://www.ncbi.nlm.nih.gov/books/NBK83241/ accessed 2-2-20

[5] *Diagnostic and statistical manual of mental disorders: DSM-5*, (Arlington, VA: American Psychiatric Association, 2013).

[6] "What Aces/Pces Do You Have?" accessed 9-12-20, https://acestoohigh.com/got-your-ace-score/.

[7] J. Davidson and R. Smith, "Traumatic Experiences in Psychiatric Outpatients," *Journal of Traumatic Stress Studies* 3 (July 1990): 459-475.

Part III:

Intrapsychic Experience: Safe and Stable with Your Thoughts and Emotions

CHAPTER 5

YOUR INNER HELPING RELATIONSHIP

In this chapter, we empower and strengthen what may be our most important relationship: the one we have with ourselves.

To review and get oriented: This healing journey is guided by the classic trauma recovery model with its three components: "Stay Safe and Stable," "Remember and Grieve," and "Reconnect and Re-engage." We are working within the "Stay Safe and Stable" component. The plan is to stay safe and stable in three key areas: the Intrapsychic world within, the interpersonal world , and the physiological world of our bodies.

In this chapter and the next, we explore what needs to be attended to in order to *be* safe, *know* you are safe, and *feel* safe in the world within. We'll explore "Parts Work" and how to use it to help you heal the intrapsychic wounds of naCCT and have a safe, stabilizing inner helping relationship.

Lovingly and effectively helping ourselves manage our thoughts and emotions provides inner safety and stability.

As we work on healing from these intangible attachment traumas, it is crucial for us to know that when we need help, we can rely on ourselves.

Early naCCTs influence how well we take care of ourselves today. Unhealed intrapsychic wounds from unresolved naCCTs block effective self-help.

Troubled intrapsychic relationships with ourselves are some of the most heartbreaking wounds from early naCCTs.

For naCCT survivors with complex PTSD, the "intrapsychic" world within does not always feel safe and stable. It's often fraught with distressing thoughts and feelings. No "home" within provides refuge. There's nowhere safe inside to go. In fact, the inner upset sometimes makes tuning in to the intrapsychic world within feel like "going into an unsafe neighborhood."

The work of this chapter will help you transform your inner environment into a really "safe neighborhood" and provide you with an inner home you can always go to.

"EMOTIONAL DYSREGULATION IS A HOT MESS"

Unfortunately, where we need internal safety and stability, too often we get "emotional dysregulation," one of psychotherapy's buzzwords of the day. Instead of "emotional dysregulation," you could say "go bananas" or "flip out," "lose it," or "go over the edge." Or, as one survivor struggling with cPTSD put it, "This emotional dysregulation is a hot mess!"

I tend to say, "get really upset."

Whatever you call it, this unfortunate state involves a tangled chain reaction, beginning with negative thoughts and emotions like shame, disgust, fear, rage, or sadness.

Instead of calming down, we stay upset or get even *more* upset. Agitated upset may alternate with shut down upset: numbness. The calming down process just doesn't happen.

As this tangled chain reaction intensifies, our inner helping relationship gets dysregulated too. We lose our loving, helpful connection within, and so we have trouble helping ourselves get regulated again. Then we get scared of our own thoughts and emotions, pass judgment against them, or turn against ourselves for not being able to get rid of them and calm ourselves down.

We may feel frantic, or we may just feel hopeless and down on ourselves.

FROM EMOTIONAL DYSREGULATION TO INNER SELF-HELP

Jenna Lee would get upset like this sometimes. Remember her? The special education teacher who came for therapy in Chapter One. She'll be our guide and model in this chapter.

Jenna Lee took helping her special education kids for granted — "It's my job!" she said — whereas helping herself seemed daunting and even miraculous to her.

Realistically, Jenna Lee was a skilled helping professional, "wise and skillful in dealing with discouraged or frustrated kids," giving them "gentle empathy and responsive assistance when they were upset."

However, when she got upset herself, Jenna Lee couldn't bring her strengths and skills home to help herself. In fact, she would lose awareness of them altogether, getting aggravated and impatient with herself, forgetting what a good helpful person she was, and calling herself "spoiled" and "selfish" instead.

To understand the uplifting process of going from dysregulated to regulated, let's take a more detailed look at what happened in that therapy session in Chapter One, when she was really down on herself:

(The earlier scene with Jenna Lee is in italics; my comments are in the regular un-italicized font.)

I reminded her, "Children often feel upset like you do right now, and they aren't shy about letting their feelings show. I wonder. . .what do you do when your little special ed kids have hard times like you're having right now: when they're frustrated and stuck being negative, withdrawn, scared — and don't know why?"

Invited to pause and remember helping those upset, dysregulated kids, Jenna Lee began to reclaim both her helping *skills* and her helper's *attitude*:

Jenna Lee brightened.

Her whole being shifted. She perked up, sat up straighter. Her voice softened. Even her clothes seemed to drape more fashionably on her energized body.

"Oh my heart goes out to them," she answered. "I squat right down to their eye-level. I talk in a soft voice and try to connect with them and draw them out."

It was easy to picture her doing this, being so natural, graceful, and capable that kids would draw comfort from her: they would see her as bigger, stronger, and wiser than they were. And kind. Just what kids want and need in a helper.

When Jenna Lee's helper skills and attitude came back on line, she was a little startled to remember just how helpful and caring she often was:

"She stopped abruptly. "Oh, wait a minute! . . . "

She interrupted herself, struck by the contrast between how she had been with her pupils and how she was being with herself:

"I wouldn't tell them that they were wrong or bad for feeling upset."

"So you try to comfort a child who feels as upset as you do now," I said, "and you try to understand what they're upset about?"

Tears filled her hazel eyes and hung there, glistening. She said quietly, "When those kids are upset, I'm really gentle with them."

She seemed to realize she'd veered off track.

Veering off track is normal. That's why we install GPS navigation systems in our cars. Sometimes when we're driving along, counting on our GPS to get us where we want to go, we veer off the route. The GPS voice serenely repeats, "recalibrating, recalibrating," and then it directs us back onto the correct route to our destination. In just that way, Jenna Lee was recalibrating, finding her way back to her own helper attitude and capabilities.

It's normal for those helper skills to just go missing sometimes. No blame, no shame. When it happens, we can be as matter-of-fact about veering off track as the unflappable GPS voice that calmly guides the driver to "recalibrate and resume."

TENDER TEARS

When Jenna Lee did get back on track, she got in touch with her competencies as a special education teacher, with her heart, her loving kindness. As her students would have put it in their straightforward language, Jenna Lee stopped "being mean" to herself and started being "nice."

When she felt the contrast between the "mean" attitude she'd fallen into towards herself and the "nice," gently effective way she acted with the children, tears came to her eyes: She realized how profoundly her skill and caring had gone missing when she had needed them herself.

I think her tears are tender tears. Tears of sorrow for abandoning herself. Tears of regret for being mean to herself. Tears of relief for coming back home to herself. Tears of compassionate self-love.

NOW YOUR TURN: CLAIM YOUR PERSONAL RESOURCES

As we saw with Jenna Lee, helping ourselves restore intrapsychic safety and stability begins with claiming our helping skills, impulses, and attitudes, all of which we then bring home to help ourselves.

Jenna Lee took that first step when she vividly remembered, almost re-experienced, her State-of-Being when she was helping her upset students.

Like Jenna Lee, many naCCT survivors become helpers, some in the acknowledged helping professions: therapists, healers, counselors, trainers, teachers, advisors, coaches, or consultants; many others in the more subtle helping professions: beauticians, bartenders, receptionists, virtual assistants, account managers, customer service representatives, and the like.

In addition, many naCCT survivors provide skilled, loving, helpful parenting to really upset children.

If you have a green thumb, you have a powerful helping capacity in relation to plants. Similarly, if you cook or garden, repair cars or computers, untangle shaggy pet fur or people's financial accounts, edit or proofread, knit or do woodworking, then you know what it's like to be a helper: attentive and capable, confident and calm.

REVIEW YOUR RESOURCES: SKILLS, QUALITIES, AND POWERS

Enjoy the feeling of security that comes with having the resources you need to meet challenges successfully, that confident "I can handle this" feeling. Remember: You survived!

Like Jenna Lee, first strengthen your faith in your power to help yourself. Get back in touch with your helper attitude and skills. You have inner resources. Take a minute here to review a few of them.

Notice what kind of help you tend to give. Is it help exploring?

Comforting? Pep talks? Problem solving? Practical help like a car ride or financial loan? Cuddles and hugs? Advice? Encouragement? Information? Comforting words? Gifts? Entertaining? Jokes?

This might be a good time to go back and review the strengths you claimed in Chapters Three and Four. All those strengths are available to you *all* day, *every* day, for the rest of your life. And for a good price, too!

Sometimes it's a good idea to actually pick up a pen and paper and write down your strengths and helping skills. Some mysterious power in the act of writing seems to intensify the brain's belief in their existence.

This simple sentence stem works wonders; just fill in the blank:

"At least once in my life, I have [_____]."

What popped into your mind? "Comforted a child?" "Cleaned up a mess, calmly"? "Rescued a casserole that didn't come out right the first time?"

If you feel silly doing this exercise or worry that someone will find what you've written and think you're silly, you can always write it on a napkin which you can later toss into the recycle bin. Not silly. *Smart!*

To reclaim your resources, you'll, of course, mentally review your work resume. But don't stop with job skills. Here are some other simple ways to identify your strengths:

- Acknowledge all the ordinary, taken-for-granted life skills you've developed since the day you were born: reading, grooming, banking, arranging transportation, shopping, computing, socializing, googling.

- Even though you probably don't remember developing them, give yourself credit for mastering all the grown up skills you worked so hard to develop as a toddler, skills and capabilities you didn't have as a baby: turning over from your stomach to your back; walking, talking, feeding yourself.

- Include mental and emotional soothing and regulation skills: replacing insecure thoughts with secure thoughts, using creative distractions, relaxation, meditation, exercise, and so forth.

SELF-TALK SCRIPT: USING YOUR SKILLS TO HELP YOURSELF

So, you have skills. Can you bring them home? Can you use them to help yourself? Our relationships with ourselves form the heart of self-help. Try out this basic Self-Talk Script:

"I help myself. I can help myself. I do help myself."

"PARTS WORK"

Let's look at a feature of that Self-Talk Script: it implies an inner relationship. If I say "I help myself," there's the "I" part that helps and the "myself" part that gets helped.

Even though I know I'm one person helping myself, my words suggest a relationship between two people. Lots of expressions used for the way we treat ourselves work this way: "I feed myself; I wash myself; I groom myself."

Some people might protest, "I'm not two people. I'm a whole person. I don't have multiple personalities like 'The United States of Tara' on TV, or that woman, Sybil, in the movie."

True. And yet, the way we speak reflects the way we experience ourselves.

Relationships between parts of ourselves are built into these reflexive verbs: the "I" part acts upon the "myself" part. "I badger myself, or pamper myself, or starve myself, or beat myself up."

In my case, for example, I do feel like there's a *part* of myself that badgers me and a *part* of myself that *gets* badgered. There's a Ricia part who pampers and a Ricia part who *gets* pampered.

Some people think of these "parts" as representations of different internal processes: different drives, functions, neurological networks, or inner states of being.

Some people compare these "parts" to "wearing different hats" that match the different roles they play: a chauffeur's hat when they take the kids to the sleepover, a baseball cap when they're kicking back with the gang, or a crown when they're in total charge.

Talking about the inner parts of an individual as though those parts are separate people has a long-standing tradition in psychotherapy and self-help. From the psychodynamic Id, Ego, and Superego, through Transactional Analysis' Inner Child, Inner Adult, and Inner Parent parts, to the exiles, "Self," and protectors used in today's Internal Family Systems approach, therapists have used "parts" to represent how we think and feel inside.

Some people give these parts concrete form by thinking of them as actors in an "intrapsychic play" or members of an "intrapsychic family."

Working with the relationship within is sometimes known as "Parts Work."

Internal relationships between "parts" of the self can function in the same way that external relationships between people function. They can be harmonious, hostile, conflictual, or equal, for example.

For those of us who do self-help, "Parts Work" really makes sense: the part that helps and the part that gets helped have a real relationship to each other.

I love parts work. I love how "Parts Work" makes it easy to understand what's going on inside. I love how we can use pillows, or puppets, or even real people to act out these parts. I love how we can do "Chair Work with Parts," where each part gets its own chair, and we can move from chair to chair as we get in touch with different parts of ourselves.

I invite you now to do some "Parts Work" with your inner helping relationship. This work provides a good antidote to emotional dysregulation. It can strengthen your ability to bring your skills home so you can say with confidence, "I help myself. I *can* help myself. I *do* help myself."

Let's begin. What about those inner relationships?

WE ARE BONDED TO OURSELVES FOR LIFE

Sometimes I have to remind myself: "You are the one person you will never leave and never lose."

As long as I live, there I am with myself. The relationship of "I" to "myself" is primary — permanent, enduring, abiding, forever, till death do us part.

I am my own most significant other.

Wherever I go, there I am.

Our inner relationships to ourselves are more permanent than marriage. You can't get a divorce from yourself. (Though many of us often try to.)

FOR BETTER OR WORSE, YOU MIGHT SAY

Like marriages, our relationships to ourselves contain positive and negative aspects.

Sometimes the relationship between inner "parts" goes well: You take good care of yourself. You're your own best friend forever. It feels like being in love. When you wake up in the morning, when you lie in bed at night, you feel good.

If you could put the good feeling into words, those words might say something like this: "I'm so glad I have me in my life now. I take good care of myself. I protect myself. I'm the boss of me. I am so blessed to have me on my team. I'm a catch! And whenever I want me, there I am!"

And sometimes this inner relationship doesn't go well at all. Sometimes it's awful.

"Wherever you go, you are burdened with yourself," wrote Christian religious philosopher Thomas á Kempis 600 years ago, and many of us find it's true for us today.

ASSESS YOUR INNER RELATIONSHIPS

How do *your* inner parts relate to each other? Do you find yourself predominantly in "honeymoon heaven" or "pre-divorce hell"?

Are you "your own best friend"? A harsh "frenemy"?

Do you flip flop between these two extremes or maintain more moderate fluctuations on a more even keel?

Do the different aspects of your self get into prolonged conflicts with each other? Does one part assess a situation as safe and another part assess the same situation as dangerous? Does one part want to move towards someone in a friendly way and another part want to move toward the same person aggressively? Does one part strive for self-expression while another part protests, "No way!"

Some therapists call this "intrapsychic conflict." Many naCCT survivors with cPTSD suffer from "intrapsychic conflict." We get upset. Sometimes we get dysregulated.

One the positive side, do different parts sometimes work harmoniously together? Do they cooperate, with all parts functioning together as a whole to cope with challenges, seize opportunities, and pursue dreams?

Can you be a responsive witness, a good parent, a wise counsel to yourself?

CAN YOU BE YOUR OWN INNER HELPER?

Many people seek out therapy or self-help because their inner helping relationship has gone bad, lacks strength, or scarcely exists. These seekers aren't getting enough inner help to manage their present life challenges, let alone to dream and plan effectively for a brighter future.

With the goal of creating a safe "inner home," we'll focus on the inner helping relationship between the "I" part that helps and the "myself" part that gets help.

First, Inner Helper, the "I" part that helps.

SPECIFIC WAYS YOUR INNER HELPER CAN HELP

Here's a list of helpful ways we can relate to ourselves, what the "I" part can do for the "myself" part.

Read through this list of self-help functions. What can you offer yourself? Ponder each item.

Notice what the "I" part of yourself — the Inner Helper part — feels able to provide. "Hey! I can do that." Mentally put a heart next to those functions you feel you feel secure about providing for yourself. Put lots of hearts next to those that you feel *very* secure about.

And what about the self-help functions that the Inner Helper part of yourself finds challenging? Acknowledge to yourself, "I'd like that." And because these are skills your Inner Helper can develop as you continue healing, you can also say to yourself: "I'm not so good at that yet, *but I can learn!*"

You can:

- Be gentle with yourself
- Compassionately come alongside yourself
- Soothe yourself
- Provide yourself with safety
- Endorse your accomplishments
- Acknowledge your strengths
- Treat yourself with respect
- Be patient with yourself
- Help yourself stay within loving limits
- Repair your relationship with yourself
- Explain to yourself how early trauma relates to your present troubles

- Reassure yourself that you're safe
- Restore your thoughts and emotions to balance when you get upset
- Restore your body to balance when you get upset
- Protect yourself
- Problem-solve for yourself
- Validate your perceptions, interpretations, and hunches
- Provide food and shelter for yourself
- Provide excitement, soothing, or entertainment for yourself
- Guide yourself
- Empathize with yourself
- Reflect yourself
- Love yourself
- Evaluate yourself
- Encourage yourself
- Keep yourself on task and on track
- Nurture yourself
- Teach yourself
- Coach yourself
- Understand yourself
- Explain yourself to yourself
- Stick up for yourself
- Praise yourself
- Celebrate yourself
- Just "be present" for yourself

"OUTSIDE THE BOX" RESOURCES

Sometimes you'll think outside the box and come up with unexpected ways of helping yourself. This happened for a woman I'll call Deena.

She was a new client, new to me and to psychotherapy. Like Jenna Lee, Deena had gotten upset, dysregulated, and lost touch with her strengths and skills for helping herself. She knew she was upset and couldn't find her way back to stability.

"I'm so agitated thinking about it," she said. Her Inner Helper had been decommissioned, and she was frantic, trying to come up with a way to manage her response to disturbing information she'd just received.

"How will I function at work tomorrow? I'm so worked up. My heart rate's through the roof. Forget blood pressure. And how will I even *get* to work? I'll be a wreck, feeling like a caged animal trapped on the subway!"

When I asked Deena how she usually managed stress, she surprised me: "I shoot hoops," she said. "Basketball. Or hit the gym. . . . .[Long Pause] People tell me to sit and focus on my breathing, but it doesn't work. It makes me feel like a wild animal in a tiny cage. I need to blow off all this energy. . . ." [Longer pause, during which her gestures become more organized, and she appears more grounded, more settled into her center. Has her Inner Helper kicked in and come back on line?] . . . ."Do you mind if I do some pushups?"

"Here? Now?" I asked, revealing my "inside the box" thinking. I'm a psychotherapist, and I was stuck inside a psychotherapist box where talking was *the* method for calming down. Gyms were for pushups. Psychotherapy offices were for talking.

Clearly, my client knew herself and what she needed better than I did. Her Inner Helper went outside the box and came up with a better plan for her.

Persuasive, focused on what she needed, Deena replied, "Yes, here. I'm so wired. I can't shoot hoops here in your office. Pushups."

"Well. . . .OK," I replied, *very* tentatively. "Can you talk while you're doing pushups?"

I watched — probably stared — as she moved from her chair down onto the hopefully clean-enough office carpet.

I said, "I can't believe you're doing those pushups AND talking to me. . . ."

I stared some more, then observed, "You definitely do seem calmer."

"*Much* calmer," Deena said, still doing pushups. "I need to blow off all this energy. Hoops and workouts are best. Running's not bad. . . .Wait. . . . tomorrow I could run. There's no stigma to running. I could carry my running shoes on the subway tomorrow. If that 'caged animal' feeling comes over me while I'm on the train, I can get off at the next stop, exit the subway station, and go for a run until I've worked myself down. Then get back on the subway. Eventually get to work.

"And once I'm at work, no problem: everybody runs. We even have a shower. No one will think twice about me going for a run and showering when I get back. I can do this."

Deena's Inner Helper, initially decommissioned by anxiety, came back on line, and Deena brilliantly solved her own problem. Something had worked. I hadn't done much, mostly "just been there," listening, paying attention, asking a few questions, saying "OK" to her doing pushups.

I marvelled at how fast Deena's skills came back, as she went from being dysregulated to being regulated, planful, creative in her self care.

On the checklist of "Specific Ways Your Inner Helper Can Help," Deena could check off several items: She began with "just being present for herself." She also "restored her body to balance when she got upset." She "compassionately came alongside herself." She "kept herself on task and on track." She "understood herself:" what she needed, how her upset worked. She "guided herself." She "problem-solved for herself." And she ultimately provided herself with inner safety and stability.

THE PART OF YOU THAT NEEDS HELP

We've spent some time focusing on the "I" part of "I help myself," the part that helps.

Let's now devote some energy and attention to the troubled part that sometimes needs help, the "myself" part of "I help myself."

The "myself" part that needs help is sometimes referred to as the Inner Child because, to survive, dependent children obviously need help. If you like this Inner Child image, use it. Ignore it if you don't.

As you've been reviewing your Inner Helper's many helping skills, the part of you that sometimes needs help (the Inner Child) may have been peeking out and observing that process. How does that help-needing part feel at this point, observing the Inner Helper part stepping forward, becoming stronger and more helpful?

At this very moment, your "myself" part that needs help stands on the threshold of meeting with a part that gives help.

How does that help-needing part feel about that meeting? About actually receiving help? Are you aware of wanting help with something now?

Let yourself imagine that where you were dismissed, you will be attended to. Imagine interest where there was indifference; enthusiasm where there was scorn. Imagine warmth where it was cold; kindness where it was harsh; "niceness" where it was "mean;" and deep presence where there was nothing at all.

Draw out that part that needs help. Give that part a voice.

Maybe do some "Chair Work with Parts." Set out a new chair at your desk for the part that needs help. Set out a keyboard or some paper and a pen, physically move into that chair, and let the part that needs help do some journal writing.

Is that little part that needs help all open-hearted receptivity and satisfied longing? Would this be the movie sequence that pulls on our heart strings, where the little part that needs help and the Big Helper awkwardly meet, shyly smile at each other, then laugh, have a tender hug, and all is well at last and forever after?

MAYBE NOT.

In my work as a therapist and in my own personal growth, I sometimes get fooled because I naively think this great new inner helping relationship will blissfully come about and solve everything.

And then it doesn't.

I forget this is real life.

From my unrealistically optimistic mistakes, I've learned to make a space for an angry child who asks, "Where have you been? Why didn't you come when I cried for you?"

I've learned to make space for an apprehensive and suspicious child whose behavior embodies the saying, "Once bitten, twice shy."

Or make space for a child who's really good at covering up anger and suspiciousness with a smile.

At the threshold of this new helping relationship within, it's *normal* to be ambivalent; *normal* to think "Yes, it sounds great," on one hand and "no, she'll never pull it off and really help me" on the other. It's *normal* to think "What a phony" or "Don't jostle me, I'm used to it the way it is" or even "I don't want to make this mess any worse. Go away!"

My realistic take-away: Make space for these real-world aspects of the inner parts that needs help. Welcome them. Come alongside them. Get to know them.

NOT A FAIRY TALE

If the inner part that needs help isn't ecstatic about meeting the Inner Helper, isn't anticipating a happy-ever-after Fairy Tale outcome to this meeting, there's a reason.

Recall that trauma is about danger; naCCT is specifically about danger in early attachment relationships; and cPTSD from naCCT is about staying alive after actually experiencing danger and a trauma state in those essential early relationships.

Recall also that the key tip-off to naCCT in Chapter Two, "Is This

You?" was a disturbing answer to the question "When I was little, what happened when I got upset?" Here that answer becomes relevant.

For many naCCT survivors, what sometimes happened when we got upset back then wasn't very good. The response we got sometimes made matters worse. It might even have been awful, an actual naCCT of Unhelpful Help.

Maybe an early Lifeline Person didn't have time for our troubles, pooh-poohed them, and shamed us for having them. Who wants to get shamed again?

Maybe the looks and gestures, the tone of voice, the "vibe," or the quality of touch was scary. Who wants to get scared again?

Or a parent nagged or sneered or just went missing emotionally when we were having a hard time, when we made a mistake or couldn't understand something. We were scared that person would abandon us, and emotionally they did. Who wants to risk being emotionally abandoned again today?

To cope — no, to *survive* — in these early, absolutely essential relationships, our deep survival instincts guided us to come up with a complex network of strategies for handling what we perceived as threats. Deeper than our conscious mental operations, our brilliant bodies instituted "survival policies" that came to function almost like reflexes for warding off possible dangers.

Rather than risk being scared, shamed, or emotionally abandoned, maybe we "body-learned" to burst into nervous laughter instead of crying.

Or maybe we learned to stare vacantly at the floor or get engrossed in a toy instead of rushing to cling to a parent who had rebuffed us in the past.

This protective warning system with its "survival policies" led an early-bird reader of this book to think of the expression, "Danger, Will Robinson," a popular catchphrase from the 1960's American TV show *Lost in Space*, in which a boy named Will Robinson develops a close bond with a robot who protects him by warning "Danger, Will Robinson, Danger!"

The phrase caught on and was commonly used to alert someone that what they were about to do could be dangerous.

With cPTSD from naCCT, it's as though our survival policies warn, "Danger, help-needing part, danger!" when we need help, seek help, or even find ourselves in the presence of a potential helper.

With deeply embedded survival policies like these, the help-needing part may not be open and receptive to Inner Helper at all.

In fact, like a well-trained child's "I don't take candy from strangers," the help-needing part's survival response might be more like "No way! Back off."

Taking all this into consideration, a realistic model for this meeting between your Inner Helper and the part that needs help might be that of a very complex and difficult "adoption:" An open-hearted grown up, eager to love, adopting a very wary little child.

TROUBLING REVERBERATIONS FROM EARLY NACCTS.

When you spend time with your help-needing part, memories of what you experienced as a child might start to come up. You may hear echoes and sense shadows of your early relationships with mother, father, or other Lifeline Caregiver.

Maybe the "myself" part that needs help is remembering upsetting times of turning to people for help long ago and getting rejected, neglected, or ignored.

If you find yourself remembering what happened when you were upset long ago, you face a decision: What to do about those memories now?

STAY IN THE PRESENT OR REMEMBER THE PAST?

Here is where you might find yourself feeling pulled to go "out-of-sequence" to the "Remember and Grieve" component of the trauma-healing model.

Vividly re-experiencing your backstory can be tough, even dysregulating and destabilizing. Is it better to set the backstory aside and concentrate on staying safe and stable? Or better to remember and grieve?

If you stand far back, maybe even going into the inner refuge you created in the Safe Space Imagery process, you can sense whether you'd be better off going more toward setting your backstory from childhood aside for now or more toward delving deeper into that story.

Here are a few Self-Talk Scripts to help you step back and consider whether to focus on your present experience or give your attention to your past. Try each Self-Talk Script out. Which one meets your present needs best?

SELF-TALK SCRIPT FOR SETTING THE BACKSTORY ASIDE AND WORKING WITH THE "STAY SAFE AND STABLE" COMPONENT

"Hmm. . . . .my upset now could be related to my naCCT backstory. I'll acknowledge that it's there, maybe just keep saying to myself, "Flashback; this is a flashback." And then I'll set it aside for now. . . . .or attempt to."

SELF-TALK SCRIPT FOR WHEN YOU ATTEMPT TO SET YOUR MEMORIES ASIDE, BUT THEY WON'T STAY ASIDE

"Hmm. . . . Those memories don't seem to want to be set aside. It's like they're insisting, 'I need attention now!' Maybe they want me to know something. I'll give them a little attention and do a one-sentence answer to that "What happened when I got upset when I was little?" question. I'll use the list of naCCTs from Chapter Four, "Psychoeducation." Or maybe give it a label, like 'Flashback to disturbing memory of naCCT from long ago.'"

SELF-TALK SCRIPT FOR OUT-OF-SEQUENCE JUMP TO WORKING WITH BACKSTORY "REMEMBER AND GRIEVE" COMPONENT

"I know this is out-of-sequence because I'm working in the 'Stay Safe and Stable' component right now, and this is 'Remember and Grieve' work. But I want to give attention to this backstory. I don't want to set it aside. I'll take responsibility for feeling unsafe and getting destabilized. . . . maybe I can manage to tell the story and stay safe and stable. I want to work with that backstory now. That part of me needs attention right now. I'm going to risk it."

Whatever you decide, ultimately it's a good idea to keep on reading this chapter, and continue working to stay safe and stable and strengthen your inner helping relationship.

CHECK BACK WITH THE PART OF YOU THAT HELPS, YOUR INNER HELPER

Meanwhile, your Inner Helper part is about to meet the part of you that needs help. What's going on for your Inner Helper? It might be a disturbing time for that part too, raising concerns like, "Uh oh! This inner part that needs help could turn out to be a real handful."

Take heart. Here are some tips for your Inner Helper:

TIP #1: USE THE MAGIC AND POWER OF "HMM. . . ."

Consider the Magic of "Hmm. . . ." It's the subtly powerful gesture of the one who ponders, index finger to temple; the one who isn't all bent out of shape, but takes it all as manageable; who leans forward with interest and pays attention; who is mindful. Curious. Non-judgmental. Aware. Open to brainstorms and occasional flashes of brilliance.

You might picture the famous statue of "The Thinker." You might picture a meditator sitting on their meditation cushion.

"Hmm. . ." represents the following powers:

• Interest, curiosity, clarity, wisdom

• Gentle sustained focus of attention inward

• Exploring, understanding, empathizing

• Witnessing; self-reflecting

Get in the habit of going "Hmm. . . ." That's all. Just hang out there with yourself, present, interested, saying "Hmm. . . ."

Imagine yourself pausing and settling down. You stand back. Observe. Witness. Just be present and aware. You might imagine going to the sanctuary you created with your Safe Space Imagery process.

Experiment with the Magic and Power of "Hmm. . . ." Pick something that happened to you this week and practice going "Hmm. . . ." as you contemplate it.

If you meditate or have a mindfulness practice, using the Magic of "Hmm. . . ." will feel quite familiar to you! You've been doing it all along!

If you have read this far, you've got this power. You've been implicitly using the Magic of "Hmm. . . ." periodically as you've been reading this book. Own it!

TIP #2: IMPRESS THE PART THAT NEEDS HELP WITH ALL THE POWERS AND CAPABILITIES OF THE INNER HELPER

You know how little kids look up to big kids — want to hang around them and be like them? And how they regard "big people" as all powerful, mighty, even God-like?

Author and personal growth speaker, John Bradshaw, frequently enlisted this tendency to provide extra "Oomph!" in the inner helping relationship. Using the image of the Big Inner Adult Helper and the Little Inner Child part that needs help, Bradshaw urged the growth-seekers in his workshops to have their Inner Adult Helpers really strut their stuff, to inspire awe in their Inner Child.

Try it. Your Inner Adult has so many skills and resources, such adult wisdom, far beyond that of a child. For example, "Well, I know how to read, so I can read directions. And road signs. And story books. I know how to fix breakfast and what to do when you get a cold."

Impress Little Inner Child with Big Inner Adult's *relative* power and might: "I can reach the high shelf all by myself without standing on a stool" or "I can skip and ride a bike and swim — even drive a car."

From an infant or toddler's point of view, even your most basic skills are impressive achievements: "I know how to talk, and walk, and use the potty, and turn over."

And how about "I know how to earn money and buy cool stuff." What stuff would impress your Inner Child? Owning a flashy red sports car or sparkly high-heeled shoes with ankle straps?

TIP #3: MONITOR THE MATURITY LEVEL OF THE PART THAT NEEDS HELP

Notice when the part that needs help is really little, or just *feels* really little. Sometimes a really little part needs a really BIG adult helper to take over, to simply say, "I'll take care of this."

Adults are better at discerning the difference between what is distressing and what is really dangerous.

For example, an adult with this calming sense of perspective can explain to a child, "I know you're scared when your tummy hurts, and it feels like it will go on forever. I know your tummy hurts because you ate so much holiday candy. And I know you'll be fine tomorrow."

Sometimes the part that needs help is so "little" that words don't help. They're irrelevant. Just meaningless noise. That's when non-verbal soothing becomes powerful. Inner Helper provides wordless help, conveyed with a calm, confident presence.

Your inner helper might require a lot of help to achieve and maintain this inner serenity in the face of a frantic, young, non-verbal inner part of you that is crying for help.

Check in with your attachment to yourself right now. How much and how often can you be there with love and capability for your beloved self?

Check in with that part of yourself that would come alongside yourself to help. That part takes charge, assumes responsibility for the well-being of the relationship. How does that responsibility sit with you?

Can you commit to repairing your relationship with yourself if you lose patience with yourself? Or if you slip and mentally call yourself ugly names like "narcissist" or "borderline" or just "lazy cry-baby quitter"?

If this level of responsibility intimidates you, don't despair. Flip to the next chapter: "Inner Helper gets help." Take action to get that help for yourself.

TIP #4: PLAN WHAT TO SAY

Be prepared. Build a repertoire of helpful things to say when your troubled self needs help.

Start with this: "I'm right here when you need me." Emphasize the secure attachment bond between your Inner Helper and Inner Child, the secure bond that may have been missing in an naCCT childhood.

In your repertoire of helpful things to say when your troubled self needs help, the phrase "I'm right here when you need me" is a "must have".

From there, expand your repertoire with phrases from the list below. Choose the top three that you would most like to hear from your Inner Helper. (Yes, of course, you can have *all* of them!)

- *I'm sorry.*
- *You really matter to me.*
- *We'll work this out.*
- *What would help?*
- *You can do it!*
- *I'll help you.*
- *Let's do it!*
- *Good job! Good for you! You did it!*
- I love you.

You may be like special education teacher Jenna Lee, who had all the words — she regularly said stuff like this to her pupils — but had to struggle to say them to herself. At first, even *imagining* saying them to herself was way outside her comfort zone.

If you're like Jenna Lee, take it very gradually. Try saying these phrases to yourself out loud. Or say them silently, hearing them with your "mind's ear."

Experiment with building your own tailor-made talks to help yourself. Add your own phrases. Blend your own phrases and those above into a kind of lullaby, soothing that little part that needs help into a secure peacefulness. Or imagine giving the part of you that needs help an encouraging pep talk (perhaps while looking in the mirror): your steady eye contact, your reassuring touch, your confident voice.

Here are samples of tailor-made Self-Talk Scripts to an Inner Child part that needs help:

"I'm here to help you. We can handle this. We'll get through this. I know what to do and how to get good help. Let me be present with you and reflect you. And let me give you guidance, advice and encouragement, empathy and praise. Feel how happy I am for you when joy comes into your life. I love you, Little One."

"I love you and I'm here with you forever. And I know what you're experiencing makes sense. I won't give up trying to understand what's happening for you and helping you with it, no matter how long it takes, because you're worth it."

Write out your Self-Talk Script. Carry those written words around with you. Whisper them to yourself. Enclose them in a beautifully decorated, hand-lettered notecard. Then put a fancy stamp on the envelope and snail-mail it to yourself.

IMAGINE THE MEETING OF INNER HELPER AND INNER PART THAT NEEDS HELP

I don't know when your Inner Helper part and the Inner Child part that needs help will meet. Maybe they've already met each other. Or their meeting might not happen for a while. Their meeting might happen spontaneously and take you by surprise.

It might even happen right this minute.

Picture your own Inner Child part and your own Inner Helper together, maybe giving them their own names. For example, my legal name is "Patricia," and I have an Inner Helper named "Big Ricia" and a part that needs help named "Little Patty." Let that picture of them together settle into your consciousness. Bring this whole experience to mind when you say, "I can help myself; I *do* help myself."

Maybe draw or cut a sweet picture of a child and grown up together from a magazine, or print out an online image. Maybe put on music. Maybe bring your body into this meeting: Experiment with both moving and being very still. Maybe write a dialogue or story of the meeting.

Maybe sometime around now, you'll try bringing your Inner Helper and the part that needs help together. Stroke your own arm, or the back of your hand. Tenderly touch your cheek. Try saying these words to yourself: "I'm here to help you." Then try responding with, "Thanks, I could use some help."

BUT YOU DO NOT HAVE TO IMAGINE THIS MEETING, NOW OR EVER!

Therapists like me love to suggest role plays and dramatizations. Plenty of clients choose to say "no" to those suggestions, and healing still happens. You can just read along and skip the actual picturing of the meeting. You can do the meeting later. Or you can choose never to do it at all. Just read along and trust that the stories, ideas, and tips will sink in and do their own magic.

TENDING TO THE INNER HELPING RELATIONSHIP IS THE HEART OF THIS WORK

This relationship is the heart of the work. Come alongside yourself and all your problems and desires with love, interest, curiosity, and wonder. Realize it's *possible* to have a secure inner relationship. You have that helper capacity. Contemplate being that good helper to yourself.

Your own inner helping relationship progresses: first, you introduce the parts to each other; then, you tend that relationship by maintaining it — and troubleshooting it when necessary.

We grow this inner helping relationship one small operational step at a time. Thousands of baby steps in thousands of nanoseconds. One grain of sand at a time going through the hourglass.

When you can truly come alongside yourself with compassion, love, effective guidance, and restraint when called for, well, then some people, maybe even you, yourself — might say you are "all better."

WHEN YOU NEED MORE THAN TIPS: WHEN YOU RUN INTO TROUBLE, TROUBLESHOOT!

If you worked with a mental image of the meeting, how did it go? Did it go well? Do you now feel happy? Warm? Touched?

What if the meeting didn't go so well? Do you feel irritated? Discouraged? Welcome to the real world! Seriously, if the meeting didn't go as well as you'd hoped, remember that troubleshooting is part of tending your inner helping relationship. When you run into trouble, trouble shoot! Your Inner Helper can get help. More on that in the next chapter.

Meanwhile:

GOOD WORK!!

You've done a lot of good work: reviewing your resources, thinking about "parts work," facilitating a meeting of your Inner Helper and your inner part that needs help, and checking in with both of them.

How does it feel to have read *all that* and thought and felt *all that*? What did it take for you to hang in there with it all? What stood out for you?

Be sure to credit yourself for all you've done.

COMING UP NEXT: INNER HELPER GETS HELP

Now, time for a break? Stand up, stretch your legs, rest your eyes, get a refreshing drink of water, and just feel good about taking care of your precious self. Over and over and over.

CHAPTER 6

INNER HELPER GETS HELP

Realistically, the inner helping relationship sometimes runs into trouble and self-help tips just aren't enough. For those of us with non-physically-assaultive, attachment-based Chronic Covert Trauma in early relationships with caregivers, taking care of ourselves can be hard.

Inner Helper may easily run out of resources, become exhausted, flummoxed, or upset.

Some naCCT survivors find themselves asking, "Why do I have to help myself? I want *them* to help me. That's not fair. Makes me mad and sad."

Some survivors experience conflicts between how they want to help themselves today and the way their caregivers helped them in the past; they're confused about which way of helping is "the right way."

Still other naCCT survivors report that this inner helping relationship feels so unfamiliar that it's uncomfortable. It feels stilted, clumsy, or even ridiculous.

It's normal for Inner Helpers to be troubled by the aftereffects of naCCT. They may have had poor early role models and consequently not know how to help today.

It's *also* normal for troubles in early naCCTs in outer relationships to be echoed in troubled inner relationships today. Outside then; inside now. Inner Helper might even feel annoyed with the part that needs help, resentful of having to always be the one who helps.

Difficulties in helping ourselves are to be expected after childhood attachment traumas of any kind, from horrific physical assaults to subtle, albeit well-intentioned, traumatic misattune-ments and unhelpful help.

It's normal for all these troubles to arise as you address taking care of yourself.

And yet, although it may be normal, having trouble with the whole process of helping ourselves can lead to discouragement. And being understandably discouraged when establishing and maintaining a secure inner helping relationship just isn't happening, it's also normal to ask, "Why bother? Why not just give up?"

BUT WAIT! HELPERS CAN GET HELP!

It's a good thing Inner Helpers don't need to be superheroes with a cape and infinite superpowers.

As you work with your inner helping relationship, you may find yourself appreciating how much real, human helpers need other helpers. Parents need helpers. Teachers and therapists consult with peers and supervisors. They seek out continuing education and have walls lined with professional books they can turn to. In the tradition of taking care of the caregiver, good helpers ask for, receive, and use help.

Getting help is also an intrinsic part of team sports. Successful players welcome assists. As an avid sports fan pointed out to me, team sports like basketball, ice hockey, water polo, and even Ultimate Frisbee honor both the player who scores *and* the teammate who enables the score. The fact that the helpful teammate officially "gets an assist," which is recorded and tracked in team statistics, recognizes that successful players succeed *with help*.

In summary, getting help is a reputable, honorable thing for helpers to do. Here's a Self-Talk Script for that:

SELF-TALK SCRIPT FOR SEEKING HELP

> *"Good for me! I recognized I was having a tough time. I can actually pat myself on the back for taking my helping responsibilities so seriously that I overcame all those shaming self-criticisms and decided to look for help."*

WHAT KIND OF HELP?

So, on to getting some help. What kind of help is available?

HELP PROTECTING THE INNER SELF-HELP SPACE

Your meeting of Inner Helper and the part that needs help can go wrong if there's no suitable mental "Self-Help Space" available for them to meet together. Unfortunately, this often happens.

A good analogy would be that of an agency therapist assigned to help clients in an "office" that turned out to be a hallway lined with vending machines.

People would keep cutting through the "office" space, using the vending machines, eavesdropping on the session, butting in, asking questions, making suggestions, giving advice, taking over, and just making a helpful one-on-one therapy session impossible. Wouldn't it be good to close some doors, put the vending machines somewhere else, stop people from barging in?

MIRIAM'S STORY

Not having Self-Help Space available was the predicament of a woman I'll call Miriam. She consulted me because she needed the psychological safety and security of a good inner helping relationship, but it just wasn't happening.

Her Inner Helper wasn't connecting with her part that needs help, whom she called her "wounded child."

She explained that her "wounded child" was having trouble believing *any* positive helper could exist *at all* because her previous helpers — her parents and her psychiatrist — had not been helpful. They had instead, in Miriam's words, been "emotionally abusive."

Miriam identified part of her problem as "loyalty" to these emotionally abusive people. She felt like some magnetic force pulled her irresistibly towards them. Even though in many ways they had failed to help her, they had functioned in the *role* of helpers. Miriam's loyalty took the form of an unrealistic, ultimately treacherous, belief: "Only they can take care of me."

Because both Miriam's Inner Helper and her wounded child "kind of" believed this was true, her inner helping relationship was *overwhelmed* and *over-run* by images of her parents and her psychiatrist actually taking over the helping relationship space, leaving no room there for her *own* Inner Helper, who was now feeling invisible and powerless.

As Miriam described it, her "abusive" parents and psychiatrist were like squatters, moving in and refusing to leave. In another image, her mental space had become like a country invaded and occupied by problematic self-defined helpers whom she regarded as unhelpful helpers, even as "abusers."

Miriam's "Loyalty Problem" was making it hard for her to clear a private space where her Inner Helper could take care of her wounded child.

Miriam identified what she needed in order to stay safe and stable with a secure inner helping relationship: A "Boundaries Ritual" to protect the inner Self-Help Space from invasion and free herself from that magnetic bond.

So, she asked me for help: "Ricia, maybe you could help me write letters to previous helpers who don't fit my needs today. Or maybe we could create a 'Letting Go' ritual where I don't allow those so-called helpers into my current Self-Help Space.

"I need something concrete and physical. Maybe you could do a role play with me, or I could use a pillow representing someone I'm not inviting, and I could tell myself and the pillow that I'm choosing new helpers.

"I need to formally release myself from my past inappropriate help, tell myself and the pillow I'm making new choices now."

She also sensed that working with this psychological Boundary Ritual might bring up feelings she didn't like: maybe grief and anger for having had "such hurtful" helpers; maybe guilt for not allowing those helpers into her Self-Help Space.

MIRIAM'S SELF-HELP SPACE CLEARING PROCESS

We considered possible concrete physical "Boundary Rituals." One possibility: Something like a throw rug could represent her Self-Help Space. Pillows or puppets representing unhelpful helpers could role play attempts to entice, bribe, or intimidate her into letting them into her mental space.

The unhelpful helpers might wheedle, love bomb, and guilt-trip her, insisting "Only we can help you," trashing her new way of helping herself, frightening her with predictions of a dreadful future without them.

As Inner Helper asserted her rightful place in Miriam's self-care, there might be some raised voices and boundary tussles. Or Miriam's Inner Helper could be diplomatic, saying (perhaps with exaggerated civility), "Thank you for your concern, and for the time and energy you devoted to helping me in the past. I need a different kind of self-care and help going forward, so I need to say 'No, thank you'."

Miriam weighed her options for her concrete physical "Boundary Ritual." Eventually, instead of moving and speaking in a role play with pillows, she chose the action of writing a separation letter.

So, Miriam wrote. Two letters, actually. One was passionate: angry, explosive, sometimes raging and sometimes "snotty" and cold, clearly spelling out all she had suffered and the new boundaries she was setting forth. The second letter was logical: a calm, balanced appreciation of what her difficult former helpers *had* given her, and a clear effective statement of her new boundaries. She would decide later whether she would send an actual letter to them.

COMMENTARY ON MIRIAM'S PROCESS:

Miriam wrote the letters to her parents and psychiatrist, but also, deeper down, Miriam wrote those letters to herself. In those two letters, one passionate and one logical, she firmly stated her commitment to herself.

Although Miriam didn't actually do her concrete, physical "Boundary Ritual" with the role play and pillows, imagining it may have helped Miriam to strengthen her own Inner Helper and firm up her protective boundaries.

Imagining is a low-risk way of taking a step toward change. Miriam had imagined strong boundaries around her Self-Help Space. Maybe she'd pictured herself effectively protecting that space, standing up for herself, demonstrating that "they" were, in reality, not the only source of help.

Miriam also got help acknowledging specific actions she had taken that showed she had an effective, attuned, caring Inner Helper:

- She had recognized her "wounded child" needed help.

- She had recognized her Inner Helper also needed help.

- She had brainstormed possible ways to solve her problem.

- She had formulated a request and reached out to ask for help.

- She had made a decision and acted effectively on that decision.

- She had maintained core safety and stability throughout the whole problem- solving process.

In her boundary work, Miriam firmly established herself in the Inner Helper role and claimed her legitimate authority in that role.

She mentally came face to face with the sadness, anger, and guilt that setting boundaries and clearing her Self-Help Space would probably bring up in her, and she committed to taking care of herself when she felt those difficult emotions.

NOW YOUR TURN:
KEEP YOUR INNER SELF-HELP SPACE CLEAR

Do you resonate at all with Miriam's story? It is so common to have previous occupants in your mental Self-Help Space and to feel anger, sadness, guilt, or fear about this. People call these previous occupants a variety of names: ghosts, haunts, squatters, party crashers. And they use a variety of names for the Inner Helpers who protect the boundaries: Ghostbusters, gatekeepers, bouncers, guardians, protectors.

Let Miriam's story inspire you: Say "No" to unhelpful helpers. No squatters. No backseat drivers. Even if you feel loyal to them and to their unhelpful ways, no unhelpful helpers allowed!

Do any of Miriam's brainstorms for protecting her Self-Help Space suggest strategies for you to use?

WHAT ABOUT TURNING TO OTHER PEOPLE FOR HELP?

Other people can be so helpful, especially in person. Just being in the physical presence of someone else who cares can make a difference. Another person can provide a caring look, an understanding nod, or the touch of a hand. Maybe a hug, or a shoulder to cry on.

Unfortunately, other people can *also* say or do things that trigger naCCT survivors. I call these behaviors "People-Triggers."

Other people are beyond our control; we can influence them, but not control them. Realistically, we can't prevent them from doing something that triggers us.

So, there's an element of risk for naCCT survivors in turning to other people for help.

You probably don't need me to point this out to you, because you've probably already noticed that People-Triggers can happen — or maybe you've experienced them yourself.

This unfortunate People-Triggering can even happen in relationships with therapists and other helping professionals, because helping professionals are people, and people can trigger naCCT survivors.

However, the risk of People-Triggers doesn't mean you disconnect from society and become an island. We are social creatures, after all. It just means that an naCCT survivor is less likely to get triggered by seeking help that doesn't involve direct interaction with other people.

For example, you might be the kind of person who, when you're driving around lost, likes to ask someone for directions; whereas some other people prefer to consult with their car's GPS navigation system. You might call a friend for a recipe; whereas someone else might get the recipe on line. If you want to be super-cautious, hold off on turning to other people until your inner helping relationship is solid. Until then, to be super-free of People-Triggers, use the GPS for driving directions, and go on-line to get the recipe.

Staying safe and stable while seeking help from other people will be addressed later in Chapter Ten. Once you can rely on a sturdy, caring, effective inner relationship between your Inner Helper and the part of you that needs help, you'll have a reliable resource for handling challenges that can happen when turning to other people for help.

So, we'll begin with some relatively low risk, People-Trigger-free, kinds of help for the Inner Helper: We'll begin with this book.

THIS BOOK AND ITS HEALING PROCESS

Your immediate resource right now for healing PTSD from intangible attachment trauma is this book you're reading or listening to. I wrote this book directly to you, dear Fellow NaCCT Survivor, to help you deal with the specific and unique problems that arise from naCCT.

You can read this book or visit my website *ChronicCovertTrauma.com* anytime 24/7.

ME, RICIA FLEMING, NACCT SURVIVOR, AUTHOR OF THIS BOOK

Of course, I'm one of your resources. I am a partly-healed wounded healer myself — been there, done that, got-the-T-shirt. My healing process was long and is still incomplete. It took place over decades, with help from many sources, including many friends and guides in many books.

On my journey, I've learned my way around the cPTSD from naCCT territory and developed some skill at navigating it. I've found a few ways that worked. And now, in my role as author of this book, I am sharing these ways here with you. I can function as a guide for you on your journey.

THE RELATIONSHIP BETWEEN YOU AND ME

You and I have a relationship, but we don't have individual face-to-face interactions. That lack can be frustrating. You can't make in-person requests, receive feedback, or benefit from getting my attuned responses to you.

However, that lack of interaction can also be freeing: You don't need to take my possible response to you into consideration. (This is really beneficial for co-dependents.)

This book is a private "refuge" for you. Here you can react any way you want to, and no one will see. You can get bored, skim over sections, skip entire chapters, and I won't know it.

You can get furious and disgusted with me. I won't get hurt or be mean to you if you say I'm an idiot, slam the book shut, and throw it across the room. And I won't shame you if you change your mind, go get the book off the floor, and start reading again. Because we have no direct interaction, when you come back to the book, I'll be right there, ready to pick up where you left off and continue your healing work.

But help for Inner Helpers is not limited to me, this book, and/or my website. There are many varieties of help that are free from the risks of direct interaction with other people.

OTHER PEOPLE-TRIGGER-FREE SOURCES OF INFORMATION

As I'm writing to you in 2021, I know of no other material that is dedicated specifically to validating and healing the unique wounds from these non-physically-assaultive, attachment-based Chronic Covert Traumas.

But sources of valuable information relating to *aspects* of naCCT healing do exist.

I've listed six broad categories of those sources below. This list is not a ready-made, one-size-fits-all list of helpers for Inner Helper. Instead, you can draw on these categories to create your own personal resource list of Inner Helper's helpers that work best for you.

PEOPLE-TRIGGER-FREE RESOURCES #1: BOOKS

Books were my Inner Helper's primary source of help. My "helpers in books" often came through for me. The advisors, authorities, experts, and fellow strugglers in books answered my distress calls. They helped me understand that I made sense. They gave me perspective, facts, encouragement, and, perhaps most important, they validated me. They helped me think straight and calm myself down.

Relationships with authors via their books are fairly safe. An author's ideas, style, or stories can trigger you, but you probably won't get People-Triggered by their actual interpersonal behavior. As with me and this book, you can shut any author's book if it annoys you. You can return it to the library unread. If you get mad at it, you can leave it someplace and just forget about it. You are also free to retrieve the book and start reading again if the feeling passes.

So turn to your friends and helpers in books. Scan your shelves for both your favorite tried-and-true books and those you've set aside and forgotten.

Check out brick and mortar bookstores, admittedly hard to find in this electronic day and age..

Go online for books, workbooks and eBooks, manuals, audiobooks.

Go to the library. Check out the professional literature on trauma and attachment. This material is not secret. These books are available for anyone to read. This means *you*. Assert your right to plow through pages of jargon to extract valuable information and be inspired by case histories.

Some libraries catalogue their books according to the Dewey decimal system. For books on trauma, check out the 616.85 section. In U.S. libraries using the Library of Congress cataloguing system, the trauma section is RC552 and the section on attachment is BF575. If you can find a library that lets you wander around in the stacks, you'll find lots of help.

PEOPLE-TRIGGER-FREE RESOURCES #2: INFORMATION SOURCES OTHER THAN BOOKS

Check out Internet webinars, websites, on-line videos and podcasts, radio and TV presentations, in-person forums and lectures. All of these are good sources of information. And they are all reasonably People-Trigger-free because you can shut down the computer or leave the venue whenever you want to.

You can go to events that don't require interaction with other people. There's a long, respectable tradition of attendance at lectures. You can attend telephone and zoom conferences without participating. You can participate anonymously. You can "lurk" on internet forums. On big teleconferences, you can remain anonymous by muting yourself and turning off your video.

Depending on your needs at the time, your Inner Helper can obtain up-to-date information and common-sense advice for various specialties: parents, coaches, teachers, therapists, managers, leaders, and more.

Mommy blogs are great resources for Inner Helper when she's functioning like a loving, helpful mother.

Sites such as *PsychCentral.com* and *GoodTherapy.com* provide mental health help. You can get a lot of information about trauma from the International Society for the Study of Trauma and Dissociation website *http://www.isst-d.org* and from my professional group, NESTTD (New England Society for the Treatment of Trauma and Dissociation) at *https://www.nesttd-online.org*.

PEOPLE-TRIGGER-FREE RESOURCES #3: YOUR FORGOTTEN HELPERS FROM THE PAST

Review skills from previous personal growth and transformational work you've done. Introduce today's Inner Helper to your own knowledge, attitudes, and skills that may have been marinating, incubating, or germinating in darkness underground.

Welcome these reinforcements from your past. Take them off the shelf and dust them off so your Inner Helper can use them and apply them today.

Substitute your own helpers from the past in place of those in the sample Self-Talk Script below.

SELF-TALK SCRIPT: WELCOMING HELPERS FROM THE PAST

"I've been building my inner helping relationship all along, even if I haven't been directly focusing on healing cPTSD from naCCT — haven't even known about it. All the personal development work I've done. The meditation, the yoga and Tai Chi, the 12-Step and cognitive behavioral work, all that has helped me develop my Inner Helper skills, my awareness of my feelings and thoughts, and my openness to receiving help; all that will stand me in good stead in my recovery.

"Developing those skills has not been a waste of time and energy. It's made me a better healer and more receptive to healing. Good for me! I can transfer those skills."

PEOPLE-TRIGGER-FREE RESOURCES #4: YOUR SAFE SPACE IMAGERY

You have an inner refuge you can access anytime. It's your mobile pop-up sanctuary, the one that you created during the Safe Space Imagery process. It's easy to forget it's there. Pop into it now, just to remind yourself it *is* there and to get in the habit of using it. Your Inner Helper can go there to refresh, relax, and recharge anytime.

PEOPLE-TRIGGER-FREE RESOURCES #5: YOUR HIGHER WISDOM

It's been said, "God helps those who help themselves." As you develop your skill at helping yourself, your Inner Helper may welcome help from a source of greater wisdom. This source might be thought of in various forms and be given different names: Higher Power/ God/ Allah/ Great Mother/ All That Is/ Source/ Wiser Self/ Holy Spirit/ the Mystery.

Sometimes people experience that source of help as outside of themselves, and sometimes people experience it internally as a spiritual aspect of themselves.

A wealth of resources facilitate tapping into this higher wisdom: religious liturgy and ritual, retreats, classes, books, guided meditations, and even mind/body/spirit practices like yoga.

The humble practice of simply pausing and using the magic of "Hmm. . . ." sometimes opens people up to receiving insights that break through the confines of ordinary thought patterns.

Many religions have a practice that you can use to contact and receive guidance. Someone once told me "Prayer is talking to God, and meditation is listening to God."

I've personally known people who've regularly received guidance by going to their Bibles and letting their fingers be guided to words that bring a greater wisdom to their earthly troubles.

Many people are helped by looking at art, film, and dance or by listening to music or spoken poetry. Others find that creating art themselves connects them to higher wisdom.

Connecting to nature also provides many people with inspiration and wisdom: Sitting by running water. Listening to birdsong. Walking in the elements, feeling the wind and the rain and the sun and looking up at the sky. Even clipping herbs from your kitchen garden or looking at a potted plant or a window box filled with flowers can provide connection to the greater web of life and encourage a broader perspective on your own life.

Mindful work is another path followed by some people for opening to a more vast and transformational awareness. Instead of focusing on the breath or a candle flame, they "Chop wood, carry water." Try routine repetitive chores: sweeping with a broom, dishwashing with a sponge, washing the floor with a scrub brush, scouring a sink. Even routine keyboarding, filing, and xeroxing. Or chopping vegetables. Done mindfully, any of these can cut through inner chatter, open awareness of larger truths, and invite a wiser, more transcendent point of view.

PEOPLE-TRIGGER-FREE RESOURCES #6: YOUR "EARTH ANGELS"

This final category of People-Trigger-free resources recognizes the deep psychological significance and comfort that seemingly ordinary things can provide for us.

"Certain special objects function for us as 'Earth Angels,'" according to Shaun McNiff, a leader in expressive arts therapy for more than three decades and University Professor at Lesley University.

At a workshop he invited us to reflect on special objects in our lives that he gave the name "Earth Angels." We went around the room, each person telling of a rock they found at the beach long ago, a set of photographs, or an old shawl they treasured and that seemed to help them in hard times and inspire them. Call in your "Earth Angels." Gather them around you.

HEAVY WARNING HERE: WHAT'S COMING UP COULD BE TRIGGERING, BUT TAKE IT SERIOUSLY. . . .

SUICIDE CRISIS

This is very serious. Take it very seriously. If there is any possibility that you could — impulsively or planfully — hurt yourself, treat it like an emergency. It is.

And here is a special consideration for naCCT survivors with our sensitivity to People Triggers:

Telephone Hotlines and Hospital emergency rooms are operated by people, and, as we know painfully well, interactions with people can be triggering for people with naCCT-sourced cPTSD.

Getting People-Triggered by a well-intentioned but unskillful or unattuned helper on a hotline or in an emergency room can lead to a vicious cycle in which the level of crisis increases and the risk of becoming even more dysregulated and destabilized than before reaching out becomes very real.

So, what is your best course of action? Even here, be aware of your special sensitivities to getting People-Triggered. It might come down to "I could end up getting People-Triggered, acting more and more dysregulated, and feeling very embarrassed, but at least in a hospital emergency room they will help me stay alive to continue my healing journey on another day."

INNER HELPER'S HIDDEN HELPER

Now I invite you to witness a happy story of someone who got help where she expected trouble:

In my experience, it's rare to find an naCCT survivor who doesn't have some version of a harsh inner critic. Here are some of those critics' common names: The Judge; the Skeptic, the Nag, the Blue Meanie; Worry Wart; Nit-Picker; Mean Mom; the Crab; and "I'm- only- trying- to- Help- You-Dear."

Sometimes, like Jenna Lee in the upcoming story, these survivors are surprised to discover a helper hidden in that Inner Critic.

JENNA LEE'S INNER CRITIC

We've seen how Jenna Lee sometimes cuts off her self-criticizing and comes lovingly and helpfully alongside herself. But, being human, she can't do it *every* time. It's an uneven process, one day discouraging, another day pretty good, the next day maddening. Two steps forward, one step back.

As you know, Jenna Lee and I have done the foundational Inner Helping relationship work. Her Inner Helper and the part that needs help have met and worked successfully together. She has used the mindfulness Magic of "Hmm. . . ." to observe what's going on within herself. She's really good at this.

She is also really good at portraying her inner conflicts with role plays. Unusually good. "It's fun and it's enlightening," she says. I think she should have been a playwright because she is so good at dramatizing what goes on inside. She creates characters and understands what motivates them. She improvises and has them say lines that really convey what they're feeling and what they want.

Where some people would use puppets, and some other people would make "Pro and Con Lists," Jenna Lee likes to work out her indecision and inner conflict by setting up "Chair Work with Parts," where she intentionally moves from one chair to another chair when she speaks from different internal parts of herself.

Here's a "Chair Work with Parts" session with three "parts": There's Inner Helper. There's the part that needs help — she's given this part the name "Little NeedsHelp." And a new character will make an appearance: the Inner Critic.

Here's how her healing dramatization unfolds:

JENNA LEE'S "CHAIR WORK WITH PARTS"

This session begins with Jenna Lee criticizing herself. Again. Her thoughts and feelings are spiraling down the drain of learned helplessness and low self esteem. Again she's lost contact with her strengths, her helper skills and attitude.

"I'm such a loser," she says, "I get all upset and emotional, dysregulated — that's the word they're using these days. Such an ugly word, like I'm a broken down machine. I hate getting dysregulated. I can't calm myself down, and I upset everybody else."

We set up the room for "Chair Work with Parts." As usual, we put out pillows on two folding chairs: one for her Inner Helper, one for "Little NeedsHelp."

As we're setting up, she comments, "Just knowing I'm getting help is bringing me a little out of panic mode. It's so awful to have to manage these states entirely by myself."

After the chairs are set up, she surprises me: Instead of beginning as she usually does, by sitting in Little NeedsHelp's chair, she plunks herself down in Inner Helper's chair and says, "Speaking from my Inner Helper, I just can't manage all this. I'm overwhelmed and exhausted.

"I need a consult. I'm in panic mode, a dysregulated mess, bringing everyone down with my gloom and negativity. I just want to give up and quit. I'm such a loser."

Although Jenna Lee is sitting in her Inner Helper's chair, it sounds like her Inner Critic has come into the room. So we set up a third chair, and Jenna Lee looks around for a suitable pillow to represent her Inner Critic part.

"I'll use this," she says, picking up a black velvet pillow that she sometimes strokes while she's talking in sessions.

Jenna Lee flips the soft black pillow over, revealing its reverse side of neutral burlap. "This ugly burlap side bothers me — that's why I always turn it over when I get here for a session. But this ugly side is *perfect* for an inner critic — scratchy and harsh."

Once we have the chairs and pillows set up, she outlines her plan for the "Chair Work with Parts." She'll use the mindfulness magic of "Hmm. . . ." to work with Inner Helper and Inner Critic. Her inner part that needs help — "Little NeedsHelp"— will just observe.

JENNA LEE'S CHAIR WORK BEGINS

Jenna Lee moves to the chair she's designated to represent her Inner Helper. She faces the pillow with its harsh scratchy side up, and says, "Inner Critic, I have something to ask you. What's going on with you when you say Jenna Lee's such a loser, getting all dramatic and emotional?"

Jenna Lee moves to the Inner Critic's chair, holds the pillow, and answers, "Yes, Inner Helper, I *certainly do* say Jenna Lee is such a loser for getting all dramatic and emotional. She just behaves like a spoiled little princess, a four-year-old Drama Queen. Self-indulgent. She needs to get herself under control.

"And you want to know what's going on when I do that?. . . .Hmm. . . . OK. I'm trying to get Jenna Lee to shape up. Nobody likes Drama Queens. She needs to get herself under control."

Jenna Lee moves back to the Inner Helper's chair and responds, "So, Inner Critic, I hear you saying Jenna Lee needs to shape up. You remind her that nobody likes a drama queen. Is that pretty much where you're coming from?"

Back in the Inner Critic's chair, holding the scratchy burlap pillow, she releases a torrent of criticism: "Yes, Inner Helper, that's exactly where I'm coming from.

"I'm trying to get Jenna Lee to pull herself together, stop bothering people and making a nuisance of herself. It bothers people when she behaves like that, needy and demanding, expecting special treatment. Nobody wants someone like that around. She needs to get herself under control, calm down, be the way people like —"

Jenna Lee interrupts herself. "Wait!" she says, jumping up out of the Inner Critic's chair and turning towards me, "Inner Critic is actually trying to *help* me."

I respond, reflecting only what she's already noticed herself: "Well, it's interesting how clear your Inner Critic is about intending to protect you, to save you from being disliked and shunned."

Still standing, Jenna Lee continues to think out loud, "I *do* hate to be annoying, to be someone nobody wants around. I can be a real gloom cloud. A super spreader of gloom."

I marvel as I watch her process unfold, her mindfulness skills and her helping wisdom kicking in. She's on a roll.

She continues, "I'm glad my Inner Critic wants to help me be liked. But she could be a little nicer about it. Some coaches build on strengths, motivate with praise. Others motivate by shaming, though they call it 'challenging.'

"Maybe my Inner Critic needs a continuing education class on effective coaching. . . .motivating. Oh. Wait a minute! I've taken those classes. My Inner Critic knows that stuff."

"INNER CRITIC, YOUR WAY ISN'T WORKING"

Jenna Lee sits firmly down in the Inner Helper's chair and says, "Inner Critic, we're on the same team. We're both helpers. But your way of helping isn't working.

"Your way is like the athletic coach who says, 'Listen up, you bunch of losers. You couldn't fight your way out of a paper bag.' That kind of coach hopes the team will fight back, will go 'We're not losers; we'll show you!'

"But look, Inner Critic: Around here, that kind of coaching doesn't seem to work. Around here, encouragement works! Understanding works!"

When Jenna Lee's feedback to her Inner Critic winds down, I ask her how Inner Critic takes what Inner Helper just said to her.

Jenna Lee moves to the Inner Critic chair, picks up the scratchy "ugly" pillow, holds it on her lap, and says, "How do I take what Inner Helper just said? Hmm. . . . Well, I definitely want a positive outcome. In that sense, Inner Helper and I are on the same team."

As she speaks, I notice she's flipped the scratchy Inner Critic pillow over to the soft velvet side and begun making little circles in the black velvet with her index finger.

Still speaking as Inner Critic, she continues, "And I do coach like that. Adult. No nonsense. Strong."

She glances over at Little NeedsHelp's chair, and observes, "And that way of coaching doesn't seem to be working. That's a fact. Hmm. . . ."

Inner Critic faces Inner Helper's chair, asks, "Are we really on the same team?"

Jenna Lee switches to the Inner Helper's chair, looks directly at Inner Critic, and says, "Yes. I thought we were enemies, Inner Critic. But we're really not. We're in this together."

Jenna Lee gets up and crosses slowly back to the Inner Critic's chair. Sits down. Takes a deep breath. Her breathing is calm and steady. Long pause. "Hmm. . . ."

She sits for quite a while, then, still as Inner Critic, she says, "I wanted her to belong, for people to want her around. I thought what I was doing with her would make that happen."

Another pause. Even longer this time. Inner Critic looks toward Little NeedsHelp's chair, sits up straighter, takes another deep breath, releases it in a measured exhale.

Jenna Lee sits in the stillness of the exhale, and finally speaks, still as Inner Critic." I'm tough," she says. "I'm strong. This needs to be fixed and *I'm fixing it.*"

With that, she turns, slowly and deliberately, toward Little NeedsHelp. Still as Inner Critic, she leans forward and places a hand on the arm of Little NeedsHelp's chair. Her portrayal is so vivid and accurate that I can almost picture a forlorn little girl sitting there in that chair.

In a low voice, articulating every word carefully so what she says is very clear, Jenna Lee as Inner Critic addresses Little NeedsHelp.

"I'm so sorry," she says, "My intentions were good. I wanted to help you and I screwed up. I was clumsy and I hurt you and I scared you. Let me help you feel safe and confident again. You matter so much to me."

COMMENTARY ON INNER CRITICS

Jenna Lee's Inner Critic turns out to be well-intentioned, responsive, and flexible. Once her positive intent has been discovered and appreciated, this Inner Critic becomes a helper.

It's sweet — and very healing — when an encounter between Inner Helper and Inner Critic resolves like this one did.

When this happens, we need to de-pathologize inner conflict and remove the sense of danger from it, even though it's true that Inner Helper and Inner Critic are going to need many planning sessions together to balance Jenna Lee's needs for self-expression with the needs of the people she's with. But now Jenna Lee's Inner Helper and her well-intentioned, reformed Inner Critic can do that hard work together as members of the same team.

However, not all Inner Critics are so well-meaning and nice as Jenna Lee's. Some of them look, sound, and behave like duplicates of the meanest, most troubled aspects of an naCCT survivor's mother, father, or other Lifeline Caregiver.

Some Inner Critics have to be kept away for a while. Boundaries have to be set and protected. In a dramatization, pillows representing those hostile critics can be firmly placed outside the boundary, communicating firmly "if you are hostile, you must stay back."

Determining the niceness of an Inner Critic calls for much work, patience, and wise, realistic assessing.

ন্ধ

YOUR "FIRST-AID KIT:" SPECIFIC PEOPLE-TRIGGER-FREE ACTIONS

Here's an on-going project for all your inner parts to do together. Your Inner Helper, the part that needs help, the well-intentioned Inner Critic, and Inner Helper's Helpers can all collaborate, brainstorm, and build their relationship by doing this uplifting project together.

Brainstorm ways to soothe and manage distress on your own: "What I can do as an individual to stay safe and stable within myself without risk of getting triggered by another person."

Then assemble a "Virtual First-Aid Kit" of specific People-Trigger-free actions. The process of developing, maintaining, and using these kits is responsible self-care, as natural as travelers carrying first aid kits, or loving parents leaving emergency instructions and phone numbers for the baby sitter.

Here are some "Virtual First-Aid Kit" suggestions:

- Listen to music.

- Walk by the ocean or elsewhere in nature.

- Run in place

- Cook a meal

- Write in a journal
- Art journal or SoulCollage
- Sleep
- Check out a comedy club
- Visit a library
- Take a brisk shower or a luxurious bath
- Hand wash dishes
- Read inspirational literature
- Breathe, meditate, pray
- Groom a pet
- Sit with "Earth Angels"
- Enjoy a cup of tea
- Use Safe Space Imagery
- Make lists

MAKE LISTS AND ADD TO EXISTING LISTS:

The last item, "Make Lists," deserves highlighting and expanding. So many people are helped by the simple act of making a new list or adding to an existing one. Some of my favorite subjects for lists are these:

- Ways to manage inner upset
- Ways to calm down
- Ways to get energized
- Ways to contact higher wisdom
- Sources of psychoeducation
- Sanctuaries and other places I can visit or imagine visiting
- Compliments and actual successes
- Favorite sayings, memes, quotes
- Gratitudes

- What nourishes me
- What entertains me
- Music playlists

INNER SELF-HELP POLICY FOR PROMOTING SAFETY AND STABILITY

Now that your Inner Helping Relationship is growing stronger, it's time for me to share a good self-help policy for promoting inner safety and stability, and also to suggest you adopt something like it for yourself:

If you're doing parts work using the model of an Inner Helper and an inner helped part, the ultimate guiding ideal and self-help policy is:

"All parts that need help get helpers."

"All parts" includes Inner Helper, and since Inner Helpers can easily forget to seek help, they can be written right into the policy:

"All parts — including Inner Helpers!! — that need help get helpers."

Inner Helper's Helpers sometimes need helpers too. For example, a wisdom guide might need to consult a wiser teacher or a book of wisdom.

If you think of your inner part that needs help as an Inner Child, then another way of wording this guiding ideal and self-help policy is:

"Every Inner Child needs an Inner Grownup."

or, maybe, more specifically,

"Every Inner Child needs an Inner Parent"

or, even more specifically,

"Every Inner Child needs an Inner Mommy"

and/or

"Every Inner Child needs an Inner Daddy"

A broadly applicable way of expressing this policy is simply:

"Whenever I'm troubled, I provide help for myself"

Although I've made adhering to this policy a guiding ideal in my own recovery, I often fail to come near that ideal. Sometimes an inner part needs help but no help comes — none from outside and none from inside. Then the part that needs help ends up "doing some emergency crisis thing" like stuffing her face or blurting out something she would be much better off keeping to herself.

When I notice one of those "emergency crisis things" has happened, I take it as a call to give my relationship to myself some special attention.

And I try to remind myself that a guiding ideal is not a target goal; then I congratulate myself for successful progress and keep on going forward in that positive direction.

CONGRATULATIONS!

As we near the end of this section on how to stay safe and stable in the Intrapsychic realm of thoughts and feelings, be sure to acknowledge the gains you've made in these important areas. A few of them are spelled out for you here:

- You've strengthened your relationship with yourself, the relationship you'll never lose and never leave.

- You've created a secure bond within to counteract the fear-filled atmosphere surrounding trauma.

- You've brought some healing to the attachment wound of cPTSD from naCCT.

- You've claimed your own significant helping skills and attitudes.

- You've gathered skills and tips for relating to the part of yourself that needs help.

- You've learned about "parts work" and observed "Chair Work with Parts."

- You've established the basis of a safe "home" within.

- You've provided a clear inner Self-Help Space, free of intruders or unhelpful helpers from the past.

- You've amassed a reliable collection of People-Trigger-free resources.

- You've equipped yourself with tools for meeting the challenge of "emotional dysregulation."

- You've made other gains you may want to emphasize and celebrate now.

- You've enhanced your ability to provide yourself with effective, loving care.

The work you're doing in this chapter is healing in itself. It helps you to regulate yourself, to avoid the dreaded "emotional dysregulation," get yourself back into balance, and manage intrapsychic cPTSD symptoms.

You deserve every scrap of pride and self-endorsement you can muster for every little micro-increment of recovery as you move along this path toward secure attachment to yourself.

Coming alongside yourself as an effective helper is an ability you'll be strengthening as you continue this work. Delight in the many rich, loving ways to build and benefit from a secure attachment with your ever-more-beloved self.

Remember: Providing self-care, self-help, and self-regulation really *is* a long-term project. Embrace every success at this beginning stage and look forward to getting better and better as you move forward.

"BUT I DON'T WANT TO BE A HERMIT!"

This intrapsychic work with the inner helping relationship is also the core for all the other things you will do here in recovery.

In this part of your recovery, we've focused on managing thoughts and feelings within. You've been urged to be very mindful of the distinction between resources that are free of People-Triggers and those that pose risks of People-Triggers, and to stay safe and stable by simply avoiding People-Triggers.

Your Inner Helping Relationship is getting solid, secure, and reliable. With this preparation, it's time for expansion into the world of relationships with other people. As your relationship within gets more reliable, and more comfortable, you'll have an increasingly secure foundation to support the transformational healing of early relationship wounds.

COMING UP:

Next chapter, we dig into the issues relating to the "a" in naCCT, the "attachment-based" issues in relationships with other people.

Many of us naCCT survivors have experienced danger in our deepest, earliest, closest, most crucial relationships. How does cPTSD from these early attachment-based traumas in relationships with our Lifeline Caregivers negatively impact our adult relationships with other people? And what do we do about that?

We'll dare to confront People-Triggers, and we'll brave the challenges and ultimately reap the deeply rich rewards of relating with other people.

And as you venture into the next chapter, take this secure thought with you: At the same time that you are relating externally to other people, you are *always* relating internally to yourself. So, your increasingly secure relationship with yourself will facilitate increasingly good relationships with other people.

Part IV:

Interpersonal Experience: Safe and Stable with People

CHAPTER 7

IDENTIFY PEOPLE-TRIGGERS

We've explored the intrapsychic world within and how having a secure inner helping relationship helps regulate thoughts and feelings.

Now let's turn to the outer world, where relating to other people adds another element to the challenge of living with cPTSD from naCCT.

How to maintain safety and stability while relating to other people?

ON TO THE CHALLENGE OF RELATING TO OTHER PEOPLE

Picture this: In the play, *No Exit*, written by French existential philosopher Jean Paul Sartre and performed in Paris, 1944, during the Nazi occupation, a man and two women — all three with histories of reprehensible behavior towards other people — have been condemned to hell.

One by one, these three strangers are brought together in a small room to begin their eternity of suffering. However, the suffering of Sartre's doomed characters isn't the expected physical pangs of hellfire. Trapped together forever in that small room, they torment each other in a twisted love triangle fraught with jealousy, malice, and contempt.

They are *each other's* instruments of eternal suffering.

One prisoner sums it up:

"So this is hell. I'd never have believed it. You remember all we were told about the torture-chambers, the fire and brimstone, the 'burning marl.' Old wives' tales! There's no need for red-hot pokers. Hell is — other people!" [8]

The phrase "Hell is other people" caught on.

A Google search for the phrase in 2021, seventy-seven years after the play was originally performed, yielded 817 *million* responses. This high number suggests that, like the characters in Sartre's play, ordinary people in real life today find themselves sometimes feeling that "hell is other people."

PEOPLE-TRIGGERS: WHEN "HELL IS OTHER PEOPLE"

Because our traumas happened in relationships with other people, we naCCT survivors are exquisitely attuned to what goes on in our relationships with people. So, naCCT triggers aren't backfiring trucks that sound like explosions; naCCT triggers are more likely to be People-Triggers: interpersonal situations that hearken back to early threats in our attachment relationships with parents or other Lifeline Caregivers.

People-Triggers can present problems in relationships. Take Nadia and Bruce, for example. They have fun together, help each other out, genuinely care about each other. But listen as they describe studying together:

Nadia says, "I make a friendly comment. Bruce doesn't respond at all. He just goes on reading. This happens a few times. I sink into a funk, feeling unloved, worthless, boring. I rack my brain trying to come up with something Bruce would find interesting. Then I offer to make him some popcorn."

Bruce says, "I find it very annoying when Nadia interrupts my reading. It's rude and thoughtless. I want to shout, 'Dammit! Stop badgering me.' It takes all my restraint to just take a deep breath and keep reading."

Nadia is sensitive to inattention and interpersonal abandonment — in her words, to "people who don't respond, who emotionally abandon me." That's her People-Trigger. And she responds with driven pursuit and attempts to arouse interest and engagement with that person.

Bruce is sensitive to intrusions and interruptions: in his words, to "people invading my time and space." That's his People-Trigger. And his response is often suppressed shouting and tight-lipped withdrawal.

Bruce triggers Nadia, and Nadia triggers Bruce. Their "People-Triggers" interlock.

INTERLOCKING PEOPLE-TRIGGERS

Like Nadia and Bruce, Marilyn and Rosemary struggle with interlocking People-Triggers. Also like Nadia and Bruce, they are close, turning to each other for companionship, and for comfort and understanding. They are both out-going. They maintain a warm, friendly household and have a rich circle of shared family and friends.

However, they sometimes feel tormented by each other:

Rosemary says, "I express one little worry, and the next thing I know I'm drowning in this tidal wave of so-called help from Marilyn. She has to be in control, has to know better, has to have a better way of doing everything, a 'helpful' suggestion for improving everything I'm proud of figuring out on my own. She has to be the boss."

Marilyn says, "Rosemary is always in some kind of a jam. And I patiently listen and listen to her troubles and think about what would help her. But instead of taking my advice, she gets mad at my suggestions and then goes right back to her scatter-brained way of doing things, the way that gets her into those messes in the first place. . . .and then I have to listen to her new troubles. *But* if I don't make *any* suggestions, she says I don't care."

Rosemary's "People-Trigger" is "people foisting advice on me and talking to me like I'm a child." And her response is to get flustered and start "screwing things up."

Marilyn's "People-Trigger" is "flustered adults worked up about their troubles." And her response is, first, driven helpfulness and then rejected withdrawal.

Marilyn triggers Rosemary, and Rosemary triggers Marilyn. Their "People-Triggers" and responses interlock and create a zone of chronic trouble in their relationship.

Interlocking People-Triggers are very common, especially with people who are coping with the aftereffects of interpersonal traumas.

NEEDING PEOPLE IS NORMAL

"People who need people," asserts Barbra Streisand in her Grammy Hall of Fame song, "are the luckiest people in the world." Some people disagree. They feel burdened by needing people. They feel stigmatized and ashamed for "being needy" and "having abandonment issues."

"It shouldn't get to me," these people say.

If you criticize yourself — or others criticize you — for having other people matter so much to you, take heart! Here's de-shaming news from the neurophysiology of attachment: Our human bodies are wired for connection!

When we care about our connections to other people, we're in alignment with our bodies. Those connections are *supposed* to matter to us. Maintaining relationships with other people is part of our hardwiring for survival.

Here's the research:

RESEARCH FINDING #1: SOCIAL ENGAGEMENT SYSTEM

In 1994, biobehavioral scientist Dr. Stephen Porges presented the trauma treatment community with ground-breaking research powered by tools like PET scans and fMRIs. Porges' research demonstrated that we have a neurological system for connecting with other people built into our bodies.

This anatomical system goes by different names: the Social Engagement System (SES) or the Ventral Vagal (rhymes with "bagel") Nerve Complex.

Only animal species with the ability to breastfeed their babies have this system.

This Ventral Vagal/Social Engagement System is right there functioning the minute we are born, and it stays with us throughout our lives.

When psychotherapists talk about the Ventral Vagal system, they're referring to a long nerve — cranial nerve X, the Ventral Vagal nerve — that begins in the ventral part of the primitive brain stem and connects the anatomical parts of this Social Engagement System to one another.

Our hearts, lungs, mouths, middle ears, eyelids, jaws, neck, vocal cords, and throat all receive messages from this long nerve.

We use the Ventral Vagal/Social Engagement System to connect with other people. We use it to tilt and turn our heads. We use it to show expression on our faces, to talk, to sing, to change our tone of voice, to babble, coo, and flirt. We use it to ignore background noise and focus on our conversations with others.

When we're upset, this Social Engagement System is our first response system. People turn to other people for protection, love, and comfort. Babies cry for their mothers. Children run to their mothers. Adults turn to other adults. Some adults turn to their therapists.

This system is powerful. It wields the subtle power of calmness and connection. Lest you doubt this power, let me tell you that the subtle force of the SES/Ventral Vagal system can even override the overtly mighty fight or flight response.

This Ventral Vagal/Social Engagement System is so powerfully calming that, as researchers at the University of Exeter in the UK discovered, it works even when we aren't physically close. They discovered that our physical distress diminishes even when we just look at pictures of people receiving comfort from other people.[9]

[Note: As I write in 2020, during the COVID-19 era with its hygienic masks and physical distancing, it's heartening to recognize that we have used creative ingenuity to assure that our social connections — albeit often electronic — are still treasured and thriving.]

NOW YOUR TURN:
SOCIAL ENGAGEMENT SYSTEM QUESTIONS

Reflect on your own experience with your own Ventral Vagal/Social Engagement System. Have you ever felt comfort simply by being with other people when something disturbing was going on?

Recall positive experiences such as being on a team or in a book club, volunteering with a group, or being part of a social action or support community.

Have you had an experience of being helped by a friend face-to-face, at a meeting, or even on line? Think back to a time or two when you received such an assist.

Remember, too, the big comforts: the reach out when you had an illness, a breakup, even a death or other serious loss.

And also recall even the littlest of assists:

- like the time someone held a door open for you, or let you borrow their pen.

- or when a skilled customer service rep said, "I understand how upsetting that can be, and I'm sorry you had to go through that," and you sensed they really *were* sorry.

And remember the times you've assisted someone else:

- like the time you calmed down a relative, friend, or colleague who reached out to you when they were upset.

- or even the appreciative nod from the driver of the car you motioned in front of you.

How did you reach out to ask for help? To receive help? To provide help to someone else? How did your body feel? What look did you see in the other person's eyes?

Take note of the small wave of calmness that comes to you when you remember those moments of helpful connection. Maybe you breathe a faint sigh of relief. Maybe your energy level lifts. Maybe you even feel your tight muscles relax.

RESEARCH FINDING #2: NEUROLOGICALLY, SOCIAL PAIN EQUALS PHYSICAL PAIN

Being connected soothes us. And being — or even *feeling* — left out really hurts.

Neuroscientific research provides evidence that social connections are important and that when something goes wrong in those connections, getting upset makes sense.

We now have mounting scientific evidence that the social pain of being excluded is biologically equivalent to physical pain.

For example, research done in 2004-2005, described in "'Why It Hurts to Be Left Out: The Neurocognitive Overlap Between Physical and Social Pain," showed that being in social pain activates an area of the brain traditionally associated with processing physical pain. [10] (That area is the posterior insular cortex, if you like to know this sort of thing.)

The Social Engagement System and the physical pain system overlap in our nervous systems.[11]

Thus, neurophysiological research supports our everyday experience: being left out hurts.

Our bodies are actually hard-wired to keep us alert to our social well-being.

Our connection to each other is so crucial to our well-being that being cut off from other people is sometimes used as punishment — often severe punishment, as when someone is ostracized, banished, cast out, shunned, or imprisoned in solitary confinement. Think, for example, of Tim

Robbins' character, Andy Dufresne, in "The Shawshank Redemption" being given another month in "The Hole" (solitary confinement) to "think about" his offense to the warden.

Both physical pain and social pain can indicate danger, a threat to our well-being, perhaps even to our survival. Both kinds of pain signal that something is wrong. Ask the office worker omitted from the email communication loop. Ask anyone who's ever been shunned for not belonging to the majority culture. Ask just about anyone who's ever been a teenager or the left out kid on the playground or the one sitting alone on the school bus: they will confirm that social pain reads as "Danger!" It warns us that something is wrong with our relationships with other people.

Just as physical pain alerts us that something *physical* needs attention, so social pain alerts us that something *social* needs attention. We may also hope that social pain motivates us to fix the problem, to find some new way to get connected and belong with our fellow people.

Both this social pain research and the Ventral Vagal Social Engagement System research offer scientific support for our experience that people need people. Relationships with people are vitally important. Judging by the ways our bodies are wired to work, it seems we're supposed to be this way. Our bodies are hard-wired for relationships, and People-Triggers make biological, survival-based sense.

SURVIVORS IDENTIFY PEOPLE-TRIGGERS

Here are few examples of survivors identifying their People-Triggers. The strong adult responses to these relatively minor situations were later tracked back to naCCT patterns in childhood, when similar relationship troubles could constitute major life-threatening stress, involving the Ventral Vagal /Social Engagement System and the social pain system.

These strong adult reactions in the present made sense as post-traumatic hair-trigger responses that had been "wired-in" during the past naCCTs.

Jenna Lee:

"Sometimes my lead teacher's feedback just gets to me. Even though I'm pretty much overqualified for my job, I get afraid of doing something wrong and being let go. Like last night, I was lying in bed, replaying the way my lead teacher had corrected me that afternoon. I tried to remember where I'd learned to do it the way I did, the way she criticized. Finally I had to get up and look at my training notes to see if I maybe I really *did* do it the wrong way that afternoon."

Me, Ricia:

The interpersonal relationship didn't even have to be face-to-face. A sign could do it. When I was a cigarette smoker, I used to see red when I saw signs that said 'Thank you for not smoking.' I obsessed over how illogical they were. So tricky. So sneaky. Sort of twisted. And it bothered me that no one else but me seemed bothered by those twisted requests. I schemed to get someone to agree with my aggravation: Why can' t they just say, 'No smoking'?"

Fran:

"I was at one of those workshops where we had to turn to the person next to us and share our hopes for the day. I turned to three people and every one of them already had a partner. I finally partnered up with another 'orphan' way over on the other side of the room. But I think it got to me, because during the coffee break I couldn't connect with anyone, and I ate lunch by myself."

Margo:

"I was brought up in a strict religious household. My family valued lofty serenity and composure. I felt pressure to "always be good." To "rise above my little troubles." To "let go of anger."

"Turn the other cheek" was the motto for dealing with insults, especially subtle insults from my parents and siblings.

"Although I no longer practice the strict religion of my childhood, sometimes a talk given in my meditation center will trigger me, especially when the talks stress detachment, forgiveness, and the importance of not getting angry.

"I was even triggered when I overheard a little boy on a playground say he hated his playmate, and his mom told him to 'try to find something about him you like.' I felt a flash of panicky rage come over me. That mom's advice was a perfectly reasonable suggestion for coming to a balanced view of a friendship, but it got to me."

WHAT TO DO ABOUT PEOPLE-TRIGGERS?

Be prepared.

You can take care of yourself and cope with People-Trigger s by first anticipating triggering and then having a plan in place for calming yourself and restoring your equilibrium if you do get triggered.

We'll cover anticipating People-Triggers in this chapter and later we'll cover planning how to cope with People-Triggers.

The first step in managing triggers and flashbacks is identifying them. But, although People-Triggers are everywhere, it's not so easy to identify them.

IDENTIFYING TRIGGERS AND FLASHBACKS TO NACCT CAN BE VERY DIFFICULT.

Because naCCT People-Triggers tend to be ordinary, everyday occurrences between people, the risk of triggering in many everyday situations is hard to avoid. And recognizing them as triggers can be very difficult. Why is that?

One reason it's hard to know you've been People-Triggered is that an naCCT flashback doesn't *seem* like a flashback. Triggered naCCT survivors with cPTSD can suddenly find themselves in a bad mood. Or hopelessly despairing. Or even trying to manage a sudden uprising of hate and rage that they'd been taught as children "must not be expressed." An naCCT flashback can just come out of the blue for no apparent reason.

When this happens, past pain has overtaken present social reality, and the survivor is flooded by old grief, sadness, hurt, anger, disgust, and/or terror.

Furthermore, the People-Triggers leading to naCCT flashbacks aren't obvious. Like the interactions that caused the original trauma, these People-Triggers are embedded in ordinary everyday social life. No backfiring trucks; no flashing knives; no screeching brakes; no aggressive physicality; no overt sexual gestures. No interpersonal violence or physical fights. Just a slight turning away, a funny look, a social snub.

And these People-Triggers are functionally covert. Hidden. Hard to identify as trauma triggers. Their ordinariness, their mildness, their apparent triviality keeps them covert. What the survivor has gotten upset about seems too trivial to take seriously. Taking it seriously would just be something *else* to be ashamed of.

So the naCCT People-Trigger is overlooked. Minimized. Dismissed as a cause.

Flashbacks to intangible traumas are often so subtle that neither the naCCT survivors nor the people they're relating to know "for sure" that they've been triggered.

The good news: Forewarned is forearmed. Once people know they have experienced trauma, they can be "on alert" for flashback triggers, and once people are "on alert," they are more likely to identify a flashback trigger for what it is.

Forewarn yourself! Identify your own People-Triggers. Make a list of interpersonal situations that are distressing but not dangerous for you, ones that can scare you into thinking they are dangerous.

Don't be blindsided! De-mystify the triggering process. Make it ordinary, everyday, mundane, and manageable! Make the covert triggers overt. Identify the subtle triggers so you won't be blindsided.

ON TO THE LIST OF PEOPLE-TRIGGERS

To facilitate the difficult first step of identifying flashbacks, I've gathered together a list of distressing things that naCCT survivors may perceive as dangerous threats in the present, long after their childhood naCCTs are over.

These are real People-Triggers I've personally experienced or witnessed other people experience as triggers.

This trigger list is long. Note how commonplace the triggers are. Remember that it's normal for such common, seemingly trivial things to send normal people with naCCT histories into flashback tailspins, numbness, or frenzies.

As you read through the list, note what triggers *you*. Also note the person whose behavior triggers you and what your relationship is. Intimate partner? Your kids? Your parents? Close friends? Co-workers? Neighbors? Authority figures? Your therapist?

"PEOPLE-TRIGGERS" (INTERPERSONAL PET PEEVES THAT "PUSH MY BUTTONS")

- Little rudenesses, well-intentioned but clumsy remarks
- "Weird" looks and gestures, especially if somewhat hostile or abandoning

- Being "force fed" a positive mental attitude
- Coercive cheerful jollying
- Well-intentioned advice such as "calm down," or "you don't need to be upset," or "forgive for your own sake," or "think of something else," or "focus on your breathing," or "let it go"
- Someone else's extreme serenity, "holier than thou," "more serene than thou," "more peace-loving than thou"
- Negative feedback
- Someone receiving something I've been longing for but don't have
- Being left out
- Being lectured to
- "Know it all" behavior
- Creepy interactions
- Lack of agreement
- Direct disagreement
- Being misunderstood
- Not being able to follow what someone is saying; feeling confused
- Belittling of any sort, snottiness
- Being argued with
- Having mistakes pointed out; being corrected
- Not being chosen
- Someone changing the subject
- Feeling "out of sync" with the people I'm with
- Being shamed or judged for being upset or distressed
- Someone "raining on my parade"
- Teasing
- Having what I said twisted into something I didn't say
- Realizing the person I'm talking to doesn't "get" me
- Being interrupted
- Being told "don't worry"
- Feeling "used"
- Scrambled communication
- Other person's responses miss the point
- Difficulty following or understanding what someone is saying
- Someone seems not to be following or understanding me
- Being told I'm not capable of something I really *can* do quite well

- Having an accomplishment minimized
- Being "dissed"
- Being told "just do it"
- Being unrealistically encouraged
- Receiving shame-based pep-talks: "you aren't a wuss who can't do this"
- Being put on the spot, having to speak or stand up or be looked at
- Being challenged to explain myself or my position on something
- Being asked to do something for someone
- Hearing someone else, especially an enemy or "frenemy," be praised
- Physical contacts, being touched, not touched, moved aside
- Sensing that another person "looked at me funny"
- Unfair blame
- Being sharply spoken to
- Telling a joke that received no laughter, while another person's joke did
- Realizing a listener presumes to understand but doesn't
- Being where everyone else was upset and their upset was contagious
- Tangential responses
- Being caught in a bind, "damned if I do and damned if I don't"
- Being interrupted
- Receiving faint praise when hearty congratulations are called for
- Having an accomplishment overlooked or one-upped

INTERPERSONAL ABSENCE

- No one there
- Lack. Wanting. Waiting. Unsatisfied. Abandoned. Ignored.
- Wanting a kind of interaction or responsiveness that just isn't happening
- Experiencing long pauses before response to what I've shared
- Receiving no response at all to what I've shared
- Being rejected, left out of the loop, skipped over
- Having someone look away while I was speaking
- Being excluded
- Feeling lonely, especially in the presence of other people

- Longing for soothing, comfort, help
- Waiting for someone who is late
- Having plans cancelled with little notice or last minute
- Being "ghosted"
- Not being thanked
- Having to ask for help

INDIRECT PEOPLE-TRIGGERS

- Discontinuation of product, service, or menu item
- Favorite checkout person or receptionist quits
- Loud noises; din
- Too many people; crowds
- Long lines, long waits
- Traffic, driving rudenesses, cut offs
- Being kept "on hold" during a phone call

SENSORY INDIRECT PEOPLE-TRIGGERS

- Someone wearing a particular style of clothing, even the particular drape of a woman's blouse
- Being touched, brushed up against, handshake
- Tone of voice; voice quality; accent, dialect, regional speech, slang expressions
- Perfume, body lotion, body odors, sweat in the subway or crowd
- Background noises from a playground, sports, or party

SURPRISING TRIGGERS: EVENTS THAT SEEM LIKE THEY WOULD MAKE ANYONE HAPPY ACTUALLY TRIGGER SOME PEOPLE

(The classic case of surprising triggers is the research done by Matina Horner in the 1970's on women's "fear of success": College women responded to story prompts such as "woman finds herself at top of first year medical school class" with stories like "she feels happy at first but then her classmates beat her up and she is maimed for life.") [12]

- Success: (Like the woman student getting high marks on exam)
- Having fun; exuberance; loud laughter
- Being praised
- Being complimented

- Being chosen as a winner
- Being singled out as special
- Feeling proud: good-looking, smart, talented, popular, accomplished

There is a collection of these People-Triggers on my website: https://ChronicCovertTrauma.wordpress.com/people-triggers/. You can go there and contribute your own. Sharing your People-Triggers might help you, and it certainly will help other people to know they aren't the only one with that trigger.

Identifying People-Triggers is a learnable skill. At first, these People-Triggers may not even register in your awareness. Eventually you become skilled at "coming alongside yourself" and noticing them.

With time and practice, survivors get better and better at sorting out what part of present day distress is due to People-Triggered flashbacks to the past and what part is due to present feelings in response to present circumstances.

A NOTE ON PEOPLE-TRIGGERS AND PSYCHOTHERAPY

At some point, you may choose to enlist a therapist to help you heal cPTSD from naCCT. In the classic therapist-assisted PTSD healing model, the relationship with the therapist is viewed as a core source of safety and stability. Therapist and client work together to build a safe relationship.

However, building and maintaining a safe relationship in therapist-assisted recovery can be challenging. The therapy relationship itself can become fraught with problems arising from intangible attachment traumas. (Some of you may even be reading this book because of problems in a therapy relationship, past or present.)

The therapy relationship is vulnerable to the aftereffects of naCCT in ways it isn't vulnerable to aftereffects of blatant trauma. Here's why that is:

If a person endured a traumatic car crash or natural disaster, it's highly unlikely that in their therapy they would encounter triggers that would remind them of car crashes, rising flood water, or wildfires.

If a person endured blatant physically assaultive traumas in their past, their therapy would be safe from triggers reminding them of those traumas simply because under normal circumstances therapists don't physically assault their clients.

However, triggers stimulating reminders to naCCTs are, unfortunately, quite likely. Note how many of the items in the list of People-Triggers could easily happen between therapist and client. A well-meaning therapist could easily misunderstand a client, or inadvertently use an expression or make a gesture that occurred as part of a client's early naCCT.

Furthermore, a history of blatant, physically assaultive trauma in Lifeline relationships doesn't confer immunity to naCCT People-Triggers in therapy. Why? Because those physically assaultive traumas usually include naCCTs, and therapist's actions or failures to act can trigger reminders to those naCCTs.

INTERLOCKING TRIGGERS IN A THERAPY RELATIONSHIP

And it's not only the client who can experience People-Triggers during therapy. Therapists are trained to manage their responses and to seek supervision and/or therapy when their own issues come into play in a therapy relationship. However, therapists are human, and naCCT is so prevalent and so covert that a therapist can be People-Triggered by a client. This means that both therapist and client can be struggling with subtle, even unidentified, opened wounds at the same time, trying to protect themselves and stay safe.

Unidentified and unresolved interlocking triggers in a therapy relationship present serious challenges. If they continue, the therapy relationship may come to feel, and may even become, more than can productively be managed. The therapy relationship can then become another relationship where "Hell is other people."

If you decide to go the therapy-assisted route, the work you are doing here with this book and the awareness you are cultivating can help your therapy go well, and help you take care of yourself if it runs into this kind of difficulty.

ATOMIC CHAIN REACTION OF TRIGGERS

These People-Triggers can interact in ways that can be very challenging and hard to manage. Sad to say, this often happens.

Sometimes an external People-Trigger can set off an *internal* chain reaction of distress: thoughts, feelings, memories, expectations, or rules that "need to be followed." Sometimes even contemplating a course of action related to people can function as a trigger.

These chain reactions of triggers can become complex and

overwhelming. They remind me of the classic popular science demonstration of an atomic chain reaction: A room is filled with mousetraps loaded with ping pong balls. When one mousetrap is triggered, the ping pong ball flies out of that mousetrap, lands on another loaded mousetrap, and sets that ping pong ball flying, until the room is full of flying ping pong balls.

COULD YOU USE A HUMOR BREAK NOW?

If you can use a few fun and educational laughs right about now, check out this video reconstruction of the ping pong ball and mousetrap chain reaction, done with all the professional glitz of network television on "900 Mousetraps Unleashed with Science Bob on Jimmy Kimmel Live" https://www.youtube.com/watch?v=XIvHd76EdQ4. Start at 1:00.

Or go to "Monsters of Schlock" "Mousetrap Ping Pong Ball Nuclear Fission Chain Reaction - SCIENCE: Unexplained!" https://www.youtube.com/watch?v=bEmb0HDHHIc&feature=youtu.be.

There you'll see a bunch of guys in safety goggles and hearing-protecting earmuffs experiencing what could easily represent a very upset, dysregulated trauma survivor dealing with a chain reaction of triggers.

The commentary to this video reads "We first saw this chain reaction demo in a video at the Atomic Testing Museum in Las Vegas. . . .there were tonnes [tons] of these style of video on YouTube. . . .but they were missing the one thing we were dumb enough to do. . . .stick your face in it!"

This video can give you a weird, validating picture of the overwhelming nature of a chain reaction and help you to say, "No wonder I have a hard time!"

Does it help to say to yourself, "Oh no, now I'm having an Atomic Chain Reaction of triggers and flashbacks?"

DISTRESS RESPONSES TO PEOPLE-TRIGGERS

PSYCHIATRIST GABOR MATE'S PEOPLE-TRIGGER AND HIS DISTRESS RESPONSE TO IT

Hungarian-Canadian psychiatrist Gabor Mate (he pronounces it *mah tay*), internationally renowned speaker and author of four books, including *When the Body Says No* and the award-winning *In the Realm of Hungry Ghosts*, generously shares one of his triggers and his Distress Responses to it with readers of his book *Scattered: How Attention Deficit Disorder Originates and What You Can Do about It:*

"My voice quickly falters when someone as much as averts his eyes from me while I am speaking with him," he writes. "My words lose connection and dry up, like water trickling into sand."[13]

Dr. Gabor Mate views this trigger and response pattern as a symptom of his own Attention Deficit Disorder. Behind his pattern of shutting down in the face of withdrawn attention is his personal backstory, which he investigates and pieces together in order to make sense of the way he is. Here's what he discovers:

[Warning: Possible triggering regarding Nazi Holocaust]

First, the historical facts. In January of 1944, little Gabor Mate, known as Gabi, was born into a Jewish family in Budapest, Hungary. Two and a half months later, the Nazi invasion and occupation wiped out two-thirds of Hungary's Jewish people.

To those horrific historical facts, he adds personal family history gleaned from photographs, interviews, and a diary his mother kept for him while he was an infant. When he grew up, she gave him the diary, but he didn't read it until he was in his fifties. "A powerful ennui and drowsiness would come over me whenever I opened the diary, and that was seldom," he says, and goes on to explain: "It must have evoked painful emotions I was not prepared to re-experience on the conscious level."

When his mother was almost eighty, he finally asked her to read the diary out loud, and he recorded and translated her reading into English. Here's what he learned:

At the time of little Gabi Mate's birth, his father had already been sent to a Transylvanian forced-labor camp.

When the Nazi occupation of Hungary began, two and a half month old baby Gabi began crying non-stop. His mother called the pediatrician, who said, "All my Jewish babies are crying." Dr. Mate reflects that those babies, including himself as a baby, obviously had no cognitive knowledge of war or genocide, but they absorbed their parents' anxiety, "drank it in with their mother's milk, heard it in their fathers' voices, felt it in the tense arms and bodies that held them close. They inhaled fear, ingested sorrow. Yet were they not loved?"

To answer his own question, he opens his chapter "An Utter Stranger" with a photo of himself at four months old with his mother. This photo sums up the heart-breaking and well-nigh inevitable naCCT thrust upon children who are born to loving parents embedded in atrocious social and political contexts that invade and impact the personal intimate bonds between babies and their Lifeline People.

In the photo, mother is wearing the yellow star, the "badge of shame" required by the Nazis, and bending "toward her son with an expression of soft, loving absorption." Mate comments: "If in the photograph the love may be seen in my mother's face, her fear and worry are reflected in mine."

As a Jewish baby in Nazi-occupied Hungary, he clearly suffered what we could call "naCCT of Omission of Attuned Attention." In a remarkable understatement, he says, "My mother and I had little opportunity for normal mother-infant experiences."

Mate doesn't blame his mother: He has compassionate understanding for her preoccupation with genocidal horror and survival terror. Of course, she had little available attention, let alone consistent empathic attunement, to give to her infant boy. His relationship with his mother was clearly a case of trauma, but not abuse.

Five months after little Gabi Mate was born, his mother's parents were killed in the gas chambers of Auschwitz. Neither the fate of her husband nor that of her sister, who had also been sent to Auschwitz, was known. His mother felt such despair she wanted to kill herself.

At this time, she and little Gabi, along with many other Budapest Jews, were forced to move into an overcrowded "star house" marked with a yellow star of David. She made plans for little Gabi to be secretly adopted by a gentile couple if she were sent away. "I will give up my son when they're here to throw me into the cattle train," she said, "not one second before."

In the midst of all this personal horror and loss, her milk dried up, and she had to stop nursing Gabi.

Mate also learned from his mother that when he was an eleven month old toddler, she sought safety for the two of them in a different place: a filthy, overcrowded office building, called a "protected house," offered by the Swiss embassy. Among the many Jewish people struggling to survive there, with overflowing toilets, body lice, and scarcely enough to eat, was a Jewish man with a non-Jewish wife whom Gabi's mother didn't know.

Horrifically aware that she, too, might be sent to the death camps, Gabi's mother became frantic about his survival. So, on a desperate impulse, she entrusted him to the Jewish man's non-Jewish wife. This helpful stranger pushed Gabi in his baby carriage through downtown Budapest to his mother's cousin's house outside the ghetto. There he remained for three weeks in relative physical safety.

Gabi and his mother both survived, but the ending of his mother's story is troubling: Mate says he learned from her that instead of the joyful mother and toddler reunion one might expect, he "responded as if she were an utter stranger to me. I would not so much as look at her for days."

GABOR MATE MAKES SENSE OF HIS RESPONSE

Like many of us, Dr. Gabor Mate gets help from people, face-to-face and through books. To deal with this story of his non-response to his mother, he turns to psychiatrist John Bowlby, pioneer attachment researcher, and Bowlby's study of small children who, like Mate himself, were separated from their mothers because of family emergencies. Bowlby's study lets Mate know that he wasn't alone in not responding to his mother: All the children in the study showed some of what Bowlby called "defensive attachment": "Two seemed not to recognize mother. The other eight turned away or even walked away from her."

Mate brings Bowlby's research home to his long-ago personal situation. In circumstances similar to his, other children responded the same way he did. He's not the only one. After normalizing his own response as a toddler, Mate says, "The response of the infant to the fathomless anxiety of physical or emotional separation from the parent is either rage or withdrawal, or a combination of both in sequence."

He then brings this abstract information home: "This is how I have many times reacted in similar circumstances. Being activated, I am sure, was anxiety and rage from my first year of life when my mother was emotionally dissociated, and particularly from our three-week separation just around my first birthday."

HOW THIS APPLIES TO HIS PEOPLE-TRIGGER AND DISTRESS RESPONSE

Bringing compassion, understanding, and self-attunement to his own present-day trigger and Distress Response, Mate reflects on how these early experiences connect to his adult Attention Deficit Disorder — "What I do know is that I can make sense of my ADD traits when I consider them in the light of this formative period of my life." Specifically, it helps him make sense of the way he shuts down, his "voice quickly falters," and his "words lose connection and dry up" if his listener's attention drifts away from him.

Mate turns to a colleague, child psychiatrist Stanley Greenspan, whose relevant observations on the life-long impact of "seemingly trivial gestures" from late infancy he quotes:

"For the rest of our lives," Greenspan says, "should someone stare at us blankly, gaze off into space, or remain mute, we begin to feel confused, rejected, perhaps even unloved. Very sensitive individuals may even find their thinking becoming disorganized, their sense of purpose gradually dissolving." [14]

After quoting these normalizing words from his colleague, Mate closes his chapter with the simple statement: "My experience, precisely."

THE CHAIN OF VALIDATION

Did his fellow psychiatrist's words help Gabor Mate legitimize his Distress Response to his listener's wandering attention?

I, Ricia, certainly felt some of my own personal distress legitimized by Mate's story.

I felt kinship with Mate because I have also shut down like that when someone looked away while I was talking. I have also experienced the abrupt loss of interest and engagement with that person. Like Mate, I have also lost my connection to what I was talking about. Suddenly it no longer mattered to me.

Before reading Mate's account, I had felt shame and confusion about my shut-down response .

But when this man whose book I was admiring confessed that the same thing happened to him, my shame lifted as I thought, "Me, too. I'm not the only one." I joined Mate in saying, "My experience, precisely."

I thought to myself: "Maybe this is an understandable human thing to have happen to you, to me. This is normal. This is what happens to humans on planet earth." Whew! I felt relief.

Discovering you aren't "the only one" is a powerful experience: It enabled me to reassure myself with this Self-Talk Script:

SELF-TALK SCRIPT: "I'M NOT THE ONLY ONE"

"I'm not the only one who responds in disturbing ways to seemingly trivial — superficially trivial, that is — situations that trigger anxieties imprinted in my memory long ago. It's normal for seemingly trivial gestures from late infancy to impact us for the rest of our lives."

ARE YOU A WELCOME NEW LINK IN THE CHAIN OF VALIDATION?

The chain of validation began when Greenspan validated Mate.

Another link was added when I took normalizing comfort from Mate's words.

This Chain of Validation may progress not only from Greenspan to Mate to me, but maybe also to you, dear reader. You may be taking comfort as their words pass through me to you. You may find yourself saying, "Me too. My experience, precisely."

And you may add yet another link to the Chain of Validation as you go on to provide comforting validation to another naCCT survivor.

It's a lineage of comforting and empowering validation being passed down from one recovering survivor to another: *"For people with early attachment traumas, Distress Responses to People-Triggers are normal!"*

NOW YOUR TURN

YOUR PEOPLE-TRIGGERS AND DISTRESS RESPONSES

We move on now to identifying *your* typical Distress Responses to your People-Triggers.

While you were going over your triggers in the lists provided previously in this chapter, you probably became aware of how you react to those triggers. Some of these Distress Responses may be identical to the "signs and symptoms" that you inventoried in Chapter Two: the "out of the blue depression." The chronic tension headaches for no reason. The bad habits that won't budge. Maybe those "signs and symptoms" are Distress Responses to People-Triggers.

To explore this possibility, make a list of your standard problematic response patterns when you're triggered by other people. Do you generally "under-react" or "over-react?" What are your typical ways of responding to these triggers: your physical sensations, thoughts, emotions, expectations, impulses, actions.

YOUR TYPICAL DISTRESS RESPONSES

Do you:

- Shut down?
- Withdraw?
- Argue?
- Attack?
- Investigate?
- Self-medicate?
- Get out of there?
- People-please?
- Talk fast and smile?
- Go along to get along?
- Get confused?
- Get busy?
- Seek help?
- Curl up into a ball?
- Cry?
- Go online?
- Head for cover?
- Set a trap?
- Faint?
- Throw a punch?
- Space out?
- Look for someone to blame?
- Eat? Smoke? Drink? Shop?
- Run?
- Lie down?
- Lie low?
- Get sick?
- Go numb?
- Act calm?

- Get really left-brained and rational?
- Get intellectual?
- Look for logical flaws?
- Start explaining something?
- Something else?

How do other people describe your responses? What words have they used? Has someone said that you "Get hysterical"? "Throw a hissy fit"? "Get up on your high horse"? "Turn into a human computer?" Even: "Go out with your gun loaded for bear." Do you agree with their descriptions? Others' choice of words may be quite pejorative. Still, can their "feedback" be at all useful to you?

Be aware of your standard response patterns, especially ones you might want to delete from your repertoire for both your well-being and better relationships with other people.

PEOPLE-TRIGGER AND DISTRESS RESPONSE STATEMENT

At this point, you have a list of your People-Triggers *and* a list of your typical Distress Responses to those triggers.

You can work with these lists to formulate People-Trigger and Distress-Response statements like this for yourself:

"When I encounter this People-Trigger [_____],

my Distress Response tends to be [_____]."

There's a kind of magic to these statements of awareness.

Gabor Mate might complete the People-Trigger and Distress Response Statement this way:

"When I encounter this People-Trigger [someone looks away and stops listening to me],

my Distress Response tends to be [my voice falters, words lose connection and dry up]."

SELF-TALK SCRIPT: "I PROTECT MYSELF WITH AWARENESS"

"Good for me! Identifying triggers and Distress Responses to them is the first step in managing them. Every time I can acknowledge a pattern of trigger and Distress Response and create one of those People-Trigger and Distress Response statements, I am building protection from being caught off guard and blindsided."

WHAT'S NEXT? REMEMBER THAT YOU ARE A WORK IN PROGRESS.

Remember, it takes a lot of skill and healing to be exposed to a trigger without actually having a flashback or other Distress Response. You are still learning.

SELF-TALK SCRIPT: "I'M MAKING PROGRESS"

Endorse yourself for even the smallest of gains. Acknowledge your milestones. For example, you might say:

"Good for me. At least I noticed I got triggered. Even though it took me three days, I finally did realize it, and in former days I wouldn't have noticed it at all."

Later you'll even be saying:

"Good for me, this time I noticed I got triggered right after it happened. That's progress."

WHAT TO DO ABOUT PEOPLE-TRIGGERS?

The next step in staying safe and stable around people is changing those patterns, having a plan in place for calming and reassuring yourself and restoring your equilibrium if you do get People-Triggered.

Break apart the fused links between trigger and Distress Response. Put a little mental space between the trigger and the Distress Response. Loosen that densely packed soil, plant seeds of dreams. That's where intervention is possible.

As your recovery progresses, here's a kind of Self-Talk Script you'll find yourself saying:

SELF-TALK SCRIPT: FROM TRIGGER TO ANNOYANCE

"I don't like what they're doing, and I don't like what they're saying. It used to really trigger me. I still don't like it, but now I stay pretty safe and stable and just try to figure out the best way to respond."

COMING UP: TIME FOR A BREAK AND A STORY

You've worked hard. After all this, you may have done enough self-scrutiny and stock-taking for the time being. Set the lists aside. Let your answers and insights lie fallow for a bit. We'll come back to them later.

I invite you to come with me now to a place devoted to healing. There you'll observe some People-Triggers, some Distress Responses, and some recovery. You'll observe two incidents of people getting triggered in relationships and what they did when they were triggered.

You'll see people stay safe and stable. You'll also see people remember and grieve. And you'll see people reconnect. The components aren't happening in a rigid sequence, one step completed, another step begun. All the healing components weave together in this up-coming episode of real life healing.

NOTES

[8] In *No Exit and Three Other Plays*, trans. Stuart Gilbert (New York: Vintage Reissue edition, 1989), p. 45

[9] "Brain's Response to Threat Silenced When We Are Reminded of Being Loved and Cared For," University of Exeter, Nov. 7, 2014, http://www.exeter.ac.uk/news/featurednews/title_420975_en.html

[10] Naomi I. Eisenberger and Matthew D. Lieberman, "Why It Hurts to Be Left Out: The Neurocognitive Overlap Between Physical and Social Pain," in *The Social Outcast: Ostracism, Social Exclusion, Rejection, and Bullying* (New York: Psychology Press, 2014).

[11] Christopher Bergland, "The Neuroscience of Social Pain," *Psychology Today*, Mar 03, 2014, https://www.psychologytoday.com/us/blog/the-athletes-way/201403/the-neuroscience-social-pain.

[12] Vivian Gornick, "Why Radcliffe Women are Afraid of Success," *New York Times*, Jan. 1, 1973, https://www.nytimes.com/1973/01/14/archives/why-radcliffe-women-are-afraid-of-success-research-by-matina-horner.html.

[13] All quotations here are from Mate, *Scattered,* pp. 88-92, 254, and 263.

[14] Greenspan, 1997, quoted in Mate, *Scattered*, p. 255

CHAPTER 8

CHRONIC PAIN GROUP ADDRESSES PEOPLE-TRIGGERS

With this newly-focused awareness of your People-Triggers, come listen to a story about working with these triggers in a healing environment.

The story is about people whose growth is woven together as they bring healing to their interpersonal traumas, lessen the power of these People-Triggers, and move toward greater well-being.

This story is a kind of reality-based fiction, anchored in my twenty years of providing psychotherapy groups in a four week, live-in rehabilitation program for people challenged by debilitating chronic pain.

The way pain happens in our bodies is mysterious, so mysterious that chronic pain often cannot be explained by anything the eye can see or medical tests can reveal.

Yet, the pain is *very* real. This is the basis for Chronic Pain Syndrome, well recognized in the medical world. In the United States alone, according to the Centers for Disease Control and Prevention (CDC), in 2016 over fifty million adults suffered from chronic pain.[15]

In order to respect confidentiality while giving you a sense of what really happens in a psychotherapy group like this, I've created fictional characters, born from the true facts about more than four-thousand real people — both patients and staff. The only literal, historical character in this story is me.

This story will recreate for you a day in my life as I was coming to appreciate and honor the mysterious power of naCCT.

But maybe this story is not only about me and the people in the Chronic Pain Program. Maybe it's your story, too. As you read along, note when something touches you. Especially note if you find yourself thinking, "I'd like to experience something like that."

THE PAIN PROGRAM STORY

When our story begins, it is evening in an urban hospital. Patients are milling about between dinner and the evening psychotherapy group I'll be leading.

In the pain treatment program, my formal job title was "Psychomotor Therapist" in the "Biopsychology" Department. My formal job description was to help people "address the psychosocial factors impacting chronic pain." In plain English, my job was to help people talk to each other and take part in healing role-plays that brought together parts of life that we so often put in separate compartments — the "bio," the "psyche," and the "social," or the body, the soul, and relationships with people. A more accurate name for the group might have been "The Whole Life Group."

The patients milling about before the group begins are all wearing street clothes. Some are hooked up to IV tubes; a few others are in wheelchairs or pushing walkers. Many appear healthy enough to be mistaken for hospital staff or visitors. Yet, all are challenged by chronic pain.

Behind the nurses' station, in a tiny staff room, a young man wearing a stethoscope around his neck sits glumly in front of a cafeteria tray. This is Jason, the evening nurse who assists me in the psychotherapy group. Jason is also my friend. We're finishing dinner together.

"So, I have no good reason to be upset," he says, pushing aside his Styrofoam dinner tray and glancing out the door, where patients are lining up for their medications before heading off to our group.

"Especially compared to these folks with chronic pain," Jason continues, raking his fingers through his thick black hair and scowling, "the situation with Chief Jones that keeps me awake on nights before team meetings is relatively trivial. I have no right to complain."

"Working here sometimes makes me feel that way too," I reply, "especially when I get worked up over something relatively trivial. . . . and then start comparing myself to people who 'really' have a good reason to be miserable.

"But, Jason, maybe you *do* have a reason to be upset," I continue, "This isn't the first time I've heard about your sleepless nights before your team meeting days. Even if Chief Jones did choose you over all those other people to be his assistant, you *still* might have a good reason to be upset . . . I mean, lying awake, thinking he regrets choosing you for the team at all, even that you should find another line of work, well, *something's* going on."

"No," Jason interrupts firmly, "I should be happy. I have a good job. I'm on a great treatment team, headed by the best team leader. Everyone says Jones is the best. So what if he dismisses what I say in the team meeting? So what if everyone thinks he's brilliant, and he thinks I'm not cut out for this work at all? I'm just another privileged guy whining about nothing."

Just then another nurse pops her head into the tiny staff room. "Sorry to interrupt," she says, "News bulletin about Nick. He's in your group tonight. Today his test results came back with bad news for him — no tissue damage. So, the procedure he was counting on for pain relief won't work. He's really disappointed. Major setback, convinced that nobody believes his pain is real."

In the nightmare world of chronic physical pain, as in the world of naCCT, there is no tangible cause or evidence of suffering. Hospitalized for disabling physical pain, many of these people, like naCCT survivors, can't point to any tangible cause for their suffering, and those who suffer may feel challenged to prove it's legitimate.

On TV commercials, other people's pain is easy to perceive and validate: images show jackhammers drilling into throbbing heads, and flames leaping from throbbing tennis elbows.

However, in real life, other people's pain offers no such visual evidence. Like someone enduring naCCT, only the sufferer perceives the pain and knows from experience how real that pain is.

Although chronic pain syndrome is now recognized as a real problem by the medical treatment community, the pain patients themselves, with no material "proof" of their suffering, feel vulnerable to being dismissed as "fakers" and "freeloaders."

And like survivors of intangible trauma, people with chronic pain have often been lead to feel they have "no right to be upset."

For example, even with the special license plates on their cars, some people disabled by chronic pain have heard passers-by in parking lots snarl at them, "Hey, scumbag, those spaces are reserved for disabled people who really need them." Some patients joke grimly about getting a leg cast or a neck brace "just to show I really have something wrong."

The invalidation is so upsetting that even a diagnosis of a herniated disk or a damaged nerve has been welcome news because it "proves" the pain is legitimate.

"Now that Nick's tests have come back negative," the nurse continues, "he's terrified that people will decide his pain isn't real, and his treatment will be terminated. Since this afternoon, his pain level and his angry hopelessness have both soared, almost to where they were when he came here from alcohol detox. He blew up at his AA sponsor this afternoon, according to his buddies Michelle and Carlos, the other two of 'the three musketeers.'

"Now he's talking about leaving the hospital against medical advice, getting some relief from 'his old friends in the bottle.' I told him that before he takes off, he should go talk it over in your group."

With these words, the nurse ducks out of the room.

Jason looks up from the congealed dinner on his plate and our eyes meet. "Actually, I can relate to Nick," he says. "It's really tough when it looks like there is no legitimate reason for your pain, and nobody's taking it seriously."

I reply, laughing with some self-recognition, "Especially when the main person refusing to take your pain seriously is you, yourself."

We're all so clear about the need for validation when it comes to other people. But we often forget to care for ourselves, to take our own pain seriously, to recognize that it's real and has causes that don't show up on tests or respond to surgical procedures.

When we catch ourselves struggling with feeling that our pain is invalid, that's when we need to remember what people with chronic pain have taught: even if it doesn't bleed, bones aren't broken, and tests still come out negative, pain is real if it hurts. And if it hurts, it deserves compassion and healing care.

BOTH OVERT ABUSE AND NACCT: NICK'S STORY

Both Jason and I glance at the clock. 6:45. Our talk will have to wait. It's time to join eleven patients in the dining room, push the chairs into a circle, and spend the next three hours helping patients help each other.

As the patients gather, the mood in the room is tense. Although they come for rehabilitation of chronic physical pain, many patients also have histories of trauma and abuse, which may have become embodied in such conditions as tense muscles and disordered neurochemistry.

This means that childhood trauma and abuse may now be contributing to their total chronic pain experience. In this group we help adults trace their chronic pain to whatever sources may be fueling it.

Last week, the mood in the group had been tender. The patients helped Nick's special buddy, Michelle, as she grieved the sexual abuse and emotional indifference she had suffered from her father.

This week, the air crackles with Nick's suppressed rage. In his early thirties, Nick suffers from chronic neck and shoulder pain that began three years ago after a motorcycle accident. Yet he is still strong and muscular because he still does as much physical therapy exercise as he can manage in spite of the pain.

In a flimsy, molded-plastic chair, Nick sits with his powerful blue-jeaned legs stretched out in front of him, his painful right shoulder hitched up even nearer to his ear than usual, his arms folded across his navy t-shirt. In this position, he has generated a "no trespassing" zone around himself: the chairs on either side of him are vacant.

A small woman and a wiry young man walk into the room. They're Nick's special buddies, Michelle and Carlos. The three are so close they've been nicknamed the "three musketeers."

Michelle grins at Nick and says, "Hi, Smiley," as she and Carlos cut through the middle of the group and slip into the two empty chairs.

As often happens in the presence of safe people, Nick's mood and manner shift dramatically. He says, "It's a good thing you got here, Michelle, after you talked me into coming. I'm only here tonight because of you and what you did in this group last week. Telling us about your father; that took guts."

"Yeah," Michelle says, "It was pretty bad last week, but now I'm glad I worked on it. . . .Tonight's your turn, Nick. You've got to talk."

The group begins. Sitting between Carlos and Michelle, Nick gradually tells his story through a role play. He turns to Jason, whom he trusts deeply, and asks, "Will you role play the part of the physician I met with this afternoon?"

Jason says, "Yes, I'll role play that physician for you."

Following Nick's directions, Jason says the physician's triggering words: "I'm sorry, Nick. No tissue damage showed up on the tests. You'll have more success with the biofeedback, physical therapy, and relaxation training than with the medical procedure you wanted."

Then Jason pretends to close a medical chart and set it aside, signaling that the meeting is over.

Nick turns to the group and says, "That doctor just closed my file, and then it was like I was gone, even while I sat there. I wasn't even a person. He looked at me like I was a file cabinet. A waste basket."

Then turning to Jason, who's still role playing the physician, Nick says, "Make your eyes go blank."

Jason seems to know what this means. He slightly curls his upper lip, raises his eyebrows, and lowers his eyelids. He briefly glances at Nick; then, seeming to pull window shades down over his eyes, he turns away.

Something about the blank expression in those eyes. The indifferent look on that face. . . .It reminds Nick of bad times with his father.

Feeling safe with this group of people he's come to trust, Nick tells about his father. From the time Nick was a little boy, he'd been physically abused by his father.

"Dad did the best he could," says Nick. "I know what alcohol can do. My dad would often get drunk and rant and rave, banging doors and yelling back at the TV. When I cringed or whimpered, he would sometimes just look at me with contempt, then turn away from me like I didn't exist.

"But sometimes he'd come at me, his eyes blazing, neck muscles bulging. He'd push his big face up against mine and bellow, 'No son of mine's a sissy!' And sometimes he wouldn't stop at just yelling. I remember once when he had to take me to the hospital, he hissed at me, 'You tell that emergency room doc you fell while you were playing, if you know what's good for you.'

"He'd yell at me or hit me or 'X' me out of existence. I couldn't do anything to make it right. If I cried, I could get hit. If I stood up to him, I could get hit.

"And even worse than getting hit was knowing that he didn't care how I felt. It didn't matter to him at all. I didn't matter. That was the worst part. All that mattered was the booze. I learned to harden myself, stuff my feelings down, even if I felt like crying inside."

Stuffing down and holding back tears and rage uses a lot of muscles in the upper body, just where Nick was injured in his accident. In spite of himself, Nick winces as the tightening muscles increase his pain. "I just locked it all up inside. I wouldn't give him the satisfaction of seeing I cared."

"You hid your caring," says Michelle softly, "but you still cared."

Indeed, Nick still cared. He remembers one time he cared, after his father sobered up and came to Nick with remorse in his deep brown eyes, pleading with Nick to forgive him. As Nick begins to tell what happened, he asks Jason to shift from the role of the physician to the role of Nick's father, pleading, "Nicky, just tell me what I can do to make it up to you, and I'll do it."

Of course, Nicky wanted his father to stop drinking, to stop beating him, to just love him. Yet, as his childhood story unfolds, he remembers longing for one special thing from his father: "Come watch me pitch for the Wildcats," says a slightly higher, smaller voice than we are used to hearing from Nick. Little Nicky wanted his dad in the bleachers, cheering him on, watching him pitch. He wanted to see his father's brown eyes shine with pride and hear his deep voice say, "That's my boy!"

Nick's own brown eyes fill up as he relives what actually happened that day at the ball park. "I thought those headlights were his green Ford pulling up at the corner. But a lady got out and went into the convenience store. After the seventh inning, the ice-cream truck left. Then I knew he wasn't coming."

Nick's deep voice cracks, "Dad said he'd come today." It's as though we travel back twenty-five years and watch a little boy's heart break. "He would've been proud of me. I'm a really good pitcher. But now he's drunk again, and he's not here. I don't care if he hits me. I don't care what happens. He *promised* me, and now he's not here. He just doesn't care."

HONOR THE DISTRESS, NOT THE TRAUMA

Nick's story illustrates several things. First, obvious physical trauma and naCCT often occur together.

Second, when they *do* occur together, the obvious physical traumas are so bad that the subtle naCCTs seem too trivial to get upset over. Trips to the emergency room are obviously traumatic. By comparison, what's a little thing like a moment of inattention or a no-show at a ball game?

So the subtle non-physical trauma is hidden, and the incidents that cause it are labeled "nothing to get upset about." In this way, psychological naCCTs like Nick's can get hidden by the glare of horrifying physical abuse.

"People focus a lot nowadays on the abuse. What happened? What did this person actually do to you?" says mental health clinic director Dr. Lauren Slater. A survivor of both overt physical abuse and intangible trauma, Dr. Slater knows first hand the devastation of emotional pain. She reveals in her 1996 memoir *Welcome to My Country* how she grew up terrified in one of Boston's loveliest suburbs:

As a child whose passive father failed to protect her from her mother's rage, Lauren Slater got socked, punched, dragged by the hair "and all that stuff." Yet, when she reflects on why she had to be hospitalized five times for bingeing and purging down to eighty-eight pounds and for compulsively cutting her arms with a razor, she doesn't point to the physical abuse. Instead, she says, "What really stands out in my mind is the quality of being humiliated, verbally, over and over and over again."[16]

Nick had faced much of his father's alcoholism in his Alcoholics Anonymous meetings. He was wise to the ways of alcohol from his own experience with drinking. He had received support for grieving his father's unpredictable physically-abusive outbursts. But until tonight, a piece of the puzzle hadn't been faced. That missing piece was the profoundly *traumatic* impact of his father's chronic neglect, indifference, and emotional abandonment.

In the group, Nick's fellow sufferers respond to his story with compassion, the true compassion that's a spontaneous response of the heart to suffering:

Nobody says much. Just "Yeah" and "That sucks." Wise through their own pain and healing work, and sensitized by their own struggles to get validation for their pain, they know that Nick's emotional trauma deserves as much compassionate validation as the violence he suffered from his father. So they sit quietly with Nick and offer him the simple attention and loving kindness that allow him to feel the full force of his grief.

During the silence that follows Nick's work, I meditate on the undeniably traumatic nature of emotional pain.

Before I had the concept of naCCT to help me dignify the profound distress of intangibly-caused traumas, I tended to make sharp distinctions between physical pain (terrible) and emotional pain (unpleasant). The people in the pain program taught me that wasn't true.

After telling a hair-raising story of physical trauma and blatant abuse, a patient would sometimes say, as Nick had just said, that the accompanying emotional pain was "even worse."

On several occasions in past groups, I had asked if any of the patients would rather face a surgical cure than work in the group on their emotional pain. Each time, I had been shocked to see that most patients' hands went up. "Maybe I'm shocked because of my inordinate dread of surgery and physical pain," I'd thought, "Or maybe I need to get their message that facing emotional pain is really seriously bad."

I continued to make sharp distinctions between physical pain and emotional pain. Then one day after group, a man with intense back pain and a blatantly traumatic childhood came over to me and said, "Some of us patients were wondering: Have you ever had chronic pain?"

Feeling guilty, alien, ashamed of the good luck that protected me from physical pain like his, I did a classic psychotherapist's "answer- a- question- with- a- question" dodge: I asked him, "Why do you ask?" Then I braced myself to hear him answer, "Because you have no right to presume to understand us and help us if you haven't been through what we've been through.".

Instead, he answered, "You understand us. We wondered if it's because you've had chronic pain yourself."

I was startled. And I was so touched by his "You understand us" statement that I blurted out the simple truth: "I've had chronic emotional pain."

He smiled knowingly, nodded, and said, "*That's* why you understand us."

Like me, many naCCT survivors resonate with survivors of blatant trauma. No surprise. The dramatic outer events differ greatly; but the inside distress is so similar: the traumatic state, the terror, the helplessness, the long-lasting scars.

Back in the group, the quiet meditative mood runs its course. Nick stands up. "I want a 'Do Over,'" he says. "A little honest make-believe like we did for you last week, Michelle."

Nick turns to Carlos, "Will you role play an Ideal Father for me? Stay sober and watch me pitch."

Carlos, of course, can't wait to play that part. He jumps out of his seat and says, "I'm your friend in real life, and I'm happy to role play your Ideal Father. Can I improvise?"

"Sure," I say, a little nervously because we don't usually improvise: it's too risky. But an intuition tells me to let this one happen because Nick and Carlos are so attuned to each other. "Go for it."

"I'm so proud of you," says Carlos as Ideal Father, buddy-punching Nick on his good arm, then flinging his arms around him. "You did great! Of course I came. You're much more important to me than any booze could ever be."

Nick responds, "You saw me?"

"I was over there by the bleachers, and I saw you," replies Ideal Father. "I saw that fabulous strike out at the end of the eighth inning, that's 'Most Valuable Player' stuff. You must be feeling great right about now."

Nick is silent, letting the scene sink in and do its healing work.

Carlos, as Ideal Father, puts his hand on Nick's shoulder and asks, "How's that pitching arm? It got quite a workout. We'll have to take care of it. Maybe a little ice for it when we get home."

I, Ricia, think to myself, "I couldn't nag him about using ice, but a fellow sufferer from chronic pain can, and he'll listen."

Ideal Father continues, "I see your teammates and the coach are all giving you the Most Valuable Player treatment. You worked hard for this. It was great to watch you, son."

Both men are into the role play now, having a great time.

Michelle, meanwhile, can hardly contain herself. She jumps up and asks Nick, "Can I role play your Ideal Mother?"

"And how about some Ideal Teammates?" some other group members call out, eager to provide Nick with an experience he only dreamed of as a child.

Nick grins as Michelle and the rest of the group are already on their feet.

Then Nick turns to Jason, "Role play my Ideal Coach. I want you to meet my folks."

Jason doesn't miss a beat. As Ideal Coach, he turns to Ideal Father and says, "You must be Nicky's dad. Great to meet you. Nicky won the game for us today."

A few moist eyes can be seen in the room. Everyone has spontaneously joined in the celebratory role plays, cheering for Nick, playing the parts of team members.

Nick himself is quiet, getting used to the real magic of this loving, healing make believe, his whole being recalibrating and taking it all in.

"Hey!" he says, "My pitching arm could use a little ice."

It's a make-believe love fest. And the healing it provides is "for real."

Tomorrow, when I arrive at the pain program, Nick will probably still be there, not out drinking. He'll probably be calmer, his pain level will probably have gone down, he'll be in possession of another piece of his real life story, and he'll make more sense to himself.

JASON'S STORY: "I KEEP FORGETTING I HAVE A GOOD REASON TO BE UPSET."

On this high note, the group ends. Jason and I retreat to the tiny staff room and debrief about the group: what happened for the patients. . . .and for us.

"Playing that part for Nick helped me with my own stuff," Jason says, "The patients didn't laugh at Nick. They didn't say, 'Come on, that's nothing to be upset about' or 'You're just taking yourself too seriously.' They were really kind to him, the way they took his emotional pain so seriously. Respected him for showing it. And look at how happy they all were for him at the end. The love in that room.

"And role playing that doctor helped *me*. Seeing how it all started with that doctor's dismissive look, and the way he turned away, setting Nick aside. How that triggered an emotional flashback for Nick."

Jason starts making jagged doodles on a page of nursing notes as he talks: "I *know* about flashbacks. But I'm blindsided by them when they happen to me in the midst of my daily life.

"You know how upset I've been about my supervisor, Chief Jones," he says. "Well, thanks to Nick I got the whole picture of what was really getting to me about him. And I feel like a jerk for getting blindsided *again*.

"When Nick asked me to make my eyes go blank, I knew just how to do it because I watched my father blank his eyes out like that. Like he pulled a window shade down in front of his eyes and I became invisible."

Jason had told me about his dad, about his job at the factory where he was proud of being Union Steward. There were great benefits, including a scholarship to school for Jason. I've heard about the good community of other people active in the union, how some of the families would all go on picnics together. In the summer when the factory closed down, they would all go for their two weeks of vacation together.

Jason had also told me that his dad was "really needy" because he hadn't gotten much attention as a boy, but he covered over the neediness by being outgoing and "the life of the party." In this community, Jason's dad was a leader, even somewhat charismatic. Other kids thought Jason was lucky to have him for a dad.

But Jason's dad looked different from Jason's point of view.

Jason continues, "In his warm, fun-loving way, my dad was really pretty narcissistic. Sometimes he just wouldn't stop. When I was really little, he'd sing and make funny noises and funny faces; I remember how he'd wiggle my toes and blow bubbles with his lips on my stomach. People thought he was such a good loving dad, but sometimes it made me frantic.

"A part of me would be screaming, '*Make him stop!*' even while I was giggling and laughing and sort of shrieking with delight.

"Still, he was my main, well, my *only* source of physical play and delight because mom only had eyes for him, the star of the family. And he would go cold if I didn't give him the attention he wanted — and God forbid if I asked for some attention for myself."

Jason's doodles are getting smaller and tighter. "At parties Dad used to do parodies of popular songs, and if I joined in at his invitation, that was great. I could add to his glory, and even get to bask in the sunshine of his glory myself. I had to be talented, but not too talented. Not talented enough to overshadow him.

"Once I put together a bunch of parodies of TV commercials and sang them at a union picnic. Everyone was eating watermelon and spitting out the seeds. I started with the toothpaste commercial. People stopped spitting out the seeds, stopped eating the watermelon and started grinning, then laughing. They thought it was funny and I was good.

"Probably no one else there even noticed how Dad hurt me, but I'll never forget the hostile look in his eyes when I finished, and he said in this flat, dull voice, 'That's very nice, Jason.'

"Then he turned to my best friend and tousled his hair. He picked my little sister up and sat her on his knee. He could 'X' me out just like that, so subtly no one could notice.

"To everyone else, he was still perfectly charming. He started doing one of his magic tricks, taking a quarter out from behind my friend's ear, making it disappear behind my sister's ear. Soon every body was mesmerized by him again, and I was just standing there, dizzy, feeling like an invisible idiot."

For a few minutes, the only sounds are the scratching of Jason's pen and the ticking of the big wall clock. Then Jason continues, "The way Chief Jones doesn't acknowledge my comments in team meetings and then gets really enthusiastic about what the team know-it-all spews forth reminds me of that day at the picnic. Jones reminds me of my father. The way everyone thinks he's so great reminds me of my dad. The way we still call him 'Chief Jones,' even though he's no longer the chief of anything, reminds me of my dad.

"And most especially, the way Jones can sometimes 'X' me out reminds me of my dad.

"Jones and my dad got crisscrossed in my mind, just like Nick's father and the physician got crisscrossed in Nick's mind this afternoon. I should have recognized that."

"Where my dad was deft, had magic hands, Jones' magic derives from his brilliant mind and his way with words. But it's the same pattern of 'Don't top me or I'll "X" you right out of existence.'"

Jason stops doodling and throws down the pen. "How many times do I have to go through this? Of course, Chief Jones' boundless need for admiration reminds me of my dad. I'm not an idiot. I'm in therapy. But every time I remember how Dad was — and how I've gotten immobilized by someone who reminds me of him — it's like a revelation to me.

"I thought I dealt with all this, but here I am, back in the same place again, making the same discovery I made last week, last month. Still surprised to discover I have a good reason to be upset. I guess I have to accept that I still have a ways to go in my healing."

WORSE THAN BEING HIT?

And as for me? Like Jason, I had been impacted by Nick's work. For me, the personal impact came from hearing Nick say that knowing his father didn't care how he felt was worse than being hit.

I ask Jason, "When Nick said that was worse than being hit, worse than the beatings. . . .Do you think that's so?"

"I heard him say it," Jason says. "Why would he say it if he didn't feel it was true?"

"Do you think it's true?" I ask. "I wasn't hit."

"Neither was I, not hit. Just beaten down into a good audience and good supporting cast member. I don't know about the comparison with being physically hit, but I know it was awful. I need a Do Over. A love fest like Nick's, celebrating his pitching.

"It's hard for me to imagine a father genuinely happy for my success. I wouldn't mind being in a group where I could ask for a Do Over like Nick did. It would probably do me a world of good. Just to experience having a dad like that, so proud of me, happy for me, helping me enjoy being the Most Valuable Player for the night. Whew! What would be your Do Over?"

I think for a minute. Then I pull out one of the innumerable validating notecards I carry around in my handbag. "Hmm. . . . Invalidation is very triggering for me. I'm always collecting validating statements, like this one from a therapist named Robert Subby, listen: 'I shouldn't feel this way,' he told himself when he was upset. 'After all, I have it plenty good in comparison to a lot of other folks I know.'[17]

"My Do Over would probably be having someone big and authoritative look me right in the eye and say directly to me, 'You aren't just a little belly-acher, making a mountain out of a molehill. Even if you were never hit, you have a good reason to be upset. What some people insist is only a molehill really *is* a mountain.'"

COMING UP NEXT

People's stories influence other people. Notice how Michelle's story from the previous week influenced Nick. Nick's story influenced me and Jason. All their stories and interactions influenced my conviction that naCCT is real and merits serious resources for its healing and prevention.

In the next chapter, we'll explore how your healing can be positively influenced by the stories in this chapter. How can you use these stories to help yourself heal?

NOTES

[15] James Dahlhamer et al., "Prevalence of Chronic Pain and High-impact Chronic Pain among Adults –United States, 2016," *Weekly, Sept. 14, 2018 / 67(36); 1001-1006*, https://www.cdc.gov/mmwr/volumes/67/wr/mm6736a2.htm#:~:text=An%20estimated%2020.4%25%20(50.0%20milli on,adults%2C%20adults%20living%20in%20poverty%2C

[16] Lauren Slater, *Welcome to My Country* (New York: Random House, 1996) 85, 90

[17] Robert Subby, *Lost in the Shuffle: The Co-dependent Reality* (Deerfield Beach, FL: Health Communications, Inc., 1987), vii.

CHAPTER 9

COPE WITH PEOPLE-TRIGGERS

To live well with people, cope well with People-Triggers. As we continue to heal the attachment-based wound of naCCT, we turn to coping with People-Triggers. Let's use the stories of Nick and Jason and the group to accomplish that goal.

Their stories illustrate how people can trigger us: Jason was triggered by his team leader's snub; Nick, by the doctor's dismissal. Both Nick and Jason had People-Triggers from the "Interpersonal Absence" category: "Someone turning away." The trigger took the form of a gesture and facial expression that signified being set aside, forgotten, snubbed, dismissed, put down, rejected, or abandoned. Just not mattering at all.

That gesture or facial expression might hurt an adult, but to a dependent child it conveyed the terrifying message: "You don't matter; I 'X' you out, annihilate you; you are nothing to me."

This "You don't matter; I 'X' you out" gesture could be the "main character" of the story, the star of the show. Four relationship vignettes revolved around that gesture: Nick's and his doctor's; young Nick's and his father's; Jason's and Chief Jones'; and young Jason's and his father's.

The gesture itself is so powerful that it can overshadow and even misrepresent the real people who are making the gesture. We weren't there when Nick's physician closed Nick's file or when Jason's Chief Jones led the team meeting. For all we know, Nick's physician could really have been a nice guy, feeling awkward and sad to be delivering unwanted news, and Chief Jones could really have been bending over backwards to avoid showing favoritism toward Jason. We saw Nick's physician and Chief Jones through Nick's and Jason's eyes, and their eyes saw triggering gestures.

Let's look more closely at what happened for Jason.

JASON

[Note: We use Jason's narrative of what happened, and we give attention to what is going on inside him. At this point, the focus is not on working with the external relationship between Jason and Chief Jones. Rather than standing back and questioning the reliability of Jason's narrative or the validity of his interpretations, we come alongside Jason and his inner experience with the triggering gesture.]

Recall how subtle and hard to identify these naCCT People-Triggers are. At first, Jason didn't even realize he'd been triggered.

He didn't say, "I've been triggered." Instead, he said he couldn't sleep because Chief Jones wasn't responding to his contributions in team meetings. He went on to say that he thought Jones now regretted choosing Jason for the team and that perhaps he, Jason, wasn't suited for his chosen career after all.

Jason was blindsided by a People-Trigger.

JASON'S PEOPLE-TRIGGER AND DISTRESS RESPONSE STATEMENT

As the events of that evening's group unfolded, Jason understood he'd been People-Triggered by Chief Jones' lack of response. Jason's past trauma state, past traumatic events, and past feelings and thoughts of danger had overtaken his present reality.

Jason might complete the People-Trigger and Distress Response Statement this way:

"When I encounter this People-Trigger [my contribution dismissed by a man in authority whose approval I feel that I need],

my Distress Response tends to be [mental stewing and confusion; sleeplessness]."

When you're frazzled, using these statements can feel magical. Something about putting into words the way the various elements of the cPTSD from naCCT experience relate to each other makes it possible to think more clearly and calmly about it all.

These statements function as templates that provide structure. They can guide you to focus on important elements of the situation and understand how those elements relate to each other.

These statements also provide order, and many people find order calming. Indeed, order can prevent panic.

JASON'S BETTER OPTION STATEMENT

Jason didn't stay stuck in nights of sleepless stewing; he talked it over with me instead. So, to Jason's People-Trigger and Distress Response Statement, we'll add a Better Option Statement, a "What- I'm- Going-to- Do- About- That" Statement:

"and I might be better off if instead I [talk about it with someone]."

JASON'S "REMEMBER-THE-NACCT-BACKSTORY" WORK

As Jason's story unfolded, you may have noticed that he used elements from all three components of the classic trauma-recovery model. That's because real life recovery isn't strictly step-wise. The healing work tends to jump around from one healing component to another. Because the memories are always there and something in life can always trigger a flashback to them, remembering naCCT backstory experiences and inner states is to be expected.

That triggering "You don't matter; I 'X' you out" gesture brought Jason's own naCCT backstory into his consciousness. He recognized the "going blank" look Nick asked him to role play because his own father had used it: After young Jason's successful performance, his father had "X"ed him out with that look.

But the single incident Jason remembered hadn't caused his childhood naCCT all by itself. That single incident typified a prolonged, repetitive, chronic naCCT *pattern* of incidents in his Lifeline Relationship with his father.

JASON'S NACCT RESONANCE STATEMENT

Jason might say,

> *"These are the naCCTs that I resonate with:*
>
> *NaCCT of Omission: no praise, no sympathetic joy for my successful performance, no words like 'I'm so proud of you.' And no remorse or repair of the rupture to our relationship;*
>
> *NaCCT of Unwholesome Closeness: my dad using me as a support for his performance, but keeping me from becoming an independent "star performer" in my own right; gave me the message: 'Don't grow up'*
>
> *NaCCT of Hidden Hostility: withholding praise and sympathetic joy, inflicting social pain."*

JASON'S "VICARIOUS HEALING"

You may have heard of "vicarious trauma," which happens when an empathetic listener experiences trauma while listening to another person's traumatic experience.

Happily, "vicarious healing" also happens. I believe we often experience vicarious healing: for instance, when we get choked up at the end of a touching movie when the troubles are resolved and the important relationships are healed.

Jason experienced some vicarious healing thanks to witnessing and being a part of Nick's healing work. After vicariously experiencing Nick's healing, Jason was able to recognize that he'd been triggered. And he was inspired to imagine his own Do-Over, in which he performed successfully and his Ideal Father expressed pride and empathic joy on Jason's behalf.

JASON'S "MAKES SENSE" STATEMENT

In both his professional work and his personal growth, Jason was an experienced traveler in the realm of cPTSD. He could say, "Given all those naCCTs I resonate with, it makes sense that I would be triggered when my team leader ignores my contributions."

Yet, even though he "knows in his head" that his upset makes sense and that he's taking steps to handle it, Jason sometimes "forgets" what he knows, and therefore blames and shames himself for getting upset.

JASON'S "RECONNECT AND RE-ENGAGE" WORK

Jason also worked with the "Reconnect and Re-engage" component. He's done a lot of healing work. In spite of obstacles and setbacks, he's made many positive changes, so he connects differently now. Three new ways he connects stand out:

First, Jason talks with me about his problems: how he feels unimportant and without value and thinks that his professional contributions to his team weren't valued or valuable either. He doesn't have to hide his feelings or keep them all bottled up when talking with me.

Second, he publicly uses his performance and acting skills — the very skills his father had undermined — to help Nick tell his story to the group. He portrays with his own body the dismissive, "X"-ing him out expression and gesture that had triggered Nick.

Jason's hurtful experience with his father enables him to sensitively portray indifferent dismissal for Nick to respond to in the role play.

Third, by confronting his memories and telling me about them, he removes some of the cPTSD blocks to accurately assessing and effectively responding to his present situation with his team and Chief Jones. Jason may go on to reconnect and re-engage with Chief Jones and the rest of the treatment team in better ways after his evening's work.

AND NOW LET'S TURN TO NICK

While Jason takes a common route: talking to a friend about his present problem and naCCT backstory, Nick does more uncommon, structured work assisted by a therapist and a whole healing community. The hospital environment provided stability for Nick to safely do potentially de-stabilizing "Remember and Grieve" work.

NICK'S PEOPLE-TRIGGER AND DISTRESS RESPONSE STATEMENT

Nick's People-Trigger: Hoping for pain relief through surgery, Nick met with his physician who informed him that test results indicated surgery would not help. The physician then closed Nick's file, set it aside, and ended their meeting.

Nick could have completed the sentence about his People-Trigger and Distress Response this way:

"When I encounter this People-Trigger [someone setting me aside],

my Distress Response tends to be [getting hostile, giving up, using alcohol]."

Again, we weren't at Nick's meeting with his physician. We don't know how reliable Nick's account is. However, that relationship is not our focus at this point. In the future, Nick may choose to plan for another conversation with his physician. Right now, the focus is on coping with the *trigger*.

NICK'S BETTER OPTION STATEMENT

We know that Nick's buddy Michelle and at least one nurse made it clear to Nick that he had a better option than getting hostile, giving up, and using alcohol. Here's Nick's Better Option, "Here's- what- I- can- do- about- that" Statement:

and I might be better off if I [stayed in the program and went to this group with my buddies]."

Nick chose to act on his Better Option.

NICK'S "REMEMBER AND GRIEVE" BACKSTORY WORK

Nick's "Remember and Grieve" backstory work illustrates how people can help us heal.

His backstory work had two parts. The first part was remembering and grieving his early naCCT.

The physician's triggering gesture read as "Danger!" to Nick. Following that trigger led Nick back to his relationship with his father.

The painful process of waiting for his father and finally realizing his father wasn't going to come also meant "Danger!" to Nick. Relationship danger. His father didn't do what he promised to do. His father "set Nick aside" when he failed to show up at the game.

Nick's NaCCT Resonance Statement might be:

"I related to the naCCT called [Trauma of Omission: Set aside, dismissed, forgotten]."

Note that being an naCCT of Omission, Nick's experience has another insidious, almost paradoxical, element: NaCCTs of Omission are traumas caused by *nothing*. Nick observed the doctor setting his folder aside, whereas there was nothing to observe when his father broke his promise to come watch Nick pitch. Where Nick had expected and joyfully anticipated his father would be — physically at the ball park, watching Nick pitch, feeling proud, cheering him on —there was only emptiness.

When we know Nick's naCCT of Omission backstory, his sensitivity to being set aside makes sense.

The second part of Nick's backstory work was the Do-Over. The whole therapy group spontaneously created an ideal society, bringing team and family together, helping Nick grow up and find a valued place for himself in the world.

In the role play, Nick's whole being got a new "outside the box" experience. Instead of the usual unsatisfied longing and shame-filled loneliness of feeling forgotten, he got to experience the safety and joy of a promise kept, of a father whose promise: "I'll be there" meant he really would be there. Nick's whole being got the opportunity to experience a responsive, reliable Ideal Father whose actions showed that he cared.

NICK'S "RECONNECT AND RE-ENGAGE" WORK

Because Nick decided to stay in the program and work in the therapy group, he didn't have to pick up alcohol again. Instead, he was able to accept help and profound caring from the people in his group. He was even able to show them what had happened to him as a child, to let tears come into his eyes, and to imagine and act out a Do-Over in the center of a warm, attentive group that loved him, cheered for him, valued him, and celebrated with him. This was a major reconnection "first" for Nick.

For Nick, as for Jason, reconnecting in this new way lays down new neural pathways that can be used in the future. Taking in these new experiences, remembering them, and letting them reshape beliefs and behavior, builds a playlist of positive experiences to add to their inner memory libraries and blazes trails for future well-being.

❦

NOW YOUR TURN

As you read Nick's story, did you have moments when you found yourself thinking: "I'd like to experience that"?

Can you be inspired by how Nick was helped by people? Can you apply some of what you noticed about Nick's healing environment to your own life?

You might protest, "But Nick was in a live-in hospital program. He didn't have to take care of family and work responsibilities. He didn't even have to drive home after his session. That's nothing like my life. It was like Nick was on a retreat."

And you would be right. Nick *was* on a structured healing retreat.

But it wasn't the prepared meals or the fresh bed linens that helped Nick take that big step toward healing the aftereffects of his childhood trauma. What helped Nick was the *people*.

First, the hospital staff was comprised of concerned and capable professional helpers. Nick's recovery was important to them: He was urged to go to activities and appointments. No one called him "self indulgent" for taking care of himself this way. In fact, he was praised for participating, and if he didn't participate, he was firmly confronted for "failing to utilize the program."

Can you do for yourself some of what Nick's professional helpers did for him? Could your Inner Helper — and your Inner Helper's Helpers — provide some of this care for you?

Second, while the people on staff were important for Nick's healing, the most important people were his fellow patients: Nick wasn't "the only one" with his chronic pain problem. He had a whole live-in "affinity group," a community of people who cared, and who could relate to him and his situation.

WHAT PEOPLE-HELP NICK GOT THAT YOU CAN GET TOO

Here's a list of People-Help Nick received in his treatment program. As you read through this list, let yourself wonder whether that type of help could be available to you. (You may even notice that you're getting some of this People-Help from me through this book. I hope so.)

- People who understood about triggers, how a "trivial thing" could set off a whole cascade of physical, social, and emotional disturbances that push coping resources to the breaking point.
- People on his wavelength who understood what he was up against.
- People helping him *make sense* of what he was up against.
- People who believed his pain was real, even though there was no blatant overt cause or observable disability.
- People who understood how he'd had to protect himself, his body, his heart. And didn't shame him for it.
- People who helped him remember the connection between his present troubles and the past events that give him a perfect right to be upset.
- People who believed that emotional trauma deserves as much as much compassionate validation as the violence he suffered from his father.

BEYOND THE POWER OF THIS BOOK

Nick also got help that a book can't provide. Fortunately you too can get help a book can't provide. You can get help from:

- You, yourself
- People or beings you've put in your Safe Space Imagery
- Other people, anyone else who might pop into your mind.

As you read through the following list of the help Nick received directly from people, let yourself think, "Maybe I can get this kind of help too."

- People to help him when he got People-Triggered. He didn't have to deal with his People-Triggers all on his own.
- People who accepted the existence and expression of his difficult, negative feelings.
- People to help him tell his trauma story and work with it.
- People who dared to come close to him when he was upset, angry, or unreasonable.
- People who respected his pain and still pushed him to "keep on keeping on," even when it was really tough, and he wanted to quit.

- People like Michelle who served as a role model for him, inspired him, and let him see how to take the next brave step, as well as the healing results of taking that step.
- People who could be there when he needed "to reach for a hug instead of a drug."
- People to talk to after the group when his pain level might temporarily go up.
- People to sit quietly with him and offer him the simple attention and loving kindness that allow him to feel the full force of his grief.
- People who were happy for him when he made progress, when things went well for him.

WE NEED A SOCIAL CONTEXT FOR OUR HEALING FROM NACCT-SOURCED CPTSD

One of the many gifts Nick received from the people in his program calls for special attention here: Nick got a *social context* for his healing. The attitudes toward chronic pain in the program were different from the attitudes he encountered in the world outside the program.

Why is a social context for our healing so crucial? Because we humans are social creatures. This means we need to belong to a group of people who believe our problem is real and that healing it matters.

We need social context in the form of affinity groups, social action groups, and organizations that take the problem of naCCT seriously.

The chronic pain program provided a social context for healing chronic pain. Similarly, Alcoholics Anonymous created a social context for healing alcoholism. Even the existence of hashtags #Me Too and #Black Lives Matter indicates there are emerging social contexts for addressing those social wrongs.

Social context might provide support, practical help, information, validation, and/or language.

Social context can determine what problems we believe are legitimate and real. Having a social context provides refuge from invalidation and contempt, assures we "have a right to be upset" as well as "a right to heal."

PROGRESS TOWARD SOCIAL CONTEXT FOR HONORING CPTSD FROM NACCT

We need a stronger social context for addressing cPTSD from naCCT. Advances in both science and language offer some hope that we are progressing in that direction. We're getting data and we're getting a voice. Let's review some signs of progress in that direction:

Recent discoveries provide science-based legitimacy for taking naCCT very seriously:
- the necessity of attachment to a Lifeline Caregiver for both neurological and social development;
- the neurological overlap of physical and social pain; and
- the existence of the powerful Ventral Vagal Nerve Complex/ Social Engagement System that enables interpersonal connections.

This data from hard science confirming the importance of relationships contributes to the creation of a social context for healing cPTSD from naCCT.

Progress towards a social context is happening with our language too. Having words for things gives them a social context. Let's look at some of our new words:

Since 1980, we've had the name "PTSD, Post-Traumatic Stress Disorder." Since 1992, we've had the concept and name of "*complex* PTSD."

Having shared language protects us from social isolation, from feeling like "a freak from outer space or some kind of genetic mutation," as well as from feeling like "the only one." When we have common words, we're in a community where we all speak the same language.

Words and phrases for troubling phenomena related to naCCT have also been recently coined and are now widely used. For example, we can talk about "verbal abuse," "abandonment issues," and "emotional neglect." "Gaslighting" has become a term and concept used and understood in mainstream conversations.

Language does more than simply indicate that we *have* a social context. It also helps to *expand* the existing social context. Having new words and phrases makes it easier to give voice to new ideas, new discoveries, and new awareness. We can *talk* to each other and explore and heal together.

As you read this book, you can hold the secure thought that at the very least, you have the social context for healing provided by the group made up of you and me. You're part of this group: Me, writing. You, reading. This little group of the two of us is expanding the social context for healing cPTSD from naCCT.

Furthermore, by reading this book, by asking for it at bookstores and libraries, by using the words "intangible trauma" and the acronym naCCT, you contribute to creating a broader and deeper social context that will support your own healing and pave the way for others to heal.

MEANWHILE, WHAT TO DO WHEN PEOPLE-TRIGGERED?

What can naCCT survivors with complex PTSD do, if they don't want to be hermits, but find they get triggered by their interactions with other people?

Most people find it helps to have a plan in place to restore their equilibrium, to stay emotionally regulated. Some people's Inner Helpers really like having a streamlined, laser-like "What to do when" plan to follow, something like "If you have a fever of more than 103 degrees F (39.4 degrees C), call your physician." Those Inner Helpers might love a concise Self-Talk Script, a personal pocket-sized "diagnosis and treatment plan" like the one we'll formulate here.

Let's begin by defining your specific People-Trigger challenge using the expanded People-Trigger and Distress Statement: the one that includes a Better Option Statement.

"When I encounter this People-Trigger [_____],

my Distress Response tends to be [_____],

and I might be better off if instead I [_____]."

Your Better Option Statement can be phrased to suit you. Maybe one of the following works better for you:

- *"and a better alternative response would be [_____]."*
- *"and what I can do instead is: [_____]."*
- *"and I also have the option of [_____]."*
- *"and instead I can decide to [_____].*
- *"and what I'm going to do about that is [_____]."*

Let's look at some better options for what to do when People-Triggered.

OPTION #1: WHEN PEOPLE-TRIGGERED, "TAKE A BREAK"

In Nick's group, we had two helpful "Take a Break" policies you can adapt for yourself:

1. **Joke emergencies/ Humor Breaks:** Sometimes taking a humor break helps.

Some people are really funny, and sometimes our group had one of those really funny people as a member. When things were progressing along — deep, moving, real, disturbing but manageable — the funny person kept quiet. But when the tension level got really high, we called "Joke Emergency!" Then the funny person helped us relieve our tension with some side-splitting laughter.

You can certainly call a "Joke Emergency! Humor Break!" for yourself: Let the Internet provide humor for your joke emergencies. Keep light-hearted films and videos handy.

2. **Solitude/ Bathroom Breaks:** If the atmosphere, subject matter, or group interaction got too intense or triggering, a group member could quietly get up and leave the group at any time, no questions asked. They simply "took a bathroom break." When they felt ready to return to the group, they returned, still no questions asked.

Sometimes the stress of relating to other people is too much, and taking a break helps to cool off. Temporary separation from other people often provides relief.

Taking a break is especially helpful when you and another person are experiencing interlocking triggers, where your responses trigger each other in a very vicious cycle, like we saw with Nadia and Bruce or with Rosemary and Marilyn.

Here some naCCT survivors tell how they know it's time for them to take a break:

- Les uses a simple guide: "If I'm talking with someone, and I suddenly want a Coke, or a cigarette, or I get the urge to eat something sweet, I know I'm starting to sink, and that's a warning for me: Time to get out of Dodge."

- Sami says; "I need to learn that it's NOT SAFE for me to be around, or be close to, someone who isn't interested in my work and my activities. Always developing a new interest to match theirs could be a red flag of trouble for me. Another red flag is stopping my own work because I don't think it's as good as theirs, like when I dated a 'good' artist, and I stopped working on my own art altogether. That is a dangerous interpersonal place for my soul to be. No blame; it's just dangerous, and I need to get out of there."

- Paul says, "For me, being around people who mismanage their lives and then have a crisis is dangerous for me. At least until I learn to say 'No' and really believe that another person's inability to manage their affairs responsibly does not constitute a crisis for me. Right now, I get so pulled in to helping the other person that I put myself aside. That isn't safe for me."

- Ashley's tip-off is what she calls "Urgent Fixing." She says, "In my flashback state, I used to rush right into a triggering situation and urgently try to fix the problem. Now I stop myself at the first sign of my 'Urgent Fixing' behavior. I concentrate on staying safe and stable myself, intentionally calling on my Inner Helper to devote helping attention to myself."

OPTION #2: REVISE YOUR SAFE SPACE IMAGERY TO INCLUDE PEOPLE FACTORS

Jenna Lee tweaked and updated her Safe Space Imagery to suit a life with relationships in it. She says, "My Safe Space imagery is a work in progress: I made some additions for dealing with my abandonment issues. For example, I get magnetized by indifferent people, so I installed a 'Magical

De-magnetizing Device.' And also a 'Magical Un-Adhesive Spray,' some 'UnGlue,' and a 'De-Velcro-izer.'

"A blank stare exerts powerful suction on me, sucks me right in to that relationship, trying to get a response. So I also imagine a handheld tool that disempowers all suction. It's my 'Suction Extinguisher.' It hangs on the wall like a fire extinguisher. In case of emergency. That is the deepest threat I need protection from.

"I'm also thinking of adding some helpers who can operate the 'Magical de-magnetizing Device' and the 'Suction Extinguisher' when I'm too triggered to do it myself."

Do you want to redesign your Safe Space Imagery now, to make it work even better as you include relationships with people in your challenges to be met and delights to be enjoyed?

Do you want to include some images of absolutely reliable Ideal People in your Safe Space Imagery? Do it!

PEOPLE-HELPERS IN SAFE SPACE IMAGERY

Here are some other people-related elements that survivors have included in their Safe Space Imagery:

- "I have included in my Safe Space some imaginary ideal caregivers: Ideal Mother and Ideal Father. I haven't yet decided whether I want them to always be there, or to always come whenever I call them."

- "My safe space has a lot of helpful protectors, screeners, and evaluators, who sort, sift, and decide who comes in (if anyone at all!), how far they come in, and when they have to back off. They are sort of watchdogs, guardians, watching for things I don't yet know enough to watch out for myself. Assertiveness trainers. Diplomats. Some logicians to screen out anything that doesn't make sense. Protectors to keep the hooks out of my brain, so I can safely relate to people without being gaslighted. Altogether, these imaginary protective team members function sort of like bodyguards for my mind."

- "The only 'people' in my mobile Safe Space Imagery are the helpful parts of myself: my Inner Helper and my Helper's Helper in the form of my inner guidance. I don't want anyone in there I can't control."

- "I have all the saints and guardian angels from my early religious training. A sort of manger scene, inspired by the nativity scenes of my childhood. . . there is the happy, adoring mother; the loving, strong, protective father; the warm animals and welcoming visitors; all of us protected by spiritual forces shining all around. I used the image that always came to me when I heard 'Silent Night.' Then I added some modern superheroes. And in the very deepest center of my safe space, I imagine myself safe as a baby in the womb of the great Mother."

OPTION #3: WHEN PEOPLE-TRIGGERED, USE SELF-TALK SCRIPTS

Here are three Self-Talk Scripts you can use for staying calm when you find yourself triggered by something someone does or fails to do:

YOUR SELF-TALK SCRIPT FOR DISTINGUISHING THEN FROM NOW

First, distinguish the present person whose behavior is triggering you from the traumatizing person in the past, using this statement: *[Present person] isn't [past person.]*

Jason might say: *"[My team leader] isn't [my father]."*
Nick might say: *"[That doctor] isn't [my father]."*
Jenna Lee might say: *"[My boyfriend] isn't [my parent.]"*
You, dear reader, might say: *"[My best friend] isn't [my mother.]"*

Then add that statement to this four-element statement for remembering you are safe in the here and now:

"Fortunately, the reality is that I may feel awful, but
- *At least [present person] isn't [past person.]*
- *I'm an adult, not a child.*
- *I'm in [present place] not [past place].*
- *It's [now], not [past time]."*

SELF-TALK SCRIPT FOR BELIEVING YOU MAKE SENSE

This Self-Talk Script acknowledges the very real possibility that your trigger and the naCCT category (or categories) that you relate to are linked to each other.

"I related to the naCCT category of [naCCT category],

so it probably makes sense that I get distressed when [trigger]."

Jason, for example, might use the Self-Talk Script:

"I related to the naCCT category of [Trauma of Omission: no praise and sympathetic joy for my performance, my dad turning away from me after my successful performance]

so it probably makes sense that I get distressed when [my team leader ignores my contributions and leaves me out of discussions]."

Try creating your own Self-Talk Script for believing *you* make sense:

"I related to the naCCT category of [naCCT category],

so it probably makes sense that I get distressed when [trigger]."

It's useful to combine this Self-Talk Script for "Believing You Make Sense" with a heavy dose of the Magic of "Hmm. . . ." Really come alongside yourself with the assurance that, far from indicating your "defectiveness," the way your present troubles arose from your naCCT history makes perfect sense.

BUILD YOUR OWN SELF-TALK SCRIPT

You can build your own script for dealing with People-Triggers. Use any of the statements above, add any of the statements below and any others you've created to help yourself.

Mix and match the elements below to suit yourself:

- *"I can check in with my Inner Helper; sometimes just saying 'Uh, oh, I got triggered' helps."*

- *"I can concentrate on getting to some inner sense of safety and calm."*
- *"Being triggered is normal. It is distressing all right, but I can take the time to check out whether there really is any danger."*
- *"I'm so relieved I know about triggers and flashbacks."*
- *"I'll feel much better when this has passed."*
- *"I'm not broken. This is a natural response. I don't like it, but it's natural. I work just fine."*
- *"I can drop the danger."*
- *"Whew! I'm really lucky to have me on my side now."*
- *"I have a lot of resources for handling this situation, including my Safe Space Imagery and my Inner Helper."*
- *"I can always do something like take a bathroom break or 'remember a crucial appointment' and just get out of here."*
- *"I can take a cooling off period."*
- *"Of course these People-Triggers are trickier than the ones that came about from my own thoughts and feelings. They are trickier because they involve another person, and I can't control that other person like I can control myself."*
- *"It does help to remember that the more intimate my relationship is with my triggering person, or with the person this trigger reminds me of, the more intense my own triggering is naturally going to be."*
- *"These People-Triggers are clues, bread crumbs I can follow to my naCCT backstory."*

Does it make sense for you to write out your own Self-Talk Script? To email it to yourself? To carry it on your phone? Do whatever will help you have this calming script on hand whenever you need it.

OPTION #4: TURN TO REAL LIVE PEOPLE

And of course, other people aren't only triggering: They're also helpful. This is such a big deal that it gets its own chapter, coming up next.

CHAPTER 10

HELP FROM REAL PEOPLE

Turning to real people for help with People-Triggers is both complicated and well-worth pursuing, so let's go.

First, we need to acknowledge that help from real people in real life sometimes just happens. Or it happens in ways our own planning didn't anticipate. To illustrate, here's a step on my own recovery learning curve, showing how I got some unexpected People-Help when I was People-Triggered by my own mental images.

HOW HELP FROM REAL PEOPLE HAPPENS IN REAL LIFE

It happened for me when my car broke down.

Things didn't break down in the family I grew up in. We were careful. We kept the car well maintained: the gas tank always full, plenty of water and oil, engine purring along.

If anything more serious than spilt milk went wrong, my parents got distressed. If something of mine broke, or if I lost something, the smooth family functioning was disrupted. And that meant trouble. But my parents didn't yell, or blame, or criticize. Instead, their strained, patient helpfulness, combined with the fear in their eyes and the pained looks on their faces, conveyed that they were drained by the demands of the problem to be dealt with.

I carried this family attitude into my adult life. I could go from a smooth sailing mindset directly to catastrophic mode: Either everything was in order, or the world was quietly and absolutely coming to an end. This was especially the case when something broke down. My computer. Or my car. Especially my car.

One day I left my apartment, drove my old car out of its parking space, and felt it sputter and stop. Right in the middle of my busy street. A narrow, one-way street. My car wasn't moving. And no other car would have room to get around it.

I panicked. My Inner Helper was decommissioned. Any minute a car would come along, get stuck behind mine, and the world would come to an end.

I was flooded with worries. . . . about the *wrong* problem! Instead of figuring out how to get my car out of the middle of the street, my thoughts raced to self-condemnation: I had not maintained my car properly. I had bought an old clunker. "What's wrong with me that I can't buy a good car that never breaks down and blocks traffic?" I thought. "Everyone will hate me. And for good reason."

Fortunately, my decommissioned Inner Helper had help available. In my recovery, I'd been working on asking for help and had developed mutual aid relationships with people I could call. We "Emergency Helpers" assisted each other in turning crises into manageable challenges.

Abandoning my car, I ran back inside, up three flights of stairs, and called my Inner Helper's Emergency Helper on my only phone, the landline we used in those days.

When my Emergency Helper heard my panic, she reminded me of my real problem: the car in the road.

She also reminded me of a saying: "When a regular person's car breaks down, they call the road service tow truck; when a nervous person's car breaks down, they call the suicide hot line."

Maybe it was hearing my Emergency Helper's calm, normalizing humor, or maybe it was her reminder that tow trucks exist and they actually tow cars to repair shops. Whatever it was, my Inner Helper came back on line. I snapped out of my ineffectual, make-matters-worse panic and snapped back to reality, thinking "Realistically, no one will hate me for buying an old car that broke down, but they'll be really aggravated if they get stuck behind it."

I ran back outside, where indeed a car had gotten stuck behind mine. *Three* stuck cars, in fact. With drivers inside. Honking.

I mustered my courage, ran to the first of the stuck cars.

"I am so sorry," I said to the driver. "I panicked. My car stopped. It won't go."

I was lucky. The driver was so calm and helpful. Really understanding. I didn't have to call the suicide hotline.

He got out of his car. Two little kids also got out. They seemed happy enough, stretching their legs, running around, watching the novel proceedings: Their dad organized me and the people in the other stuck cars, and, all together, we pushed my car to an empty parking space. How often did kids get to watch that?

The family got back in their car, and as they drove off, the driver called out the open car window to me, "Don't panic, ask for help!"

I took in his words.

Not surprisingly, my old clunker conked out again. But this time, a new guardian angel on my shoulder whispered in my ear, "Don't panic. Ask for help."

My trigger was typical of real life: a mixture of a real problem — (a broken down car) — and a cPTSD problem — (a triggering mental image of my family members' distress and silent disapproval of me for having a car that broke down.)

And the People-Help I received was also a mixture: both planned-for help — (my mutual aid Emergency Helper relationships and phone numbers) — and unplanned help — (the help I received from a smart, generous stranger who not only solved my immediate car problem, but also served as my calm, level-headed teacher.)

So, help from other people sometimes happens. Let's now do what we can together in the way of planning how help from other people can happen in *your* life.

CLARIFY WHAT YOU WANT IN YOUR RELATIONSHIPS

In your real-life mutual relationships, you both give and receive help. However, for planning how to get People-Help for People-Triggers, set aside that mutuality for the time being, and bear the constructive discomfort of focusing on what *you* want.

Many naCCT survivors find that wanting others to provide something for them is a trigger in itself. Giving may be easy , whereas *taking* is loaded and therefore difficult. And forget about asking for help! Even *thinking* about it can be triggering. Asking. Receiving. Appreciating. Thanking. Using. All of these can be triggering.

Here's a list of what people typically want in relationships. Identify what you desire, need, and/or would benefit from receiving in your relationships.

Look back over your list of People-Triggers for help answering these questions: What did you want, hope for, or expect from that interaction that you didn't get? What did you get that you didn't want?

(I know it can seem dumb and redundant to actually write down your responses, and I know from experience that writing them down can help clarify your intentions when relating to your fellow people.)

What I want from someone now is:

- Just being in their presence, maybe in a coffee shop, store, or on public transportation
- Observing, not interacting, maybe in the audience at a lecture, movie, or concert.
- Casual relating, small talk, chit chat
- A shared project or activity
- A discussion of ideas
- Practical help
- Good advice and guidance
- Sharing deep feelings with me
- Talking about being triggered
- Just being there with me, witnessing and caring, while I'm expressing myself: maybe when I'm worrying, or ventilating, or ranting and raving, or crying
- Help solving a problem
- A hug
- Some sympathetic joy, being happy for me
- Fun
- Hearing someone say, "That sucks!"
- A companion in my healing work

In addition, because people are often subtly People-Triggered when they offer something to someone else and it's rejected, I want to call special attention to a powerful subtle want that needs to be noticed but is often overlooked:

- Did I want someone to want what I have to offer them, whether it was my presence, my sympathy, my advice, my practical help, or something else. Did I want to be in a relationship where I was able to give, to contribute, to be of service, to care, to love?

I encourage you to take the time to work with this delicate issue. And take pride in your attempts and in every step towards addressing what you want others to provide for you.

LIST OF POSSIBLE REAL-LIFE PEOPLE-HELPERS: WHO TO ASK?

And now, remembering that the combination of too much challenge and too few resources is what determines trauma, let's build up your people resources. We began this process with wondering how you could get for yourself some of what Nick got from the people in his program. Let's expand that process now.

Mull over people you know, have heard of, read about, or can watch on video. Imagine Ideal Mother and Ideal Father, spirit guides, role models, and more. Go online and do a little research into people and organizations that can help you.

Below is a list of possible people-resources for you, people who might provide what you desire, need, and would benefit from receiving. Completing this list is a significant on-going project, probably not one to be completed right now or in one sitting.

Here's the list: (Be sure to include contact information)

- Emergency phone #: For example, as of 2020: in the USA, call 911; in Canada: 911; in the UK: NHS 999 for life and death emergencies; NHS 111 for non-emergencies; in the European Union: 112; in Australia: Triple zero: 000

- Local Emergency room:

- Hot lines, crisis lines, Samaritans:

- Therapist:

- Spiritual Director; Religious leader:

- A friend you can call:
- Another friend you can call (If the first friend isn't available):
- An acquaintance:
- Someone who might be able to come over:
- Someone with a lot of common sense:
- Someone who can help me objectively assess my situation:
- Someone who can help me stay on track, hang in there when I'm tempted to give up:
- Someone with a soothing presence:
- Someone who can handle being with me when I'm crying:
- Someone who can handle being with me when I'm angry:
- Someone who can handle being with me when I'm feeling ashamed or guilty:
- Someone who can handle being with me when I'm frightened:
- Someone who can handle being with me when I'm feeling great:
- Someone who is good at distracting me:
- Someone who gets me laughing:
- Someone who's good with practical help:
- Massage therapist, meditation teacher, someone doing goddess work or shamanic journeying:
- Two in-person self-help groups I can attend (e.g. Recovery International, 12 Step meeting, Focusing) phone # and meeting times, locations, and directions — even if I never go:
- Yoga class, gym, track, swimming pool, drum circle, singing group, club, drop-in center:
- Someone who could benefit from my help:

Use this list as a guideline for developing your own people resources. Make a long term commitment to keep working on this list, filling in different names as you develop more relationships.

And, as you consider these potentially helpful people, you might mentally send them advance gratitude and appreciation.

HOW TO ASK FOR HELP FROM PEOPLE: SOME TIPS

1. *Only make requests if you'll be able to stand hearing "No."* Don't ask for something if you know or suspect that a refusal will send you over the edge.

2. *Break your wants down into small requests* that people can realistically satisfy (and you can stand hearing "No" to).

3. *Tailor your request to the person you're asking.* Some people will be more responsive if you wail and sob. However, many caring people are nervous around raw feelings. Sometimes even *talking* about feelings makes them nervous. Here are some ways to make it easy, (well, less difficult) for them to want to help you:

4. *Start with mild words.* Most people can stand to hear you say, "That was stressful." Stress is acceptable. Dignified. It's a place to start. Using mild words to describe unpleasant states can be a useful way to begin bringing a deeper, truer range of feeling talk into your relationships.

5. *Start with a past experience:* "It's over!" Many people find it easier to respond to hearing about an experience you've already handled in the past. All you're asking for is a sympathetic ear: "I was feeling stressed about something. Can I tell you what happened?" This approach often works better than "I'm a mess! Rescue me!"

6. *Try saying this* if you really need to cry and you're with a caring person who frequently says something well-meaning but upsetting,: "I'm so sad, and you're so caring, can you please just sit with me while I cry." If they say "OK," then let yourself cry, but not for too long. Thank them for listening.

PLAN B: WHEN SEEKING HELP FROM PEOPLE DOESN'T WORK

Have a Plan B for when someone's response doesn't satisfy your needs and desires, or if it makes a situation worse.

When getting help from other people works, it's great. But it doesn't always work. "Unhelpful Help" is a whole category of naCCT. Seeking help from other people can be riskier than helping yourself.

People aren't perfect. People are unpredictable. They are human, and that means that sometimes their responses will be "off" and we can feel disappointed. Sadly, if safety in relationships requires that we're *never* disappointed, then no relationship is ever absolutely safe. We can never be sure whether we'll get "warm fuzzies" or "cold pricklies" from other people. This includes therapists. Your best friend may be in a funk. Your therapist might be on vacation.

Because people are imperfect, and because getting help from other people is uncertain and sometimes even makes matters worse, have a Plan B to fall back on. And maybe Plan C and Plan D also.

WHEN PLAN B MEANS TROUBLE

Seeking help from other people is more uncertain than turning to some other resources, even dubious ones like substances. You may have heard the suggestion: "Reach for a hug instead of a drug." When Plan A, reach for a hug, doesn't work, some people will think, "Plan B, reach for a drug."

These people seem to turn to drugs, those chemically reliable short-term resources, almost as though they are turning to reliable helpful people. Recall that when Nick got People-Triggered, he planned to return to "his friends in the bottle."

A smoker showed me an insightful drawing that portrayed how a cigarette pack appears to an addicted smoker:

The drawing depicted the standard pack with a few cigarettes jutting appealingly out of the opening in the top of the pack. But they weren't like other cigarettes. They were still white, cylindrical, sized to fit comfortably between the fingers of a human hand. The difference? These cigarettes had friendly human faces. They were cigarette *people*! The drawing showed little smiling "Cigarette People" popping up from the pack to "help" the addicted smoker, as if they were saying, "Reach for me, I'm your friend!"

Drugs and alcohol really do "work" in the short-term. Sugar, too, is a bio-chemically reliable short-term mood elevator, a "pick-me-up" that many people consider to be a drug. The impact of drugs and alcohol is rapid and predictable. That's why these potentially addictive and destructive resources (should we call them "false resources"?) are so powerful.

We may feel like we love them. They may be biochemically soothing in the short-term. And yet we know that in the long-term they'll harm us, and, unlike people, *they will never love us back.*

To be realistic, some of us need to expect that we might be tempted to use these substances, and we need to include handling that temptation in our plans.

AN INDIRECT CONNECTION MAKES A GOOD PLAN B

In between fending for yourself and getting direct help from someone else are the indirect ways of connecting with people. Not connecting in person. Not in real time.

You may have already touched on some of these indirect ways, such as books, videos, or websites, as resources in Chapter Six. Here are some more:

- Use photos, videos, memorabilia, and/or meaningful gifts to recall safe times with other people. Listen to their voicemail messages or read letters they've sent you. Imagine being with them while you're feeling distress.

- Use your imagination to connect to figures that may not be literal people in your present life: angels, guides, fictional heroes from books, comics, and movies.

- Go people-watch in a public place, sit in a park or a coffee shop.

- Watch movies, videos, especially sweet videos about people, e.g. "family movies" for children.

- Look at pictures of people being kind, caring, and helpful to each other.

True, these indirect ways don't offer you the comfort of a direct, real-time response from an actual person. However, these less direct ways are safer, because they don't leave you vulnerable to someone's well-meaning, yet disturbing response.

So, let's put all this together to make a comprehensive, thorough plan. An naCCT survivor with cPTSD symptoms tells how she went about doing just that. Let's call her Kate. Here's her account:

KATE'S PEOPLE-TRIGGERS

"It's all People-Triggers," says Kate. "They're what set me off. I've been working on handling People-Triggers for quite a while now, and on getting help with them.

"When I get triggered, I self-medicate with a wide variety of substances and behaviors: six months ago I put down alcohol, but I picked up donuts and candy bars, big time; I also buy state lottery tickets and binge-shop for clothes and books, for knick-knacks and shoes, for anything to ease the upset I'm feeling. I want to stop doing these things.

"I've completed several People-Trigger and Distress Response Statements. One of my main triggers is negative communication from other people. Probably I'm hypersensitive, over-reacting, because it's not only people I'm close to. It's *any* negative communication from *any* other people, including strangers. A bus driver who doesn't return my 'hello.' A sales clerk who looks at me funny. A server in a restaurant who's slow to serve me. I take it all personally.

"I'm choosing to work with this 'relatively manageable' trigger that happened to me recently when I went alone to a restaurant. I got seated ok, but the server didn't come to my table for quite a while and then was rude to me, looked at me like I didn't belong there.

"I got triggered and stayed upset throughout my meal. I'm so ashamed. Everything gets to me. I'm a hypersensitive mess. What I want or need is impossible. I just fall into a pit of chain-reaction triggering and flashbacks, sometimes lasting into the next day, or even longer.

"So, here's my People-Trigger and Distress Response Statement:

"*When I encounter this People-Trigger:* [snotty, indifferent, non-responsive server looks at me funny],

my Distress Response tends to be [self-medicating with substances and shopping]."

"Since I don't drink now, my self-medicating Distress Response didn't include comforting myself with a glass of wine, but I *did* order an Irish coffee without the whiskey — which is kind of on the slippery slope toward relapse, and I also ordered dessert to lift my spirits, but only a scoop of sherbet, not the hot fudge sundae I really wanted.

"But there was really more to it than that."

DEEPER TRIGGER, DEEPER DISTRESS

"I had to really use the magic of 'Hmm. . . .' to just be present with that inner part that got so triggered and upset. To spend some time with it, get to know it.

"I feel so awful when I get triggered. I just feel like sobbing. But not by myself. Crying alone is triggering for me too. That feels too heartbreakingly lonely to me.

"Finally that part that needs help trusted my Inner Helper part enough to reveal my deep, private, hidden Distress Response:

"I don't want a substance or a shopping binge, I want a *person*. Someone who understands how ridiculously devastated I get by a little thing like that.

"The funny look, the snotty indifferent non-responsive server, all led to the longing to cry and be hugged and comforted. Deep down, what I wanted was just someone being present while I sobbed.

"The depth of my longing frightened me and made me feel ashamed. It had been hidden, even from myself. I had to struggle to write out my whole Atomic Chain Reaction of Triggers, but I did finally do it. Here it is:

> *"When I encounter this People-Trigger [snotty, indifferent, non-responsive server looks at me funny],*
>
> *my Distress Response tends to be [experience the longing to cry and be hugged and comforted],*
>
> *which triggers this Distress Response: [self-medicating with substances and shopping.]*

"So it's a much more complex statement, many links in a chain, but it's also more true to my experience, which turns out to be complex too.

"Then I had to come up with better options, figure out what I'm going to do."

KATE THINKS ABOUT GETTING HELP

"I did the Self-Talk Script for believing I make sense, and my People-Triggers make sense. I remember quite a bit of my childhood, and I related to naCCT:

> *"I related to the naCCT category of [Traumas of Omission: lack of emotional warmth, physical touch and affection, and comforting, especially when I felt hurt or alone],*
>
> *so it probably makes sense that I get distressed [when a snotty, indifferent, non-responsive server looks at me funny]."*

"That statement seemed a little far-fetched at first, but I knew the rude, indifferent server wasn't the ultimate source of my longing, or of my dessert-eating and shopping. I also knew that realistically I couldn't expect to be hugged and comforted for the "immense distress" of being treated rudely by a server. It's for the deep grief of the early experiences, the naCCTs, that I long for hugs and comfort.

"And I can appreciate that my longing to cry and be hugged and comforted triggered a Distress Response that had roots in my early naCCT.

"I also know eventually it will be good to work on my naCCT backstory and make really deep changes, but right now I don't want to open up those wounds, and I don't want to go back to the emotional wasteland of my childhood.

"I just want to get on top of using substances and shopping. I want relief now, before doing the deep work of healing those wounds and relational scars. Is that possible?"

CAN I GET RELIEF BEFORE THOSE WOUNDS ARE HEALED?

Kate continues: "Wanting to sob in the presence of someone else and have them hug me, comfort me, and help me get out of the pit of flashbacks and back into the present is a *big* interpersonal want. How am I ever going to get that?

"Some people have a suitable close person easily available to hug and comfort them while they sob, but many people don't. I don't.

"So, what can I do?

"Well, I turned to my lists of possible People-Helpers, and the minute

I did, the negative thoughts rushed up: Even if I could find someone, they would probably say some wrong, shaming thing like 'You aren't going to let a little thing like a rude server get you all bent out of shape, are you?' and that would set me off on another chain reaction of triggers and flashbacks. And then I would have to deal with feeling even more ashamed about getting bent out of shape over such a little thing. . . .which I *already* feel ashamed of.

"So I went back to basics, back to helping myself with my Inner Helper.

"I went over my resource list and my favorite Inner Helper helpful things to say. I especially like 'What would help?' 'You really matter to me,' 'We'll work this out,' and, of course, 'I love you' and 'I'm right here when you need me.'

"Getting back to a solid relationship with myself got me feeling back in balance; I felt safe and stable enough to plan my better options and how to get help from other people when I get triggered.

"I also realized that I could stop shaming myself about getting triggered and wanting such deep help. I have a lot of scar tissue and wounds around seeking help from people. This planning to connect with people who might be able to help me is really advanced work — in the 'Reconnect and Re-engage' component. It's a radical new way for me to connect with people. No wonder it's hard!

"So, plunging into this new territory, thinking about People-Help, I went to the "List of What I Want from People" and checked off someone to 'give me a hug,' 'say 'that sucks,' 'talk to me about being triggered,' and 'be with me while I'm expressing myself.' I also want someone else who gets easily People-Triggered, a 'Me too!' person.

"I looked over my list of possible real-life People-Helpers, especially someone to be with me while I'm crying.

"I wish I still had my dog to come lick my face when I cry.

"But I *do* have someone in my life who can stand my crying, and who usually says pretty much the right thing to get me safely grounded in the present. That person is my therapist. She can stand it. But she doesn't hug. And I have to wait for an appointment with her.

"I'm also friendly with a woman in my gym who's very warm. She hugs. Maybe I can get a hug from her.

"And I do know someone who is a good listener. She might not let me sob, but she might give me a little hug or a pat on the back. A virtual hug over the phone. At least a heart emoji in an email.

"And as for wanting a 'Me Too' person, I can open up the subject with some people I already feel sort of comfortable with. Maybe start small with asking 'Do you ever get kind of stressed out when a server is rude to you?' or say 'It bothered me when a server was rude to me' and then ask, 'Has anything like that ever happened to you, where a bad feeling lingered after someone was rude to you?' I can even say, 'I think I got triggered.'"

KATE, TWO WEEKS LATER

"So, I've been working on my Better Options for the past two weeks. Here's what I can do if a server is indifferent or rude to me, and I get triggered:

"I can have dialogues with my Inner Helper and my Inner Child. Use my resources for being safe and stable with myself.

"I can use my Safe Space Imagery as a mobile 'pop up Refuge.' Since it's all in my mind, I can use it right in the restaurant.

"Then there's my phone. I always have my phone. It's ready with the 'Now, not Then' Self-Talk Script, all typed up and filled in for this very situation:

> *"Fortunately, the reality is that I may feel awful, but*
> - *At least [this rude unresponsive server] isn't [my mother]*
> - *I'm an adult, not a child.*
> - *I'm in [this restaurant] not [the dining room where I grew up].*
> - *It's [right now, 5 o'clock today], not [40 years ago]."*

"And that brings me to my Patchwork Quilt of Help from other people.

KATE'S PATCHWORK QUILT OF HELP

"I ultimately came up with a comforting patchwork quilt of possible helpful responses from people. I targeted my plan for coping with a rude server in a restaurant, but it could apply to lots of other People-Triggering situations. I'm very proud of my patchwork quilt plan, actually.

"I set up some indirect People-Help: On my phone, I put together a personal photo album of me with other people I've been close to over the years — including lots of photos of my dog that died three months ago — and I'm saving photos that touch me in newspapers or on line.

"I also put together a music playlist, and I have some touching videos of 'unlikely animal friendships.'

"In addition, I've also flagged and pinned some warm emails. So, right after a People-Trigger, I can take out my phone and re-read these safe connections with people.

"If the Safe Space Imagery and the photos and the emails don't work, and I still feel awful, I have more plans, Plans C and D. I need a whole alphabet of plans.

"I want to connect with people. Even though I know they aren't predictable. Booze was predictable. Candy bars and donuts are predictable. People are not predictable, but I want to connect with them anyway. Sometimes an outer person helps me to do my inner work. Ultimately, it's really private, inside my own consciousness, but having another person just being there helps me to do that.

"I talked to some other people about getting triggered, too. One woman could relate; she said I can just text her: 'People-Triggered!' and she'll understand.

"That means I can have some direct contact with helpful people even while I'm in the restaurant. I can email or text people from my phone, privately, silently, no embarrassment of being overheard whining about my hurt feelings. I have a contact list of people I can connect with, right on my phone.

"I can make an appointment with my therapist, any time, on-line. Feel some security knowing I have that set up.

"Oh, and I learned there's a grief group through my vet's office for people who've lost their pets! I'm checking that out. I really miss that dog.

"I've been imagining good connections with people. Some people from my AA program understand having strong reactions and can handle tears. Though they might come down on me for the Irish Coffee, even though it was made without alcohol. Still, I can try them.

"I can start small. Ask for a piece of what I want. I imagine the person I call lets me cry on the phone for a few minutes. I might still be craving a cryfest, but being with me while I sob and sob might be too much for this person. So I imagine saying, 'Thanks so much for just being there. I feel relieved, just letting some of that out.' Then I move on.

"And here's my favorite Plan B for if I don't calm down during my meal, if I leave the restaurant still feeling out of balance. The weather is warm these days and the sunset is late, so I look for someone walking a dog. I go up to them and say, 'What a great looking dog. Can I pet it?'

"I get to pet the dog. Probably doesn't lick my tears away, but petting it makes me happy and maybe the dog's happy, too. Then I say to the dog's owner, 'Thanks, your dog's terrific. Have a nice day.' That's all. Keep it simple.

"Then, I sit down with myself and my Inner Helper and I say to myself, 'Good for me. I was feeling isolated and triggered and starting to go through the time tunnel into a flashback or into my addictions, and I intervened. I stopped myself. I did it! I found a friendly person and a dog I petted. I took action to help myself feel better by relating to other beings.'

"I'm hoping that as I get better at handling triggers, and maybe do some "Remember and Grieve" work with the original naCCTs, I'll feel less frantic and more just annoyed if a server looks at me funny.

"Oh, and look at this! Remember the warm woman at my gym? I told her a mild version of how I get upset by rude strangers and waitstaff, and she could kind of relate. That felt good. And then she gave me something I think is going to be really helpful to carry around with me. I'm not Catholic, but she is, and she gave me this tiny, sweet medal and said, 'Keep this; the Blessed Mother will comfort you, and you won't feel alone.'"

NOW YOUR TURN

How about you? Would you like to bring Kate back for a Q and A session? Can she serve as an inspiration for you to create better options for yourself and put them into action? Her account shows the specific elements that go into planning to get help from other people. The sheer length of her account shows that this planning is a lot of work.

To begin your own planning, come alongside of yourself and normalize being triggered and distressed. This is foundational and always available. You can use a general statement:

"I have a possible naCCT history, so it probably makes sense that I get distressed when [trigger]."

Or you can be more specific, putting a trigger and the naCCT category or categories you relate to in the blanks:

"I relate to the naCCT category of [naCCT category], so it probably makes sense that I get distressed when [trigger]."

The way your present troubles arose from your naCCT history does make perfect sense. These troubles might include finding that your Inner Helper is not functioning at the usual level of helpfulness.

YOUR PEOPLE-TRIGGER, DISTRESS RESPONSE, AND BETTER OPTION STATEMENT

Define your challenge with the People-Trigger and Distress Response Statement:

"When I encounter this People-Trigger [_____].

my Distress Response tends to be [_____]."

If you discover a Chain Reaction of Triggers, make a note of your additional triggering links, whether they are People-Triggers or intrapsychic triggers like thoughts and feelings. Write down whatever "gets to you" or "pushes your buttons."

Use as many missing links statements as you need. Add more if you discover a long chain of triggers.

"And then that Distress Response triggers this other Distress Response:
[_____],

which triggers this other Distress Response: [_____],

which triggers this other Distress Response: [_____]."

Then choose one Distress Response to explore and start brainstorming with the Better Option/ "What- I'm- Going- to- Do- About- That" Statement:

"and what I'm going to do about that is: [_____]."

YOUR OWN PATCHWORK QUILT OF HELP

Looking over all your resources and all your desires and needs for help, brainstorm your own wise alternative responses to People-Triggers.

Put it all together into a Patchwork Quilt of Help. You can let the plan take shape mentally. Or you can use Kate as a model, and write your Better

Options out as a cohesive action plan.

Use the options outlined in these last two chapters: namely, take a break; use your Safe Space Imagery, (updated to include people factors); and work with your Self-Talk Scripts.

You also have at your service all the strategies and skills you've developed earlier in your recovery: the ones from earlier in your work in this book, plus all those that you've discovered and cultivated elsewhere in your life. They're all yours, 24/7, anywhere you go!

Next, begin to turn outward to other people for help. As Kate did, clarify the kind of help you would like from another person. Pace yourself with wise compassion as you do this work.

Then look over the list of People-Helpers you've been gathering. Plan how to reach out to some of these real live humans for help. Maybe write out a script for what you can safely and effectively say, for the actual words you could use. You can, of course, use some of Kate's language if it suits your purpose.

Then it's time to take action steps in the real world. They can be really tiny. Baby steps.

Be sure to have abundant backup: your Plans B, C, and D, at least. The indirect ways of connecting with people by looking at photos, films, and memorabilia can be good backups.

When you do reach out to people, regardless of the outcome, congratulate yourself for each courageous act. Daring to take new actions in an area where you have naCCT scars is significant, advanced healing work.

Take a moment to stand back and mentally review your Patchwork Quilt of Help. You now have a process you can use to stop People-Triggers from bringing a sour note to otherwise sweet relationships.

This process can also help you realistically assess what relationships you would be wise to step back from and what ones you want to deepen. As triggering lessens, clarity about present relationships increases.

Attempts to improve basically good relationships are also more successful as your triggering diminishes. Even if the other person gets triggered, your People-Trigger-free state can prevent interlocking triggers.

As your skill at staying safe and stable with People-Triggers increases, look forward to making further gains as you work in the "Remember and

Grieve" and "Reconnect and Re-engage" trauma healing components. You can realistically anticipate using the healing work in these components to come to a joyful place of rich, authentic, mutually respectful and loving relationships with other people.

UP NEXT: IMPACT OF NACCT ON THE BODY.

This work with people and People-Triggers now draws to a close.

So far we've explored two of the three realms we set out to explore. First we explored the inner helping relationship within the intrapsychic realm of thoughts and emotions, and we've now explored the interpersonal realm of relationships with other people. Next, we look at the physiological realm: how our bodies respond to trauma.

The pressing question here is: "What happens when you are actually safe, you *know* you're safe, and yet your body isn't *feeling* safe?"

Sometimes we get physiologically dysregulated, and it feels impossible to calm down enough to use the Magic of "Hmm. . . ." or any of the plans we've worked so hard to develop. We may be able to say with intellectual confidence and belief, "This situation is an aggravation, not a life and death emergency," but our bodies remain cranked up or down, ready to respond to danger. We find we haven't returned to comfortable and balanced functioning.

How can we come alongside our *physical* selves in an effective, loving way? To explore the answer to that question, we turn now to the physiology of threat. What is the impact of naCCTs on our bodies?

Part V:

Physiological Experience: Safe and Stable with Your Body

CHAPTER 11

BODY-BASED TRIGGERS, SOUL MIRRORS, AND MEDICAL CONDITIONS

So far in this book, we've addressed staying safe and stable with thoughts and feelings within ourselves, where Inner Helper helps the part that needs help. We've also looked at staying safe and stable when relating to people. We looked at coping with People-Triggers and getting help from other people.

In this part of the book we're adding the mind-body connection. What are the physiological aftereffects of naCCTs on our bodies?

OUR BODIES ARE AFFECTED BY OUR RELATIONSHIPS

"My issues are in my tissues," quipped an naCCT survivor with cPTSD, reflecting on her stressed-out physical condition. She's right: abandonment issues, co-dependency issues, self-care issues, even existential issues of meaning and purpose — all can be embedded in the tissues of a survivor's body.

We turn our attention now to the connection between distressed tissues in our bodies and the attachment issues of naCCT. Our everyday intuition about the connection between the state of our relationships and the state of our bodies shows up in the way we describe our feelings about people:

- "They make me sick."

- "Work is a headache; my co-worker's a pain in the butt."

- "Am I shouldering too much responsibility?"

- "I was itching for human contact."

- "To preserve our relationship, I bit my tongue, choked back my tears, and swallowed my anger."

The impact of early relationships with caregivers on our developing bodies is profound. Even naCCTs, which involve absolutely no direct physical assault — even naCCTs of Omission, in which there is *no interaction at all!* — profoundly impact our bodies.

Yet the *connection* between childhood naCCT and adult bodies often goes unrecognized, and the *role* played by early naCCTs in our physical well-being as adults is unacknowledged. This is another way in which naCCT is functionally covert.

Although this profound connection between our adult bodies and childhood naCCT is often covert, I witnessed it in action both professionally, throughout twenty years providing body-oriented psychotherapy to people hospitalized for chronic physical pain, and fifteen more years providing psychologically-informed bodywork and massage therapy to adults seeking stress relief; and personally, in my own experience living in my own body these many years. I can testify that connection is powerful.

You, too, can understand and use this connection between the attachment issues of naCCT and your physical well-being. Whether or not your medical provider understands and uses this connection in your treatment, you can use it to help yourself.

NACCT IMPACTS BODIES: PHYSIOLOGICAL AFTEREFFECTS OF NACCTS

The links between attachment issues and physiology need to be brought to light. That's the aspect of your recovery addressed in this chapter. We'll dig into understanding what's going on with a body that's been impacted by intangible trauma.

Present-day physical troubles reflecting the impact of yesterday's naCCTs may include medical conditions, chronic pain, addictions, and even troubling moods like anxiety, panic, and depression.

Think back to what you inventoried about yourself in Chapter Two, "Is This You?" Notice how many troubles were based in your body. The work you're doing with this section of the book will help bring the hidden links between early naCCT and adult physical issues out into the open where they can be recognized, acknowledged and addressed. We'll explore:

- Sensory Triggers from outer environment

- Soul Mirrors

- Medical problems, especially those serious enough for a doctor visit

- Body-State Triggers from inner environment

As you read about the physical impact of naCCT, come gently and appreciatively alongside the force of life in your physical body. Hold your body-based troubles compassionately in mind. Hold them with curiosity and kindness. Invite well-being to come to the issues in the troubled tissues of your body.

SURVIVORS REFLECT ON IMPACT OF CHILDHOOD NACCT

Reflecting on naCCT's physiological impact, a survivor says, "I was always inwardly bracing myself for some covert emotional attack or subtle deprivation, while outwardly I played the part of a well-adjusted child. All that inward bracing took a toll on my body."

Another says, "I lived in a straight jacket made of my muscles, and my will power was the boss of my body. I wanted to scream, throw a fit, bite and spit and scratch, but I wrapped my muscles tightly around my impulses and 'worked hard' and 'played nicely' with everyone."

"Something's always going wrong with my body," says another. "Even when I was a kid. Especially when I was upset. Then my troubles went right to my body. If I was scared, I got stomach cramps. If I couldn't do my homework, I threw up. Overwhelmed and heart-broken? I came down with a head cold: runny nose and sore throat that felt a lot like crying."

Yet another adult with an naCCT history wonders, "What was I breathing in, when I was living in that dry cold atmosphere? People were polite. Accomplished. Responsible. But I was living touch-deprived in a love desert — no snuggles, no 'I love you,' everyone shrink-wrapped in plastic . . . . sometimes I feel like I don't have a physical body at all."

ALARMS INSTALLED YESTERDAY, TRIGGERS TODAY

Life experience becomes embedded in the body. You may have heard the saying "Biography becomes biology." How does this happen?

A long chain of cause and effect links yesterday's non-physically-assaultive relationship trauma with today's physical problems.

When we were really little, even before we learned to talk, even before our conscious brains came actively on board, our bodies were learning what was dangerous and what to do to stay alive.

As we continued to grow, unbeknownst to our conscious brains, the tissues and care-giving systems of our developing bodies were hard at work installing alarms to protect us from abandonment.

With these alarms installed, our adult bodies have wired-in response patterns that spring into action whenever they receive a message, "Threat detected!"

As we've seen, these alarms that warn "Threat detected!" can come from many sources. They can come from interactions with people: For example, an interpersonal alarm detecting an attachment threat like being ignored can lead to a body-based defense response such as shutdown or panic.

And alarms that trigger bodily responses can also come from thoughts and emotions from our inner environment. For example, the thought-trigger: "I'm not good enough" or the emotion-trigger: "I'm afraid I'll be left alone" can lead to physical depletion and fatigue.

SENSORY TRIGGERS FROM OUTER ENVIRONMENT

Information from our senses can trigger "Threat detected!" messages. For many people, particular physical qualities function as Sensory Triggers. Here are a few examples of Sensory Triggers that can come at us from the external world:

- Voice qualities: pitch, raspiness, speed, accent, and so forth

- Sounds: toys, machinery, electronics, music, animals, wind and other nature sounds, even gatherings of people

- Colors of such items as nail polish, wall paint, or articles of clothing; your "unfavorite color"

- Messiness; disorder; e.g. Crooked picture on wall

- Certain tastes, loved or violently hated flavors

- Weather, temperature, humidity, pollen count, smoke or fumes in the air

- Temperature of a room; muggy, dry, or stale air quality

- Smells, especially food, body odors, cleaning products, cut lumber and grass, mildew, plants, medications, gasoline

- Vibrations: car, train, washing machine, air conditioner, fan, vacuum cleaner

- The "mouth feel" of certain foods: mushy, tough, crunchy

- Tactile: textures of clothing, bedding, furniture, other surfaces

- Feel of water: bathwater, shower, rain, swimming pools, ocean waves.

- Songs, melodies, lyrics, pictures, sculptures, movies, other works of art

People have reported being "allergic to sunshine," afraid of fog or high wind, depressed by rain, even "creeped out by the long shadows of late afternoon."

You may wonder if objectively positive physical qualities can function as Sensory Triggers. Yes, they can: because objectively positive qualities can be subjectively associated with negative naCCT experiences. Very unpleasant conversations can take place at gourmet meals. A chronically belittling person can wear a heavenly designer fragrance. Don't be fooled by objectively positive physical qualities.

Much of our misery comes from being caught unawares by a physical quality functioning as a subtle Sensory Trigger. Like the scary soundtrack in a horror movie, information from our senses can set up an expectation that something bad is about to happen to us.

So, be prepared. Carry your list of Sensory Triggers around with you for a week, gathering helpful information about yourself. Notice the physical qualities that trigger you. You might try to find one trigger of each type. (Sort of like going on a scavenger hunt). Notice what thoughts, emotions, sensations, and impulses are triggered by those qualities.

Forewarned is forearmed. The more we notice and pay attention to our own personal Sensory Triggers, the more we protect ourselves from being caught off guard and blindsided by them.

SOUL MIRRORS

These Sensory Triggers have a cousin that you've probably experienced. This phenomenon happens when we're stirred in a particularly meaningful way by something outside ourselves. It might be a photograph, a painting, a poem, or song lyrics. This experience is different from "regular" appreciation of art. It's special, almost uncanny. It might be a scene from a movie or even a vignette from real life that leads to recognizing: "Hey! That's exactly how I feel! It's like seeing my insides reflected outside of me; an X-ray portrait of my soul."

This phenomenon was clearly important for naCCT, so, of course, I wanted to write about it for you. But it had no suitable name.

These particularly meaningful sensory experiences were called "objective correlatives" by the poet T.S. Eliot, because they objectively correlate to our inner emotional experience. That name caught on in the literary and visual arts worlds, but nobody I talked to outside of those worlds could relate to it. I needed a name people could relate to and use when they wanted to talk about their experiences with this phenomenon.

Finally, it dawned on me. They are "Soul Mirrors!" Just as looking in a mirror gives us feedback that helps us know our visual selves, so these Soul Mirrors help us know our psychological selves.

These days, when I sense that my inner experience is being reflected by something I hear, read, or see, I call what's reflecting me a "Soul Mirror." We can add that name to our vocabulary for talking about naCCT. Throughout this book I'll be using the name "Soul Mirror," and I urge you to start using it too.

EXAMPLES OF SOUL MIRRORS

Soul Mirrors often happen with a piece of music, especially for teenagers, who are changing so fast and challenged by so much. A particular song by a particular artist can convey a whole teenage State-of-Being — physical feelings, emotions, impulses, sensory experiences, moods, and happy or heartbreaking relationship circumstances.

For me, the teenage Soul Mirror song was Elvis Presley's "Heartbreak Hotel." I loved the way my teenage angst was reflected in the sobbing quality of the voice, in the image of a transient living space — a hotel, not a home — dedicated to loneliness and heartbreak.

What song does it for you?

Besides songs, a movie or even a sequence from a movie may be a Soul Mirror. Many people have mentioned the therapy sequence from "Good Will Hunting." They report feeling surprised, confused, relieved, often tearful, when Robin Williams' therapist character forcefully asserts to Matt Damon's guilt-ridden PTSD character "It wasn't your fault."

MUNCH'S PAINTING "THE SCREAM" AS SOUL MIRROR

A particularly resonant example of this Soul Mirror experience is Edvard Munch's painting "The Scream." Many people have a shock of recognition when they look at that eerily accurate portrait of their inner emotional experience.

Although it was painted over a century ago in 1892, "The Scream" is an icon of our times. As an indication of its current value to us, in 2012 the color pastel version sold for $119,922,500 US dollars.[18]

"The Scream" is so popular today that you can now buy rubber "Scream" face masks and full body costumes; "Scream" shower curtains and pillows; Do-it-Yourself "Scream" Paint-by-Numbers kits and inflatable life-sized "Screams."

"Life had ripped open my soul," the artist Edvard Munch wrote about his creation of "The Scream." He described walking with two friends in Oslo, Norway, when "the sun went down. . . .a flaming sword of blood cut open the firmament. . . . And I felt a huge endless scream course through nature."[19]

The scream of a soul being ripped open by life is conveyed in the twisted shapes, the head like a skull, the eyes and mouth frozen unnaturally wide in horror. The vibrating lines imitate the shaking legs, the knocking knees, the chattering teeth, the overall quaking of Munch's experience.

The power of "The Scream" also resides in its silence. Do we resonate with our own inner silent scream, never expressed and never heard?

SOME SOUL MIRRORS LINK PAST AND PRESENT

Some Soul Mirrors have the power to flash us back through time. Just as the songs we loved as teenagers can carry us back to those days, so these Soul Mirrors can link a survivor's past and present experiences. As if by magic, they can conjure up a whole State-of-Being and a particular era in our lives, including our thoughts, feelings, moods, sensations, dreams and nightmares, and the relationships that were so important to us back then.

Recognizing these Soul Mirrors helps us come alongside ourselves. They can reveal our deepest longings and tip us off as to what we had to learn to cope with as children.

EXAMPLE OF A SOUL MIRROR THAT LINKS PAST AND PRESENT: AN INDIFFERENT MOTHER HOLDING HER BABY

A professor's comment and a Soul Mirror experience in an art history class helped a client of mine understand her childhood naCCT on a body level.

Her professor had projected a Renaissance painting of a Madonna and child onto the classroom screen and commented, "This painting portrays a Madonna who was more of a court lady than a mother."

My client, a dancer I'll call Claire, didn't have an image of the painting to show me, but she found a way to convey her experience: she jumped up and grabbed a little pillow off the sofa, placed it indifferently on her hip, and turned her body away from it and the baby it represented.

Claire held the pose for a minute, then sat down and said, "That court-lady Madonna was my mom. I don't know how that baby Jesus in the painting felt, but I know exactly how I felt: Awful. Invisible. Like I didn't exist."

A REAL-LIFE SCENE MAY ALSO BE A SOUL MIRROR

A survivor of well-meaning, fussy parents reported watching a mother and father with a little girl in a cafeteria: "The little girl was maybe two, dressed like a little doll. She held herself very still and looked up at the ceiling while her mother dipped a napkin in the water glass and used it to tidy up the little girl's mouth after each messy mouthful.

"I heard the father say, 'For every bite of spinach, you can have a bite of cake when you're done.'

"As I witnessed this scene, I could feel my body stiffening and a trapped sensation came over me, like being surrounded and pressed in upon and having to be very careful not to make any wrong moves."

When have you felt a Soul Mirror reflect your inner experience? Was it a piece of music? A scene from a movie? A picture? Can you conjure up the whole experience when you think of your Soul Mirror now?

MEDICAL PROBLEMS

In addition to our post-traumatic stress responses to Soul Mirrors and Sensory Triggers, the physical impact of our childhood naCCTs may extend to present day medical problems.

Statistics show that stress is rampant among people with medical problems. In 2013, the Journal of the American Medical Association published an article titled "When Physicians Counsel About Stress: Results of a National Study." The research results indicated that between 60% to 80% of doctor visits showed a probable relationship to stress.[20]

Here's one physician's opinion about stress from non-physical attachment traumas:

"The quantum shift in endocrine and immune responses resulting from these 'trivial' events," says rehabilitation neurologist Dr. Robert Scaer, "may sow the seeds of many common somatic diseases and emotional disorders throughout the lifespan." [21]

WHAT BODY TROUBLES CAN BE AFTEREFFECTS OF NACCTS?

What specific diseases and disorders might grow from the "seeds" sown by these "trivial" events? According to Dr. Scaer, symptoms of trauma "reflect a dysfunction involving the brain and most of the regulatory systems of the body — autonomic, endocrine, and immune."

This means that unresolved naCCTs could sow problematic seeds of dysfunction in any of the following systems:

THE BRAIN

Dysfunctions involving the brain could include problems remembering, learning, thinking, reflecting, self-calming, problem solving, understanding, processing information from the senses, paying attention, and even speaking.

THE AUTONOMIC PART OF THE CENTRAL NERVOUS SYSTEM

The autonomic part of the central nervous system regulates the heart, intestines, breathing, blood vessels, liver, kidneys, bladder, pupils, urination, defecation, sexual arousal, sweat, saliva, tears, blood pressure, body temperature, metabolism, electrolyte balance, and body fluids.

The autonomic nervous system also regulates the fight or flight response as well as mood disorders such as depression and anxiety.

THE ENDOCRINE SYSTEM

The endocrine system controls all the glands. It distributes hormones throughout the entire body to every cell that has a receptor for that particular hormone. So the endocrine system is involved in diabetes, hypoglycemia, as well as dysfunctions of thyroid, metabolism, growth, sexual development and function, and sleep. Disorders in the endocrine system also contribute to mood disorders such as anxiety and depression.

THE IMMUNE SYSTEM

And of course the immune system defends our bodies from attack. When the immune system becomes dysfunctional, it can fail to protect us from attack. Or, in auto-immune conditions, it can incorrectly identify our very own cells as the enemy and lead us to attack our own bodies.

In addition to these regulatory systems, other systems in our bodies where childhood naCCT could sow seeds of adult problems include the following:

THE MUSCULOSKELETAL SYSTEM

This system provides structural support, upright posture, and movement. It includes muscles, bones, tendons, ligaments, joints, and fascia.

Included in musculoskeletal problems are muscle tension and spasms; trigger points and tender points; restricted movement or inefficient movement leading to wear and tear on joints with bone painfully rubbing against bone; misalignments; and areas of diminished sensitivity or numbness.

In my own work, both as a massage therapist and as a psychomotor therapist treating chronic pain, I often saw people become aware of a connection between their chronic musculoskeletal pain and the social and psychological pain they were experiencing.

"Muscular armor" is a term given to us by Wilhelm Reich, Alexander Lowen, and other Bioenergetics investigators. Like a suit of armor between the inner and outer worlds, chronically braced muscles hold back impulses to act in ways that have lead to trouble in the past. Especially held back and kept inside are impulses to express anger, fear, disgust, sexuality, and grief.

Once the armor is in place, we don't have to exert any intentional effort to stop ourselves from saying or doing something we might later regret. The muscular armor does it for us. Muscular armor may even freeze the diaphragm and muscles of the ribs to limit breathing.

Dr. John Sarno, physician, researcher, and author of four books on pain, has helped many people with his clinical treatment, research, and writing on the impact of suppressed emotions, particularly anger, on pain related to the musculoskeletal system.

THE SKIN

Have you ever had to deal with someone who "got under your skin" or "made your skin crawl?"

Aftereffects of early trauma can be implicated in problems with our skin, our largest organ and the boundary between our inner and outer environments. Skin problems can include blushing, goose bumps, rosacea, psoriasis, fever blisters, and, of course, hives.

"I didn't think reading that chapter about naCCT would bother me," apologized an early-bird reader of this book. "Even though I promised you I'd have feedback by today," he explained, "I had to stop reading. About halfway through the chapter, these itchy, burning welts broke out all over my arms and back. Hives. This isn't the first time I've gotten hives when I've gotten upset."

Of course, he did give me feedback: simply reading about these naCCTs gave him hives.

THE GASTROINTESTINAL DIGESTIVE TRACT

Are there some ideas that you just "can't swallow?" People you just "can't stomach?" Ever get butterflies in your stomach? Have a "gut feeling" about something, or a "gut-wrenching" experience?

One hundred million nerve cells line the gastrointestinal digestive tract. That's more than in either the spinal cord or the peripheral nervous system. No wonder some people call the nerves of the gastrointestinal tract the "gut brain."

"Stress can affect every part of the digestive system," says Digestive Health Center Medical Director Dr. Kenneth Koch.[22] Stress is implicated in esophageal spasms, acid stomach, nausea, diarrhea, constipation, cramping, and inflammation. It can also make irritable bowel syndrome (IBS), peptic ulcers, and Gastroesophageal reflux disease (GERD) worse.

In addition to impacting specific organ systems, childhood naCCT also influences adult conditions of chronic physical pain, addictions, and mood disorders.

CHRONIC PHYSICAL PAIN

When pills and tablets don't work, when surgery doesn't result in a cure, when nothing shows up on tests, chronic pain persists. It is a complex problem that manifests in the physical body, but it involves much more than that. Although the specific internal structures and processes that drive chronic physical pain remain in large part a mystery that researchers are working to solve, stressors, and especially traumatic stressors, are implicated as significant suspects.

SELF-MEDICATION THROUGH ADDICTIONS

Like chronic physical pain, addiction is complex and not limited to the physical body.

Many people can testify to the connection between addictions and attempts to self-medicate for a variety of intertwined physical, psychological, and interpersonal problems. Both behavioral and substance addictions persist, at least in part, because they provide us with some control over the state of our body's sensations, moods, and functions. This control, in turn, helps us manage stress and pain.

I can testify to the presence of early naCCT issues in my eating, coffee-drinking, and former two-pack-a-day smoking habit. They told a wordless story about efforts to take care of myself — to be present, to care, to respond, to soothe.

MOOD DISORDERS

This overview of "somatic diseases and emotional disorders" that may develop from seeds sown by "trivial" traumas concludes with mood disorders: anxiety, mania, and depression.

Mood disorders involve a whole State-of-Being, a miserable package of distressing emotions; disturbing thoughts; characteristic uncontrollable energy levels; and changes in pain perception, sleep patterns, sexual behavior, and sociability.

They are strongly influenced and regulated by the human nervous system: brain, spinal cord, and the network of nerve cells linking all the parts of our bodies together.

Mood disorders are so prevalent and troubling for naCCT survivors that they will be the focus of two upcoming chapters.

TO SUM UP THE IMPACT OF
NON-PHYSICALLY-ASSAULTIVE TRAUMAS
ON THE PHYSICAL BODY, YOU COULD PRETTY MUCH JUST SAY,
"THESE TRAUMAS AFFECT EVERYTHING."

BODY CHECK-IN: SAY "HELLO"

Let's bring that general information about human bodies home to our personal relationships with our own bodies.

We can begin by simply checking in with our bodies.

In working with naCCT recovery, this check-in may be as simple as giving a nod to our bodies and saying a brief "hello" in passing: "By the way, how is your body feeling as you talk about this? Are you holding your breath? Are your hands balled into fists, heart beating fast?"

A typical brief check-in is illustrated by this fragment of an exchange with a client dealing with anxiety. I'll call her Zoe. She explores what would happen if she said "hello" to her scared feelings.

"Something awful could happen," Zoe said, quickly adding, "That's not really true. Rationally, I know I'm not in any danger at all. I'm just afraid."

"So, knowing rationally that you're not in any danger at all, can you check in with the scared feeling? Where is it in your body?" I asked.

"In my stomach. My throat. Clutching at me," Zoe said.

"Even though you know rationally that you're not in any danger at all, it feels like there's a scared feeling clutching at you, in your throat and your stomach," I reflected back for her.

Looking down at her jiggling foot, she said, "I feel frantic, like I want to jump out of my skin."

For some people, joining the emotion with the bodily sensation is very disturbing. Zoe was one of those people, so that was enough saying "hello" to the sensations for that day. We might back off, say "good bye" to the troubling sensation, and switch to action plans, reviews of past successes, or even physical movement around the room: maybe getting a glass of water or looking out the window — all strategies previously established in Zoe's repertoire for stress relief.

From this brief "hello" to her body state, Zoe's awareness tolerance could gradually increase. She could become quite good at choosing when to approach her embodied emotions and say "hello" to them, and when to distract herself and back off. Having more choices, she could begin to feel safer; and feeling safer, she would be able to tolerate staying longer with the disturbing physical state.

Some people check in with their bodies by using a structured Body Scan meditation, in which they gradually direct attention to various parts of their bodies, often beginning at the feet and progressing to the head, just saying "hello" and noticing comfortable, relaxed areas as well as areas of discomfort.

Guided body scans and scripts for recording your own abound on the internet.

NO PHYSICAL ASSAULT, BUT STRONG PHYSICAL IMPACT

This is a good time to dig a little deeper into how our relationship issues become embodied in our tissues.

IMPLICIT PROCEDURAL LEARNING

It's easy to limit our understanding of "learning" to school work and job training, tasks we intentionally direct our brains to master.

It's easy to ignore the learning that goes on without any conscious intention to learn — and often without any awareness that we *are* learning or even *what* we have learned.

This unconscious learning, known as "implicit procedural learning," is based on "implicit memory." Familiar examples include learning to tie shoelaces, walk up stairs, or ride a bicycle. This kind of learning is also responsible for the familiar "child see, child do" phenomenon, for those embarrassing moments at a church picnic or in a physician's crowded waiting room when Mom witnesses her favorite swear words coming out of her frustrated four-year-old's mouth.

Much of this implicit procedural learning serves our drive to survive. It enables our bodies to adapt to a world with naCCT in it. Our bodies are like well-functioning human biocomputers. If we're in stressful, threatening, or traumatizing circumstances, then our brilliant bodies will learn procedures for staying alive under those specific circumstances.

For staying alive when we're little, the overriding rule of safety is "Stay attached to Lifeline Caregiver!" Our brilliant, survival-driven bodies learn to behave in ways that keep our caregivers close by and responsive to us. If our bodies used words, their survival learning might be expressed like this:

"They're nice when I smile, so I'll smile."
or:
"They go away when I cry, so I won't cry."

This lesson isn't learned in just one incident. It's repeated over and over and over. It's cumulative. Compounded. Chronic. This repetition deepens our learning.

Staying attached to a Lifeline Person takes precedence over just about everything else.

When our behavioral strategies "work" and our Lifeline People stay responsive to us, our bodies receive messages of well-being that tell us, "Keep doing this; it's keeping you alive!" They experience relative well-being overall, even while feeling a little cramped or uncomfortable.

Comfort — and even health — may be sacrificed to maintaining safety by staying attached to a Lifeline Person. So, for instance, as toddlers we may have learned to stay awake and keep acting bouncy and cute even when our over-tired little bodies actually needed rest.

Maintaining a secure attachment to a Lifeline Person also takes precedence over honestly expressing our true feelings. So we learned to smile when sad. We learned to squash the crying after the times we cried and cried and Mommy got fed up and went away.

We learned to shut down, to lie low, to crank up our energy, to gurgle and babble, or to smile and laugh — all in accordance with what our bodies learned would keep us attached to our Lifeline Person.

Our bodies gradually perfected these survival procedures. Skillfully and automatically, these procedures handled being chronically slighted and set aside, or always being "in the way," or getting teased when scared. We handled the absence of comforting hugs and snuggles; we coped with being pushed to cheerfully build another tower of toy blocks before having a chance to cry over the tower that collapsed.

THE DOWN SIDE OF THESE SURVIVAL PROCEDURES

Unfortunately, even as we master these survival procedures, our bodies' repertoire of responses shrinks. We stick to those procedures. We don't take chances on responding a different way. So, we become more prone to getting stuck in reaction patterns that wear a body down, or keep it too long in a particular state, even though overall health requires flexible responses to actual changing conditions.

To make matters worse, as life goes on, getting stuck in a rut of tried and true attachment-preserving procedures may undermine our resources for dealing with new interpersonal challenges.

Take Yvonne, for example: When she was little, Yvonne slowed her responses and lowered her energy level to match her depressed mom's needs. As time went by, Yvonne became stuck in a rut with her slow responses and low energy level, and being stuck like that made it hard for her to take part in activities with other kids in school and with other adults once she grew up.

Or take Randy, for another example. He had been trauma-taught as a baby to stifle the cry for help that alienated both his parents. Later on, requests for help stuck in his throat and he couldn't ask for help when he needed it.

This stifling process is so commonplace that we even have an expression for one of its most widespread results: We get "choked up." We almost start to cry, but stop ourselves by contracting the muscles in our throats and squeezing our windpipes so hard that no sound comes out. Why would anyone want do this to their body?

Maybe because they learned as children that crying could be dangerous, maybe it went along with Mommy turning away, or Daddy shouting "Shut that baby up!"

At first, choking back tears might be intentional, along with holding the breath and stiffening the upper lip. If the threat happens repeatedly, choking back tears becomes automatic, almost like a reflex, and we find ourselves "getting choked up."

We acknowledge all three elements: the emotion itself, the impulse to express the emotion by crying, and the muscular inhibition of that expression. Ultimately, the common use of the everyday expression "getting choked up" normalizes the armoring process of inhibiting crying to get along socially. It conveys that we are both tender enough to feel the tears come up and civilized enough to choke ourselves back from expressing them.

Thus it becomes perfectly normal — "civilized," actually — to choke up ourselves in order to block the expression of tears at a tender moment.

Unhealed trauma and its corresponding adjustments in our bodies gather force. As we continue learning and adjusting to attachment relationship demands, we may be moving farther away from what will be good for us as adults later on.

Furthermore, the adjustments we make to cope with our ongoing early traumas may render us less resourced and more vulnerable to later traumas. It's a vicious cycle. You may have heard the saying "The rich get rich, and the poor get poorer." It's also true that if trauma isn't healed, the traumatized get more and more traumatized.

WISDOM THEN, WOUNDS TODAY

So, are these learned procedural adaptations wounds, or are they wisdom?

Consider, for example, the body-based procedural adaptation of anxiously watching with shallow breathing, suppressed emotion, and a people-pleasing attitude for the tiniest sign someone is getting impatient and about to go away. This adaptation might have helped a child with a moody, fragile, or impatient parent to survive by keeping that parent close by. For that child, this response pattern was wisdom at work.

In an adult, however, the same response pattern might be more like a wound. Anxiously watching with shallow breathing, suppressed emotion, and a people-pleasing attitude for the tiniest sign a temperamental partner is getting impatient and about to leave can turn an adult into an unassertive, even psychologically abused, co-dependent "doormat." And what toll will that way of relating take on a body?

Wisdom or wound? Stuffing down emotions that frightened away a caregiver was wise in childhood, but stuffing down emotions as an adult might reasonably be considered a wound.

How about cranking up energy to keep a tired little body acting bouncy, perky, and "lovable?" Wise for a child, when being cute secured love, delight, and connection with Mommy and Daddy, Grampy and Grammy, and all the visiting aunts and cousins and family friends. However, for today's grown-up adrenalin-depleted naCCT survivor, that trauma-taught, survival strategy of driven cheerfulness might be considered a cPTSD wound.

BODY-STATE TRIGGERS

Among these post-naCCT wounds are Body-State Triggers, another illustration of our relationship issues becoming embodied in our tissues.

When being in certain body- states caused problems in childhood with parents or other Lifeline Caregivers, those body states started to feel dangerous: Something bad could happen again. For example:

- When I felt angry back then, something bad happened. If I feel angry now, something bad could happen again.

- When I laughed my head off back then, something bad happened. If I laugh my head off now, something bad could happen again.

- When I wanted a hug and reached out for one back then, something bad happened. If I want a hug and reach out for one now, something bad could happen again.

Who wants something bad to happen again? No one.

So, to prevent something bad from happening again, our bodies install alarms to signal "Danger! Stop!" when we feel angry, start laughing, or reach out for a hug.

After that installation, feeling angry, laughing, or reaching out for a hug will set off an alarm. In this way, body states become Body-State Triggers. Our bodies have been trauma-taught to adapt to a world with naCCT in it.

Body states that can become Body-State Triggers include:

- Being sick, injured, or having a physical weakness or malfunction

- Needing medical or dental care

- Being tired, drifting off into sleep

- Experiencing body processes such as sexual arousal, bathroom actions "peeing" and "pooping," sweating, blushing, stammering

- Being in an overall state such as high energy, discomfort, or fatigue

- Making certain movements or gestures

- Feeling too hot or too cold, especially if other people claim to be comfortable

- Being in a certain position such as squeezed into a subway, bus, or plane, or even being in a particular yoga posture.

A woman I worked with liked to schedule a session after going to the gym because so much came up for her as she moved through a workout. Many body states triggered her.

Blushing is a wide-spread body state that easily becomes a Body-State Trigger. That's what happened to Carl. As far back as he could remember, his brothers had teased him about his blushing, but it turned to serious shame when he was fifteen:

As Carl sat at the long cafeteria table having lunch with his friends, including two of his brothers, a popular girl, the target of Carl's secret crush, came over to ask about homework. The blood rushed to Carl's face, giving away his secret. His friends ("frenemies?") teased him mercilessly as the girl stood awkwardly at the table, and he tried to find a way to disappear.

After that day, Carl's blushing became a serious Body-State Trigger. As an adult, even thinking about the possibility of blushing intensified his social anxiety.

UNCONSCIOUS BODY-STATE TRIGGERS

In addition to body states we're aware of, there are the body states we aren't aware of — levels of hormones, neurotransmitters, allergens, vitamins, and minerals, for example. Although our conscious brains aren't aware of these body states, they are revealed in lab reports, and our internal data sensors monitor them carefully for any sign of trouble. Shifts in those states can function as deep Body-State Triggers we are entirely unaware of.

Although new details about the deep internal processes whereby our bodies turn body states into Body-State Triggers are rapidly being discovered by researchers, in our day to day lives we individual naCCT survivors leave handling this process to the body itself. Like most people, we let our cells, tissues, and organs do their job outside of our conscious awareness, hopefully protecting us from harm, regulating our bodies' temperature, and keeping all the systems of our bodies purring smoothly along.

Just as an industrial park outsources landscaping and facilities management, or a municipality contracts for building and grounds services, we treat our cells like brilliant environmental engineers and maintenance crews, as whole operations management services to which we've delegated the responsibility for safeguarding our physical well-being.

Our cells, tissues, and organs, including the subcortical brain's cerebellum, limbic system, and brain stem, take care of the detailed operations; they don't need us to micro-manage them. Like any facilities management or housekeeping service, it's a background operation. So, deep within our bodies, alarms are installed and responded to and adjustments are made, all beyond the scope of our conscious awareness.

DOUBLE WHAMMY: BODY-STATE TRIGGERS AND PEOPLE-TRIGGERS TOGETHER

There is no universal pattern whereby body states become Body-State Triggers. Different people develop different Body-State Triggers. Take being injured or sick, for example: some naCCT survivors remember being pampered when they were injured or sick. For some of them, that was relationally almost a happy time because it was the one time they got genuine tender loving care. The body state of injury or sickness doesn't become a Body-State Trigger for these people.

Other survivors remember being sick or injured as both physically and relationally painful, maybe because they were yelled at for being careless or accused of pretending to be sick to get out of school or chores. The social danger that gets attached to the anxiety attack, the headache, the fatigue, or even the irritable bowel adds another layer — the cPTSD symptom layer — on top of the initial physical problem. As adults, these people may have both Body-State Triggers and People-Triggers related to being sick or injured.

Combine intrinsic medical unpleasantness with an naCCT People-Trigger and a Body-State Trigger, and life gets really painful. Say, for instance, your tooth hurts. Add to that pain the People-Trigger derived from a parent's negative reaction to you having a toothache — maybe they were impatient with your crying, or afraid of possible dentist's bills, or angry and yelling at you for not taking better care of your teeth — and the pain is additionally bad: Toothache pain plus Body-State Trigger pain plus People-Trigger pain.

Sometimes a particular body state functions as a Body-State Trigger only when relating to a particular type of person. Sami, for example, was soothed and comforted by her mother when she cried, whereas her father raged and shamed her by calling her a cry-baby. As an adult, feeling the impulse to cry functioned as an alarming Body-State Trigger for Sami only when combined with the People-Trigger of being around a loud, aggressive man like her father.

What was your family culture's attitude toward sickness or vulnerability? Towards accidents?

ANGELA'S CHAIN REACTION OF TRIGGERS

Once we add Sensory Triggers and Body-State Triggers to the mix of intrapsychic triggering thoughts and feelings and interpersonal People-Triggers, the potential for Chain Reactions of Triggers boggles the mind and poses a huge challenge to the body.

For instance, a physical injury can trigger childhood fears of an impatient parent's irritation and rough handling, plus thoughts like, "I should have been more careful, look at all the problems and expenses this accident caused" or even "I can't do anything right." These fears, in turn, can trigger a panic, a shutdown, an urgent impulse to have a drink or do some online shopping, and even more physical distress.

Or a body state of elation and pride — maybe after winning a gymnastic competition, a beauty pageant, or an academic award — can trigger a fear of being cold-shouldered by envious family members, and that fear can trigger an angry, self-protective impulse to strike out and punch an envious sibling; that impulse, in turn, can trigger guilt feelings and muscular blocking of the punching impulse.

An anxious client with a nervous stomach that's been troubling her since childhood had that very Chain Reaction problem. I'll call that client Angela. She explains, "I looked at the Atomic Chain Reaction video, the one with all the ping-pong balls in the mouse traps. [23]

"It's like my mind is full of mental mousetraps set with ping-pong balls, ready for some trigger to set them into explosive action. I imagined labeling all the mouse traps and ping-pong balls with all my alarms and triggers. I couldn't do it. It seemed like practically anything could trigger practically anything else."

Angela explains a bit of her history: "When I was a child," she says, "my nervous stomach would keep me home from school and away from family outings. And because of me, other family members sometimes missed family outings too.

"My parents, my mother especially, worried about me. Maybe she was also a little impatient and even disgusted with me sometimes. But mostly she cared. She took me to doctors, specialists, and alternative healers. None of them found anything that would respond to surgery or medications. 'Just nerves,' they said, 'Stress.'

"Now, as an adult, I have a nervous stomach, shortness of breath, trouble sleeping, and heart palpitations. I work with a physician and a nutritionist to address those problems. I watch what I eat and use ginger tea, breathing, meditation, and exercise to keep my stress level down.

"But the faintest twinge of sour stomach or queasiness triggers my anxiety and sets off a chain reaction of triggers. I've been working to come alongside myself mindfully when this happens.

"Here's a typical chain reaction: Queasiness is a Body-State Trigger that flashes me back to my mother sighing, worrying, fussing. . . . and to hearing my big brother groaning, "Angela's sick again.'

"And even though I'm usually in my apartment and not at their house when an attack happens, I *feel* the presence of my mom and my siblings and their attitude toward me. I feel it so vividly that I fall into guilt, aggravation, and fear they'll abandon me. It also triggers shame about my disgusting, always-something-wrong-with-it body. And that triggers anger at them. And at my body for being so screwed up. And then guilt for being angry.

"And all that stuff triggers worse stuff in my body: cramps, clenched stomach muscles, gagging. Those physical states set off emotions of dread and longing, and thoughts like 'I'm a bad, worthless person who'll always be a burden to anyone who cares about me.'

"My Inner Critic guilt trips me for all the times I made my mother worry — and also for getting irritated by her worried, controlling behavior. The inner conflict between my poor overwhelmed Inner Helper and that Inner Critic rages on, and I end up with a tension headache on top of my stomach trouble."

"So, everything triggers everything.

"The upside is that I'm beginning to understand how interconnected my troubles are. I actually did a good job of explaining those interactions, didn't I?

"Maybe it's not as bad as the mousetrap and ping pong ball Atomic Chain Reaction video. I am untangling all the triggers. I am getting better at labeling them when they get activated. And soothing myself. I've actually made progress, and I'm not giving up.

"And by untangling the whole history of my nervous stomach, I'm digging up the roots of my relationship problems too. Overall, I'm actually feeling hopeful."

NOW YOUR TURN

Once we take the triggers at the level of the body into account, the potential for chain reactions of triggers grows pretty overwhelming. And we survivors are often overwhelmed. So let's explore how to use all the information in this chapter to counteract overwhelm.

Let's begin right now with giving your body direct attention and care. Check in with the state of your body and do whatever works to restore balance. If you are feeling:

- **Geared up physiologically to fight or flee, to mobilize?** Discharge by tapping your foot, running in place, vigorous cleaning, jogging, pushups.

- **Fearful or uneasy?** Stand up and shiver and shake your arms and torso, like a dog after a swim.

- **Teary?** It might be time for a good cleansing cry.

- **Tired?** Let yourself rest in safety until you feel somewhat refreshed.

Remember the work you did much earlier in this book with your Inner Helper, your inner part that needs help, and your Inner Helper's helpers. Your relationship with yourself offers help with distressed body states. Keep that inner helping relationship activated as you proceed.

Remember all your skills: "the power of Hmm. . . ," the actions in your first aid kit for what you can do for yourself as an individual. And remember all the Self-Talk Scripts you used with yourself.

TAKING STOCK OF PHYSIOLOGICAL NACCT AFTEREFFECTS

So, let's look over the physiological aftereffects discussed in this chapter and take stock of how they relate to *you* and the impact of naCCT on *your* body. You might want to write about your responses.

YOUR SOUL MIRRORS

Make note of anything that functions as a Soul Mirror for you. Keep in mind that Soul Mirrors can be positive as well as negative. They can reflect remembered experiences, imagined experiences, and even experiences you long to have.

YOUR MEDICAL CONDITIONS

Take note of your present medical conditions. Include addictions, both substance and behavioral. Include chronic pain. Check out questionable body-problems with a medical professional. Get help to either address or rule out medically addressable problems.

Stand back and take a panoramic view of your overall medical history. Is there a pattern? Do your medical challenges tend to occur in a particular system of your body? Is there a family pattern?

YOUR SENSORY TRIGGERS AND DISTRESS RESPONSES

Flip back to the list of Sensory Triggers at the beginning of this chapter.

If you think of something that works as a Sensory Trigger for you, experiment with putting that into the Trigger and Distress Response Statement:

"When I encounter this Sensory Trigger: [_____],

my Distress Response tends to be [_____]."

[Note: "I want to get away from it," "It excites me," and "I feel weird and yucky" are perfectly reasonable, expectable Distress Responses.]

YOUR BODY-STATE TRIGGERS AND DISTRESS RESPONSES

As we survivors know from painful experience, long after the original trauma is over, something can trigger the body-based alarms, which may, in turn, set off long, complex sequences of responses. And even though we may not even be aware of the alarm going "Threat detected!" we're painfully aware of our distress.

To bring more awareness to this process, try working with the Body-State Triggers listed earlier in this chapter. Don't overwhelm yourself with this. Maybe do a few items; then stop, and make a note to come back here later. Here are three ways to work with this list:

1. Look for **People-Triggers** associated with Body-State Triggers: As you read through the list, notice the interpersonal element. Who was around when you felt this way before? Could something that person did or failed to do be a People-Trigger linked to that Body-State Trigger?

2. Look for **Intrapsychic Triggers**, those feelings and thoughts you might experience in connection with a particular Body-State Trigger.

3. **Sentence Completion using the list:** Select one of the sentence beginnings below and complete it with one of the different body-states on the list:

Something bad could happen if I am in the body state of: [_____].

A body state I'm scared of is: [_____].

A body state that could mean relationship trouble is: [_____].

A body state that bothers someone is: [_____].

A body state that could mean danger is: [_____].

A body state that upset Mommy is: [_____].

4. **Free Writing:** Write one of the phrases above and just keep on writing. You might experience a rush of expression, or you might stop with a single sentence.

If you identify a Body-State Trigger, fill in your Trigger and Distress Response Statement:

"When I encounter this Body-State Trigger: [_____],

my Distress Response tends to be [_____]."

YOUR PARADOXICAL BODY-STATE TRIGGERS

Give special attention to the paradoxical, surprisingly negative, body states — the ones that are objectively positive, but trigger Distress Responses for you. Feeling proud, expansive, flirtatious, sensual, exuberant, or even curious often falls into that category.

> *"A body-state many people might like but could be a Body-State Trigger for me is: [_____].*
>
> *When I encounter this Body-State Trigger: [_____],*
>
> *my Distress Response tends to be [_____]."*

YOUR PERSONAL POSITIVE BODY STATES

While we're addressing body-states, take this opportunity to treat yourself to remembering or imagining enjoyable ones. Body states you like feeling. Ones that make you feel safe. The tranquil luxury of a bubble bath, perhaps, or the virtuous exhaustion after a workout. Even the mellow ease of contentment.

You might start with how your face feels when you're smiling, and enjoy the good feelings that radiate out from that smile to your whole body.

These are your personal positive body states. You can bring these enjoyable states to mind whenever doing so would please or soothe you.

YOUR CHAIN REACTIONS OF TRIGGERS

With all this attention to your triggers, have you become aware of any Chain Reactions? Sensory Triggers and Body-State Triggers might fill in a missing link in a Chain Reaction you've already identified. Some puzzling distress states that seemed to come out of thin air might make sense as Distress Responses to Sensory Triggers or Body-State Triggers.

YOUR BETTER OPTIONS

Let's turn now to planning how to deal with your body-based, post-naCCT challenges.

First, keep in mind that these challenges happen in the natural course of events. They are indicators that your self-care processes have worked effectively to support your instinct for self-preservation.

Next, it helps to put these physiological aftereffects in a larger context. What is the big picture?

Other factors besides naCCT impact our physical bodies. The naCCT elements interact with other factors such as disease, injury, accidents, and genetics. It's good to keep this wholistic perspective in mind and include attention to these factors in your self care.

Physiological, psychological, and social factors are all braided together in our lives. It isn't realistic to expect to work on one area in isolation from the others. They all interact. As you work on one area, other areas are affected.

You may have noticed that as you work on the psychological and social factors, your body distress challenge may go up. If you "self-medicate," your urge to do so may increase.

With this inter-relatedness in mind, notice if your body gets more comfortable — or less — as you go near certain thoughts, feelings, impulses, and relationships.

Use that interrelatedness! Calming thoughts can calm your body. Good connections with people can bring balance and ease to your physical self. Instead of a vicious cycle or a Chain Reaction of Triggers, you can enjoy a vitalizing cycle.

Knowing about the mind-body-social interconnections and giving them mindful attention can help you stay safe and stable as you heal.

Focus on discovering where you can intervene in order to improve your life. Keep chunking these body-based post naCCT challenges down into small elements you can successfully cope with. Gradually you'll unpack the symptoms, acknowledge the triggers, untangle them, and slowly de-activate them.

1. SAFE HELP FROM OTHER PEOPLE

We know connecting with others has an effect on our bodies, sometimes for better and sometimes for worse. Review the patchwork of people-resources you gathered and listed earlier: your list of people you can directly connect with and their contact information; your list of indirect ways to use your Social Engagement System without risking unpleasant direct responses from other people; your backup "Plan B" for when human imperfection and fallibility get in the way of the response you'd hoped for.

2. SAFE SPACE IMAGERY

Incorporating what you've learned about body-based challenges, update your Safe Space Imagery with body-balance restorers. Maybe some comforting explanations, either written out or gently explained by one of your Inner Helper's Helpers. Include soothing processes for body-based troubles. Do you want to add a spa? A gym? Some bodyworkers and trainers? A vegetable garden? A labyrinth for walking meditation?

3. PAYING DIRECT ATTENTION TO YOUR POST-NACCT BODY

3A. CHECK-IN: BODY SCAN

First, take some time to say "hello" to your body. You might do a self Body Scan. Tune in to your body mindfully, with curiosity, wonder, and kindness. You might choose to listen to one of the many guided body scans found on YouTube and various podcasts. Or you might look into body scan scripts and record one for yourself using your own voice.

A helpful technique you might try is direct communication with your body as though it is a part of you that you can have conversations with. Have your Inner Helper ask your Body Self, "What do you need now?" Try to listen and respond with wisdom, and sometimes with loving limits, if your Body Self gives a reply like: "I want to go to sleep now. Or maybe to eat."

Let your ever-increasing knowledge about how naCCT can impact your body increase your compassion for your own post-naCCT body.

You will be tuning in to your body, listening to the messages from your body. You will become a brilliant, kind, helpful observer of the states your body is in. You will also get to know and integrate body with mind, with heart or meaning.

What account of what happened to you is being carried in your body? If you befriend your body, you befriend your life experience.

Maybe your body hasn't gotten the message yet that it's safe now. The coast is clear. The threat has been removed. Can you intervene to let your body know that it's safe?

3B. RESTORING YOUR BODY TO BALANCE

Inventorying your physical problems and sensitivities can be de-stabilizing. To bring your body back to comfortable and balanced functioning, work with your Inner Helper to use the body-based resources already available in your toolkit.

Balance-restoring activities involve simple decision-making you know you can do well. It's good when they require just enough attention and movement to anchor you in the present and remind you that you are basically capable. They might include simple household or workplace chores such as handwashing dishes, sweeping with a broom, making copies, dusting shelves, or stacking firewood.

Make a list of things you can do to activate calm *mental* functioning: for example, sort laundry, do Sudoku puzzles, collect rocks, organize your spice rack, or follow a recipe.

And here are some techniques that address the state of your body directly:

• BREATHING

Breathing always helps. Just remembering to breathe helps. Use Mindful breathing or a Yoga breathing technique.

• GROOMING, EATING, HYDRATING

Have a drink of water. Prepare, serve, and eat something. File your nails, floss your teeth, or brush your hair. Almost any simple everyday self-care activity will do.

• ENGAGING SENSES

Some people find it helpful to distract themselves from their stressors by focusing their senses on details in their present environment. For example, "list three sounds you can hear right now" or "look for five green objects in the room."

• USING CALMING SENSORY INPUT

Crunch ice chips, dim the lights and lie down under a weighted blanket, push on a wall or squeeze a stress ball, soothe yourself on a swing or in a rocking chair, suck a thick milkshake or smoothie through a straw.

• MOVEMENT, EXERCISE, AND PLAY

Hit the gym, dance floor, or bike path. You've heard so many times about the benefits — both physical and psychological — of exercise. And movement, exercise, or play can also provide some relief in the form of distraction.

- **MEDITATION AND MINDFUL MOVEMENT**

Meditation and mindful movement such as Yoga, Tai Chi, and Chi Gong have helped many people stay safely embodied, as have labyrinths and meditative walking, especially in nature.

- **MASSAGE AND OTHER BODY WORK**

Try kneading the tense muscles in your forearm after a long keyboarding session, or gently rubbing the muscles around your temples and jaw. Even self-massage releases the calming hormone oxytocin. Or treat yourself to professional massage therapy. Many massage therapists today have been trained to provide trauma-sensitive treatments.

- **ENERGY WORK**

You could also use techniques based on the body's energy meridians. Emotional Freedom Technique (EFT) and Tapas Acupressure Technique (TAT) are both taught on internet.

Survivors also have found help with Reiki healing, which you can learn to do on yourself through reasonably priced in-person training.

Professional healers also provide Reiki, Emotional Freedom Technique (EFT) and Tapas Acupressure Technique (TAT) as well as Acupuncture and Shiatsu.

- **SLEEP**

A quick trip to the internet supplies all the information needed to confirm Shakespeare was right when he spoke of "sleep that knits up the raveled sleeve of care." Restorative sleep repairs the tangles and unravelings of life, especially post-naCCT life with all the challenges of cPTSD. In addition to a restful night's sleep, legitimize a cat nap or "a nice lie down" as a wise way of caring for a body that has become frazzled and out of balance.

You probably do many of these things already. Even so, you may find they have a different feel if you bring to them an awareness of naCCT's on-going stressful effect on your body.

You can do some of these right now! They are always available for you to use.

And for long-term physical well-being, of course keep doing the healthy eating, movement, exercise, rest and relaxation, spa treats, and general self-care you've been providing yourself.
And, investigate these:

- **BODY-BASED PSYCHOTHERAPY:**

Pesso Boyden System Psychomotor, BioEnergetics, Psychodrama, EMDR (Eye Movement Desensitization and Reprocessing), SensoriMotor, Somatic Experiencing and, of course, the expressive therapies, including play therapy, art therapy, drama therapy, music therapy, and dance therapy.

- **SOULFUL MIND/SPIRIT BODYWORK:**

SomatoEmotional Release/ Craniosacral therapy; Feldenkrais, trauma informed massage; physical therapy and osteopathic manipulations.

YOUR SELF-TALK SCRIPT: "IMPROVING MY PHYSICAL HEALTH BY HEALING COMPLEX PTSD IS WORTH A TRY"

"Present physical problems, even mood disorders, sure seem linked to these early non-physically assaultive traumas. What happened back then in my outer world with people could have impacted this body I'm living in today. Maybe an naCCT experience is being carried in my body today. As I try to improve my physical condition, resolving complex PTSD is an avenue I could explore. It could turn out to be really helpful. Maybe I can even afford to feel a little more hopeful."

NOTES

[18] Chris Michaud, "Munch's 'The Scream' sells for record $120 million," Reuters, May 4, 2012, https://www.reuters.com/article/us-thescream-auction/munchs-the-scream-sells-for-record-120-million-idUSBRE84200M20120504

[19] Quoted in *Panic: Origins, Insight, and Treatment*, ed. Leonard J. Schmidt and Brooke Warner (Berkeley, CA: North Atlantic Books), 239-40.

[20] A. Nerurkar, A. Bitton A, R.B. Davis, R.S. Phillips, G. Yeh, *JAMA Intern Med.* 2013; 173(1):76-77. In https://jamanetwork.com/journals/jamainternalmedicine/fullarticle/1392494.

[21] Robert Scaer, *The Trauma Spectrum: Hidden Wounds and Human Resiliency* (New York: Norton, 2005), 42 & 62.

[22] *Kenneth Koch, quoted in* https://www.everydayhealth.com/wellness/united-states-of-stress/how-stress-affects-digestion/ Medically Reviewed by Kareem Sassi, MD, Last Updated: 10/16/2018.

[23] You can see this for comic relief on "900 Mousetraps Unleashed with Science Bob on Jimmy Kimmel Live," start at 1:00, https://www.youtube.com/watch?v=XIvHd76EdQ4 or "Monsters of Schlock" video adds a human face in the middle of all that. Everyone is laughing, https://www.youtube.com/watch?v=bEmb0HDHHIc

CHAPTER 12

THE RESIGNATION STUPOR

Continuing to explore intangible trauma's long-lasting tangible effects on our bodies, we move on from Sensory Triggers, Soul Mirrors, medical problems, and Body-State Triggers, and we zoom in for a close-up of moods. Many people with cPTSD from naCCT have problematic recurring moods, even if they haven't been formally diagnosed with a mood disorder.

For a closer investigation of post-naCCT moods, I'll begin by sharing with you my therapeutic work with my most challenging client: Myself! Maybe you'll relate to some of this.

PROBLEMATIC MOODS

Before awakening to the reality of complex PTSD from naCCT, I was challenged by problematic moods that I never dreamed were connected at all to trauma. Like many naCCT survivors with unidentified cPTSD, I didn't link "What's wrong with me?" to "What happened to me?"

Looking back to that time, I now I understand that naCCT had indeed caused what rehabilitation neurologist Dr. Robert Scaer called a "quantum shift" in my body's regulatory systems. But all I'd known back then was that bad moods sometimes came over me "out of the blue." Shameful moods. Seriously problematic moods. Two in particular.

One of those problematic mood states revolved around my Inner

Critic's painful reminders of how I was supposed to be: According to the white American Protestant values I'd soaked up from my culture, enshrined in motivational poems like Longfellow's "A Psalm of Life," I was supposed to be "up and doing. . . .still achieving, still pursuing. . . .leaving footprints in the sands of time."

But when this problematic mood state came over me, I wasn't "up and doing" anything at all. I didn't care about anything at all. I was stuck: Apathetic. Listless. Moping around, feeling low, maybe depressed, definitely apart somehow from the regular flow of human life.

I called this state my "swimmy feeling." To me, "swimmy" meant swooning, fainting; it meant unanchored; it meant me without gravity, without orientation. "Swimmy" also meant a vague fear of not being able to muster enough energy to do some as-yet-undetermined task in the future, even if my life depended on doing it.

This listless, "swimmy" mood state was represented by a line from another poem, but definitely not a motivational poem. In this state, I related to the part in John Keats' "Ode to a Nightingale" where he says, "I have been half in love with easeful Death."

I understood the appeal of just "easefully" letting go into a painless swoon beyond willpower, beyond pushing, guilt-tripping, or shaming, beyond struggle.

But, also like the poet, I was only "half in love with easeful Death." I was also half terrified of that swoon into extreme rest. In fact, I sometimes felt uneasy about letting myself rest at all.

So, I went back and forth between the listless "swimmy" state and the frantic "don't-rest-be-up-and-doing" state.

Because being "up and doing" seemed like a state to be proud of, my Inner Critic focused my shame and negativity on my listless "swimminess."

"IT'S ALL ABOUT ADRENALIN"

It went against then-current psychotherapeutic theory to think that my troubles were related to trauma or to post-traumatic stress. In those days, people only talked about the agitated response to trauma, with no mention of "freeze" states. It was all about adrenalin, the hyped-up "fight or flight" response.

So, stuck in the limited knowledge of that era, I believed that PTSD meant agitation: being coiled tight, feet tapping, fingers drumming, ready to spring. PTSD meant heart palpitations, chest constrictions, hair-trigger explosions into action.

And stress? I believed that stress caused "Type A" problems like heart attacks in high-energy, driven people; not weird low-energy mood states in people like me.

No way was my distress Post-Traumatic Stress Disorder.

BAD GENES OR BAD CHARACTER

How my thinking went at that time is, sadly, a fairly common mindset even today. I concluded that my problematic giving up, my not trying hard enough, my depression — whatever it was — must be one of two things:

- Either it was some biological malfunction, probably genetic,

- Or I was a person of bad character who just didn't try hard enough, a lazy, self-indulgent slug.

Slothful. That's what I was. And isn't sloth one of the Seven Deadly Sins?

And speaking of sins, what about the cigarettes, sugar, and caffeine I used for an energy lift? Once I was in a self-blame tailspin, I added "undisciplined, self-indulgent addict" to my list of character flaws. Gluttony, right up there with sloth, among my deadly sins.

It had to be sloth, gluttony, or bad genes.

HELP FROM FRIENDS IN BOOKS

As I wrestled with shame and self-disgust about my depression and swimminess, help came to me from books.

These "book friends" helped me appreciate the way trauma had affected my body. What I learned changed the way I viewed my troubles. It was like learning the world wasn't flat.

Here's what happened:

In a little book called *Freedom from Stress,* author Phil Nuernberger described a stress state that he called the "Possum Response." [24]

I stared at the pages, somewhat in disbelief. The symptoms of this Possum Response were so familiar: loss of muscle tone, mental lassitude, slowed heartbeat, inactivity. Pretty much what happened to me. Pretty much the opposite of that adrenalized fight or flight state I'd associated with stress.

Yet this expert said this Possum Response was a state of stress. He even suggested that this stress state might be implicated in asthma. Asthma! I had had an asthmatic reaction to cats in my early twenties. Maybe I was one of the people who got possum stress instead of adrenalized chicken-with-its-head-cut-off stress.

My book helper, like the helpers on the mythic hero's quest, also gave me an empowering word: the scientific term for the Possum Response. He called it "parasympathetic dominance."

A name! A clue! A magic phrase!

"Parasympathetic dominance" was my "Open Sesame." This magic phrase would open the way to hidden treasures that would help me understand what was going on with me and my moods.

My Inner Helper went into high investigative gear.

I RESEARCH PARASYMPATHETIC RESPONSE

In those days before the internet, my investigation took me deep into the university library stacks. There I dug through the physiology books' diagrams, charts, and dry scientific terminology, looking for the secret of "parasympathetic dominance."

I was rewarded with priceless information that helped me make sense of my troubles and find a way to solve my chronic bad-mood problem. To spare you that digging, I share my discoveries with you here. Some of those discoveries might be disturbing. This might be a place for a Trigger Warning.

My discoveries began with the autonomic nervous system and its two branches.

There's the familiar sympathetic branch, the branch that drives us to be "up and doing" or to crank out adrenalin and go into fight or flight. This branch is such old news that my gym has a class called "Adrenalin," and we all know that means "high energy."

Opposing the sympathetic branch is the less famous parasympathetic branch.

When the parasympathetic branch is in charge, its nerves send messages that instruct the body to "rest and digest." The muscles relax. The heart beat slows down. Blood pressure and body temperature drop. This state is usually associated with well-being: peaceful, serene, harmonious, relaxed, at ease. Sometimes people try to reach this state by meditation to get relief from stress.

When life is going along smoothly, we rhythmically alternate between the "get up and go" of the sympathetic branch and the "rest and digest" of the parasympathetic branch.

However, when we're stressed, the nervous system responds with extremes of those states. Sometimes it responds with an extreme adrenalized fight or flight state, which can become disorganized "running around like a chicken with its head cut off."

And sometimes when we're stressed, the parasympathetic branch with its extreme response takes over.

ANIMALS' PARASYMPATHETIC RESPONSE TO THREAT

This extreme response is "Parasympathetic Dominance." Extreme "Parasympathetic Dominance" has a dark side associated with danger.

Some animals go directly to Parasympathetic Dominance when they are threatened with attack. They don't even try to fight or flee.

Take, for example, the original "Possum Response." When the grey furry possum's alarm system detects a hunting coyote, owl, or bobcat nearby, the possum immediately loses consciousness. Its bodily processes slow down so much that it appears to be dead.

Possums aren't the only animals that shut down instead of fighting or fleeing. Pigeons can be petrified by snakes. Geese freeze when turned over onto their backs. Chickens, too, may remain motionless for hours after being attacked and then released by their chief enemy, the hawk.[25]

Chipmunks with no place to hide from an approaching snake "play possum" for up to half an hour. In this state, the chipmunks' heart rates may plummet from their normal 210 beats per minute to only 30 beats per minute.[26] Even when the snake crawls under their bodies, they don't move.[27]

This parasympathetic "Possum Response" is a normal, natural response with survival value. It conserves the possum's energy. And because it also prevents the inert animal from being noticed by predators, this parasympathetic "Possum Response" often saves the hunted animal's life.

My Inner Helper's take-away from this research so far: This parasympathetic "Possum Response" is *definitely not* a genetic defect or a sign of bad character.

HUMANS' PARASYMPATHETIC RESPONSE TO THREAT

I learned too that humans may also respond with extreme parasympathetic "possum responses" in the face of danger.

DR. LIVINGSTONE'S STUPOR

The Scottish physician David Livingstone related one such incident in his memoirs.[28] Christian missionary and explorer in Africa, Dr. Livingstone was a popular British hero of the late 19th-century Victorian era. In 1844 he was living in the village of Mabotsa, in what is now South Africa.

The village cattle were being wiped out by lions.

At night, lions leapt into the cattle pens. Even in daylight, they attacked the herds. So Dr. Livingstone and a group of men from the village went out on a lion hunt.

When the men were about 30 yards (roughly 27 meters) from a lion, Dr. Livingstone aimed his gun and fired.

The village men cried out, "The lion is shot. Let's go to him."

But Dr. Livingstone could see that although the lion had indeed been shot, it had not yet collapsed. Behind the bush its tail was raised. The lion was still alert and dangerous.

As Livingstone was reloading his gun, the lion sprang. It grabbed Livingstone by the shoulder and dragged him to the ground.

The lion did eventually collapse, and Livingstone did live. But the attack was serious. Being a physician, Livingstone was later able to describe his wound precisely: "Besides crunching the bone into splinters, eleven of his teeth had penetrated the upper part of my arm."

Livingstone tells us how he felt in the jaws of the lion with eleven teeth gripping his upper arm:

"Growling horribly close to my ear, [the lion] shook me as a terrier dog does a rat. The shock produced a stupor similar to that which seems to be felt by a mouse after the first shake of the cat. It caused a sort of dreaminess, in which there was no sense of pain nor feeling of terror, though quite conscious of all that was happening. It was like what patients partially under the influence of chloroform describe, who see all the operation, but feel not the knife. This singular condition was not the result of any mental process. The shake annihilated fear, and allowed no sense of horror in looking round at the beast."

At this point, Livingstone was conscious; he had been seriously attacked by a predator and was facing death, yet he felt:

- no fear

- no horror

- no pain

- no terror

He compares his "peculiar state" to that of a surgical patient: awake, aware, anesthetized, in a sort of "dreaminess" or "stupor." Like many trauma survivors, Livingstone told his trauma narrative many times. In another version he describes this "peculiar state" as one of "placidity," a word I associate with calm, peaceful, unruffled tranquility or quiet serenity. Hardly the way I would expect to feel when gripped in the jaws of a lion, with eleven of its teeth digging into my shoulder.

MERCIFUL STUPEFACTION?

The peacefulness that appears to accompany this state beyond all struggle has been compared to the peacefulness reported by people who have had near death experiences. At its extreme, this parasympathetic response appears to be akin to trances, hypnosis, dissociation, and other states at the frontier of our understanding of consciousness.

When death is inevitable, as consciousness itself begins to diminish, the extreme stupefaction of this response provides doomed creatures, large and small, animal and human, with relief from terror and anguish.

It appears that our bodies are prepared to cope with the horrible possibility that neither fight nor flight will ward off a threat to our well-being. Our bodies, wiser than our conscious minds, are ready with the parasympathetic response.

This response relieves the enormous strain the emergency "fight or flight" mobilization puts on the body, mind, and spirit. The frantic behavior, the pounding heart, the racing thoughts, all calm down as the doomed individual yields to fate and surrenders.

Dr. Livingstone, the Christian missionary, concluded, "This peculiar state is probably produced in all animals killed by the carnivora, and if so, is a merciful provision by our benevolent Creator for lessening the pain of death."

Decades later, Dr. Livingstone was echoed by a combat veteran who miraculously survived in the trenches of World War One. "Our minds froze, grew numb, empty and dead,"[29] he wrote of his experience expecting to die. "The senses," he recalled, "become clouded and conceal the worst."

This combat veteran, like Livingstone, concluded that a benevolent force was providing the doomed soldiers with a peaceful death. He called this mental numbing a "merciful stupefaction."

STUPEFACTION: MERCIFUL BLESSING OR FATAL CURSE? RESIGNATION CAN LEAD TO DEATH

But this "merciful stupefaction" poses a danger of its own. When there is still some possibility for life-saving action, stupefaction works against survival. In a stupor, you fail to take any action at all.

In an extreme example from the animal world, threatened chickens have been known to enter such a profound stupor that they don't wake up to look for food and ultimately die of starvation.[30] Stupefaction prevents action and thereby leads to death.

Humans, too, may fail to take life-saving action. Take, for example, a driver whose car is stalled on the railroad tracks. Instead of actively handling the dangerous situation, the driver — perhaps mesmerized by the oncoming train, perhaps sinking into a stupor of inevitable doom — may fail to even try to move the car off the tracks.

Transitioning from "fight or flight" to resignation can lead to giving up prematurely, when there is still reason to hope.

In an ironic turn of phrase, Marty Seligman, the father of positive psychology and the researcher who gave us the concept of "learned helplessness," describes this extreme resignation state as "death by relaxation."[31]

Not actively suicidal, but simply passive, longing for ease, release, and perhaps oblivion, the exhausted arctic traveler may lie down in the snow and go to sleep, never to awaken. From my own experience resonating with the poet Keats who was "half in love with easeful death," I recognized that danger lurked in that longing: "I could just give up, lie down, let go, and die."

Merciful stupefaction could certainly be a mixed blessing: attractive, tempting in its promise of relief from painful struggle, and yet deadly, in its abandonment of all life-preserving effort and hope.

GIVE UP? OR KEEP ON GOING?

At this point, I'm cutting into this account of my discoveries to invite you to check in with yourself.

My explorations into the parasympathetic dominance took me to some very disturbing places. Those explorations were spread out over time. Even as I write about them for you now, I take a lot of breaks. Walks in the warm sunshine, robust housecleaning, conversations with good friends remind me I'm still alive. I mention this to you now because you may be finding this reading very intense. You can always take a break. Now!

Are you feeling alive and ready for further explorations? Then let's go on. . . .

DOOMSDAY SIGNAL EQUALS "GIVE UP!"

In cases of predation in animals, total surrender is sometimes marked by a clear turning point.

Consider, for example, what happens when a zebra is attacked by a pack of wild dogs. One of the dogs grabs hold of the zebra's upper lip with its teeth. As if receiving a Doomsday Signal, the zebra then stops struggling, stands still, and surrenders to its fate.[32]

As with animals, so it is with humans. Something functions for us like that zebra's Doomsday Signal. It's almost as if there's a turning point, where humans think, "Give up. It's hopeless." They then stop struggling for their lives and yield to inevitable doom.

A person in this state lets go of motivation, life skills, strategies, planning, and effort. The system of self defense shuts down. Nothing seems to matter anymore. Even the will to live ebbs away.

A turning point to a fatal Resignation Stupor of doom was observed by an American Army physician imprisoned by the Viet Cong. He witnessed a fellow prisoner of war, an outstandingly rugged Marine Corporal, plummet rapidly from determination into despair.

This rugged Marine suffered from a skin disease and malnutrition that had wasted his body down to 90 pounds (roughly 41 kilos or 6.4 stone). Yet every day the Marine had carried his own weight in local vegetables long distances in his bare feet. Instead of complaining or collapsing under this forced labor, he had soldiered on, following his own orders: "Grit your teeth and tighten your belt."

Then this determined Marine learned that his expected release date had come and gone, but he had not been released.

This information worked like a Doomsday Signal for him. It signaled: "Your struggle is hopeless. You are doomed."

Abruptly, he stopped functioning. He refused to eat. He soiled the bed where he lay in a stupor with his thumb in his mouth. Although he suffered no injuries, his skin turned blue and he quietly let go and died.[33]

Trauma victims may seem to just go away mentally or emotionally from what's happening to them. World War II soldiers used the phrase "the two-thousand yard stare" to describe the numb, anesthetized look of a man who no longer cared. Spacy, dissociated, essentially not there. This quality of "not being there" is so striking that an observer of this state suggested that maybe the soul departs from the body during extreme traumatic stress, leaving behind only a robot-like shell.

Henry Krystal, a medical doctor who survived the Nazi concentration camps himself and went on to do pioneering work with other survivors, observed that in this state both physical and mental activity, including initiative, judgment, and emotions, come to a standstill so extreme it could be considered "a state of walking death." [34]

Other survivors of the Nazi extermination camps reported that some prisoners gave up so completely that they didn't even try to stay warm, find food, or resist beatings. "These prisoners were viewed as 'the living dead.'"[35]

PSYCHOGENIC DEATH AND THE RESIGNATION STUPOR OF DOOM

Indeed, in its extreme form, the Resignation Stupor may be linked to psychogenic death, that is, death with neither apparent physical reason nor observable damage to tissues from injury or disease. According to physicians and other trained medical professionals who have witnessed these psychogenic deaths, they appear to result from psychological causes. The cause of death seems to be a Doomsday Signal. The victims die believing that they are doomed to die no matter what they do.

Perhaps the most dramatic psychogenic deaths attributable to the parasympathetic Resignation Stupor of doom are those that a less respectful era called "voodoo deaths,"[36] those that follow a curse or violation of a taboo. Group members who violate a taboo held sacred by their community are cast out, cursed, and banished from the society they need in order to survive.

One man discovered that he had been tricked years before into violating a taboo. This discovery served as a Doomsday Signal for him. In less that twenty-four hours after his discovery, he died.[37]

Another example closer to home: A woman psychiatric patient who hadn't spoken for ten years was moved to the "exit ward" when the walls of her "hopeless ward" were being painted. In her new ward, where people went just before they were discharged, she prospered: she not only spoke, she actually became quite talkative.

Unfortunately, the painting job was completed. The woman was moved back to her old "hopeless ward." Within a week, she died. When no pathology was discovered in the autopsy, the suggestion was offered that she "died of despair."[38]

The sad ending of her story fit with the "hopeless" label given to her by powerful authorities in her social world: Was this "hopeless" label a kind of curse that functioned for her as a Doomsday Signal?

WHEN THE DOOMSDAY SIGNAL COMES FROM INTERPERSONALLY POWERFUL PEOPLE.

Another disturbing case suggests a possible psychogenic death and Doomsday Signal might have come from a respected medical authority: A physician gave a man the diagnosis of metastasized cancer that had spread throughout his body. A doomsday diagnosis. The man died believing the physician's diagnosis. After the man died, however, the only cancer found in an autopsy was a 2 cm. (slightly less than an inch) cancerous nodule in his liver.[39]

An American psychiatrist reported another case suggesting a Doomsday Signal from a powerful person:

A strikingly healthy 38-year-old "mama's boy" began to pull away from his mother. First, he married. Then he decided to sell the business he and his mother managed together. When he told her about this decision, she replied, "Do this, and something dire will happen to you." Two days later, in spite of having such a healthy respiratory system that he hadn't even had a cold in ten years, he suffered an asthma attack. Undaunted, he sold the business. His asthma attacks got worse. Then a psychiatrist helped him understand the link between his mother's behavior and his illness, and his asthmatic condition began to improve. However, one fatal afternoon, he told his mother that he was about to reinvest in another business without her help. Again she told him to prepare for "dire results." An hour later, he was found unconscious, gasping for breath, and beginning to turn blue from oxygen deprivation. Twenty minutes after that, he was dead.[40]

In this case involving a man's relationship with his childhood Lifeline Person, one wonders: Were the mother's words a prediction or curse for breaking away from her and going out on his own? Was his death an instance of psychogenic death? Did his mother's words function as a Doomsday Signal?

All these instances indicate that the Doomsday Signal doesn't have to point to doom in the jaws of a predator, or on a battlefield, or in a concentration camp. It can signal doom in the form of broken social bonds to a group or to an individual person.

An individual's Doomsday Signal can be a mother's curse or a doctor's diagnosis. It can be the expiration of a deadline. The signaled doom can be exile, or severance of *any* connection a person simply can't survive without.

RELATIONAL RESIGNATION STUPOR — THE END OF A RELATIONSHIP

What about people who are said to die of broken hearts? The threatened danger has come to pass. The separation has happened. Can the loss of a love relationship lead to a Resignation Stupor or even a psychogenic death?

In people ranging in age from teenagers to elders, despair after the loss of a love certainly can lead to a feeling that life is no longer worth living. Heartbroken after the breakup of their first romance, teenagers often lament and plead "I can't live without your love."

Widows and widowers, even those with a rich storehouse of memories and faith in an afterlife, confront the fact that death means the absolute end of an earthly physical relationship. The day of the beloved spouse's death is the day of doom itself: "You are gone from my arms forever. For the rest of my days on earth, I will always be physically without you." Not a Doomsday Signal, but the cold reality of being doomed to live with the absolute irreversible impossibility of being together on earth again.

Do widows and widowers die *of grief*?

This common belief received some statistical confirmation from research by the Harvard School of Public Health. Using data from 12,316 participants, these researchers found that, in the three months after their spouses died, widows and widowers were actually 66% more likely to die than people whose spouses were still alive.41

Are the deaths of those widows and widowers extreme instances of the link between relationship distress and physical distress?

Bereft parents have also been known to stop living after the death of a beloved child. A fairly recent celebrity instance was the actress Debbie Reynolds' death from a stroke on Dec. 28, 2016, just one day after the death of her daughter Carrie Fisher. Debbie's son Todd Fisher said his mother willed herself to die, having told him in her final hours that she "wanted to be with Carrie."[42]

Implicated as a factor in these deaths of these people left behind could be a Resignation Stupor due to the real impossibility of ever again being with a person they feel their lives aren't worth living without. It may well be that the deaths of those bereaved people should be counted among the psychogenic deaths related to the Resignation Stupor.

COMING UP:

Whew! The information provided in this chapter by my friends in books has brought us through some profound and possibly disturbing territory. Parasympathetic Dominance. Possum Response. Resignation Stupor. Psychogenic death. Merciful Stupefaction. Doomsday Signals.

Because this research on parasympathetic dominance and the Resignation Stupor is heavy, I've made the chapter short.

Congratulate yourself for staying with this material!

We'll put this information to good use in the next chapter, where we'll take up its relevance to our individual personal struggles with problematic post-naCCT moods.

NOTES

[24] (Honesdale, PA: Himalayan International Institute, 1981), 69-73.

[25] Martin Seligman, *Helplessness: On Depression, Development, and Death* (New York: W.E. Freeman and Co., 1975), 171.

[26] Dubovsky, Steven L., *Mind-body Deceptions* (New York: W. W. Norton & Co., Inc., 1997), 280.

[27] Seligman, 172.

[28] All Livingstone references can be found in James Macaulay, *Livingstone Anecdotes* (London, Religious Tract Society: 1886), 36, available as a free ebook, https://books.google.com/books?id=vbsTAAAAQAAJ&printsec=frontcover&source=gbs_ge_summary_r&cad=0#v=onepage&q&f=false.

[29] K. Jaspers, *General Psychopathology* (Berlin: Springer Verlag, 1923); Translation, (Chicago: Univ. of Chicago Press, 1963) p. 367, quoted in Henry Krystal, *Integration and Self-Healing* (Hillsdale, NJ: Analytic Press, 1988), 151.

[30] Henry Krystal, *Integration and Self-Healing*, 116.

[31] Seligman, 172.

[32] J. Malcolm, "African Wild Dogs Play Every Game by Their Own Rules," *Smithsonian Magazine 2* (1980), 62-71, quoted in Krystal, 116.

[33] Seligman, 166. A similar account is also given by the psychiatrist Viktor Frankl, *Man's Search for Meaning*, 74-77.

[34] Krystal, 145.

[35] Judith Lewis Herman, *Trauma and Recovery* (New York: BasicBooks, 1992), 85.

[36] The classic source for the discussion of this phenomenon is the paper written by the Harvard physiologist Walter Cannon in 1942 "'Voodoo' Death," *American Anthropologist*, 44, No. 2 (April-June, 1942) 169-181. Also Martin Seligman, *Helplessness*, 166-188, and Henry Krystal, *Integration and Self-Healing*, 144, cites instances of psychogenic death and states "psychogenic death is much more common than one would suspect and has been reported many times since Cannon's (1942) famous paper on 'Voodoo Death.'"

[37] Cannon, 170.

[38] Seligman, 175-176.

[39] C.K. Meador, *South-Med-J*, Mar: 85(3): 244-7.

[40] Seligman, 175-176, originally reported by J.L. Mathis, "A Sophisticated Version of Voodoo Death: Report of a Case," *Psychosomatic Medicine 26 (*1964) 104-107.

[41] https://www.hsph.harvard.edu/news/hsph-in-the-news/widowhood-effect-greatest-first-three-months/.

[42] Brent Lang, "Todd Fisher Opens Up About Deaths of Carrie Fisher and Debbie Reynolds," https://variety.com/2018/film/news/carrie-fisher-debbie-reynolds-todd-fisher-star-wars-1202847902/

CHAPTER 13

FALSE ALARMS, NOT DOOMSDAY SIGNALS

After all this research, let's bring the focus back to us naCCT survivors dealing with cPTSD. What help did we gain from the magic words "parasympathetic dominance?" How does this research into the Resignation Stupor help us make sense of our troubles? I'll share first, and then it will be your turn.

To recap the story so far: Wrestling with shame and disgust about intractable bad moods that seemed to come out of nowhere, I'd concluded that either I suffered from some biological malfunction, probably genetic, or I was a lazy, self-indulgent slug who just didn't try hard enough. Then I received this information from my friends in books.

I resonated with the possums, and the chipmunks, and the chickens that keeled over into a stupor. I could relate. I identified. It applied to me.

I resonated with Dr. Livingstone's word for the way he felt when trapped in the jaws of the lion: "stupor." It described my depressed, apathetic, "half in love with easeful Death" state precisely. Even though I hadn't been literally doomed in the jaws of a predator, feeling hopeless, helpless, and resigned to inevitable doom had a familiar feel to it: "Don't bother. Give up. It's hopeless."

So I began referring to my state as a "stupor" too. It sounded more dignified than "my swimmy state."

I also felt an eerie resonance with Resignation Stupor descriptions like that given by psychiatrist and concentration camp survivor Henry Krystal, especially when he said, "Physical and mental activity came to a standstill, including initiative, judgment and emotions." He'd called it a "state of walking death."

And psychologist Marty Seligman's ironic phrase, "death by relaxation" *really* scared me. Sounded a lot like my phrase "half in love with easeful death." It went right to my fear of resting. What if I gave up too soon or laid down to rest, fell asleep, and never woke up ?

AVOIDING "DEATH BY RELAXATION"

This fear of "death by relaxation" had played a part in my very persistent cigarette-smoking and sugar-eating habits.

I didn't *want* to die; I wanted to live! One way to avoid death by relaxation would be to avoid relaxing. So I pushed back against the impending Resignation Stupor of Doom by commanding myself: "Don't relax! Don't rest! It's dangerous!"

Cigarettes picked me up. Sugar did too. Furthermore, an urgency to my eating, as if I had to eat for my life, suggested the existence of a Chain Reaction of Triggers: eating sugar was triggered by fear of rest and relaxation, which was triggered by an impending or beginning Resignation Stupor.

I "hung on for dear life" to cigarettes (and, after I quit smoking, to sugary snacks) for a reason: By frantically cranking up my energy level, I was protecting myself from "death by relaxation," from the "merciful stupor" that could kill me.

Realistically, of course, I knew that rest and relaxation weren't going to kill me, so I created this sensible, realistic Self-Talk Script:

MY SELF-TALK SCRIPT FOR "IT'S SAFE TO REST"

> *"Maybe not every impulse to stop struggling indicates a dangerous drift into a Resignation Stupor. What if I explored safe rest and relaxation? Let myself get refreshed? If I'm tired, maybe it would be safe to just lie down and rest, even to go to sleep until my body returns to balance."*

Unfortunately, this sensible, positive self-talk was only moderately successful. I needed to dig deeper. So, even though my "swimmy" Resignation Stupor state scared me, I repeatedly called on my Inner Helper and used the magic power of "Hmm. . . ." to come alongside it.

A WHOLE STATE-OF-BEING

As I paid closer attention, I learned that state was not *only* a troublesome mood. Not *only* a low-energy body state. Not *only* bleak thoughts and depressed emotions. My present-day bad-mood version of the Resignation Stupor was an entire State-of-Being, including mind, body, feelings, sensations, "vibes," energy level, heart, and spirit.

Although that State-of-Being was wordless, I'll try to put it into words:

- I've been abandoned.

- No one will ever come.

- I'll never get what I need.

- I don't matter.

- I could die.

I was experiencing a vivid, body-based attitude of interpersonal despair, feeling alone, abandoned, doomed. As though my body had assessed the situation as hopeless, I was giving up.

WAS THERE A TRIGGER FOR MY RESIGNATION STUPOR?

In addition to paying attention to my inner state, I also paid closer attention to what had happened in my life around the time when I found myself in that state. As you probably suspected, those moods didn't come "out of the blue." With their distressing thoughts and "swimmy" feelings, those moods had often come after something upsetting happened with someone else. . . .

But. . . .

not necessarily *right away* after it happened.

I might function all right initially, but notice a day or two later: "I've sort of been feeling off and out of it since then." Or, unable to let a social incident drop, I might notice recurring worries: "What did she mean by that? What should I have said? How should I have acted?"

Interpersonal incidents like these got to me:

- Having my conversation partner's attention wander;

- Getting an evasive runaround instead of a direct answer to a question;

- Being left waiting a long time in my physician's exam room;

- A customer service representative not understanding my problem;

- A friend cancelling a planned get together at the last minute.

All these suspected triggering incidents involved interpersonal non-responsiveness, conveyed not only verbally but also non-verbally through facial expressions, gestures, body positions, voice quality, and even spatial arrangements. The naCCT category this pattern brought to mind was Trauma of Omission; sub-type "Nobody there."

Could these incidents be People-Triggers, working for me like Doomsday Signals? I put one of these suspected triggers into the Trigger and Distress Response statement:

> "When I encounter this trigger [_Conversation partner's attention wanders_],
>
> my Distress Response tends to be [_Resignation Stupor_].

That statement seemed to describe what happened, but the intensity of the Distress Response was embarrassing. "Come on," I would say to myself, "These present-day situations are irritating, but they're hardly life-threatening catastrophes. . . . Talk about overreacting to a triviality!"

TRIVIAL FOR AN ADULT, BUT NOT TRIVIAL FOR A HELPLESS INFANT

Actually, the relatively trivial nature of my suspected Doomsday Signals provided a clue, a tip-off.

Maybe those present-day, seemingly trivial incidents flashed me back to a time when a troubled or, even worse, _broken_ bond with a Lifeline Person would have been life threatening. . . . when I was little and couldn't survive unless someone took care of me.

Responses that might be called "inappropriate," "annoying," or even "ridiculously over-reactive" in an adult make perfect sense for babies or little children. Screaming when a caretaker doesn't come is good survival self-care for babies. So is clinging when a needed caregiver pulls away. And when screaming and clinging fail to bring the timely care that babies need, it makes sense for them to give up.

WHAT IF I'VE BEEN TRIGGERED INTO A FLASHBACK TO A RESIGNATION STUPOR?

Had that happened to me? Could I have flashed back to when I was a baby and something went dangerously wrong with my lifeline connection to my essential caregiver?

Had I been one of those infants who, when they appeared to be settling down into sleep, were really sinking into a despairing Resignation Stupor, as though the best that could realistically be hoped for was a merciful stupefaction leading to a pain-free death?

Describing my experience that way seemed over-the-top and melodramatic from an adult point of view. However, I remembered an essay I'd read back in school by Donald Winnicott, the pediatrician and psychoanalyst who coined the phrase "good enough mother." Arguing that "anxiety is not a strong enough word" for the troubles we encounter as absolutely dependent infants, he'd called these troubles "primitive agonies."[43] That didn't sound trivial. "Primitive agonies" sounded like something to be taken seriously. Sounded, in fact, like trauma.

"WHAT COULD HAVE HAPPENED TO ME BACK THEN?"

I had some general information related to my early history:

- I'd observed and experienced through the years how my family was not "touchy-feely," was in fact uncomfortable with physical displays of affection.

- And I knew how pediatricians advised parents to care for their babies during the era when I was born: bottle-feed them carefully on schedule and let them cry themselves to sleep. Back then, parents' well-intentioned adherence to physician's guidelines meant babies spent lots of time alone, waiting. This could be a cause of primitive agony for a dependent baby. Not "abuse" perhaps, but quite possibly a "traumatic lack of response."

Throughout my life, I'd viewed my family as reliably responsive, certainly not "abandoning." Nobody left me waiting in school yards or at bus stops. If they said they would be there, they were there.

But maybe on a *body response level* as a baby, I had felt abandonment terror. Maybe my infant body "knew" in some cellular way that I could die if they failed to do something absolutely essential to my survival — if I didn't get fed when I was hungry or picked up when I cried, or even if they went away, misunderstood me, looked bored or impatient, or didn't smile back when I smiled at them. I might have felt doomed, abandoned, forgotten, waiting for a response that didn't come.

Obviously I didn't die back then. . . . *but* my non-verbal, body-based self-care system might have installed a warning system complete with Doomsday Signal to protect me from future abandonment threats.

My infant body could have learned to protect me from things my rational adult brain thought were merely inconvenient, annoying, trivial, maybe even amusing, including the quirks and rudenesses of other people, including the wandering attention of my conversation partner.

I didn't remember the actual, childhood learning experience, but my alarm response showed how well I remembered the lesson I'd learned.

To put this idea in simpler language: Like Pavlov's dogs who learned to salivate when the bell that rang at feeding time stimulated them, my body learned to respond with a Resignation Stupor to the stimulus of a Doomsday Signal such as my Lifeline Person's blank look or my inner state of unsatisfied need.

STATE-OF-BEING FLASHBACKS HAPPEN IN THE PRESENT

Past and present had gotten blurred. Although the experiences that had felt like immanent doom had occurred in the past, the Doomsday Signal alarm rings in the present; I get triggered and go into a Resignation Stupor today.

The experiences of past child and present adult are brought together in State-of-Being Flashbacks — "SBF"s I sometimes call them, for short — Distress Responses that include everything about how it was, being me, way back then in moments of interpersonal despair.

These SBFs are so all-inclusive that it can be difficult to identify them as flashbacks and quite easy to think this State-of-Being is "just the way I am".

My SBFs encompass body state flashbacks, mood flashbacks, and emotional flashbacks.

They even encompass cognitive flashbacks to the way my mind worked back then when I was little, including my limited reasoning abilities, my beliefs about the nature of people and situations I found myself in, and my understanding of how the world worked. In an SBF I could flash back to all-or-nothing thinking, to impulsively sizing people up simply as either "nice" or "mean," and assessing adults generally as all-powerful and all-knowing.

When I found myself as an adult feeling listless and "swimmy" following a distressing interpersonal incident, I could say to myself, "Maybe this whole miserable package including depression, hopelessness, swimminess, spaciness, and abandonment feelings is a State-of-Being Flashback." I could use the concise NaCCT Flashback Statement to explain myself to myself:

> "I may have been triggered by recent [conversation partner whose attention wandered]

> into a [Resignation Stupor]

> that could be a State-of-Being Flashback to a past [naCCT of Omission: Chronic Lack of Response]."

THE BEST BENEFIT OF THIS RESEARCH

Thanks to what my friends in books had taught me about parasympathetic dominance and the Resignation Stupor of doom, I could stop feeling defective and hopeless. I now knew there could be much more to my troubles than bad genes and bad character.

"You are in a flashback" is very different from "You are lazy, genetically defective, sinful, and just plain bad."

Even if bad genes and bad character were also factors, early trauma was definitely implicated as a factor in my present difficulties. My difficult moods could certainly be State-of-Being Flashbacks triggered by Doomsday Signals installed when something that happened with my parents had terrified me.

Understanding how my apathetic moods, listlessness, and so on were related to a traumatic threat to survival increased my self-compassion.

Thinking of my troubles as trauma-based took away some of the stigma and self-criticism and stopped the flow of shame and self-blame.

Until those feelings lifted, I hadn't realized how much they had blocked my healing. Now I could rise up from shame and say "Wait a minute! These moods I'm so ashamed of are trauma symptoms. I am up against a strong force of nature."

Now I could stop trashing myself and devote my energy towards lovingly and effectively helping myself instead.

I began to replace my old "stinkin' thinkin'" with more wholesome, self-respecting, realistic thoughts. Sometimes my Inner Critic even acted more like an encouraging Inner Coach, working in partnership with my Inner Helper.

I could also stop blaming myself when the cures I'd invested in failed to cure me. The assertiveness training had helped, and the meditation, the quitting smoking, the therapy: all had been beneficial in many ways; they just hadn't touched the real naCCT problem.

It was as if I'd been giving myself palliative care, and now a real improvement — maybe even a cure — was realistically possible.

NOW YOUR TURN

How about you? What is your experience with this Resignation Stupor? Have you ever put yourself down, thinking that getting into this state shows that you have serious character flaws or some genetic trouble that you're stuck with and can't do anything about?

If you've had this thought, I'm enjoying picturing you now breathing a sigh of relief, letting go of your shame and blame, feeling the lightness as they lift, enjoying your newfound freedom and possibility.

If you don't relate to this Resignation Stupor state, just read along with as much interest as you can muster. As you'll see in the next chapter, the self-regulating and self-understanding techniques you read here may come in handy later for dealing with other troubling trauma-related states.

If you do relate to this state, the rest of this chapter provides you with a mini-workbook to help you apply the knowledge you've gained so far to the challenges of your present life.

Keep in mind that like all workbooks, this mini-workbook simplifies a very complex problem and may not do justice to your real life situation. Just let these exercises provide you with a basic structure for getting clear about your problem and what to do about it.

Putting this non-verbal material into words is empowering and integrating. Doing these fill-in statements brings your logical verbal brain to this non-verbal experience, which provides you with a feeling of control, understanding, and ultimately mastery and self-possession.

RESIGNATION STUPOR? FREEZE? OR A NAME OF YOUR OWN?

First, what are you going to call this state? Currently it's often called "freeze," which does lend itself to a nice alliterative phrase: "fight, flight, or freeze." However, some naCCT survivors protest that what they experience doesn't feel like being frozen.

Bottom line: We need names that fit our experiences. What name captures *your* experience of this state?

You probably won't use the technical term "dorsal vagal parasympathetic dominance," but maybe "freeze" *does* work for you.

A woman I described this state to recognized it immediately. She dropped her head to her shoulder, unfocused her eyes, and let her mouth flop open and her tongue loll out. "Oh," she said, "that's my clunk." Someone else called it "my abandonment trauma"; another person used the clinical term "dissociation." How about "collapse"? "Spacey"?

Experiment with putting your label for this state into the basic Distress Response statement:

> *"A Distress Response I sometimes have is: [Resignation Stupor/ Possum Response/ your own label]."*

Does this statement feel true for you?

WHAT ABOUT YOUR TRIGGERS?

At this point in your recovery journey, you're probably pretty good at trigger identification, so try this mental experiment: Take a minute to identify a time you experienced this state. (It might have been when you were reading this material.) Holding that time gently in mind, ask, "Could I have been triggered?" and check yourself. (And, yes, something you just read could be a thought-trigger!)

YOUR TRIGGER CHECKLIST:

- Intrapsychic Triggers, including thoughts and/or emotions
- People-Triggers
- Sensory Triggers
- Body-State Triggers

Often a combination of triggers sets us off. For example, did it make a difference that a People-Trigger happened on a foggy day, or when something smelled like Mom's hand lotion, or talk radio was playing in the background?

Remember Jason, who helped Nick in the pain treatment program? His distress arose from a combination of his positively energized body state, his proud thoughts and feelings, and a People-Trigger.

As a child, Jason had learned that feeling pride in his performance was followed by his father's hurtful behavior, typified by the time at the picnic: After undermining Jason with faint praise, Dad had reclaimed his own "Charismatic Star" status in the limelight by doing a magic trick and magnetizing the attention of Jason's best friend. Jason had been left feeling deflated, forgotten, and alone.

When Jason grew up, a state of realistic pride and confidence in being chosen to be part of a highly esteemed team functioned as a risky State-of-Being for him. He'd learned his childhood lesson too well. When his self-confident pride met with a People-Trigger like the subtle dismissals from his team leader, Jason could sink into hopeless resignation and abject worthlessness in a nano-second.

The Resignation Stupor itself can also function as a Trigger. You saw that happen in my case, how feeling like I was starting to go into a Resignation Stupor triggered my fear of rest and relaxation.

How complicated and entangled this triggering process can become! You can make it manageable by initially focusing on one possible trigger — (maybe one of the People-Triggers you've worked with earlier) and filling in your Trigger and Distress Response statement:

"When I encounter this trigger [Your possible Trigger],

*my Distress Response tends to be [Resignation Stupor/ Possum Response/
your own label]*

Is that what happens? Does this statement need to be expanded
somewhat in order to feel like an accurate description of your experience?

YOUR RESIGNATION STUPOR STATE-OF-BEING FLASHBACKS

Experiment with thinking of your Resignation Stupor as a State-of-Being
Flashback:

*"This [Resignation Stupor/ Possum Response/ your own label] could be a
State-of-Being Flashback."*

Does that feel like it could be the case?

Recall that State-of-Being Flashbacks are all encompassing, so check
for what are sometimes referred to as "mood flashbacks" or "emotional
flashbacks."

Also check for elements that could be called "cognitive flashbacks."
These might include extreme either/or thinking, forgetting present day
resources, finding yourself easily swayed by other people's opinions, or
seeing the outer world as vast, complex, and intimidating, while
experiencing yourself as small, helpless, and needy.

How do you feel about regarding your experience as a possible State-
of-Being Flashback, a *trauma aftereffect* that you could address with trauma
healing?

ACKNOWLEDGE YOUR NACCT BACKSTORY

If it's a State-of-Being Flashback, what is it flashing back to? Acknowledge
your possible naCCT Backstory with an naCCT Resonance Statement:

"An naCCT category I feel some resonance with is [naCCT category]."

You can find the basic list of naCCT categories at the end of Chapter
Four, "Your Recovery Begins: Psychoeducation." You can use either those
category labels or your own words, whatever descriptive language best
expresses your own personal naCCT history.

YOUR NACCT FLASHBACK STATEMENT

For a concise summary of what may be happening for you when you get triggered, put all the elements together in the naCCT Flashback Statement:

> *"I may have been triggered by present [Trigger]*

> *into a [Resignation Stupor/ Possum Response/ your own label]*

> *that could be a State-of-Being Flashback to a past [naCCT Category].* "

Some other ways to say this:

- *"What I'm experiencing may be a State-of-Being Flashback to Resignation Stupor, triggered by reminders of my naCCT experience."*

- *"Maybe distress in some present-day relationship triggered me into a State-of-Being Flashback to a time I felt hopeless and doomed in my early attachment relationship."*

- *"Have I flashed back to a time when struggling seemed futile, when I collapsed into the Resignation Stupor?"*

SELF-TALK SCRIPT: "I KNOW WHAT TO DO AND I CAN DO IT"

It's time to turn this awareness into action. We're now expanding the Better Option Statement to a "What-I'm-Going-to-Do-about-That" Statement":

> *"When I encounter this trigger: [_____],*

> *my Distress Response tends to be: [_____],*

> *and what I'm going to do about that is: [_____]."*

YOUR SELF-TALK SCRIPTS

One effective thing to do is use Self-Talk Scripts. They turn general information into personal working wisdom. These scripts helped me, and they can help you apply what you're learning to the challenges and opportunities life offers you.

So here's a cornucopia of Self-Talk Scripts for you to modify and use to take loving care of your distressing feelings, thoughts, and/or sensations.

While recognizing that objectively you are reasonably safe and capable in the here and now, use these scripts to stay anchored in present reality and to reassure and calm yourself. Mix and match them. Tweak them to suit yourself. Create some of your own.

You may find you return here often, leafing through these Self-Talk Scripts, soaking in the confident, steady assurance and calming, normalizing language they offer.

SELF-TALK SCRIPT: "INNER HELPER IS HERE"

Now that you understand the State-of-Being Flashback process, you'll find it easier to calmly and confidently reassure yourself.

> *"Maybe back then nobody came, but I am here for myself now! My Inner Helper is always here and gets stronger, wiser, and more lovingly effective every day. And the part of me that needs help is becoming better and better at asking for help and being open to receiving it. "*

Remind Inner Helper that you have many options. You might think of them as Inner Helper's Helpers.

You have already found ways to provide yourself with Safe Space Imagery, safe help from other people in your Patchwork Quilt of Help, and self-help actions you can take on your own. In Chapter Eleven, you added a toolkit of body-balance-restoring activities such as relaxed breathing, exercising, calming sensory inputs, or even simply lying down and going to sleep.

SELF-TALK SCRIPT: "IT'S NOT HOPELESS! WAIT! THERE'S HOPE!"

It's important to remember that your present situation is far from any interpersonally despairing situations of your past. You can intervene directly today with this realistically encouraging Self-Talk Script:

"You aren't doomed! Don't give up! Don't listen to the Doomsday Signal!"

or you can switch pronouns from "you" to "I" and say:

"I'm not doomed! I felt doomed then, but I survived. I wasn't doomed then after all, and I'm not doomed today!"

Vary the pronouns according to your varying needs. You can stand in front of a mirror and address yourself using "you." You can say the scripts silently, privately, to yourself using "I."

Sometimes one way just seems to work better. Switching pronouns is an easy way to increase your attunement to yourself using self-talk.

SELF-TALK SCRIPT: NORMALIZE AND EXPLAIN THE FLASHBACK PROCESS

When you find yourself nervously wondering, "What's going on? What's happening to me?" you can intentionally replace insecure thoughts with secure thoughts.

Use your ever-increasing knowledge and resources to provide yourself with reassurance that what you're experiencing makes sense. You can use all those naCCT statements you formulated earlier. Incorporate them into Self-Help Scripts that help you understand what's happening to you.

Experiment with having your Inner Helper, or one of Inner Helper's Helpers, create a calming explanation beginning with the words:

"What you are experiencing is normal and natural, even though it's distressing. . . ."

To normalize and explain the flashback process to yourself, include some of the following:

- *"Remember that's it's normal for people who've experienced naCCT as kids to have been trauma-taught stuff that leads them to experience triggers and flashbacks as adults."*

- *"Maybe this is a flashback to when my learning was body-based and non-verbal, before my nervous system had developed enough to make movie-type memories. That would explain why I don't have memories of learning this."*

- *"Maybe one of my naCCT wounds was this body-based, trauma-taught tendency to give up in certain situations with certain people."*

- *"Furthermore, this impact has been "covert" in that it has been hidden in my body. It has continued to be covert in that there is no obvious connection to traumatic experience."*

- *"Of course this is hard for me and feels odd. Early attachment to my Lifeline Person is the zone I had trouble with when I was an infant learning to make sense of my world. I am addressing deep learnings about how to stay alive. It's not a walk in the park."*

It's worth taking time to explain yourself to yourself. Explanations can be comforting to receive and empowering to deliver.

FALSE ALARM: ANNOYING BUT NOT DANGEROUS

Yesterday's Doomsday Signals are often today's False alarms! So be sure to ask, "Is what's scaring me a false alarm or a true Doomsday Signal?"

A false alarm is annoying, but not a threat. We ignore alarms when we know they don't mean actual danger. Think of how often you walk by a screeching car alarm.

To illustrate, let me tell you what happened once in a hospital psychotherapy group that met on the top floor of a high-rise hospital. In case of a fire, evacuation to safety would have been a nightmare.

One evening just as our group was about to begin, the fire alarm went off. Truly alarming. Ear-splitting wails and flashing lights. Everyone froze. People dependent on walkers. People in wheelchairs. People on gurneys. The terror was palpable: racing hearts, pale skin, held breath — waiting for what would happen next.

The door opened and there stood Danny the Security guard. Capable, tall and muscular, always calm. Safe "Danny from Security," in his dark blue uniform, standing in the doorway.

He stood for a minute, looked around the room, then spoke.

He did not say "Evacuation procedures are beginning."

He said instead, "There's no fire. It's a false alarm. We are waiting for the city firefighters. Safety procedures require the city fire department to turn off the alarm. Please bear with the noise. All is well. There is no fire. The noise will stop as soon as the officials arrive to turn the alarm off."

We were stunned for a moment as the real assessment of the situation sank in: Safe. No fire. The pounding hearts slowed down to normal. Frozen muscles braced for a crisis began to relax.

The alarm still shrieked and the lights still flashed, but people began breathing again. Someone cracked a joke and a few people laughed. The psychotherapy group process started up: Someone had a family problem they wanted the group's help with. We shouted helpful responses over the noise.

But it was only noise, not a nightmare of danger, mayhem, and possible death. Annoying, obnoxious, even ear-splitting, but, still, *only noise.*

We got engrossed in our process, so engrossed that we felt surprise when someone said, "Listen! The fire department must have come and gone. It's quiet in here."

The lesson: Sometimes we need our personal "Danny from Security" to come and tell us that there's no danger and the annoying alarm will soon quiet down. When we read safe situations as dangerous, we drain our resources and produce unnecessary stress.

So call on your Inner "Danny from Security" to help you distinguish a Doomsday Signal from a false alarm.

SELF-TALK SCRIPT: "FALSE ALARM, NOT DOOMSDAY SIGNAL!"

It takes work to differentiate the threatening past from the relatively safe present. When triggered into a Resignation Stupor State-of-Being Flashback, the "Threat detected! False Alarm" Statement provides reality-based reassurance:

In my case, I could say:

> *"This [conversation partner's attention wandering off] could be a False Alarm, not a Doomsday Signal."*

Use your own trigger to complete the statement as it applies to you:

> *"This [Trigger] could be a False Alarm, not a Doomsday Signal."*

If it is a false alarm, not a Doomsday Signal of true present danger, you are probably in a Resignation Stupor State-of-Being Flashback.

You can craft your own calming self-talk from these statements:

- *"The Doomsday Signal is often a False alarm. It's not a true Doomsday Signal."*

- *"It's been set off because of old wiring or old programming (depending on the analogy) that needs to be updated to align with current reality."*

- *"Hooray! Present day reality to the rescue!"*

- *"My alarm system was set to assess present day hassles as "doom," and so it sent a Doomsday Signal to the rest of my body."*

- *"The present day situations that trigger the old alarm system are usually just annoyances my adult resources can deal with."*

- *"Whew! Relief! I'm reasonably safe and only have to deal with the annoying alarm response itself: my own shut down State-of-Being. It's really annoying, but I'm not on the threshold of doom."*

- *"And remember: I did survive! I wasn't doomed after all".*

You can turn your reassessment of the present-day trigger into a reassuring sing-song chant:

"For an adult, an inconvenience;
For a baby, life and death."

or this variation:

"For a baby, Doomsday Signal;
For me today, a False Alarm!"

To remind yourself that false alarms are distressing but not dangerous, you can call upon the popular slogan that "FEAR" is an acronym standing for "False Evidence Appearing Real."

You can also visualize the word "danger" inside a circle with a diagonal slash cutting across it: The universal visual representation of "No Danger!"

You can even expand this reassuring visualization into some meditative mark-making and symbolic cutting-and-pasting. Here's how:

1. Write the word "Danger!" or "Doom!" on a piece of paper in big menacing letters;
2. Draw a thick circle around the word and slash across it with a thick diagonal line;
3. Meditatively go over the lines you've made until the sense of danger fades;
4. On another piece of paper, write the words "False Alarm" in even bigger, more powerful letters;
5. Cut out the words, "False Alarm"; and
6. Right over the words "Danger!" or "Doom," glue the words "False Alarm."

You can vary the process by replacing the words "False Alarm!" with "State-of-Being Flashback" or even "Annoying SBF!" to remind yourself that what seemed to be a Doomsday Signal was in fact an annoying SBF.

SELF-TALK SCRIPT: "NOW, NOT THEN"

For more "Reality to the Rescue," use the "Now, Not Then" series of statements you've been using since it was introduced for coping with People-Triggers.

"Fortunately, the reality is that I may feel awful, but
- *At least [the present person] isn't [the past person].*
- *I'm an adult, not a child.*
- *I'm in [the present place] not [the past place].*
- *It's [the present time], not [the past time]."*

SELF-TALK SCRIPT: "I HAVE RESOURCES NOW"

Another calming "Now, Not Then" factor is all the resources you didn't have back then but do have now.

"I have options now that I never even dreamed of back then. I'm not an abandoned child, not a baby who can't even turn over by myself."

"I'm not helpless and hopeless now. I may have been triggered into a hopeless-feeling Resignation Stupor, but the fact is that I now have power and I have options. I know how to come alongside myself, and I can act on my own behalf. I don't have to give up.

"I know how to cope with flashbacks and triggers: Get centered and grounded. Move my body or shift positions at bit. Stay safe in the Here and Now. Label flashbacks and drop the danger. Use all my skills. Go through my lists of resources and mobilize some of them.

"I also know how to get more help. I know how to get help from books. I've been putting together a Patchwork Quilt of Help and resources of all kinds."

You can expand this further by writing out some of the specifics in your Patchwork Quilt of Help. Remember all the awareness, skills, and resources you have now that you didn't have before. You are developing Working Wisdom. It might help to take time to inventory and appreciate its many components now.

SELF-TALK SCRIPT: "THANKS TO INNER HELPER'S HELPERS"

"My Inner Helper has so many Helpers and I notice myself feeling gratitude towards them and appreciating them being available. I am thankful to my inner resources like determination and perseverance and commitment and courage. And I'm thankful for my outer resources, for other people in person or indirectly through books and websites, for nature, for spirit. Giving thanks to them all feels so good."

SELF-TALK SCRIPT: "I CAN ASSESS MY PRESENT SITUATION REALISTICALLY"

You may be asking, "What if my present situation is really dangerous? What if I'm trying to relate to someone who really isn't good for me?"

That's an excellent reality-based question, and here's a Self-Talk Script to address it:

"Maybe the person I'd hoped to build a relationship with is just not suited to my dreams. Maybe I need to lower my expectations for this relationship or even say 'good bye.'"

"Maybe my hopes for my present relationship really are doomed, but that doesn't mean I'm doomed. I may be sad and feel grief, but realistically, I

have myself, and all my resources, and I can develop a good relationship with a suitable person in the future."

SELF-TALK SCRIPT: "THANK YOU, BODY-SELF"

Appreciate your body and its wisdom, its history and truth. NaCCT has remained covert in part because its story hasn't been revealed in movie-type memories. This secret naCCT story has been held in the body. The issues have been held in the tissues.

"Thank you, Body-Self, for your wisdom and skill in developing responses to threatening situations and taking initiative in self-preservation. Thank you for holding truths of my life experience. Thank you for sharing your secrets with me, for revealing what has been hidden and helping to make overt what has been covert. Thank you for sending out S.O.S. cries for help, for letting me be aware of what's happening with you."

SELF-TALK SCRIPT: "GOOD FOR ME!"

"Good for me! I'm paying attention to my Body-Self and listening to what my body is communicating to me. We're building a trusting relationship with each other. I understand that, whether or not I was actually physically assaulted, my precious body has been impacted by any naCCT I experienced, so I'm really gentle and patient with it. I'm proud of myself! I've haven't given up. I've persisted and made great gains. Good for me!"

YOUR PARTICULAR PREDICAMENT AND THE FULL DEFENSE CASCADE

Your issue may not be the low-energy, listlessness, and giving up of the Resignation Stupor. The Resignation Stupor is only one of many physiologically-based traumatic states of being.

Maybe you get ramped up, adrenalized, hyperalert and hypervigilant, or pulled in many directions all over the map, or just "feel like a nervous wreck."

In the next chapter, you'll read about the full spectrum of natural self-preservation responses to threat that are built into our bodies.

Maybe one of them, or different ones at different times and

circumstances and with different people, will sound like a State-of-Being you sometimes find yourself struggling to manage.

NOTES

[43] "Fear of Breakdown" in David W. Winnicott, *Psycho-analytic Explorations*, (Cambridge, MA: Harvard University Press, paperback edition, 1992, copyright 1989) 89.

CHAPTER 14

THE DEFENSE CASCADE

In this chapter about the "Threat detected!" states we revisit in Soul Mirrors, memories, or flashbacks, we continue to consider how to stay safe and stable with the aftereffects of naCCT, with specific focus on the physiological aftereffects of traumas that involve no direct physical assault.

THE DEFENSE CASCADE: WHAT HAPPENS WHEN WE'RE IN DANGER

In the previous chapter we got a close-up of the Resignation Stupor/ Possum Response and saw how that State-of-Being relates to cPTSD from early naCCTs. The Resignation Stupor is one of our many built-in survival responses to threat.

These survival responses, sometimes grouped together and called the "Defense Cascade," can be activated by any threat, not only by threat of physical attack. A thought or emotion can activate these responses, and so can Sensory-Triggers, Body-State Triggers, and People-Triggers. If someone looks at you funny, for example, or takes a long time responding to you, or starts bossing you around, a survival response could be activated.

And as we also saw with the Resignation Stupor/ Possum Response, any of these Defense Cascade states can be a State-of-Being Flashback or reflected in a Soul Mirror.

JENNA LEE'S EXPERIENCES WITH PHYSIOLOGICAL BODY-BASED, SURVIVAL-DRIVEN STATES THREAT RESPONSES: THE DEFENSE CASCADE

Paying attention to these Defense Cascade states of being helped Jenna Lee make sense of what was happening to her, enabling her to respond wisely, lovingly, and effectively when she found herself in one of these states. How this happened for her is shown in two episodes.

The first episode takes place after Jenna Lee watched a documentary about the wildebeest (pronounced *WILL' duh beast*) migrations across the African plains.

Wildebeests are large silvery-brown antelopes with big heads, shaggy manes, and curved horns. They look like a cross between a water buffalo and a deer. The documentary showed a herd of over 3,000 wildebeest migrating to new grazing lands. Crocodiles at the river's edge, lions and hyenas in the distant brush, and vultures circling above all waited for a vulnerable wildebeest to weaken and collapse.

Wildebeest babies can start running with their mothers in the herd ten minutes after they're born. And if one gets separated from its mother, it's so desperate to get reconnected that it will run toward anything that moves, even a safari van. Even a predator like a hyena. [44]

JENNA LEE'S "BABY WILDEBEEST" SOUL MIRROR

"It was the babies," she said, hugging herself and rocking slightly as she spoke. "Something happened to me when I watched those wildebeest babies. So many of them die. They get trampled by the herd, or the crocodiles and lions that prey on the migrations kill them.

"Actually, one baby in particular got to me, one that got separated from its mother.

"The poor little thing was so alone in the midst of that thundering herd, trying so hard to keep on running to connect with its mother, but you could tell it wanted to collapse.

"One time it slowed down and almost crumpled on those spindly little legs. You could see its eyes roll up for just a second in that moosey-looking head. Then it looked around, sort of confused, and staggered on again.

"While I was watching that poor exhausted little thing, running, running, running, trying to find its mother before something terrible happened, that awful feeling I get sometimes started to come over me."

HER THERAPY PROGRESS UP TO THAT POINT

Jenna Lee had been working courageously in therapy, building a secure inner helping relationship and getting to know herself more compassionately.

Although she still "got meanly aggravated" with herself sometimes when she didn't measure up to her own standards, she could often tease out the hidden helpful intent of her Inner Critic.

She had identified many of her triggers:

External People-Triggers like someone's exasperated sigh, thin compressed lips, or a certain clipped tone of voice her lead teacher sometimes used;

Her own Body-State Triggers, such as "getting all worked up," that set off an avalanche of worries. Feeling her own impulse to cry or to complain to others frightened her;

Her internal intrapsychic triggers, including not only upset feelings like anger and sadness, but also thoughts like "I get too worked up. I need to calm down. What's wrong with me?"

She had also become aware of her tendency to *force* herself to put on a happy face. She knew she worked "almost unreally hard" at being "good" and maintaining her composure, reminding herself, "Don't complain, don't yell, don't get that choked up voice."

She had explored how pressuring herself to be positive — cooperative, careful, unperturbed — played out in her present life and fed on her fears and insecurities, leaving her in an unsure, questioning state both with the main teacher, the authority figure, on her teaching job: "Will I be fired?" and with her boyfriend: "Will Mike break up with me for sure this time?"

With her increased self-awareness and her newfound self-compassion, Jenna Lee could be present with herself and recognize the way the baby wildebeest reflected her State-of-Being.

JENNA LEE EXPLORES HER SOUL MIRROR

"As I watched that baby wildebeest, I could feel myself speeding up — heart beating fast, and all that. It was like seeing a movie of my insides, like my own muscles were straining to keep on running.

"But I definitely wasn't caught in a flashback. That baby wildebeest was one of those Soul Mirrors, reflecting what I felt inside. Right on the edge between panic and complete collapse, like the blood's draining out of me. It's not even safe to stop and feel the terror; if you stop, you're doomed. You have to just keep going. I totally identified with that little wildebeest."

Instead of brushing this strange feeling of kinship aside, Jenna Lee explored it. What did she have in common with an animal that spends most of its life in motion, migrating from water hole to water hole on the African plain?

Jenna Lee thought for a minute, then said, "You know those extreme survival sequences in movies? Where two buddies are, say, struggling through a blizzard in the mountains, desperate to escape from some disaster, and one buddy turns to the other and says 'I can't make it, you go on without me.' The other buddy says, 'No, I won't leave you here to die! Come on!' That's how it was for that poor baby wildebeest: one part exhausted, collapsing, and giving up; and another part pushing through the exhaustion to reconnect with its mother.

"And that's how it is for me — like I have both those buddies in my head, arguing with each other. I feel that 'give - up - NO! — keep - going!' tension inside of me a lot. . . .maybe all the time."

Jenna Lee paused for a moment, then clarified. "Well," she said to me, "I push myself to keep going, but not with actual physical running. I just push myself to keep on being cheerful, being good, maintaining my 'Positive Mental Attitude.'

"It's exhausting.

"But easing up would be like the baby wildebeest collapsing: I could get relief from the exhausting struggle to be cheerful and good, but I could also die. Maybe not literally — no lions or crocodiles are lying in wait for me — but it feels like life or death."

THROUGH THE SOUL MIRROR TO AN INCIDENT FROM CHILDHOOD

"Watching the baby wildebeest's life and death struggle was like vividly re-experiencing that time I've told you about, when my family and I made a rest stop at that horrible restaurant on the way to the lake. I realized that baby wildebeest perfectly portrayed my frantic State-of-Being back in that restaurant: the aloneness, the urgency, the feeling of danger."

BUT FIRST, THE DEFENSE CASCADE

Before you hear what happened to Jenna Lee at the rest stop, I want you to know about the Defense Cascade, so you can bring to Jenna Lee's second episode a comprehensive overview of what our bodies do when our survival is threatened.

What's coming up next reads like a textbook, but don't be fooled: Knowing the trauma-related states of the Defense Cascade empowers you to recognize, label, and cope with your State-of-Being Flashbacks to those states.

WORKING WITH THE DEFENSE CASCADE

As you read through these states, you might find it helpful to mentally put a check next to those you personally recognize. You might find that they are related to the states you inventoried as problematic in Chapter Two, "Is This You?"

Some thought questions to keep in mind regarding these states:

- Does one or more feel familiar to you? Give you that "Oh, yeah, been there!" feeling?

- Do any of your moods seem to correspond to one of these trauma states?

- Have you experienced one of them in a flashback? These Defense Cascade states might feel familiar to you because we often end up in one when we are triggered into a flashback.

- Do any of these states match any of your past Soul Mirror experiences?

- Have you ever experienced one of these "Threat detected!" states when you were, in fact, objectively pretty safe?

CAUTION: STAY SAFE AND STABLE WHILE READING THIS MATERIAL

As you read this material, "text book-y" as it may be, you may find yourself getting unpleasantly stirred up. Triggered. What to do? You know the drill, and it bears repeating here:

If you do get triggered, focus on the fact that you are literally safe in the present.

Call upon all the resources you have to help you: Safe Space Imagery, Inner Helper, Self-Talk Scripts, body-calming techniques, your lists of safe people and stabilizing actions you can take.

And remember: You can always stop reading. You can skim this material. You can skip it and come back to it later. You are in charge.

HERE ARE THE DEFENSE CASCADE STATES AS I'VE COME TO UNDERSTAND THEM

Some aspects of my organization of the Defense Cascade states, like the fight or flight states, are quite mainstream and widely accepted. Others, like the berserk State-of-Being, the ambivalence zone, and the Resignation Stupor terminology are idiosyncratic to me. Including trauma bonding in the defense cascade is also idiosyncratic to me.

For each state you'll get a name, some information about the state, and then a description of what a person in that state might notice. For some states I also include typical naCCT triggers.

So, here they are, the Defense Cascade States:

SOCIAL ENGAGEMENT SYSTEM:

❑ TEND AND BEFRIEND: (VENTRAL VAGAL; RELATE AND RELAX)

This is our first line of defense. When we feel threatened, we seek safety by moving closer to another person or group of people.

This state is regulated by one branch of the vagal nerve that starts inside the head and wanders throughout the upper torso. This nerve has two branches that do two very different things:

One branch, the dorsal branch, controls the Resignation Stupor discussed in the previous chapter.

We met the other branch, the Ventral Vagal "relax and relate branch," way back when we explored People-Triggers. To recap: recent neuropsychological investigations have indicated that this ventral branch controls a whole system of nerves and organs called the Social Engagement System (SES) that we use to stay close to other people. The actions controlled by the Ventral Vagal nerve include talking and listening, singing, tilting our heads, expressing emotions on our faces, and making eye contact. The Social Engagement System is the optimal arousal zone. It is usually dominant in humans. It can sometimes override and put the brakes on both the sympathetic "fight or flight" response and the dorsal vagal "Resignation Stupor" responses.

To sum up the Ventral Vagal/Social Engagement System's involvement in naCCT: When we're threatened, connecting securely with other people can calm us down.

What you might notice in Social Engagement System: When you've been upset, have you experienced the urge to connect, to reach out, to cling, to talk it over, to band together, to get someone on your side? Have you noticed how a good response from another person can calm you down? Or that sometimes even remembering being with someone has calmed you down? Even picturing a secure connection with an historical figure or imaginary companion can be calming.

As you continue reading about defensive reactions to threats, you can activate this system by picturing your bond with other people who are also reading this material and recovering from the aftereffects of early naCCTs.

***

ALERT READINESS TO ACT

❏ STARTLE REFLEX

Unconscious; takes place almost instantaneously in the brain stem. For example, a man reported freezing in his tracks while on a hike. When he looked down on the path in front of him, he saw a rattlesnake. His startle reflex had protected him by commanding his muscles to stop moving even before he consciously perceived the threat.

What you might notice in the startle reflex: You won't notice this state because it happens so fast and in such a primitive part of the nervous system. Before your conscious "thinking" brain is aware of danger, you jump, turn your head, or blink your eyes. Like the man noticing the rattlesnake, you might notice a danger *after* your startle reflex has acted to protect you.

❏ ORIENTATION REFLEX

Similar to the startle reflex; however, the orientation reflex is conscious and responds to a less surprising stimulus.

What you might notice in the orientation reflex: You're aware of being still as a statue, alert and ready to act, searching for an answer to the question "What is it?"

Typical naCCT triggers for both startle and orientation reflexes might be noticing an odd, critical expression on someone's face or having the conversation stop when you enter a room.

***

ADRENALIZED, MOBILIZATION ZONE

"Threat detected! Do something — *anything* — to stay alive! Do it right now!"

This is the well-known **"Fight or Flight" response**: adrenalized; controlled by the sympathetic branch of the autonomic nervous system. Pupils dilate, distance vision improves, body temperature rises, heart rate and blood pressure increase, muscles tense up, perception sharpens.

This fight or flight response enables people to perform phenomenal feats of strength and endurance — (like legendary frantic mothers lifting cars off their children) — feats they would never be able to perform under ordinary circumstances.

What you might notice in both Fight and Flight: Urgency; high energy, all systems aroused and activated. Sort of "hyper," manic, revved up, ready for action. Could illustrate the saying: "When the going gets tough, the tough get going." Could feel like anxiety, or panic, or like a "chicken with its head cut off."

❏ FIGHT

Occurs if you think you can win, if you're trapped and can't flee, or if you learned a fight response to a particular stimulus.

What you might notice in Fight: Aggressive impulse; hostility; jaws clenched; temple throbbing; hands balled into fists, ready to fight.

Typical naCCT triggers might be criticism from others; social frustration; a disrespectful remark, argumentative tone, or domineering gesture.

❏ **FLIGHT**

Occurs if you think you won't win, or if you learned a flight response to a certain stimulus.

What you might notice in Flight: Impulse to "get out of there": to hide, leave the room, or run for cover.

Typical naCCT triggers might be someone with a red face and pulsing veins, gesturing aggressively; or someone making menacing remarks in a booming voice.

❏ **SCARED STIFF, "PETRIFIED," TURNED TO STONE**

Typically lasts only a few seconds. In this state, as in "fight or flight," the sympathetic branch of the nervous system is aroused, but here you're "petrified" to move lest you provoke an attack. This state is also referred to as "attentive immobility" and sometimes, confusingly, as "freezing."

What you might notice in the Scared Stiff, "Petrified" state: High muscle tone, readiness to fight or flee, and uncertainty about which way to move or what to do.

Typical naCCT triggers might be any of the above fight or flight triggers.

***

IMMOBILIZATION ZONE

❏ **RESIGNATION STUPOR**

A response to an inescapable threat, or a strategy of last resort, when active defense responses like fighting or fleeing have been bypassed or simply have failed.

This is the Resignation Stupor state we explored in the previous chapter: Similar to depression, with a drop in respiration, heart rate, and body temperature.

Controlled by the parasympathetic branch of the autonomic nervous system, specifically the dorsal branch of the vagus nerve.

Some traumatologists consider this a traumatic dissociative state. Dissociation, or cutting off a part of one's experience from consciousness, ranges from simply "spacing out" to the extremes of dissociative identity disorder (DID) like that experienced by the woman in the notorious movie "Sybil."

What you might notice in the Resignation Stupor: fear, coldness, numbness and inability to feel pain, uncontrollable shaking, eye closure, dissociation, feelings of unreality, as well as feeling trapped, powerless, hopeless, or doomed. You might experience either stiff, rigid "tonic immobility" or limp, ragdoll-like collapse, like Dr. Livingstone's in the jaws of the lion.

Typical naCCT triggers might be interpersonal "Doomsday signals:" abandonment threats, being misunderstood, being ignored, unattunement, unrelenting criticism, unresponsiveness, insensitive and tangential responses. Also silent treatment; "no shows"; being "ghosted" or walked out on; and even actual break-ups.

***

AMBIVALENCE ZONE ("BABY WILDEBEEST FEELING")

❑ **"Do or Die;" Push Forward or Pack it in; Give up or Keep on Going**

In the ambivalence zone, the "Keep on Going" of fight or flight pulls in one direction and the "Give Up" of the dorsal vagal Resignation Stupor pulls in the opposite direction.

What you might notice in the ambivalence zone: feeling frantic one minute, keeling over the next; an internal war between going valiantly onward and giving up. The urge to give in to the Resignation Stupor battles with the urge to override it and keep on trying in the face of exhaustion.

❏ TOTAL CONFUSION

The Social Engagement System (SES) drive to get close to someone for interpersonal safety becomes involved and adds another dysregulating force.

Children strongly feel the impulse to run to someone bigger and stronger for protection: to "run to Mommy," or call out "Daddy, help me!" Total confusion is not uncommon in children because their need for care drives them to attach to parents and other Lifeline Caregivers, even when the caregivers' behavior is uncaring or even threatening.

What you might notice in total confusion: Chaos of forces and impulses; chain reactions and simultaneous triggers and defenses all pulling and pushing at the same time in opposing directions; or the three-way tension among going forward aggressively into "fight," going forward dependently into attachment bonding, and running away into "flight."

Typical naCCT triggers might be any type, because all types of naCCT triggers can lead to this confusion. Triggering is especially common if a needed caregiver is frighteningly harsh, aloof, or just doesn't make sense.

***

TRAUMA BONDING (ALSO KNOWN AS CAPTIVITY BONDING, STOCKHOLM SYNDROME, OR BETRAYAL BONDING)

❏ TRAUMA BONDING

Trauma bonding is a mysterious — almost uncanny — twist on social engagement. It occurs in situations where one person holds real power over another, often the power of life and death. The person in power may threaten the other person and display both the intention and the ability to carry out those threats.

The powerless person believes — often is *led to believe* — that both escape and successful counterattack are impossible.

Trauma bonding can occur in battered women locked into abusive relationships, in captivity and hostage situations, and between dependent children and the caregivers who traumatize them.

Once trauma bonds are formed, the will to oppose gives way to obedience, docility, perhaps even servility. As the bonds intensify, the powerful person, no matter how objectively loathsome, may begin to seem charismatic, even god-like and worthy of devoted admiration. Some hostages have expressed the desire to marry their captors and others have put up bail for their captors.[45]

Trauma bonding in these difficult situations occurs often enough in mentally strong and healthy people to be considered a "normal" response.

What you might notice in trauma bonding: Loss of self-sovereignty or personal agency. Illogical positive feelings of admiration, loyalty, and shared values towards a menacing, destructive person you experience as having power over you. Hunger for occasional moments of intermittent positive gratification such as little token kindnesses. May even feel like love.

You may also notice breakthrough shame about the force of the trauma bonds and the thoughts and feelings that go with them.

Typical naCCT triggers might include being stuck "captive" in a job, marriage, business contract, lease, or membership agreement with bosses, co-workers, business partners, spouse, other family members, landlords, roommates, or organizations.

***

BERSERKER STATE

❑   **"GOING BERSERK;" MELTDOWN; "OUT OF MY MIND;" "FREAKING OUT"**

Berserk — a mysterious super-animated state characterized by surges of immense unrestrained power — is not usually included in the "Defense Cascade" of stress and trauma states. On the fringe of the trauma literature, the berserker state is, in fact, not talked about much at all. But it's been around for a long time.

Berserker state in combat soldiers:

The phrase "going berserk" was used by the thirteenth century Icelandic poet Snorri Sturluson, describing how certain warriors would go into battle:

With "shivering and chattering of their teeth, changing of color in the face, full-blown rage and fury accompanied by noisy grunts and howls," the berserk fighters "rushed forwards without armor, bit their shields"[46]

Centuries later, in 1994, psychotherapist Dr. Jonathan Shay described the primal unstoppable rage some of the Vietnam veterans he treated had experienced in combat. Shay looked back over 2800 years to Achilles, the warrior hero of the Greek epic, *The Iliad*. He found both Achilles and those present day Vietnam veterans had "gone berserk" in battle.

Dr. Shay places the berserk state at the heart of a soldier's most severe injuries: "it imparts emotional deadness and vulnerability to explosive rage to his psychology and permanent hyperarousal to his physiology — hallmarks of post-traumatic stress disorder in combat veterans."[47]

Berserker State in Animals:

A "paroxysm of dying rage"[48] was Dr. David Livingstone's name for the behavior of the wounded lion that attacked him in Africa. The lion had been fatally shot, but did not immediately lie down and die. Between the wounding and the dying, the lion first attacked Dr. Livingstone, then turned on one of the African villagers, and even attacked a third man before falling down dead.

Similarly, a doomed prey animal with absolutely nothing left to lose, right before the jaws of the predator clamp down, sometimes explodes into one wild uncharacteristic frenzy of fight behavior. For example, the search term "mouse fights back at cat" turned up over three million Google results, of which many are videos with titles like "This Mouse is Fearless" and "Epic Mouse Fights Back."

Berserker State In Children:

Sometimes impatiently dismissed as "tantrums," toddler's out-of-control episodes of explosive rage have a berserk quality.

The name "meltdown" more accurately describes what the out-of-control child is experiencing — yelling, crying, writhing, thrashing, flailing, spasming, or lashing out.

What you might notice in the berserker state: Feeling overwhelmed. Going crazy with aggression. No regard for consequences. May feel like a superhero, willing to risk everything to right a wrong or avenge an atrocity.

The berserker state has an absolute quality to it. Unstoppable. Beyond reason or argument. Feels elemental, primal. An uncontrollable force that cannot be denied.

You might even relate to the phrase "the wild courage of despair," which American author Edgar Allen Poe used in his short story "The Masque of the Red Death" to describe the doomed revelers' attack on the costumed figure of the disease that would destroy them. Because they know they are doomed to die of the Red Death, the revelers have nothing to lose at that point, so they throw away cautious restraint and attack with unbridled ferocity.

Other words used to describe this state include "out of control," "possessed," or "over the edge." People are said to "pull a nutty," "lose it," or "freak out."

Typical naCCT triggers might be a "damned if you do, damned if you don't" interpersonal situation you can't get out of and/or can't resolve.

***

QUIESCENT IMMOBILITY

☐ **DEEP STILLNESS; EXHAUSTION**

A state of profound inactivity; inertia; dormancy. Occurring in a safe environment after severe stress or injury, quiescent immobility promotes rest and recuperation.

Like the berserker state, quiescent immobility is not often included as a trauma-related State-of-Being. However, the Harvard Review of Psychiatry's thorough "Fear and the Defense Cascade," a thirty thousand word article the size of a small book with two hundred and twelve footnotes, *does* include this state and offers this vignette:

> *Phillip was a 40-year-old accountant who told of having been neglected and abused as the only child of an emotionally dysregulated mother with drug and alcohol problems. As an adult, he distanced himself from her unpredictable, often violent behavior and connected primarily with work and his significant other. Then his mother called him wanting to connect and be forgiven. Phillip didn't report much emotional response to his*

mother's call, but his partner said that for a few days after the call Phillip slept a lot, withdrew from people, and had little energy, appetite, or motivation. Phillip was puzzled, but "only in hindsight did he attribute it to the contact with his mother." [49]

During my ten years of university teaching, I heard many first year students hint at this experience after interpersonally stressful holiday visits to their families of origin. They called their post-visit exhaustion "crashing" or "being wiped out." Had traumatic stress been a factor in their deep exhaustion?

What you might notice in quiescent immobility: Profound exhaustion, inertia, apathy, withdrawal from people and activities. You might also notice lack of appetite.

You might be knocked out by exhaustion once you're out of harm's way and you can safely devote all your energy to recuperation.

Typical naCCT triggers might be any prolonged or profound interpersonal stress.

USING THE DEFENSE CASCADE IN REAL LIFE

Let's return to Jenna Lee and translate this Defense Cascade material into naCCT realities. We'll find out what transpired emotionally for her as she watched the film and experienced her "Baby Wildebeest feeling."

After some time and a lot of work in therapy, Jenna Lee had come to a more complex view of her family. She still viewed it as civilized, still orderly, but no longer the one-dimensional, "happy family" she had described in her initial therapy session.

One disturbing memory stood out. She called it "that unfortunate start to our least successful family vacation ever." But until she watched the film, that memory was detailed but flat — "nothing but the facts." With no strong feelings to go with the events, her narrative had been less like a real-life experience and more like a plot synopsis.

That changed when those memories of external events merged with her internal state as reflected in the Baby Wildebeest Soul Mirror. In her words, "When I had that Soul Mirror experience with the baby wildebeest, it was like a time capsule exploded and a whole living memory flew out into real life."

Here are the highlights from the therapy session in which Jenna Lee reclaimed her experiential truth about her complex family relationships. You'll notice her account is unusually detailed. She wasn't in a court of law where she was sworn to tell the truth, the whole truth, and nothing but the truth. She was reconstructing her subjective experience as it vividly came back to life for her.

JENNA LEE REMEMBERS THE TIME AT THE REST STOP RESTAURANT

"We were driving to the lake for the summer, right after school got out. I'd just finished first grade, Marie had just finished third. And Sammy was really little then, babbling away to himself in his own weird language. We were all jammed into Mom's maroon station wagon with the beach gear, golf clubs, and tennis racquets.

"Everything was going wrong with this vacation. At the last minute something came up at Dad's work and he couldn't drive up with us. He was going to fly up the next day. So it wasn't the usual arrangement with Dad at the wheel and Mom in the passenger's seat next to him. This time Mom was driving. And Mom was in a bad mood.

"Marie and I had a fight, and when Mom separated us, she put Marie in the front with her and stuck me in the back with Sammy in his car seat.

"I tried to bury myself in my coloring book, concentrating on adding flowers and birds and stars all around the edges and on people's clothes. It sort of worked. But then we pulled into the rest stop, and Mom just looked back at me and said, 'Be sure you don't leave any of those crayons on the seat: I don't want a mess.'

"I remember taking Sammy's hand while Marie and Mom walked up ahead. We went into this dingy little rest stop restaurant, with cinder block walls painted a day-glow pink that didn't do a thing to cheer up the dismal place. Marie and I went into the ladies' room right next to our table. Everything in there was damp and creepy, and the light bulb in the toilet stall was out.

"Then I went to wash my hands, and there it was in the sink: A centipede.

"I froze. Then I screamed. I knew I shouldn't, but I couldn't help it. The way its disgusting legs were going."

Jenna Lee interrupted her story to show me the goose bumps on her arm. "Look, it still makes my hair stand on end, all these years later."

She waited expectantly until I said, "You were really scared."

Then she continued her story: "A minute after I screamed, Mom ran in dragging Sammy. When she saw I was only upset about a bug, her eyes got hard and her lips got thin and white around the edges. Then she did a military 'about face,' turned on her heel, and walked out of the ladies room.

"The centipede ran into a crack between the sink and the pink cement wall.

"We went back to the booth. By then I was really hyper. My seat was next to the wall, and I knew what was right behind that wall: the centipede.

"Marie knew it was there too. She also knew that in our family anybody who was scared of a harmless bug was fair game. So, while Mom was busy with Sam, Marie started teasing me, wiggling her fingers up my back like centipede legs.

"When I pushed Marie away, Mom said in her warning voice, 'Jenna Lee. . . .'

"I said 'Marie's tickling me.'

"Mom just gave me a look and slowly shook her head.

"Then Marie opened her eyes really wide and pointed at my back, like she saw that thing crawling on me. I jumped up, brushed frantically at my back. I shook my hair. I screamed, 'Get it off me!'

"When I jumped up, I must have jostled the table, because I remember Mom pounding a crumpled napkin into her saucer, sopping up the sloshed coffee, and saying through clenched teeth, 'That's enough, Jenna Lee. Act your age.'

"I sat back down. I felt like smashing Marie's smirking little face, but I knew I'd really be in trouble if I did that. So I just sat there, feeling like all the blood was draining out of me, and at the same time feeling frantic. And I was still afraid that disgusting bug would come crawling out of that pink wall any minute.

"I feel that way now, as I'm telling you about it — that horrible, back and forth, 'give- up- NO!- keep- going' Baby Wildebeest Feeling, big time. Tight chest, speedy frantic feelings mixed with a dizzy, collapsing sensation.

"I felt like I was going crazy, watching Marie smirk and Mom pound away at her saucer with the soggy napkin.

"Then, even though I knew Mom hated crying, I started to cry. I couldn't help it."

Jenna Lee had given a factual account of this experience in a previous session, but this time tears came to her eyes as she talked.

She continued talking through her tears, "It was everything, all piled on together: getting yelled at for the crayons even though I was very careful to put them away, that disgusting bug, screaming when I knew I shouldn't, then finally crying.

"I kept trying to stop crying, but I just couldn't.

"Finally Mom threw down the napkin. She picked up Sam, took Marie's hand, pushed herself up out of the booth and glared down at me with that look in her eye. Then, in her scary calm 'let's-be-reasonable' voice, she said, 'We can't have you carrying on like that. If you can't stop crying, we'll have to leave without you.'

"It was like my worst fears were coming true. I felt kind of dizzy and spacy, numb, like I was turning into a zombie. The room got dark; everything seemed flat and far away. I remember staring at the red neon sign in the window flashing 'Hot Coffee' and hearing something banging in the kitchen. My mother stopped in the doorway, turned back to me, and said, 'Jenna Lee, are you coming?'

"In my zombie trance, I got up and followed them out to the car."

When she came to this point in her story, Jenna Lee sat very still, scarcely breathing, staring blankly into space.

Then her upper lip stiffened and she seemed to abruptly shift gears. Her brows knitted behind her glasses and she said, "It still doesn't seem that bad. That's exactly what Mike says: 'That's not so bad, Jenna Lee.' I can understand why he gets so fed up with me."

Jenna Lee's partner had pooh-poohed her upset, and she, herself, was only too aware of where her rest stop experience stood on the scale of objectively horrible things that happen to people.

So, in addition to her terror, even as an adult, Jenna Lee felt ashamed: "I shouldn't let a little thing like that get to me. I mean, my mother was really stressed, and she didn't act *that* bad that day in the rest stop; half the parents you see in any fast food place on the highway act that way — I see plenty of them even slap their kids, and those kids survive."

"You survived, Jenna Lee," I said. "You were really scared, and you survived."

She sat quietly for a minute, connecting with how she had felt as a little six year old. Her features softened as she shifted moods again. She said, "It really was awful for me then, wasn't it?"

"It really was awful for you."

COMMENTARY ON JENNA LEE'S EXPERIENCE

Like many survivors with cPTSD from childhood naCCT, Jenna Lee had had trouble acknowledging the depth and legitimacy of her distress. When introducing the incident in an earlier therapy session, she'd aligned herself with her family's point of view, saying, "Once I got really hysterical over a stupid bug in the ladies room and my mother got annoyed."

Cutting her mother plenty of slack, she'd said, "That was not my mother at her best. But no one's perfect. Mom's allowed to be human."

In therapy, Jenna Lee allowed *herself* to be human, with the needs and fears of a little girl, when she faced the emotional truth of her painful experience in that rest stop restaurant and put it into words.

She then faced a double challenge:

both:

- **Continue to extend grace to her humanly imperfect mother,**

and

- **Begin to extend compassion to her little human self for enduring the trauma caused by Mom's human imperfections.**

Meeting this double challenge as an adult calls for — and helps develop — Jenna Lee's working wisdom and emotional balance.

Jenna Lee began appreciating her own point of view when she asked, "It really was awful for me then, wasn't it?" As an adult providing the emotional presence for herself that she hadn't received from her family when she was little, she came alongside herself with the compassionate recognition that her distress was both deep and legitimate.

She became aware of her whole State-of-Being in a way that linked her past and present experiences and showed what it really had been like for her that day in the rest stop restaurant.

DEFENSE CASCADE STATES IN A SIX-YEAR-OLD'S NACCT EXPERIENCE

Let's see how the unfolding of Jenna Lee's experience that day in the rest stop restaurant fits into the Defense Cascade of stress and trauma states.

These Defense Cascade descriptions provide a normalizing context and a language for self-understanding, not a medical diagnosis. They offer naCCT survivors down to earth, practical help recognizing and describing what happens to them. As you read these descriptions, you, dear reader, can use this commentary on Jenna Lee's story as a model for thinking about difficult incidents in your own life.

It's worth noting here that as Jenna Lee told this episode of her naCCT backstory, she was working the "Remember and Grieve" component of healing. This component of the cPTSD recovery model is well-named because memory's companion is often grief. Jenna Lee was feeling grief emotions, especially sorrow, anger, numbness, confusion, and disorientation.

Readers sometimes identify with her and find their own feelings and issues are getting stirred up. If you find this happening to you, remember to use all your "Stay Safe and Stable" coping skills and resources. And pace yourself. This includes, as always, taking a break.

So, here's how the Defense Cascade states apply to Jenna Lee's experience in the rest stop restaurant:

"Social Engagement System"

Jenna Lee's traumatic episode actually began with earlier on-going chronic troubles in her Social Engagement System that predisposed her to get upset later by the event in the rest stop restaurant. Even before she climbed into her mother's maroon station wagon that summer when she was six, she was under stress.

One of Jenna Lee's on-going stressors was the way her family handled feelings. Admiring strong, stoical characters who keep their feelings hidden, her family adhered to the Code of the Stiff Upper Lip: "Don't bother other people with feelings, and don't waste precious energy giving in to emotions."

By six years old, Jenna Lee had learned her family's unspoken rules: she knew she "shouldn't" scream and she "shouldn't" cry.

Growing up in a stoical family, Jenna Lee wasn't able to express her emotions safely with other people, and therefore her first line of defense against threat — turning to other people for help with her distress — was *not* a viable option for her.

In order to stay connected to her family, Jenna Lee had already learned to hide a part of herself.

Once the vacation trip began, Jenna Lee's stress grew toward a crisis. She was away from her home base, from her girlfriend next door and her secure little bedroom nook surrounded by her artwork, books, and toys.

Each little incident on the trip wore Jenna Lee down further. The usual structure of the family was broken up when Dad didn't accompany them for the start of their vacation. Mom was nervous without him behind the wheel.

When the car pulled into the rest stop, her mother *assumed* that Jenna Lee would make a mess by failing to clean up her crayons. An undercurrent of sibling rivalry between the sisters also bubbled up to the surface. And Jenna Lee had to act as caretaker for her little brother while her mother and her older sister walked ahead together, leaving her feeling both burdened and left out.

Her social engagement Ventral Vagal system was frazzled: By the time Jenna Lee saw the centipede in the dimly lit ladies' room, her feeling of security in her family had been undermined and her inner resources were wearing thin.

"On Alert" — The Startle Response

When she saw the centipede, Jenna Lee froze — a classical "startle" response. She held her breath. Her mind and senses became keenly alert as she assessed the situation: Seeing the centipede spelled danger for her, both in itself as a particularly "creepy and disgusting bug" and in the way its presence triggered states-of-being that were interpersonally dangerous for her.

Almost instantaneously, Jenna Lee's "On Alert" startle response progressed to "Danger! Threat detected!"

Social Engagement System, Again!

Even with weakened social supports, Jenna Lee's first response to danger was the primal survival behavior that nature has hard-wired into the very young: Her Social Engagement System came on board — "Threat detected! Cry for help! Connect!" Her whole being sought hugs and comforting protection from her mother. So Jenna Lee cried out for help.

For children to develop a basic sense of safety and belonging, they need to have their cries of distress responded to with loving care, and they need to cling to their caregivers until they calm down.

However, Jenna Lee's distress cry failed to bring relief. On the contrary, it brought a punishing response: Her mother impatiently turned away from her. Jenna Lee became more distressed as she faced the core naCCT danger: the absence of a secure attachment bond.

Feeling ashamed, alone in the dank bathroom with her fear, Jenna Lee was forced to manage her pain by herself. In essence, while most young animals are held by their mothers and encouraged to cling, little Jenna Lee was left to fend for herself with two perceived dangers: the bug and the angry, contemptuous turning away of her mother.

Stoical family values and present relationship tensions prevented Jenna Lee from being helped by nature's first line of defense against threat: She couldn't use her Social Engagement System defenses to calm down.

What else could she do?

The Emergency "Fight or Flight" Response: "Do Something!"

Under the influence of her sympathetic nervous system, Jenna Lee's whole being geared up for fight or flight. She thought and reacted faster. Her hearing sharpened. Her temperature rose. Her breathing got shallower and sped up. Her heart also sped up, pumping plenty of blood to her arms and legs, giving her strength and energy.

But would fight or flight actually help her?

A loving connection can't be created by brute force, so fighting couldn't help Jenna Lee. Furthermore, she knew fighting would alienate her mother even more.

What about flight, the other adrenalized response to threat?

She was threatened by abandonment, and you can't *flee* from abandonment. So, physical flight was not a realistic option for Jenna Lee either.

Neither fight nor flight can prevent abandonment.

The closest she came physically to moving her body in an urgent, adrenalized fight or flight response was jumping up, frantically shaking her hair, brushing her neck, and screaming. And that only aggravated her mother more.

Because Jenna Lee's automatic adrenalized fight or flight responses wouldn't help her connect with her mother any more than her cry of distress had helped, her mobilized adrenalized response was redeployed. Instead of helping her take action in her outer world, it was put into service within her: stopping her from expressing her distress.

Her redirected fight or flight response brought *all* her resources — her muscles, determination, and mental powers — to the task of "being a good girl."

Like someone who "bites their tongue" to avoid blurting out something they'll later wish they never said, Jenna Lee commanded her muscles to clamp down and overpower her natural urges to cling, cry, punch, yell, or even have a tantrum.

Her abdominals, diaphragm, and the muscles in her ribs had the job of stopping her from sobbing; her jaw muscles contributed to the effort by clamping together; her chin and upper lip pitched in by stiffening to block the trembling that would release her tears. Even her arm muscles helped out by clenching in order to block any impulse to strike out.

Instead of using her strength and determination *to keep running to connect*, as the baby Wildebeest had, Jenna Lee was using them *to clamp down in order to connect* with her mother.

Ambivalence Zone: The Baby Wildebeest Feeling

However, Jenna Lee's inner distress grew stronger, pushing harder for release by crying and clinging. Blocking that release became more difficult.

Exhausted, desperate, she went back and forth in the Ambivalence Zone. There she was pulled between the hyper-mobilized adrenalized fight or fight response and the immobilized Resignation Stupor. This was the picture of her State-of-Being that she saw reflected in the baby wildebeest Soul Mirror.

Confusion Zone

Jenna Lee was pulled into the confusion zone because her attachment drive to connect with her mother was still very strong, but where she needed softness and warmth, maybe even engaged correction and coaching, what came at her felt hard and cold.

Her State-of-Being at this point was one of enormous strain: emotional, social, and physical. Conflicting forces and impulses pulled her every which way: Cry! Cling! Fight! Run away! Clamp down! Express or explode! She may also have been using her muscular armor to hold back the more extreme dysregulated state of meltdown, a child's version of berserk.

She experienced internal warnings that her strength, will power, "true grit" and other internal resources were diminishing, but she wasn't yet clearly doomed.

Externally, her situation kept deteriorating: the ongoing fear of the centipede behind the wall; the everyday injustice of having her mother ignore her big sister's malicious teasing yet criticize Jenna Lee for responding to it; and the cumulative effect of all the impatient cut-offs from her mother.

So Jenna Lee began to give up, to sink into the trauma state of hopeless Resignation Stupor.

Immobilization Zone: Resignation Stupor

Feeling doomed and powerless, Jenna Lee went into a trance of interpersonal despair. She became more profoundly disconnected from both her surroundings and her inner distress. She began to feel dizzy. Her vision became blurry and dim.

In her therapy session, she compared how she'd felt back then to the strange "dreamy, foggy" state she'd experienced before a recent surgery: "They'd given me some drug and right before they wheeled me into the operating room, someone said, 'You may experience some discomfort,' and I said, 'That's all right' because I just didn't care."

Perhaps because children are usually powerless to literally escape from a stressful situation, they are likely to escape psychologically, using dissociation to blot out unbearable realities. The younger the child, the more likely this response, and Jenna Lee was only six years old.

And then came the conclusive Doomsday Signal: Her mother said, "Well, if you can't stop crying, we'll have to go on without you."

"Zombie trance"; trauma bonding

Jenna Lee was scared to death. Her mother had already emotionally abandoned her; it seemed like a small step to literal abandonment.

As she sat alone in that booth, looking up at her departing family, her throat and ribs aching from trying to hold back her sobbing, watching her world fall apart as her family literally moved away from her and threatened to leave her, Jenna Lee's worst fears seemed to be coming true.

"I felt spacy and numb," she said, "like I was turning into a zombie."

Comparing her little self to the legendary "living dead," who mindlessly lose their sense of agency and self-sovereignty and instead blindly obey their masters, Jenna Lee said, with a faint sneer of self-disgust, "In my zombie trance, I got up and followed my mother out of the rest stop."

When Jenna Lee started to slip into what she called her Zombie Trance, she began to slip into the docile, terror-based obedience that characterizes trauma bonds.

Although the concept of trauma bonding usually refers to adults in hostage-type situations, the circumstances of six-year-old Jenna Lee's zombie trance have some things in common with trauma bonding:

- She was emotionally isolated and powerless.

- Her fate depended on her mother.

- Neither fight nor flight would help her.

- She surrendered her will to her mother.

Jenna Lee was surprised and relieved to learn about trauma bonding, and how it is a disconcerting yet normal trauma response to being trapped in a stressful interpersonal situation.

COMING UP NEXT

That was a lot of information! It can serve as a potent resource for thriving after naCCT. In the next chapter, we'll apply this empowering information to present cPTSD challenges.

NOTES

44 Norman Myers, *Long African Day*, (New York: Macmillan, 1972), p. 216.

45 Bessel van der Kolk, "The Complexity of Adaptation to Trauma: Self Regulation, Stimulus Discrimination, and Characterological Development," in B. van der Kolk, A. McFarlane, and Lars Weisaeth, *Traumatic Stress: The Effects of Overwhelming Experience on Mind, Body, and Society* (New York: Guilford, 1996) 200.

46 Mark D. Griffiths, "All the Rage: A Brief Look at Berserkers," blog at *Psychology Today*, April 28, 2015, https://www.psychologytoday.com/us/blog/in-excess/201504/all-the-rage

47 Jonathan Shay, *Achilles in Vietnam: Combat Trauma and the Undoing of Character* (New York: Scribner, 1994) 80 and 98.

48 Macaulay, *Livingstone Anecdotes*, 36.

49 If you want a comprehensive treatment of the Defense Cascade, this is the place to go: 30k word article (the length of a small book) with 212 footnotes. Kasia Kozlowska, Peter Walker, Loyola McLean, and Pascal Carrive, "Fear and the Defense Cascade: Clinical Implications and Management," *Harv Rev Psychiatry*. 2015 Jul; 23(4): 263–287. Published online 2015 Jul 8. doi: 10.1097/HRP.0000000000000065 PMCID: PMC4495877 https://www.ncbi.nlm.nih.gov/pmc/articles/PMC4495877/.

CHAPTER 15

FLASHBACKS, DEFENSE STATES, AND NACCT MEMORIES

The information in the previous chapter about the Defense Cascade states can help meet the challenge of body-based cPTSD symptoms, particularly the very subtle challenge of triggered State-of-Being Flashbacks to those states. Let's check back in with Jenna Lee to see how this information benefits her.

The incident in the rest stop restaurant happened so long ago. As Jenna Lee talks about it in her therapy session, she is safe in the present, where she can use her Soul Mirror experience, her newly-vivid memory of the naCCT incident in the restaurant, and her knowledge of the Defense Cascade states to improve her present adult life. Specifically, she wants to stop getting People-Triggered by Mike.

"I get that Baby Wildebeest Feeling around Mike a lot," she says, "and when that happens, I can't think straight. There's got to be a better way to react."

To find that better way, we begin with the familiar process of identifying triggers and Distress Responses.

JENNA LEE'S TRIGGERS

Is there something specific Mike does that triggers her?

"Well, there's his obvious disrespectful behavior, his exasperated sighs, his derogatory remarks and scornful comments when I'm upset, and, sometimes, his direct threats to leave. . . .and there's something else. . . .it's something he does physically, tightens his muscles. . . .he puts up a wall. . . .is it crazy to say he shuts off his energy flow to me?"

I share with her that while the verdict isn't in yet regarding whether we pick up "energy flows" or "vibes" from each other, the work of pioneering neuropsychologist Dr. Allan Schore has certainly established the existence of subtle, body-based communication between people, beginning with "right brain to right brain" communications between mothers and their infants.[50]

Hearing this, Jenna Lee adds "Shuts off his flow of energy to me" to her list of People-Triggers from Mike.

She continues, "And then there are the inner triggers: when I 'get all worked up' or feel like crying or complaining. Or wanting a comforting response from Mike that just doesn't come. Then all my abandonment-panic buttons get pushed. I'm also triggered by my own Baby Wildebeest Feeling. It's a vicious cycle. The Baby Wildebeest Feeling triggers more intense Baby Wildebeest Feelings. It's definitely one of those atomic chain reactions of triggers."

JENNA LEE'S TRIGGER AND DISTRESS RESPONSE STATEMENT

Jenna Lee includes both outer and inner triggers in her naCCT Trigger and Distress statement.

You'll notice that her statement is not as neatly concise as examples in books tend to be. This is real life.

Jenna Lee is striving for a route to self-understanding without worrying about getting "the right answer." Her real life statement is perfectly workable, even as it sprawls and rambles.

At first, she just gets her ideas down:

"When I encounter this outer trigger: [Mike's exasperated sigh or clipped tone of voice, his blank expression and silence, his sneering and shutting off his energy flow to me, his spoken threat to leave];

or this inner trigger: [wanting comfort or understanding that isn't coming],

my Distress Response tends to be [a horrible mash-up of Baby Wildebeest Feeling, Fight, and Confusion, bouncing all over the place, maybe even a little Berserk, heading into Zombie Trance]."

She may eventually choose to streamline her statement and focus on one element, but right now the "all- over- the- place" quality is a key identifying characteristic of her Distress Response, and acknowledging it will help her recognize when she's been triggered.

BOTH PAST AND PRESENT REFLECTIONS IN HER SOUL MIRROR

Jenna Lee's Baby Wildebeest Feeling Soul Mirror reflects both the way it was back then, and the way it is now.

When she looked in the Soul Mirror, she could see her present State-of-Being:

What the [Baby Wildebeest film sequence] reflected for me in the present is [the Ambivalence Zone Baby Wildebeest Feeling I get sometimes these days when I'm triggered by Mike]

And she could also see her past State-of-Being:

What the [Baby Wildebeest film sequence] reflected for me from the past was
[The Ambivalence Zone Baby Wildebeest Feeling I got when I was in the rest stop restaurant with my family].

Thanks to her Soul Mirror experience, Jenna Lee recognized and appreciated how her present day People-Triggers correlated with her early childhood experience: The hard look in Mike's eyes, for example, and his exasperated sighs or clipped tone of voice, even the shut-off energy flow, and, of course, the spoken threat to leave, all were in a direct line from her exasperated mother.

❧

DISTRESSING TRIGGERS, HELPFUL BREADCRUMBS

Jenna Lee also recognized that those triggers and Distress Responses functioned like clues to her true emotional and interpersonal history. As she put it, "They're like breadcrumbs my child self left so I could find her."

Jenna Lee goes on to explore what she experienced as a child. She remembered a single overt incident from back then. But her trauma was not just that single incident.

Her trauma was classic naCCT — It was *non-physically-assaultive, attachment-based, Chronic, and Covert* — the cumulative impact of many incidents of unavailability, dismissal, and emotional abandonment.

When the covert pattern of naCCT-type relating became overt in the rest stop restaurant, that rare outcropping provided Jenna Lee with something tangible to point to, something that revealed the trouble beneath her family's civility.

"That threat of physical abandonment was very unusual," Jenna Lee said, "But the fear of emotional abandonment went all through my childhood. It was a way of life back then. Fear of being abandoned when I was upset.

"I'm getting a fuller, more complex picture of my childhood, of the people I grew up with. I'm understanding what really happened, what it really was like for me."

JENNA LEE FINDS HER CHILD SELF

I asked, "So what would you call what really happened back then? Can you give it a label, maybe one of the naCCT categories?"

"So much was missing," she replied. "Comfort, explanations or explorations of what was going on with me, guidance, help with handling it. And then, when I needed that good stuff, what I got instead was impatience, harshness, and hurtful abandoning responses — even a threat of literal abandonment.

"It was awful, the despair I felt when all I got was silence, blankness. . . .just nothing there. . . .or when I realized nothing — nobody, no help — was going to come.

"Then having to hide my upset for fear of being *totally* abandoned emotionally.

"My body hid stuff too, developed strategies for keeping the lid on my upset so it wouldn't show."

Jenna Lee paused, held her breath for a minute, then went deeper, "I guess I installed one of those invisible pet protection fences and put on a shock collar so I wouldn't go outside those invisible boundaries.

"I tried not to go near that longing for a response. I tried to avoid even *knowing* I had that longing.

"At least if I hid my upset from myself, didn't let myself go near the longing for someone to be there and help me, then I didn't get that 'nobody there' feeling. My strategy was 'Don't ask, don't even have any needs at all, and you won't be disappointed.'

"But that strategy didn't always work. Sometimes the longing was so strong it broke through the invisible fence. Just like it does these days, especially with Mike.

"You asked what category of naCCT did my history belong to? I can relate to so many of those categories. I had to be cheerful and pleasant, so the Pathogenic Pleasantness category fits — what with my mother always being productive, busy with something besides my feelings. . . .and her silences, always with a civilized smile. Sometimes I think the Hidden Hostilities category might fit too.

"But the worst was the fear of being left. Not getting any emotional response *felt like* being left all alone to fend for myself. Terrified. Forlorn. Heartbroken.

"It's hard to find the right words for it. I could use those psychotherapy words, like 'Emotional abandonment. Lack of deeply secure emotional attachment to parents; lack of unconditional love, of emotional safety, of attunement and empathy.'"

Finally, Jenna Lee settled on the category "naCCT of Omission," with a sub-type in her own words: "Traumatic Absence of Emotional Responsiveness."

"The jargon distances the pain," she explained. "Makes it a little more manageable."

"Using that abstract psychotherapy jargon also dignifies my distress, makes it sound legitimate."

JENNA LEE'S COMPLETED NACCT FLASHBACK STATEMENT

Jenna Lee used "naCCT of Omission: subtype Traumatic Absence of Emotional Responsiveness" to complete her naCCT Flashback Statement:

342   NO STICKS OR STONES, NO BROKEN BONES

"I may have been triggered by this outer trigger [Mike's exasperated sigh or clipped tone of voice, his blank expression and silence, his sneering and shutting off his energy flow to me, his spoken threat to leave];

or this inner trigger: [wanting comfort or understanding that isn't coming],

into a [Baby Wildebeest Feeling]

that could be a flashback to past [naCCT of Omission: Traumatic Absence of Emotional Responsiveness].

When she saw her naCCT flashback statement written out, she revised it, saying, "Cross out 'overt spoken threat to leave.' I don't need to be overtly threatened; the subtle non-verbal stuff is plenty triggering by itself.

"But I'll add that it happens when I bring up emotional concerns. Here's my revised version:

"I may have been triggered by this outer trigger [Mike's sneering and absence of response when I bring up emotional concerns],

or this inner trigger [wanting comfort or understanding that isn't coming],

into an [Ambivalence Zone Baby Wildebeest Feeling]

that could be a flashback to past [naCCT of Omission: Lack of Emotional Responsiveness]."

"There it is. All contained in that one little statement," she said.

JENNA LEE'S BETTER OPTIONS AND "WHAT-I'M-GOING-TO-DO-ABOUT-THAT" STATEMENT

Jenna Lee doesn't leave herself stranded with a clear statement of her problem but with no solution. After recognizing, understanding, and naming that difficult State-of-Being, she could lovingly say to herself, "I'm having that Baby Wildebeest Feeling now, so I'm going to double down my safety efforts because I. AM. TRIGGERED."

She then proceeds to figure out what to *do* about getting People-Triggered by Mike. She works with the expanded Better Option/ "What-I'm-Going-to-Do-About-That" Statement:

"When I encounter this trigger: [_____],

my Distress Response tends to be: [_____],

and what I'm going to do about that is: [_____].

She first comes alongside herself, connecting her distressed, triggered part that needs help with her Inner Helper. Thanks to her understanding of the triggering process and State-of-Being Flashbacks to Defense Cascade states, Jenna Lee's manner is calm, like those wise parents who know their child's after-birthday-party stomach pains are the normal temporary result of too much ice cream and cake.

She says, "I can start by calming myself down with naCCT self-understanding Statements and Self-Talk Scripts. I find that 'You Make Sense' Statement especially reassuring. It makes me feel like I'm basically sane, and that's empowering."

REFINING THE "YOU MAKE SENSE" STATEMENT USING PRONOUNS

Speaking as Inner Helper providing normalizing explanations and a calming "All is Well" perspective to her inner part that needs help, Jenna Lee first addresses herself as "you."

"You related to the [naCCT of Omission: Traumatic Absence of Emotional Responsiveness],

so it could make sense that you get distressed by [Mike's sneering and absence of response when you bring up emotional concerns]."

Later, as she integrates this understanding of what happens to her, she chooses to speak from her "I" self:

"I related to the [naCCT of Omission: Traumatic Absence of Emotional Responsiveness]

so it could make sense that I get distressed by [Mike's sneering and absence of response when I bring up emotional concerns]."

WHAT'S IN JENNA LEE'S FIRST AID KIT?

In her "What-I'm-Going-to-Do-about-That" First Aid tool kit, Jenna Lee has quite a powerful set of resources for better options. She reviews them:

"I have all my clarifying naCCT statements and Self-Talk Scripts. I know about the Defense Cascade states and how normal and natural they are, even if I've learned to attach danger to interpersonal situations that aren't really life threatening to me as a grown up. I can always remind myself 'This could be a State-of-Being Flashback.'

"Plus, I have all those stabilizing techniques we've worked on. I have my Safe Space Imagery, my pop-up inner refuge which I plan to symbolically activate with the private gesture of touching my thumb to my ring finger.

"I have my Patchwork Quilt of help and all my lists for handling People-Triggers.

"And I have my body wisdom. I can recognize my physiological responses and communicate with my Body Self."

JENNA LEE'S SELF-TALK SCRIPT: RETURN TO BALANCED BODY STATE

"My body detected something it learned was a threat long ago, and so it went into one of those Defense Cascade states. I can reassess that threat level in terms of my resources today. I lived through it back then, and it probably isn't a threat today. My body will return to balance as I come back to safety in the here and now."

JENNA LEE'S SELF-TALK SCRIPT: "DOOMSDAY SIGNAL OR FALSE ALARM?"

Coming back to safety in the here and now would be easier for Jenna Lee if she deeply believed her triggers are really false alarms. To help her deepen this stabilizing belief, I begin by asking her, "What's going on when you're triggered by 'wanting comfort or understanding that isn't coming'?"

"Comfort or understanding isn't coming at all," she replies, "not from anyone, *ever*. I need it and it won't ever come and I'll be all alone. It frightens me so much I can't think straight."

Jenna Lee may not be able to "think straight" when she's been triggered, because State-of-Being Flashbacks often include a cognitive flashback to the limited social scope and absolute all-or-nothing thinking of a child. For the duration of an SBF, this cognitive flashback component can functionally wipe out access to adult logic and common sense.

When Jenna Lee isn't triggered, however, she thinks straight and has plenty of common sense. Can thinking about this when she's calm help?

Dipping into some down-to-earth cognitive therapy work, I first sum up her response, saying, "Mike's sneering and absence of response when you bring up emotional concerns seems to function for you as a Doomsday Signal, with the horrible message that comfort and understanding will never come at all, from anyone, ever."

And then I add, "That would be an awful fate. Is that horrible message really true?"

Jenna Lee has been wondering and worrying about this for a long time. She thinks it over some more and says: "It's true to say that Mike has sneered and shut down. He hasn't given me comfort and understanding so far. It's realistically possible, even probable, that he isn't going to give me comfort and understanding any time soon, not in that situation.

"It may be realistic to expect he never will. I don't like to think about that."

Long, sad pause. . . .

"But realistically, I *could* give *myself* comfort and understanding. I *can* get comfort and understanding from someone *besides* Mike. Thank goodness. Not getting it from him isn't really a present day Doomsday Signal. It's a false alarm."

JENNA LEE'S SELF-TALK SCRIPT: "NOW, NOT THEN"

"And I can keep reminding myself "It's now, not then. When I was little, I was alone with my upset feelings, but I don't have to be alone when I remember them

today. I have my adult self, my Inner Helper. I have people — at least some people, some of the time — who are there with me.

"I really am safe in the here and now. I'm not six years old in that horrible restaurant. I'm really not a little girl who can't survive without her mommy and daddy. My lead teacher and my boyfriend really are not my parents.

"Criticized by my lead teacher isn't fired. A standoff with Mike isn't a breakup. And even a breakup isn't literally dead. It won't kill me.

"What a relief to have today's response to today's relationship realities. It's not life and death anymore."

NOW YOUR TURN

How is your Inner Helper feeling at this point? You've developed trigger management skills and strengthened your inner helping relationship. You've worked with the Resignation Stupor. Now you can add knowing about the full spectrum of natural Defense Cascade responses to threat to that powerful mix.

Knowing about the trauma-related Defense Cascade is ultimately clarifying and empowering. Maybe not right now, when it's still spinning your head. But it will be.

As this knowledge sinks in, it will help your Inner Helper to maintain a caring, capable mindset, staying compassionately and wisely present, calming you down by helping you to understand what's going on.

And as this knowledge becomes part of your working wisdom, you'll skillfully recognize, acknowledge, and work with the trauma-related defense states you've found yourself experiencing in naCCT memories, Soul Mirrors, and flashbacks.

EMBARKING ON DEFENSE CASCADE WORK

[Note: You can read through this section without doing the activities. As you read, bookmark parts you'll come back to after you've lived with this

information for a while and have a real–life Defense Cascade episode you want to explore.]

YOUR DEFENSE CASCADE DISTRESS RESPONSES

To use the Defense Cascade information in your unique individual situation, you can begin by reviewing the Defense Cascade states and note those that feel familiar to you:

Social Engagement System: Tend and Befriend

Alert Readiness to Act

Startle Reaction
Orientation Reflex

Adrenalized, Mobilization Zone

Fight
Flight
Scared Stiff

Resignation Stupor / "Freeze"

Ambivalence Zone

Keep Going or Give Up
Total Confusion

Trauma Bonding

Berserker State

Quiescent Immobility

Just as with the Resignation Stupor, your Defense Cascade experience includes your whole State-of-Being: your sensations, moods, emotions, energy level, skill level, mental level, the size of your awareness field (zoom in to details or zoom out to panoramic big picture including yourself and other people and concerns), how your mind is working (little kid or worldly-wise grown up), awareness of how fast time seems to be going, assessment of danger and the resources you have available for handling threats.

A few general questions for you to mull over as you review your experience with these Defense Cascade states:

- Is your present experience with this state a flashback? A Soul Mirror? A memory? A response to present circumstances?

- Have you noticed that some of those states happen when you don't assess any physical threat to your life or well-being, but you still find yourself in a state of defending and protecting yourself?

- What is your "go to" Defense Cascade state, the one you find yourself in most often?

- What are your "Top 3" Defense Cascade states?

～⁂

WORKING WITH ONE DEFENSE CASCADE STATE

You have the option to choose one of those states to work with here. You've already worked with the Resignation Stupor, so you might choose a different state to explore now. Maybe one that is problematic for you. Maybe the Ambivalence Zone/Baby Wildebeest Feeling you've just witnessed Jenna Lee work with? Maybe Fight or Flight, or too-frequent Orientation responses? Maybe even Confusion, Berserk, or Trauma Bond/Zombie Trance if one of those more challenging states fits your experience.

If you decide to explore this option, what's your name for that state? Does one of the Defense Cascade names fit your experience? Jenna Lee gave her experience in the Ambivalence Zone trauma state her personal name "My Baby Wildebeest Feeling." Do you have a state you've already given your personal name to? What is that name?

Put the name that works for you in the Distress Response Statement:

"A Distress Response I sometimes have is: [Defense Cascade State]."

When you think of this state, are you remembering a specific time you experienced it? Do you experience that state often enough that it's a part of your regular life, almost as if it's a characteristic of your personality?

YOUR SOUL MIRROR REFLECTION STATEMENT

If that state has been reflected in a Soul Mirror, the way Jenna Lee's Baby Wildebeest feeling was, describe the Soul Mirror and fill in the Soul Mirror Reflection Statement:

What the [Soul Mirror] reflected for me is [Defense Cascade State].

THEN ON TO YOUR TRIGGERS

People usually find that their Defense Cascade states don't come out of the blue. Something usually triggers them. Can you point to what triggered your Defense Cascade Distress Response?

Remember that triggers are often unnoticed. At first, you may simply notice that you are feeling or acting "off." So, go through the trigger checklist: internal thoughts and feelings, People-Triggers, Sensory Triggers, Body-State Triggers. Then fill in your Trigger and Distress statement:

"When I encounter this trigger [Your possible trigger or triggers],

my Distress Response tends to be [Defense Cascade State].

Identify the links in any Chain Reactions of Triggers. Add more statements if you discover a long Chain of Triggers.

And then that Distress Response triggers this other Distress Response:
[_____],

which triggers this other Distress Response: [_____],

which triggers this other Distress Response: [_____].

If the connection between a very subtle trigger and its Distress Response is so vague, attenuated, and blurry that it's difficult to discern, try using a general statement, such as "something that happened over the weekend" or "something that happened with those people" or "something I hoped would happen didn't happen."

Or just put a question mark in the blank for "trigger." Let the question mark be an invitation for awareness of the connection to reveal itself in its own good time as you continue your work.

As these links become untangled, your triggering process becomes more comprehensible and transparent, which in turn provides you with an extra boost of stability.

YOUR NACCT HISTORY: "WHAT HAPPENED TO ME?"

As you do this work, has your backstory begun to come into view? Sometimes it's almost as though the backstory is shouting, "Hey! Remember this! Deal with it!"

If a part of your naCCT trauma backstory thrusts itself into your life against your will in a flashback, or you encounter your backstory in a Soul Mirror, you have some choice regarding the depth of your response. Here are three possible depth levels:

Dipping your toe in the water:

You might imagine finding yourself in this state and discovering a note in your pocket. It's a State-of-Being Flashback possibility Statement, addressed to you and written in your own handwriting! It reads:

"You might be in a body-based State-of-Being Flashback, maybe one of those Defense Cascade trauma states, without even being aware of it."

You know not to coerce yourself to do naCCT history work, so you might just acknowledge the possibility that you're in a flashback and then focus on present-time coping.

Diving In:

Working with the naCCT Resonance Statement is a moderate depth level. You might glance through the naCCT categories in Chapter 4, identify those that you resonate with, and acknowledge

"I relate to the naCCT of [_____]."

Remember that with naCCT the trauma is a chronic pattern rather than a single event.

Put into a few words the possible connection of your Defense Cascade state with the naCCT category or categories. For example:

> *"I have an intuition that this <u>adrenalized Fight state</u> that I often get into has roots in naCCTs of Commission, specifically favoritism of my older sister and scapegoating of me."*

or:

> *"I find myself in this <u>Ambivalence Zone state</u>, and that state feels connected to naCCT of Unwholesome Closeness/ Helicopter Parenting."*

or:

> *"Sometimes I get so upset I'm <u>almost in that Berserk state</u>, and that has something to do with naCCT of Gaslighting, and naCCT of Omission of Validation."*

Taking the step of acknowledging this resonance is no small thing, so pat yourself on the back for doing so.

Diving Deeper:

Like Jenna Lee, you might decide the time is right for investigating your naCCT backstory at a deeper level. We'll really work with the naCCT backstory in my next book on the "Remember and Grieve" component of the cPTSD recovery model. Meanwhile, your level of sophistication with this material is very high at this point and you have quite an empowering set of safety and stability promoting tools now, and so you might decide to go deeper.

If you choose to remember and deal with some of this now, you'll want to pace yourself wisely.

As you dive deeper into your naCCT history, you can use as inspirational models Jenna Lee's work with her Ambivalence Zone Baby Wildebeest Feeling, my work with the Resignation Stupor, and, most importantly and powerfully, *your own work* in the previous chapters. (Yes, be inspired by yourself!)

Three different phenomena may serve as breadcrumbs that lead you back to your naCCT history. Let's look first at Soul Mirrors.

1. YOUR NACCT HISTORY VIA SOUL MIRRORS

Some Soul Mirrors reflect a Defense Cascade State that links a survivor's adult experience to childhood naCCT. This happened when Jenna Lee's frantic, desperate baby wildebeest Soul Mirror linked the way she felt in the present with Mike and the way she felt with her mom in the rest stop restaurant. As Jenna Lee did, you can acknowledge that link by creating a two-part Soul Mirror Reflection Statement: one for the present:

> *What the [Soul Mirror] reflected for me in the present is [present time experience].*

and one for the past:

> *What the [Soul Mirror] reflected for me from the past is [past time experience].*

You might explore further by adding when, where, and with whom your Soul Mirror experiences occurred.

2. YOUR NACCT HISTORY VIA EXPLICIT EPISODIC MEMORIES OF EVENTS

"Breadcrumbs" back to your naCCT history may also be in the form of what memory psychologists call "explicit episodic memories." These are memories of specific personal events that can be intentionally retrieved and put into words. These explicit memories are brain-based. When you're explicitly remembering an event, you might be conscious of "thinking," of the process going on inside your head.

Call to mind a recent pleasant episode in your life, maybe a chance meeting with someone you like. Notice that you can picture where you were, what you were doing, and how you greeted each other. You also remember the feeling of happy surprise when you recognized your friend. Or think back over the past few months and recall enjoying a delicious meal. You probably remember not only the facts — where you were, who was with you, what you ate, — but also the feelings — good, happy, "all is well" — you felt while you were eating.

Similarly, adults may recollect events from their childhood — perhaps their first day of school or a significant family gathering — and remember both what happened and how they felt.

Trauma, however, can break up the unity of memory, separating memories of what happened from how it felt. It's not uncommon for someone with cPTSD from naCCT to remember what happened at school or at the family gathering and have no memory of how they felt when it happened. The feelings have been dissociated from the events.

A purely explicit memory from which emotion has been dissociated is flat. Recall Jenna Lee's memories of events in the rest stop restaurant, before her Soul Mirror experience brought the memory to life. They were two-dimensional, cardboard, "nothing but the facts."

When experiencing these flat "nothing but the facts" explicit memories, you might find yourself speaking in a monotone. You might remain unperturbed while recounting events other people might consider negative. "It didn't really bother me," you say, "that work emergencies often made Dad miss my games, or that Mom often 'improved' my outfits with a last-minute change of accessories as I was walking out the door."

You might remember an event that you *think* could be connected to Defense Cascade State-of-Being. You know what happened, and although you don't have much emotion about it, logic tells you that it might be connected. "I guess it could be related," you might say.

3. YOUR NACCT HISTORY VIA TRIGGERED STATE-OF-BEING FLASHBACKS

The third phenomenon that can provide breadcrumbs to lead you back to your naCCT history is a triggered State-of-Being Flashback (SBF).

A different kind of memory is at work in SBFs: non-verbal body- and emotion-based (or "somato-affective") implicit memory.

With these non-verbal SBFs, you feel the whole State-of-Being you felt at some time in the past, but you might not remember what happened that caused you to feel that way.

In fact, you often aren't aware you are "remembering" at all! You just feel the mood, sensations, and emotions of a particular State-of-Being, perhaps the high-energy of Fight or Flight, or the collapsed apathy of the Resignation Stupor.

This implicit, non-verbal, body- and- emotion- based memory is crucially important for us survivors of attachment-based trauma in our early relationships with our Lifeline People.

It's crucially important to us because, as attachment researcher Dr. Daniel Stern states, "All the considerable knowledge that infants acquire about what to expect from people, how to deal with them, how to feel about them, and how to be with them falls into this non-verbal domain."[51]

Dr. Stern decided to call this interpersonal non-verbal domain "implicit relational knowing," because "knowledge most often implies conscious knowledge," whereas "implicit relational knowing is unconscious."[52] It is unconsciously learned and unconsciously retrieved. You find yourself feeling frightened or shut down, avoiding someone or disagreeing with everything someone else says, with no awareness of when or why you learned that way of relating.

Our ways of implicit relational knowing are often revealed to us via our triggers and flashbacks. To follow the guidance of SBFs back to childhood naCCT, ask "When did I *feel* this way before?"

FULL UNIFIED MEMORY OF NACCT

Sometimes after the two kinds of memories have been separated, they come back together: Your explicit, cognitive memories of events might join with your implicit, somato-affective State-of-Being memories. When the two kinds of memory come together, you *know* what happened and you also *feel* what it was like.

If you have these two kinds of memory come back together like this, you might feel like Jenna Lee did when she said, "That Soul Mirror experience with the baby wildebeest was like a time capsule exploded and a whole living memory flew out into real life."

To encourage this vivid, full, facts-and-feelings memory, try putting these two statements right next to each other:

The events that happened outside in the external world:

"I found myself remembering events that happened when [_____]."

And the internal State-of-Being:

"I found myself experiencing a State-of-Being like the one I experienced back when [_____]."

FACING YOUR NACCT HISTORY

It "gets real" when knowing and feeling come together.

Because it feels so real, this unified explicit and implicit memory combination can also hit hard. It's a double whammy.

If you've gone very deep into your naCCT backstory, you may find that you're now deep into the "Remember and Grieve" component of the trauma healing model.

As you know, working on remembering and grieving can plummet you into your distress patterns and aggravate your symptoms. Remember that grieving is more than feeling sad and crying. It may also include anger, shame, disorientation, apathy, guilt, and even disgust.

If you do find yourself troubled, remember that you have all your "Stay Safe and Stable" component resources to help you.

YOUR NACCT RESONANCE STATEMENT:

After this mini crash-course on memory, look over the list of naCCT categories in Chapter 4 again. Try out putting an naCCT category that fits your childhood experience in the naCCT Resonance Statement.

"I related to the naCCT category of [_____].

(Yes, you certainly may find that your naCCT history fits more that one category, and so you might have more than one naCCT Resonance Statement.)

YOUR NACCT DEFENSE CASCADE STATE-OF-BEING FLASHBACK STATEMENT

Putting it all together: Now, let's sum up what sometimes happens to you by creating your NaCCT Flashback Statement:

"I may have been triggered by present [trigger or triggers]

into a [Distress Response/ Defense Cascade State]

that could be a State-of-Being Flashback to past [naCCT category]."

How does it feel to just sit with that summary statement? Bring to it the magic of "Hmm. . . ." Let your awareness go deeper than the intellect.

Do doors of compassion for yourself open? Doors of insight?

This process of trying out a possible naCCT flashback statement benefits from an attitude of possibility, of "maybe" and "let's see." It's like trying on shoes or taking a car for a test drive. Maybe it suits you. Maybe not. Maybe you'll set it aside, attend to other activities, and then come back later to check it out again.

FACING YOUR CPTSD FROM NACCT

In exploring these possibilities, you are facing the symptoms and source of your cPTSD, compressed into one stark, unflinching statement.

Sometimes just being with this stark statement brings up strong feelings, memories, or a wave of grief-emotions like sadness or anger.

Sometimes it just feels weird. Or too obvious to really bother making a big deal about: "Whatever. So what?"

Facing your naCCT history may pose an even bigger challenge than managing triggers. Your history may be rocked by your realizations and your view of your world may be turned upside down.

Sometimes facing both the cPTSD symptoms and the naCCT source in this flashback statement leads to a craving, an impulse to use substances. Sometimes to feeling physical distress, a headache or digestive upset, or even getting discouraged and giving up.

MEETING THE CHALLENGE: YOUR BETTER OPTIONS/ "WHAT-I'M-GOING-TO-DO-ABOUT-THAT" STATEMENT

Every time I've asked a survivor, "What do other survivors need to hear?" they've replied with some version of, "Tell them this is really hard and takes more time and energy than you thought it would. Tell them to rest and take breaks, but never give up."

So, first and always, profoundly congratulate, honor, and celebrate your commitment, your "stick-to-it-ive-ness," your strength and fortitude for having made your way to this point.

Then give some thought to what to put in your Better Options/ "What-I'm-Going-to-Do-about-That" Statement. Coming up are some suggestions for Self-Talk Scripts to include in your safety-and-stability-providing tool kit.

THREAT YESTERDAY, FALSE ALARM TODAY

When there is a good strong separation between past and present, disturbing unconscious flashbacks and triggers gradually transition into conscious memories that you clearly recognize are over and done with. The danger and trauma are safely encapsulated in the past.

Here are a few more ways you can strengthen the separation of past threat from present safety"

1. To keep the childhood naCCT danger in the past even while addressing the cPTSD aftereffects in the present, use the Self-Talk Script: "False Alarm, Not Doomsday Signal!" Jenna Lee used earlier in this chapter.

2. Play with the image of "Memory Lane." Visualize it as an actual lane, stretching back from the present into the past, getting smaller and smaller as it recedes into the distance.

Do you want to take a stroll down Memory Lane. Or would you like to barricade the access route?

3. Call upon some of the strategies and protective devices you installed in your Safe Space Imagery. Use them to protect your "here and now "from your naCCT "there and then." For example, if you had a clear impenetrable shield around your safe space, then mentally "build" a clear impenetrable shield around the present.

4. Make a map. In addition to mental visualizations, you can also use physical materials to represent the separation of past and present. For example, you can draw or diagram a map showing the "Land of Then" separated from the "Land of Now."

5. Or designate one section of the floor of your room to represent the past and another section to represent the present. You can even label those sections by writing "Past" and "Present" on pieces of paper. Use pillows to put up strong divisions between the past and present. Then physically step into the present zone, observing how separate you are from the past.

When you're finished, be sure to return that "past section" of the room to the real present with a statement such as "This section of the room no longer represents my past."

6. Another resource for keeping the past firmly separated from the present is language. In English we have so many words and phrases relating to memory: *remember, recall, think back to, look back on, that reminds me.*

Saying "I remember that" is so empowering and stabilizing. Notice how the phrase points to both the present and the past while keeping them separate from each other. For instance, if Jenna Lee says, "I remember that awful time in the restaurant," she is actually, physically living securely grounded in the present while remembering something she experienced back in the past.

YOUR SELF-TALK SCRIPT: "I AM REMEMBERING. . . ."

"In reality, I am safe right here right now, and I am remembering some disturbing stuff that happened back in the past."

The "Now, not Then" statements we've been using provide specific contrasts between the safe-enough present and the naCCT past. Here are those statements again:

"Fortunately, the reality is that I may feel awful, but
- *At least [the present person] isn't [the past person].*
- *I'm an adult, not a child.*
- *I'm in [the present place] not [the past place].*
- *It's [present time], not [past time]"*

Let's expand the "Now, Not Then" statement to include your resources.

YOUR PRESENT RESOURCES

"Working with resources keeps me sane," said one naCCT survivor with many triggers. Why were resources so crucial to her? Because, as you recall, trauma is relative; when there aren't enough resources to meet a challenge, trauma happens. Working with resources protects against trauma.

Recall also that it's possible to have such a low ratio of challenge to resources that you're bored. An even balance of challenge to resources results in easy competence. And a moderately high level of challenge to resources can be exciting.

However, as the challenge becomes greater while the resources stay the same, the situation progresses from challenging through frustrating and concerning to distressing and sometimes, when the challenge completely overwhelms the resources, even to traumatic.

Recall too that reversing overwhelm by restoring a good balance of resources to challenge promotes safety and stability.

Because many people find they forget their resources when they are triggered, let's intentionally take stock of your present resources now and firmly establish them in your awareness so you can stay aware of them in potentially triggering situations. Here are some:

- People in real life, in books, or on the internet, whether in the present or from your past

- Animal friends, plants, favorite places

- Higher Powers within and without,

- "Reformed" Inner Critic, now Inner Helper's Helper

- Your own "first aid kit" list of things you can do on your own

- Your Safe Space Imagery

To supercharge your level of safety, especially if you're predisposed to Defense Cascade SBFs, compare how resource-rich you are today with how few resources you had for meeting the challenges you faced in the past. Starting with your increasingly sturdy, loving, and reliable inner helping relationship, try to come up with at least one resource for each of the statements below:

"Back then I wasn't [_____], but now I am [_____]."

"Back then I couldn't [_____], but now I can [_____].

"Back then I didn't have [_____], but now I have [_____]."

YOUR SELF-TALK SCRIPT: "I HAVE RESOURCES"

"I have plenty of resources today to meet challenges that would have overwhelmed and traumatized me back then.

"When I didn't have all these resources that I have now, it was overwhelming and traumatic. But with all these resources, I can think straight about the challenge facing me. Maybe I'll conclude it's a serious challenge that I'll need to muster all my resources to handle. Or maybe I'll conclude it's just an everyday hassle. Or I could even find it annoying but also kind of entertaining: From my well-resourced point of view, I might notice that there's actually something pretty funny about it all."

YOUR SELF-TALK SCRIPT: "WHAT DO YOU NEED, DEAR BODY SELF?"

Now let's turn again to the state of your body. If your body has been triggered into a state on the Defense Cascade and readied itself to handle a perceived life threat, how can you restore your physiological equilibrium?

Recall the incident you read about in Chapter Thirteen, when the hospital fire alarm was blaring its message of "Danger!" and Danny from Security came into the psychotherapy group and said to us, "There's no fire. It's a false alarm. All is well. The city firefighters will arrive soon and turn off the alarm."

Remember how we calmed down enough to do psychotherapy, even with the alarm blaring, because we knew the noise was merely annoying, not dangerous.

In coping with triggers, you play the role of "Danny from Security" for yourself. You might communicate directly with your body-self:

"Dear Body-Self, you got into a Defense Cascade state. What you thought was a Doomsday Signal was really a false alarm. We are safe now. What will help you get back into balance?"

Tune in to what your body communicates back to you. You may find you need to go back to self-help basics, strengthening your inner helping relationship.

You can also use the body-stabilizing techniques from Chapter Eleven. For example, you can solve puzzles, organize your spice rack, soak in a bath, and of course do some mindful breathing, moving, and eating. Flip back to the chapter for the full list.

Above all, you can communicate reassuringly *and realistically* with yourself about your body state:

YOUR SELF-TALK SCRIPT: "MY BODY WILL RETURN TO BALANCE"

"This body state is distressing but not a sign of abandonment or other danger. As I really feel how safe I am in the here and now, my body will return to balance."

WRAPPING UP AND MOVING FORWARD

Our exploration of the physical impact of traumas that involve no physical assault now draws to a close.

We've looked at medical aftereffects, Sensory Triggers, Soul Mirrors, Body-State Triggers, State-of-Being Flashbacks, the Resignation Stupor, Ambivalence Zone and other states on the Defense Cascade.

We've explored the profound, long-lasting impact of early relationships on our bodies. This exploration has de-mystified the way naCCT issues become embodied in our tissues.

You can now embrace your body self. If you've been impatient with your physical troubles and medical problems, if you've alienated yourself from your body, you can now connect to it in a caring, effective, and ultimately joyful way.

Extend compassion for what your body has been through and appreciate how it has served you. You are now more fully equipped to keep deepening your understanding of the profound impact of relationships on bodies, on *your* body, and relate happily with your precious body today and on into a bright and healthy future.

NOTES

[50] See, for example: Allan N. Schore, *Right Brain Psychotherapy (New York, W.W. Norton: 2019)*

[51] Daniel N. Stern, *The Present Moment in Psychotherapy and Everyday Life* (New York: WW Norton & Co, 2004) 242.

52 Quoted in Ditta M. Oliker, PhD, "This is Who and What They Are!: Exploring the Need to Deny It," *Psychology Today* blog post, November 25, 2013, https://www.psychologytoday.com/us/blog/the-long-reach-childhood/201311/is-who-and-what-they-are.

Part VI:

Owning Your Accomplishments

CHAPTER 16

GOOD FOR ME! NAME IT AND CLAIM IT

Here we are. At the end of this book and the end of the "Stay Safe and Stable" Component of healing cPTSD from naCCT. We've come far: we've looked at how to *be* safe, *know* you're safe, and *feel* safe both physically and emotionally. In this chapter, we'll sum up, celebrate, and plan for the future.

First, let's check back with Jenna Lee.

JENNA LEE'S "STAY SAFE AND STABLE" COMPONENT WORK

We've seen how Jenna Lee worked hard at strengthening a reliable, committed inner helping relationship that provided her with a sense of security. She also taught the well-intentioned part of her Inner Critic to function as her encouraging Inner Coach.

Her psychoeducation about cPTSD from naCCT served as a framework for understanding and de-stigmatizing her difficulties. She began a vitalizing cycle of taking new steps, making personal gains, and building on those gains to take additional new steps towards recovery and healing.

She completed this book's exercises: the naCCT Statements, the checklists, inventories, and self-assessments. She learned to work with the magic of "Hmm. . . ." She began learning how to take care of herself when she got upset. She identified triggers, Distress Responses, State-of-Being Flashbacks to the Resignation Stupor, Ambivalence Zone, and other states of the Defense Cascade, and she used them all as both clues to her backstory and signals to increase her self-care, including reaching out for an assist from other people.

Although this book addresses the "Stay Safe and Stable" component of healing, and therefore detailing the total arc of Jenna Lee's recovery in the other two components is outside this book's scope, we can touch on them briefly here.

JENNA LEE'S "REMEMBER AND GRIEVE" COMPONENT WORK

Jenna Lee, like many naCCT survivors, had alternated between acknowledging the degree of genuine terror she had felt, and then undercutting that compassionate acknowledgment with contempt for getting upset over such small things, which she labeled "nothing really traumatic."

Slowly, as her inner helping relationship grew stronger and more reliable, her isolated memory fragments and information from her present day triggers and State-of-Being flashbacks began to fit together like jigsaw puzzle pieces, revealing a fuller picture of her family relationships.

Jenna Lee wrestled with that more complicated picture of her "happy childhood." In the process, she came to overturn her conviction that her troubles had come about because she was spoiled and "Nothing was really wrong with my family growing up, so there must be something really wrong with me."

She gradually recognized that she had been a normal little girl, one who needed the secure attuned responsiveness all children need from their Lifeline Caregivers. A normal little girl who had felt the terrors children feel when it looks like they aren't getting the responsiveness they need.

She came to compassionately appreciate that even though as an adult she could say, "My mother didn't really mean it. She wouldn't really have left me there in that restaurant," as a child her terror had been real.

She also came to a more nuanced view of life in an imperfect universe, where situations and people are seldom, if ever, all good or all bad. She appreciated her parents having been excellent material providers and felt gratitude for the many ways they had cared for her.

And she realized that the secure material realities of her childhood had sometimes been eclipsed by a pattern of naCCT incidents, most of them much more subtle and ordinary than the one in the rest stop restaurant.

They had been subtle episodes of traumatic absence, of naCCTs of Omission where the trauma had been invisible: Jenna Lee's hidden inner state of urgency, body-based terror, and despair when the response she was hard-wired to need hadn't come.

Among the many such commonplace incidents in this naCCT of Omission pattern was one that happened when she was nine:

"Mom was standing at the kitchen sink, washing vegetables," Jenna Lee said, "and I told her I was scared of something. Funny, I don't remember what I was scared of, but I remember the sound of the water running and her vigorous scrubbing with her vegetable brush, and I can still hear her in my memory, saying, 'C'mon honey, my big girl doesn't talk like that.' She said it in such a nice way — supportive, caring, encouraging — and then she turned back to the vegetables. I get an alone feeling and a knot in my stomach, remembering.

"Mom was so impatient with fear, or crying, or *anything* that seemed weak. She said I had a tendency to feel sorry for myself, which 'just made life unpleasant for me and everyone around me.' And, of course, my big sister Marie was always teasing me when I got upset. When he got older, my little brother Sammy teased me too.

"And Dad? He might quote some positive mental attitude slogan like 'when life gives you lemons, make lemonade' which was true enough, I suppose, but it didn't make a space for me to explore what was upsetting me and what to do about it."

GRIEF: TAKING OFF THE ROSE-COLORED GLASSES

Jenna Lee had been trauma-taught to disconnect her awareness from her experience, to exile some experiences and states that her family didn't accept. She said, "When I needed help with my feelings, my serene parents, who never got upset, kind of emotionally abandoned me. That upset, scared part of me didn't have a place in my family. It was ostracized. Erased. Like it didn't exist."

In the course of her recovery, she grieved over lost opportunities for understanding, guidance, and comforting.

Although Jenna Lee had been distressed in the past, she had learned to stop herself from freely crying in the presence of someone else, even someone who might empathize and comfort her. She remembered, "Once on a school trip to Washington DC, I got upset and was crying in the hotel bathroom with the shower and the fan running so my roommate couldn't hear me. But she heard anyway, and knocked on the door.

"'Are you OK?' she asked.

"I managed to squeak out, 'I'm fine,' but now I recognize that confusing Baby Wildebeest Feeling had come over me — this time in the form of 'don't let anyone see you cry' — and that was why I kept insisting I was fine when I wasn't."

Part of Jenna Lee's healing was to honor the impulse to cry and seek comfort. In therapy, she took another brave leap of self-care when she allowed her distress cry to be expressed. The one she had learned to stifle. This time she didn't squash it. She stayed with it. Sometimes she sobbed like her heart would break. In fact, she did feel like her heart would break, almost as if she were grieving a death.

When she felt that way, she learned to call on her Inner Helper. As she touched her suffering with self-love and compassion, more healing happened. She stopped being afraid of her fear and upset. She learned it was OK to cry and to sometimes reach out and have someone else be with her in her grief.

Her moods passed more quickly. She emerged from these times of grieving feeling better, stronger, more present in her adult life, more able to connect in new, more authentic ways.

TRIGGERS & RECOGNIZING FLASHBACKS

One of Jenna Lee's major positive changes was a radical improvement in managing triggers. As we've seen, at first she hadn't been able to identify a triggered flashback as such, all she had known was that she'd felt terrible and her willpower hadn't succeeded in snapping her out of it.

As her healing progressed, she sometimes recognized a triggered flashback *after* it happened. She might look back at an episode and simply say, "I think I got triggered." Instead of being blindsided by instantaneous hair-triggered flashbacks, she could sometimes witness the process in slow motion. This enabled her to intervene and lovingly, skillfully, come alongside herself.

She got better at sorting out what were present feelings in response to present circumstances and what were flashbacks to the past. She recognized that her flashbacks were archaic blasts from the past, not contemporary warnings of real danger facing her in the present.

JENNA LEE'S "RECONNECT AND RE-ENGAGE" COMPONENT

When we met Jenna Lee in Chapter One, her body-based learning processes, operating outside of her conscious intentions, had been protecting her from triggering situations by shrinking her world. Like the electrical shocks from an "Invisible Fence" that condition a beloved family dog to stay safely in the yard, those naCCT incidents had conditioned Jenna Lee to "stay safe" by keeping her world small. There had been many places she had feared to go, things she had feared to do, and thoughts she'd been afraid to think, lest she experience one of those dreaded states.

But Jenna Lee persevered. With a mix of steady progress, dramatic leaps forward, and even discouraging setbacks, she never gave up on herself. Because she kept strengthening her secure inner relationship, remembering and grieving her past naCCTs, she reconnected to herself and to the outside world in new positive ways.

RECONNECT WITH HERSELF IN NEW WAYS

Some of those new ways were concrete and obvious: For example, she didn't just come home from work and listlessly munch on chocolate. Instead, she started riding her bike again, eventually bought a new one, joined a cycling group. Played volleyball, sometimes quite competitively. Got out some anger in a boxing class.

She also enjoyed some deeper, more profound internal changes in attitudes and expectations of herself.

For instance, her self-description at the start of therapy had been "needy," easily influenced, and overly sensitive to criticism. Her standard of emotional balance and inner poise had been unrealistically high. When she failed to meet that high standard, she had felt shame and criticized herself harshly.

With more realistic expectations, she shamed and blamed herself less, normalized "getting upset," and focused on handling her emotional reactions.

And as she got more in touch with the backstory of her Zombie Trance and Baby Wildebeest Ambivalence Zone state, she came to actually take realistic pride in having successfully suppressed her emotions in order to preserve the necessary connection with her family. "I *had to* squelch myself back then," she concluded. "And I did it. I survived. I was a strong little girl; I did what I needed to do and it was hard and I didn't give up. I was brave and strong."

She also reconnected with her body self. She gave her body a voice, paid attention to the story her body told her, listened to its messages and took them into account in her decisions. For example, when her body was in the conflicted Baby Wildebeest State-of-Being, she could ask: "What is the conflict my body story is revealing? What am I pushing myself to do? Given my goals and values, what would be my best choice of action under these circumstances?"

As her chronic shame and guilt were giving way bit by bit to self-compassion, Jenna Lee watched a news broadcast documenting the destruction following a recent flood. "That's how it is with me," she reflected, "I'm like those flooded homes. My naCCT was like those destructive waters that flooded those homes.

"And the way I used to be was like if one of those flood victims looked at her house, all damaged by those filthy, powerful flood waters, and then blamed herself for being a bad housekeeper.

"I don't have to feel ashamed or guilty. I still have to clean up after that naCCT flood, but I don't have to blame myself for the mess."

RECONNECT WITH OTHER PEOPLE IN NEW WAYS

While validating her experiences and feeling safe and secure inside herself, Jenna Lee also explored new options for acting in the outside world.

She learned to take her feelings of being hurt seriously, even to use them for assessing relationships. She could say to herself, "Wait, something is off here," ask herself, "What's happening?" and then use the Magic of "Hmm. . . ." to discover her own truth.

She gained the strength to face complex realities, acknowledge people's imperfections and shortcomings, and re-assess her relationships. She re-evaluated her old, very pernicious belief that troubles in her relationships were all her fault: "If someone isn't nice to me, that means I'm unlovable and bad."

She came to a new view: "It's not just me. It's also about them. It's not personal to me. It's also about the way *they* are."

She became more discerning in picking people she could be authentic with. She learned to say to herself, "I'm starting to get emotional with people who look down their noses at emotions. Time to get away from them or contain my emotions until I'm either alone or with safe people."

Her own family, for example, was not a safe place for her to be very authentic. Her siblings thought she was "weird" and "wasting her time" to chase down this stuff, and she learned that she only felt worse when she tried to convince them otherwise. They were the way they were, and she couldn't change them, so she abandoned that futile effort.

A TURNING POINT

One day, Jenna Lee came to a session, tossed her bicycle helmet and backpack onto the empty chair in my office, and said with a grin, "I never thought I'd be able to respond like I did.

"I used to hear people respond to their partners like that, but I never thought that I, clingy Jenna Lee, would be one of them," she continued, looking anything but clingy in her cycling pants and gloves. Delighted, struggling to believe the evidence that her dedication and hard work had paid off, Jenna Lee reminded me of an Olympic athlete staring in wonder at the digital readout of her winning score.

"You look really pleased with yourself," I said. "Tell me."

"Yesterday Mike and I had our typical 'non-fight,' where I want to talk about what's going on with us, then he shuts down, and all interaction stops.

"Even though we were in that tense place, we biked out to that Tex-Mex restaurant like we've been doing every Sunday, out where the bike path crosses the highway. All the way out there I felt lousy.

"We got one of the booths in the back, and I brought up the subject again. I wanted him to give some attention to the problem between us, like he cares about it, gets that it's a problem.

"But Mike, as usual, got really impatient. He sighed his usual exasperated sighs; he sneered his usual derogatory remarks and scornful comments; he put up his usual wall, cutting off his energy to me.

"And, as usual, I could feel myself scared that no response was coming.

"Then Mike said, 'You're just feeling sorry for yourself, Jenna Lee,' and it felt even sharper and nastier than usual. He snapped at me, 'Get off the pity pot. Or I'm leaving and you can stay here and wallow.'

"When I heard those words, that old familiar Baby Wildebeest Feeling really started to get me bad," said Jenna Lee, "You know the one I mean?"

"The one from the nature documentary?" I replied.

"Exactly. That one. I still hate it when that feeling comes over me."

She sat for a minute, curled up, comforting herself; then she shook her head with a little shiver and said, "I started to go from the Baby Wildebeest Feeling to those awful Zombie Trauma Bonds, letting Mike totally intimidate me. I felt the pressure to drop it, to sweep everything that was bothering me under the rug and just start talking about pleasant things.

"Mike stood up, making his threat to leave more real. Comfort and understanding were definitely not coming, not from him.

"As usual, I started to get dizzy, intimidated, almost immobilized. I couldn't think straight. I felt frantic, all that Ambivalence Zone push/pull confusion. I wanted to cry. . . .and to blow up at him at the same time. To express my distress, and to squash it down and be the way that pleases Mike, that makes him happy with me."

Jenna Lee uncurled and sat forward. Vitality came back into her eyes and color into her cheeks as she said, "Usually, I would start trying even harder to 'be good.' To put on my happy face. But this time the Zombie bonds didn't get me.

"Instead, I felt something shift in my brain. I could think straight, remind myself: 'I 'm feeling dizzy and stuporous now, but it's only a flashback. Distressing but not dangerous.'

"I kept saying things to myself like: 'My throat feels like I'm choking, just the way I felt back when I was six. But I'm not six . Mike isn't my mother. I have resources now I never dreamed of as a kid — not just my bike, my money, my friends, my work, my apartment, but most important, I have myself. I can take care of myself now. And if I want to get any comfort and understanding right now here with Mike, I'd better give it to myself.'"

"Mike put on his jacket, picked up his cycling glasses and helmet.

"I remembered to breathe, and just kept reminding myself, 'This is only a feeling, a mood flashback' and that put a little space between me and the feeling, like there was more to me than that feeling.

"Maybe I was feeling strong and energized from the bike ride. I remember thinking, 'Whatever happens with Mike, I've got myself. I could live without Mike if I had to.'"

Jenna Lee leaned forward and a smile lit up her face when she said, "But this time I didn't just know this stuff with my head, I felt it with my heart. I felt it in my body. The life and death need was gone! And the 'don't go, I'll be good!' desperation was gone, too!!

Jenna Lee sat up straighter. She leaned forward as she spoke. "Then I did what I thought I'd never do, never in a million years: I said, "Ok, Mike. Go. I'll stay here.'

"Mike looked shocked. Actually, I was kind of shocked myself: I sounded so calm! Confident, even."

Jenna Lee sat for a while, savoring her unexpected success, then continued her story, "We just looked at each other for a long moment. Then I reached for my pack and took out my journal.

"Mike did leave. I watched him walk through the restaurant, out the door."

Jenna Lee leaned forward and pulled her pack off the empty chair in the office. For a minute all I saw was the top of her head as she searched in her backpack. She pulled out a spiral notebook covered with her colored-pencil designs, flipped it open, and, glowing as she spoke, she said, "After he left, I got up from our usual booth. I'd been wanting some time to write in my journal. So I moved to a little table in a corner that had always appealed to me. Then I ordered some nachos and started writing.

"I'm trying to find what I wrote," she said, turning page after page filled with tiny handwriting. "I wrote a lot: a dialogue between me and my Inner Helper, some Self-Talk Scripts. A long list of my resources. Then I worked on my dreams and visions. Want to hear some of them?"

ONE OF MANY TURNING POINTS

Quite a contrast to her day with her family at the rest stop restaurant, that day at the Tex-Mex with Mike was a milestone on her healing journey. Actually, it was one of many milestones and turning points.

Jenna Lee continued to move toward a healthy connection with herself. Her sense of self became more secure, more deeply rooted, strong, whole. Powerful and empowering. Confident that she mattered to herself, her sense of how she fit into the universe also strengthened. She felt more comfortable feeling awe at life's miracles and mysteries.

At work, Jenna Lee recognized trigger incidents with her lead teacher and handled them skillfully. Eventually she got a teaching job with her own class. She even found herself sensitively mentoring a student teacher.

And what about her relationship with Mike? Although they did get together later that day, the rules of engagement and the power dynamics between them had shifted because, as Jenna Lee said, "In my head, I've always known that if Mike and I split up, I'd be really upset, but I wouldn't die. Now I know it in my body too. I finally feel it, and that changes everything."

She also said, "The way Mike is doesn't trigger me like it used to, but I need to seriously evaluate that relationship. He's got so many good qualities: not violent, doesn't do drugs, responsible, hard-working, people seem to like him. But are we really a good match?"

Their relationship was a work in progress. They had many interlocking triggers. Whether her relationship with Mike would grow to be a fulfilling long term partnership remained to be seen. As Jenna Lee's healing progressed, she would get better at balancing her needs and desires with those of other people. And she would get better at realistically assessing all her relationships.

Sometimes, during momentary setbacks, Jenna Lee would feel her old familiar terror-based need to align herself with someone more powerful, someone like her mother, and to blot out her self-compassion.

However, Jenna Lee had also learned that the world was bigger than her family and people who espoused her family's belief system. She continued to seek out people who respected emotional truth and could accept more of her. Not just in therapy, but in other groups and communities where she could develop mutually respectful and empowering relationships with others.

Jenna Lee continued to be caring and compassionate to herself, allowing herself to feel all the appropriate emotions, including rage, hate, grief and shame, that go along with surviving naCCT. The core of her self-compassion was her recognition that she really had been traumatized.

She used her knowledge of naCCT to make sense of her difficulties and to honor her valiant struggle to heal. She continued to dignify her distress. Because she knew that distress had been legitimate back then and that her difficulties in the present made sense, she dared to take her upset seriously, even in the face of sneering and very subtle mocking and dismissal. Sometimes she protested, saying, "It might not seem like much to you, but it was awful for me."

Her point of view was no longer limited to that of her family of origin. She began to ask herself, "What can I do to change what's happening?" In difficult situations, she was able stick up for herself, saying, "That hurts," and "I won't accept that kind of treatment."

Self-validating and self-accepting, taking judiciously calculated risks, she became more assertive. She held her own in relationships. She became wiser about when to keep her own counsel and when to seek an assist from beyond the small world inhabited by herself and those who would ridicule or dismiss her. She became more discerning about how much to reveal and to whom.

Her self compassion became constant; her self-validation, secure. Her healing continued to progress, slowly but surely, tiny incident by tiny incident, and she became free to grow in the direction of her dreams.

Jenna Lee's healing journey was unique to her. The specifics that worked for her may not work for everyone. Yet the overall approach brings relief and transformation to a wide variety of unique individual healing journeys. So let Jenna Lee reassure you and inspire you to journey on, resting sometimes, and, like her, never giving up on yourself.

NOW YOUR TURN

You've worked hard, persisted, steadfastly showed up for yourself. This is a sign that you are a person who values yourself. You matter and your well-being matters. For many an naCCT survivor with cPTSD, acknowledging that you matter and prioritizing your self-care is an act of great courage.

It's time to review your journey through this book and appreciate the road you've traveled and the progress you've made.

In our busy world, we often skip this vital step. We're eager to push forward. Don't skimp on your healing in this way. Instead, identify, integrate, and claim ownership of all your new skills, attitudes, and behaviors.

[Note: Possible triggering: If your naCCTs involve achievement and evaluation, praise and criticism, or jealousy, envy, or other painful comparisons, even thinking about acknowledging, claiming, and celebrating this significant achievement might be triggering. So take it easy here.]

YOUR SELF-TALK SCRIPT: "GOOD FOR ME! I DID IT!"

Remember your Better Options and "What- I'm- Going- to- Do- About- That" Statement:

"When I encounter this trigger: [_____],

my Distress Response tends to be: [_____],

and what I'm going to do about that is: [_____]."

To that statement, add congratulating yourself and taking ownership of your accomplishments:

"and Good for Me! I did it!"

Remember the enthusiasm of a child learning something new: The exuberant "I did it! Look what I did, Mommy! I read that story all by myself! I swam! I rode my bike!"

That child's excitement is about more than just learning a new skill, isn't it? It's about a whole new identity: "I'm a person who can do that! I'm a reader! I'm a swimmer. I'm a bike rider!" And even more transformational: "I'm a big kid now!"

You too have really changed. Even physically, you've changed. Thanks to neuroplasticity, your nervous system has created new neural pathways as you've done this work.

So, take some time to savor any positive shifts in your sense of who you are. Could you realistically describe yourself as wiser, more self-possessed? More confident? Empowered? More self-accepting, even self-cherishing sometimes?

CELEBRATE YOUR SELF-HELP TEAM

Take a moment to contemplate the present state of your inner helping relationship: How are you "there for yourself" these days? You've worked hard on that most essential relationship, the one you'll never leave and never lose, till death do you part. Whether you think of it as your self-help function or personify it, as I do, with Inner Helper, the part that needs help, and Inner Helper's Helpers, it provides you with your most reliable, 24/7 source of help.

You could have quit and abandoned yourself when the going got tough, but you stuck it out. And now, here you are! That inner relationship has probably become considerably stronger, sturdier, and more reliable as you've progressed through this work:

- The part of you that needs help may have become less afraid of acknowledging needs and receiving help.

- Your Inner Helper may have become more confident, more skilled at finding and receiving help to both be a *good* helper and tolerate not being a *perfect* helper.

- Your Inner Helper's Helpers may have become more clearly defined and more accessible resources.

- You may also have connected with other inner parts that pitch in and help out. Maybe an Inner Good Parent. A cheerleader, guide, or protector. Maybe even that reformed part of your Inner Critic that has been transformed into an effective Inner Coach.

- Your relationship to your physical BodySelf may also have developed, providing you with know-how and access to your natural healing powers.

Wherever you go, whatever you do, you now have this increasingly secure inner helping relationship. You bring that relationship's skills and loving presence to all the new resources you'll proceed to develop.

Celebrate this inner helping relationship. Make a special date with your beloved self. Maybe treat yourself to a spa visit featuring a professional massage. Take yourself for a walk in nature. You might prepare your favorite meal, set out candles and your best china, and enjoy your own company. Propose a toast to this precious relationship. To life!

PLAY THE "NAME IT AND CLAIM IT" GAME

As part of your celebration, enjoy playing the "Name it and Claim it" game: Claim what you now know, your working wisdom. You know the far-reaching ramifications of the human reality that to stay alive, babies need to be taken care of. You know that naCCT is serious and your troubles, however trivial they seem to others, make significant sense to you.

Reflect on the "promises" of this book from Chapter One, noting any progress you've made toward realizing them. Here they are again:

- Learning to come alongside myself.

- Learning that I make sense.

- Stopping feeling ashamed of being stuck.

- Learning my grief and pain are legitimate.

- Learning to use the tools and techniques traumatologists, researchers, and therapists have used to help survivors of overt physical trauma.

I hope you're able to say truthfully about each of those promises, "That's happening."

> *[Note: If you recognize that you've made some progress but you still feel discouraged right now, you may be in a temporary set-back or a flashback triggered by being asked to look at how far you've come. If so, it's worth taking time out to ease yourself back into the here and now by using your skills to address that trigger.]*

Let's get a little more specific about naming the gains you can claim:

You now have new words for expressing new concepts: naCCT, Resignation Stupor, People-Triggers, Body-State Triggers, Soul Mirror, State-of-Being Flashback.

You've also met new people on your journey through this book: me, Jenna Lee, Nick, Jason. Maybe one of the people who made a cameo appearance told a story that particularly spoke to you. Maybe some of my friends and helpers in books have become *your* friends and helpers in books too.

You're a person who has identified and developed resources. You now have them in your possession and have experimented with using them. Continue to inventory them, including everything on the lists you generated, your Safe Space Imagery, your Patchwork Quilt of Help, all your stabilizing naCCT self-understanding statements, and all the Self-Talk Scripts you've adapted to your own circumstances.

Feel good as you look these resources over. Mentally rehearse having them right there with you, helping you to meet challenges and seize opportunities.

You're also a person with many skills. You can do things now that maybe you couldn't do before. At least some of the time, you can soothe yourself with knowledge-based explanations of what's happening to you. You can identify and manage triggers, muster resources, calm emotional dysregulation, and normalize your difficulties.

YOUR DIAGNOSIS OF CPTSD FROM NACCT

I invite you to pause for a moment and reflect on naCCT and you. Ponder each element in the name naCCT. Ask of each one: "Does this apply to my experience?"

Non-physically-assaultive: involved no direct physical assault?

Attachment-based: took place in an essential early Lifeline Relationship?

Chronic: wasn't just once, but was repetitive, on-going, cumulative?

Covert: was hard for me to perceive and for others to validate?

Trauma: was overwhelming, resulted in me feeling terrified, confused, desperate, helpless, and/or doomed?

Does one element stand out for you? A particular combination of elements?

How does it sit with you to have "cPTSD from childhood naCCT" as a possible working hypothesis explaining some of your troubles? How does this fit your identity? Is "naCCT survivor with cPTSD" an aspect of your identity? How about "person thriving after childhood naCCT?" Or how about, sometimes, "person going forward to realize their dreams?"

YOU'VE DIPPED INTO "REMEMBER AND GRIEVE" COMPONENT WORK

As you've done your "Stay Safe and Stable" work, you've had some "Remember and Grieve" component experiences.

You've confronted three kinds of triggers with the power to flash you back to your naCCT past. You met the intrapsychic challenge of triggering thoughts and emotions; the interpersonal relationship challenge of People-

Triggers; and the physiological challenge of sensory triggers, Body-State Triggers, and the Defense Cascade responses.

At the end of the previous chapter you worked in more depth with your naCCT Flashback Statement.

"I may have been triggered by present [<u>trigger or triggers</u>]

into a [<u>Distress Response/ Defense Cascade State</u>]

that could be a State-of-Being Flashback to past [<u>naCCT category</u>]

As you've come alongside yourself with your present day experiences of flashbacks, you've become aware of how it might have felt being you back then.

You've looked over the categories of naCCT and explored applying them to your own personal history.

You probed a bit more deeply into memories. You might have dispassionately remembered objective facts and events, as if you were watching a movie. You might simply have made a mental note: "Stuff like this happened when I was a kid." Or you might have found yourself immersed in a vivid re-experiencing of a past naCCT, with all the thoughts and sensations, all the wrenching fears, heartbreak, and anger that you originally experienced back then.

Have some disturbing unconscious flashbacks morphed into conscious vivid memories of experiences that you clearly recognize are over and done with and safely stored in the past? These memories are now managed by your consciousness, which is securely in the driver's seat. Once flashbacks become memories, *you* can call them forth or set them aside, as *you* choose.

As a result of reflecting and acknowledging how your past may be influencing your present, you may have more clarity about who you are, where you've been, and what experiences played a part in shaping you. You may feel more coherent, all-of-a-piece.

YOUR GRIEF WORK

As you remembered, grief work may have been thrust upon you. Perhaps you noticed that even acknowledging "part of this triggered upset isn't about now, it's about the past" can bring up grief about that past.

Maybe you've taken off some rose-colored glasses as you faced the wounds and losses of naCCT, or maybe you've found those glasses just don't work so well any more.

If you did find yourself grieving, what form did your grieving take? Did you know you were grieving? Did you know what you were grieving for?

Did you feel upset, disoriented, or uneasy? Maybe even some strong rage, heartbreak, disgust, terror, and/or despair that you had to work very hard to handle gently and effectively?

How did you take care of yourself when you were grieving? What worked well for you? Distraction? Self-Talk? Crying and sobbing? Talking with another person?

YOU'VE DIPPED INTO "RECONNECT AND RE-ENGAGE" COMPONENT WORK

As your safety and stability have been increasing, your world of possibility has been expanding. You've probably done some "Reconnect and Re-engage" work. You may have made changes in the way you engage in life — the way you think and feel, the way you relate to yourself, to other people, even to your own body.

You might have found yourself re-evaluating attributions, beliefs, expectations, and procedures.

You might relate in new ways to the philosophical and spiritual dimension of meaning, to the big questions, the ultimate mystery of life.

To help lock in your appreciation of how your work is benefitting you, let's itemize some of these positive reconnections, beginning with new ways of relating to yourself.

YOUR SELF-TALK SCRIPTS FOR NEW ATTITUDES

Remember those harsh, self-denigrating attitudes associated with undiagnosed cPTSD that were discussed in Chapter Two? Let's re-visit them to appreciate the new, more realistic, traumatology-informed, self-respecting attitudes that are replacing them.

Here are some Self-Talk Scripts that put those new attitudes into words:

From the old troubling negative attitude cluster of confusion, bewilderment, and shame: "I've put a lot of effort into self-help and therapy, and yet I still have these troubles. How can that be? I must be mental. I don't make sense."

. . . .to new positive, reality-based self-comprehension:

"I make sense. I understand the nature of my troubles, where they come from, and why they've been so persistent."

From the old troubling negative attitude of guilt: "I must not be trying hard enough."

. . . .to new positive, reality-based enlightened innocence:

"I'm not guilty or to blame. I tried hard, but I was trying hard at some things that didn't fit. It took longer than I thought it would because it was a bigger problem than I thought it was at first."

From the old troubling negative attitude of aggravated, contemptuous impatience: "Hurry up! Are you *still* having a hard time? Get over it!"

. . . .to new positive, reality-based patience:

"I'm making good progress. It takes as long as it takes. I can take it easy. I'm progressing at a good pace for me. I'm proud of myself."

From the old troubling negative attitude cluster of sad futility, apathetic resignation, and despair: "There's nothing to do but cry. Why bother? I don't care. It doesn't matter. Meh. I'm hopeless. Nothing will help. That's just the way I am and that's just the way it is. I give up."

. . . .to new positive, reality-based hope, engagement, and motivation:

"I'm not hopeless. Where there's life there's hope. I'm not giving up. There are plenty of things I can do, plenty of actions I can take. I do care. I do matter."

NEW WAYS OF RELATING TO OTHER PEOPLE:

It might feel good to go back over your People-Triggers checklist. At the very least, you will probably find that where you used to be blind-sided and caught off-guard, you are now alert to potentially triggering situations. You are now prepared.

As People-Triggers become less activating, the way you connect with other people may also be changing. You may notice:

- Ease, even enjoyment, in circumstances where you used to feel dread;
- Sometimes reaching out instead of detaching;
- Sometimes detaching instead of reaching out;.
- Setting firmer limits;
- Relaxing rigid limits;
- Not being so "good;"
- Speaking up when your State-of-Being Flashback featured shutting up;
- Being visible in the present, even when your State-of-Being Flashback action is hiding or becoming invisible;
- A calm "No, thanks" or "Please don't do that;"
- A simple and gracious "Thanks for the compliment;"
- A daring "Would you like to join me?" or "Can you help me out?"
- Saying to yourself "He'll get over it" or "I wish we agreed on this; maybe I can influence him, but I sure can't control him" instead of "I have to calm him down and get his approval right now;"
- Having a confidence-boosting success incident, like Jenna Lee's with Mike in the Tex-Mex;
- The positive challenge of a surprising positive connection with someone when your triggers had led you to expect trouble;
- A "rupture and repair" experience, in which a relationship really did become deeper and more intimate after you processed a tough time together.

Every tiny decrease of People-Triggering is a huge step. Every time realistic irritation, concern, or discouragement replaces intense post-traumatic rage, terror, or collapse, you have evidence that the grip of triggering on your life is loosening.

Every microscopic increase in your interpersonal repertoire calls for celebration.

"THE PERSONAL IS POLITICAL"

I hope you have arrived here at the end of the book knowing that you are not alone and that your feeling of isolation is gone. Maybe you've also found yourself relating to other people on a larger social scale, reaching out, speaking up, creating a social context for healing cPTSD from naCCT.

Maybe you have even found yourself with an naCCT Survivor Mission. Maybe you offered some clarifying psychoeducation — maybe about People-Triggers, or naCCT body-state triggers — to someone who might benefit from it. Maybe you helped someone to self-identify as an naCCT survivor with cPTSD and thereby get on the road to recovery. Even using the "naCCT" acronym or mentioning "I'm reading an interesting book that says we need to take intangible traumas seriously" can increase public awareness.

WHAT NEXT?

You've reviewed your accomplishments and added them to your sense of who you are. Now what?

1. REST ON YOUR LAURELS

My first suggestion is: "Rest on Your Laurels."

Early in my career, a woman in the pain treatment program helped me curb my enthusiasm for relentless achievement. "Don't ask me right after a success what goal I'm shooting for next," she said. "Let me just enjoy resting on my laurels for a while."

With her wise request, that woman became one of my teachers, and perhaps one of yours.

Some people think "rest on your laurels" means "don't bother exerting yourself ever again," but they are wrong. Resting isn't about sinking into an endless sleep or becoming a lazy good-for nothing slug. Resting is an essential part of the rhythm of healing: phases of energy-expending exertion balanced with phases of refreshing, revitalizing rest.

"Rest on your laurels" refers to the laurel wreaths given to winners in ancient Greek athletic and musical competitions. Since then, highly honored people are sometimes designated "laureates." Think of a Nobel Laureate, or a Poet Laureate. Think of Amanda Gorman, the first U.S.

National Youth Poet Laureate, who delivered her poem "The Hill We Climb" at the inauguration of President Joe Biden.

Think of yourself as an "naCCT Recovery Laureate," crowned with a laurel wreath. Go ahead: Rest on your laurels. With each new accomplishment, you've created new neural pathways. Let them settle. Acclimate to them. Savor your accomplishments. Name them and claim them: "Good for me! I did it!"

And just rest.

2. READ THIS BOOK AGAIN

My next suggestion: Read this book again.

This book is one of your Inner Helper's Helpers. It's designed to be read and re-read, not necessarily from beginning to end like a novel, but re-read like a good cookbook, reference work, or repair manual. Like an inspirational book, to be turned to when you need encouragement, direction, or perspective.

I *want* you to read this book again. Really work it again. Read it and work it ten times! As you know, naCCT recovery is a marathon, not a sprint. Each time you read this book, you get even more out of it and become stronger, more resourced, and more deeply, lovingly, and effectively attached to your beloved self. The effect is even stronger when you also re-do the exercises.

Skip around in the book. Bookmark sections you know you will want to return to. Shut your eyes and go to a random passage. Share this book with someone else who'll be helped by it.

Every time you return to the book, you know yourself better, your skills get stronger, and your power grows.

3. RE-CONSIDER YOUR "PRESENTING PROBLEMS"

Besides resting on your laurels and re-reading this book, what else might you do next?

You might take another crack at addressing your presenting problems, those practical, immediate problems like chronic physical pain, destructive habits, or issues with work, relationships, or finances that are right there in your face every day, demanding attention and undercutting the quality of your life.

You've laid the groundwork for directly addressing these presenting problems from the inside out. As recovery work progresses, many people discover that the grip of these problems on their lives has loosened up. Have your presenting problems shrunk at all, seeming even a smidgeon less monumental and more solvable now? Do you notice any positive shifts, however small? Maybe you've been motivated to investigate a career change, learn a new skill, take up jogging.

Now that the urgency of cPTSD has let up somewhat, do you have any brainstorms for tackling those presenting problems, any places where you can intervene?

You are more resourced now for addressing them productively going forward. And we're only finishing up component one, "Stay Safe and Stable."

What previously impossible dreams can become possible after you've worked those other two components, "Remember and Grieve" and "Reconnect and Re-engage"?

4. GO DEEPER INTO THE "REMEMBER AND GRIEVE" COMPONENT

Another next step for you might be delving deeper into the "Remember and Grieve" component of trauma healing.

You might decide to dig into your naCCT backstory, getting to know the foundational bedrock of what happened to you, what it meant to you, and what you concluded about yourself and the world as a result.

Many people choose to mobilize additional resources, such as individual psychotherapy, grief counseling, or trauma-informed bodywork, for assistance in backstory work.

Profound healing and even transformation can come as you go deeper into the "Remember and Grieve" component.

5. GO INTENTIONALLY INTO THE "RECONNECT AND RE-ENGAGE" COMPONENT

As the poet Mary Oliver asks in that line we love to repeat from her poem "The Summer Day," "What do you plan to do with your one wild and precious life?"

As you worked in the "Stay Safe and Stable" healing component, some positive reconnections probably happened unintentionally. While appreciating them, your next step might be to "Reconnect and Re-engage" on purpose.

You can put what you've already learned to wise and graceful use now: Pursue new options in the present. Dream dreams, set goals, and make plans. Find and follow your bliss, your deepest happiness. Where does your deepest happiness intersect with desire and need in the world?

You might be inspired by the slogan "Don't agonize; organize!" and decide to intentionally reconnect by spreading the word about naCCT:

- Leave a review about your experience reading this book on Amazon or Goodreads or your favorite book forum,
- Make a "patron book request" for *No Sticks or Stones* at your local library,
- Share with friends on-line and face-to-face, or
- Start a group to do the reader activities in this book together.

And here's another uplifting aspect of re-connecting: If you experienced naCCTs of Omission, you got used to being deprived. Now you'll need to learn the happy lesson of how to respond to *getting* what you got used to *not getting*. How, for example, to respond when someone is there for you? Traumatic absence may have left you with gaps in your knowledge, skills, and experience. Your next step may be in the direction of filling in those gaps.

And now, the last and best of this book's "promises":
- *"Uncover the treasure that got buried along with the naCCT inside of me."*

As you continue with your healing work, eventually (if you haven't already) you'll delight in answering, "Yes, that's happening; there *is* treasure buried right inside of me, and I'm uncovering it! I'm embracing it, nourishing it, and letting it enrich my life."

BONUS: REVISIT THE "DARE TO DREAM!" PROMPTS

To help you uncover your buried treasure, I'm reprinting the Dare to Dream Prompts from Chapter Two here. Fill in the blanks with the first response that pops into your mind:

What I love picturing myself doing is: [_____].

What I love picturing myself being is: [_____].

What I love picturing myself having is: [_____].

What I would like is [_____].

What I want is [_____].

I wonder what it would be like if I could [_____].

I would like to count myself among those who are [_____].

*If you could magically change one thing, what would that thing be?
[_____].*

*If you could magically change one OTHER thing, what would that be?
[_____].*

*If you knew you would be supported in finding and following your bliss,
what would you do? [_____].*

What's your idea of deep happiness in your lifetime? [_____].

What are you joyfully anticipating? [_____].

You might write out your responses to these prompts and pin them to a vision board to help you begin living your best life.

And Don't forget The Double Bonus question: Fun and delight

*A time when I will belly laugh so hard that I snort, cry, or feel the muscles
in my stomach and my face hurt will be when [_____].*

CHAPTER 17

AU REVOIR AND BON VOYAGE

I really mean "Au revoir" — "Until we meet again." Let's make specific plans, not just "we should get together again sometime."

The best way to stay connected is through my website ChronicCovertTrauma.com.

I'd like to welcome you there and show you around, hear what you have to add to the conversation. As humans, we all share the experience of a primary bonding experience at the beginning of our lives. However, that universal early human attachment relationship experience is profoundly influenced by our extremely diverse economic, cultural, and geo-political contexts. So, we have a lot of unique experiences and points of view to talk about!

Join with other naCCT survivors on this healing journey. Get in the loop by getting on the mailing list. Send me your questions and success stories. Have input on what's happening.

Going forward, I'm thinking of doing group work, which I love, maybe offering an on-line course and/or putting together affinity group gatherings, maybe an on-line healing and transformation retreat.

I'm also thinking of writing some more. Your feedback matters. It will be significant in shaping my next offering for you. I especially want to invite you to be part of the manifestation of the next book for us survivors. What would you like to see next? I already have notes for a sequel to this book addressing the "Remember and Grieve" component. I'm also considering writing about how naCCT insidiously affects the relationship between naCCT survivors and their psychotherapists.

Please let me know your concerns about what you'd like to read next.

And maybe, in addition to your personal healing work, *you* will go on to do some writing of your own, too. This subject needs work of so many kinds and points of view. And it needs play too. So, let's collaborate! Come join me at ChronicCovertTrauma.com. Come on over!

BON VOYAGE

You, Dear Reader, have been my muse. I am not "A Writer." I am a person with something to tell you and writing has been the way to do that.

Writing this book has been part of my Survivor Mission to create a social context for healing naCCT. Your healing doesn't only benefit you. It benefits me, too. Our healing makes the world a better place for each other, a place where we're wiser, smarter, kinder, more able to connect authentically and enjoy more love, purpose, prosperity, and delight in our lives.

Thank you for listening, for connecting with what I'm saying to you here, for putting it to use in your life.

Happy trails to you. I wish you all the best on your healing journey.

Sincerely,

Ricia

PS: If this book has been helpful to you, it would also make me happy if you would hop over to Amazon and write a quick review of this book to help spread the word to other naCCT survivors. Here's the link: https://www.amazon.com/Sticks-Stones-Broken-Bones-Non-physically-assaultive-ebook/dp/B09B4HP329/

I thank you, and those other naCCT survivors will too.

ACKNOWLEDGEMENTS

I am grateful to the many friends, clients, students, colleagues, teachers, therapists, and authors whose healing influence made this book possible. It would be impossible to cite everyone who has contributed, but I do want to acknowledge several whose influence has been enormous, beginning with early supporters and believers, who caught the vision for this book from the very beginning, especially:

Despina at L Street for saying, "You should write about this."

Paula Maute, LICSW, editor and writing coach, for totally "getting it," thinking the concept was interesting and worthwhile, and encouraging me to develop and express my ideas.

Carol Goldman grasped the concept right away, thought clearly about it, enthusiastically shared many resonant ideas and experiences, intuited next steps for writing and outreach, and repeatedly convinced me to keep going.

Marya Wolfman helped me organize an overwhelming stack of early notes.
    This book would not have seen the light of day without several people who generously took the time to read and share responses to early chapters with me: Suzanne Gallant, Billy Volkman, Paul Levy, Kelley Donovan, and the folks at the Tufts St. focus group.

Thanks to the many groups that have helped me move along this path of healing and engagement. My "Beyond Coping" group, therapy and personal growth groups, women's consciousness raising groups, the folks at the House Sangha, UUCGL Choir, Funsters, ROCCs, Reiki and Craniosacral shares, Focusing, 12 Steps, and Recovery International. To Tim Towner for his group leadership and the spirit house.

To my soul sistahs Sara, Arlene, and Stephanie.

To the muses Anne Boedecker of Art Heals the Soul, Jane Militello, Martha L. Maness, Gail Byrnes, Nita Penfold, and Jane Justice.

To Andrea Schroeder of Creative Dream Incubator.com and the courageous, insightful, "midwives" in her Dream Book Mastermind. I was so fortunate to have my first video interview about the book with her and see it shared on-line.

To all the folks in the National Writers Union who helped me take my writing seriously.

To the speakers and colleagues at the New England Society for the Treatment of Trauma and Dissociation (NESTTD) for providing education, training, and resources on the effective treatment of psychological trauma, complex trauma and dissociation. And to early NESTTD readers who encouraged me to keep working so they could have this book for their clients.

The early commenters on the ChronicCovertTrauma.com website contributed more to the completion of this project than they probably knew, and their validating shares motivated me to keep reaching out beyond my personal sphere to connect with a truly world wide web.

Completing this book would have been impossible without the loving support and encouragement of many important people in my life. I am blessed to have had many caring and supportive friends, colleagues, and fellow travelers help make this dream become a reality. Here are a few:

My friends and early bird readers and responders, Karen Benner, Kelley Wilson, and Stephanie Chissler, who — tolerating innumerable awkward early phrases, typos, and failed spellchecks — took the time to read the entire rough manuscript and encouraged me to bring it to publication.

Paula Sharaga for her on-going encouragement and enthusiasm, for believing in the value of the work and the validity of cPTSD from naCCT, and for being engrossed while listening to me read my stories.

Colleague and friend Betsy Wright Loving, LICSW, for hours of mindful listening and sharing her expert professional and personal perspectives.

Beverly Kozlosky, for her unfailingly careful readings and thoughtful suggestions.

Gloria Kozlosky, matchmaker and outreacher extraordinaire.

Kit Irwin for saying "Your book is important and you need to set a publishing date."

My cherished friend, Jan Engelman, so caring and smart, for her clear thinking, thoughtful analyses, and whole-hearted encouragement in my journey to go public with this material.

Many more people contributed directly and indirectly to this project, providing various forms of helpful feedback, encouragement, and energy. Among them are Bob Hall, Richard Knowlton, Irene Glassman, Donna Grant, Diane Faissler, Anne Principe, Marc Sibella, Andy Ciarletta, Rubi, Heidi, Marie Hall, Bonnie and Ron Fishman, Debbie Davis, Jane McKenna, Don Goldman, Regina Millis, Agnes Donovan, and Didi Emmons.

I offer my heart-felt gratitude to all my students, clients, and informants who shared so much of themselves and dared to interact with me on such a meaningful and authentic level.

I gained much wisdom and healing from my friends, supporters, and guides in books, all the researchers and authors who played such an important part in my personal evolution, in particular Harry Guntrip, Alice Miller, Jean Jenson, Judith Herman, and Marsha Linehan, especially her work on invalidating environments.

I also deeply appreciate the many places that buoyed me up while I worked on this heavy subject. The beautiful woods and beaches and the sea air.

The people who were willing to accompany me into the depths.

And the singing, drumming, art-making, body-work and tap-dancing groups that kept me sane and moving throughout this long process.

I also want to acknowledge and thank my parents for bringing me to life and providing a foundation of consistent, reliable practical and material safety and well-being.

My deep gratitude also goes to underlying contributions that indirectly empowered me to begin and stay with this work. In particular:

Author Norman Waksler, for encouraging my thinking and writing.

Anitra Lavanhar, for introducing me to massage as a way of deep body-mind-spirit healing.

Jane Jacobs, for telling me the truth about the audio tape.

Ruth Yeazel for taking the trouble to understand what I was trying to say in my doctoral dissertation long ago, helping me draw out the ideas in my head and keep struggling to put them into words.

Finally, I am grateful to the vivid memory of my younger self and how she struggled when there was no book like this one available to her, and to the sustaining vision of other naCCT survivors and future readers who would benefit from this book.

ABOUT RICIA FLEMING

Ricia Fleming (officially Patricia J. Fleming, Ph.D. English Literature, triple-licensed as mental health counselor, certified social worker, and massage therapist) says "If you've been drawn to this book, I especially want you to know that I'm a partially healed wounded healer with cPTSD from naCCT myself. In this book, I share with you what I've learned personally and professionally about how to heal.

"Trained in Trauma Focused Cognitive Behavioral Therapy, EMDR, Psychomotor therapy with Al and Diane Pesso, and Psychodrama with Jacob and Zerka Moreno, for twenty years I provided mind-body based psychotherapy to help over 3,000 people hospitalized with chronic physical pain, depression, and PTSD reclaim their lives. Gradually I began to educate myself about myself, applying to my own challenges the language, concepts, and treatment techniques that helped victims of atrocities and disasters. To my amazed delight, I started getting better."

Ricia now brings together psychology, the arts, and bodywork, drawing on four-plus decades of professional service as a therapist, educator, and hands-on healer promoting human well-being, with a special focus on healing trauma.

She began with a Ph.D in English Language and Literature at Boston University, where she learned to pay close attention to the meanings people communicate through their speech and written words. While there, she also researched and wrote "The Integrated Self" and taught several hundred university students to observe, think, and express themselves.

Then on to an M.Ed. in Counselor Training and becoming a consultant and clinician in private practice, a co-director of a college counseling center, and a program developer.

She developed and delivered the "Beyond Coping" Vocational Achievement Program and wrote the group manual, which sold in women's bookstores and was used by self-led women's groups throughout the US.

In conjunction with the American Cancer Society and the Massachusetts Dept. of Public Health, Ricia provided telephone consultations to people seeking freedom from nicotine addiction at the pioneering "Smokers' Quitline" telehealth program.

Ricia is a long-time member of the New England Society for the Treatment of Trauma and Dissociation (NESTTD), where she served on the Outreach Committee and wrote the extended review and summary of "Understanding the Neuroscience of PTSD: Clinically Useful Applications" by Amy Banks, MD, for the NESTTD newsletter, available online at https://www.nesttd-online.org/resources/documents/review-banks.pdf.

She also served on the Executive Council of the Massachusetts Mental Health Counselors Assn. (MaMHCA).

Hands-on body work, with a license to directly touch, massage, and release tensions people have stored in their bodies, is the most recent addition to Ricia's healing repertoire. For more than ten years at Rolling Ridge Retreat and Conference Center, she taught wellness and provided therapeutic talk and touch using Somato-Emotional Release, massage, energy healing, and other somatic modalities.

Integrating direct body work, psychotherapeutic concepts and techniques, and personal narrative, Ricia also developed the BodyStory method. She offered BodyStory consultations to individuals and presented workshops in such venues as the Arlington Health Professionals Alliance.

Throughout, she has been fortunate to have expanded her skills and awareness via such ground-breaking in-person workshops and trainings as Internal Family Systems (IFS) with Richard Schwartz, Somatic Experiencing with Peter Levine, Sensorimotor with Pat Ogden, Polyvagal Therapy with Steven Porges and Deb Dana, Focusing with Gene Gendlin, and Dance and Movement Therapy with Norma Canner. She studied Improv for Clinicians and Counselors with the Improv Therapy Group.

She also learned directly from talks by such pioneers as Bessel van der Kolk, Judith Herman, Allan Schore, and Janina Fisher.

Believing it's important to set aside time for reflection, in her personal life she attends organized retreats at meditation centers, personal self-structured retreats, Kripalu's legendary "Inner Quest Intensive," and talks and workshops with such devoted practitioners as Sharon Salzberg, Jon Kabat-Zinn, and Jack Kornfield.

Balancing the playful and profound, she co-founded the Funsters Singalong group, facilitates SoulCollage® workshops, tap-dances, drums, and leads the community creation of large scale labyrinths for walking meditations on public beaches.